NORMAN BLUHM
METAMORPHOSIS

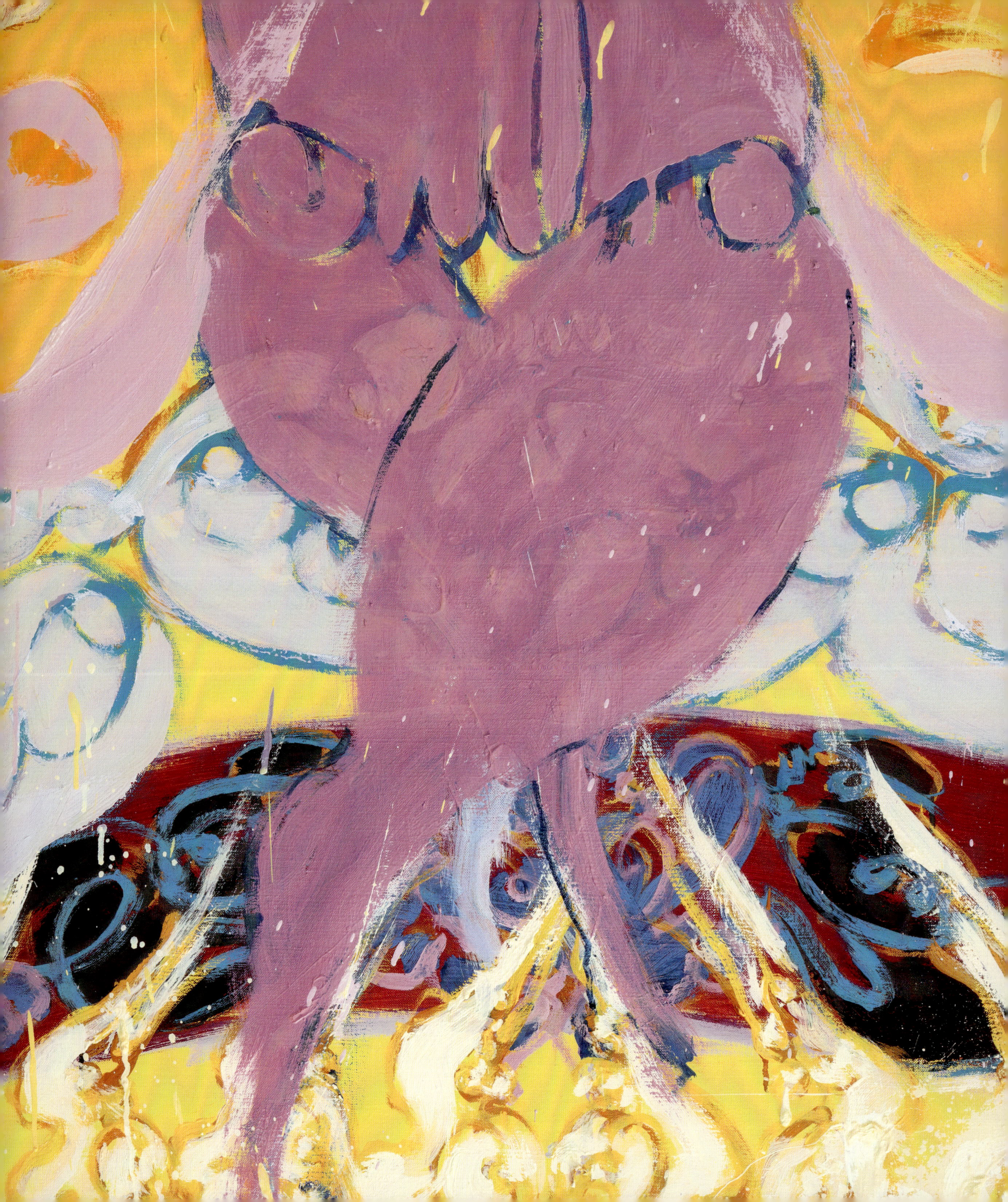

NORMAN BLUHM METAMORPHOSIS

Tricia Laughlin Bloom

Jay Grimm

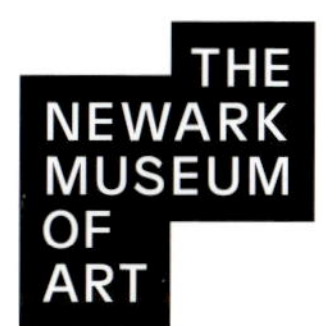

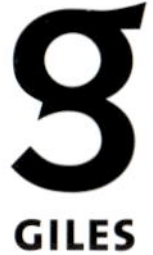

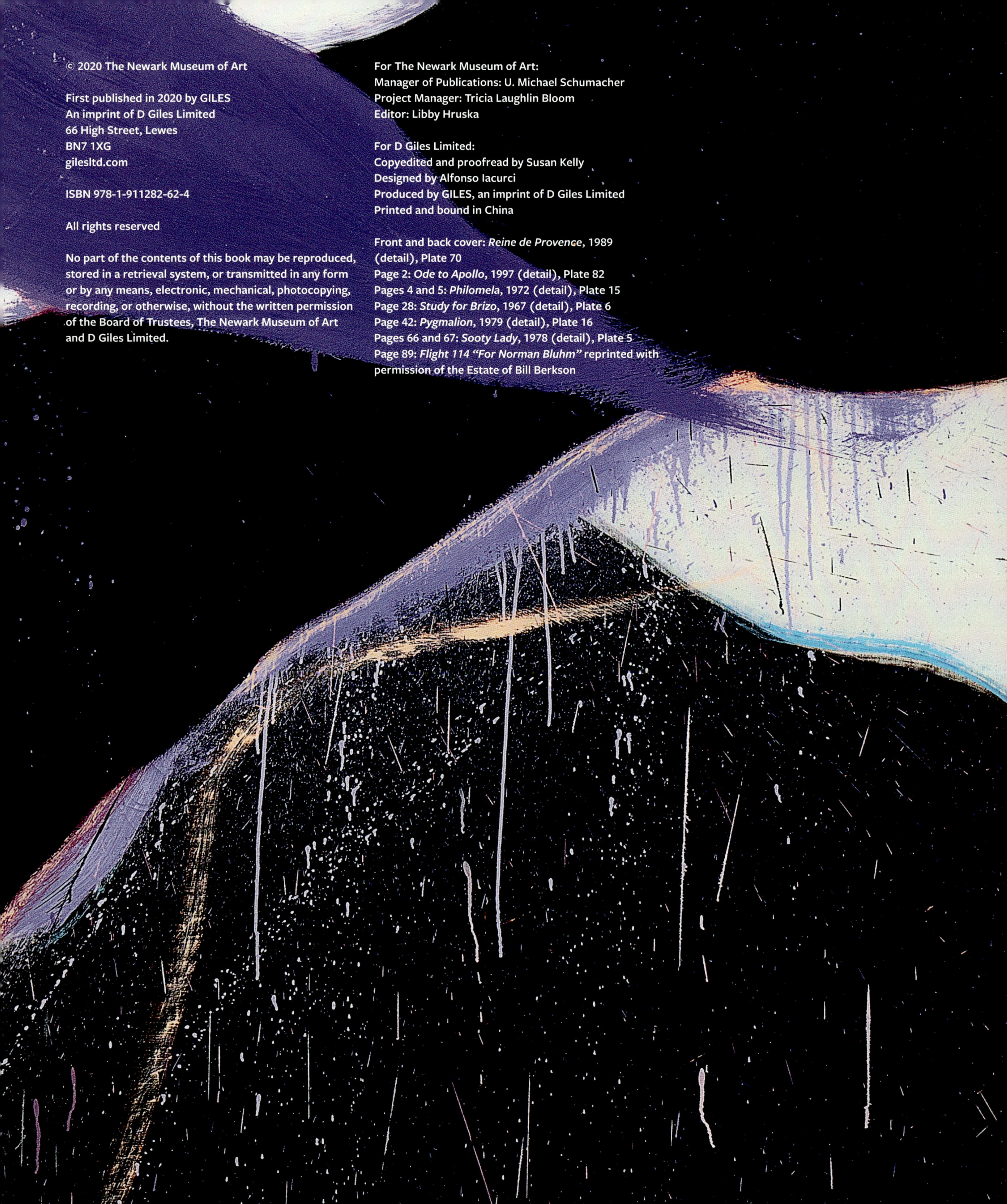

First published in 2020 by GILES
An imprint of D Giles Limited
66 High Street, Lewes
BN7 1XG
gilesltd.com

ISBN 978-1-911282-62-4

For The Newark Museum of Art:
Manager of Publications: U. Michael Schumacher
Project Manager: Tricia Laughlin Bloom
Editor: Libby Hruska

For D Giles Limited:
Copyedited and proofread by Susan Kelly
Designed by Alfonso Iacurci
Produced by GILES, an imprint of D Giles Limited
Printed and bound in China

Front and back cover: *Reine de Provence*, 1989 (detail), Plate 70
Page 2: *Ode to Apollo*, 1997 (detail), Plate 82
Pages 4 and 5: *Philomela*, 1972 (detail), Plate 15
Page 28: *Study for Brizo*, 1967 (detail), Plate 6
Page 42: *Pygmalion*, 1979 (detail), Plate 16
Pages 66 and 67: *Sooty Lady*, 1978 (detail), Plate 5
Page 89: *Flight 114 "For Norman Bluhm"* reprinted with permission of the Estate of Bill Berkson

Contents

Support

The Newark Museum of Art, a not-for-profit museum of art and science, receives operating support from the City of Newark, the State of New Jersey, the New Jersey State Council on the Arts/Department of State—a partner agency of the National Endowment for the Arts—the New Jersey Cultural Trust, the Prudential Foundation, the Geraldine R. Dodge Foundation, the Victoria Foundation, the Estate of Phyllis and Sanford Bolton, the Wallace Foundation, and other corporations, foundations, and individuals. Funds for acquisitions and activities other than operations are provided by members and other contributors.

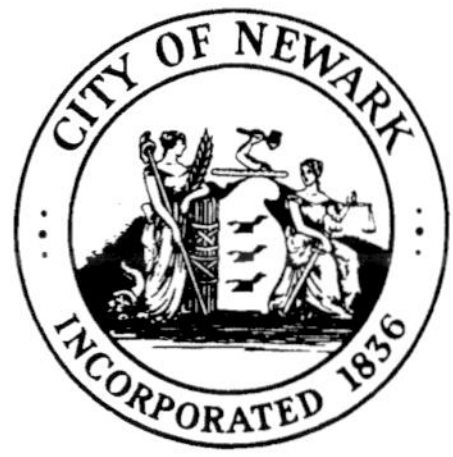

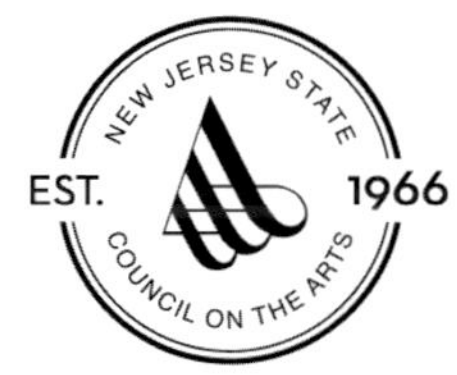

Norman Bluhm: Metamorphosis is sponsored in part by:

Eleonore Kessler Cohen and Max Insel Cohen
Hollis Taggart
Arlene Lieberman

Additional support provided by:

The Marie and Joe Melone Exhibition Fund for American Art
The Elizabeth Richards Family Exhibition Endowment Fund

Lenders to the Exhibition

The Estate of Norman Bluhm

Graham Shay Gallery, New York

Herbert F. Johnson Museum of Art, Cornell University, Ithaca, New York

Manny Silverman Gallery, Los Angeles

Metropolitan Museum of Art, New York

Neuberger Museum of Art, Purchase College, State University of New York

Whitney Museum of American Art, New York

Mr. Anthony Scotto

And those who wish to remain anonymous

Foreword

One hundred years after the birth of Norman Bluhm, The Newark Museum of Art is proud to celebrate this quintessential American painter with a long-overdue retrospective. *Norman Bluhm: Metamorphosis* is a rare gathering of Bluhm's visually arresting large-scale works that takes visitors from his earliest years in Paris to his involvement with the Abstract Expressionist movement in New York City, and on to the operatic late works he produced in the pastoral settings of his studios in upstate New York and Vermont. This is the first time Bluhm's visionary late work has been presented so fully, and in context with all stages of his earlier production, highlighting the grand sweep of his humanistic art. Along with monumental oil paintings that position Bluhm as a major underrecognized talent, the show includes numerous works in gouache and ink on paper, offering a wonderful opportunity to reflect on Bluhm's process. The subtitle of the exhibition—*Metamorphosis*—intentionally calls to mind the Roman poet Ovid's magnum opus, *Metamorphoses*, underscoring Bluhm's deep engagement with classical mythology and poetry. At the same time the vigorous and always bold brushwork on display in Bluhm's paintings captures a kind of metamorphosis, recording the organic evolution of an artist's life in paint.

Bluhm's interests ranged from boxing to brunching with the family of Henri Matisse, and his big personality shines through in this exhibition and catalogue. Through his vibrant, expressive mark-making and his references to art and cultural traditions from around the globe, Bluhm's fascination with the world around him and his joie de vivre resonate through his works. His abstract canvases have an epic quality—from the monumental scale he often worked in to the poetry and ancient myths he loved to reference—and remind us of the importance of trusting one's gut. Decades after the declaration by modern art critics that "painting is dead," Bluhm's production still feels fresh and relevant to twenty-first-century eyes. In a postwar and even postmodern art world where gender roles and the rules of representation remained rigidly binary, Bluhm reached beyond tradition and trends to create paintings that are muscular, feminine, avant-garde, and lush.

In interviews, Bluhm spoke of his aspiration to convey spirituality in his paintings, and throughout his career he abstracted from religious architecture and devotional objects including stained glass, medieval and Renaissance altarpieces, and Russian icons. He also embraced the physical world and reveled in the pleasure that color can communicate. It is fitting that this, the first full museum retrospective of Bluhm's work, is staged at The Newark Museum of Art, amid holdings that include a spectacular Tibetan Buddhist altar and Joseph Stella's futurist polyptych, *The Voice of the City of New York Interpreted*. We welcome the opportunity to share Bluhm's remarkable paintings with new audiences, to offer a critical reassessment of his oeuvre, and to pass along to a new generation the joy of painting that is his legacy.

Linda C. Harrison
Director and CEO
The Newark Museum of Art

Acknowledgments

It has been a great privilege and a pleasure to organize *Norman Bluhm: Metamorphosis*, with the help of so many colleagues. This exhibition would not have been possible without the devoted assistance of Nina and Cary Bluhm. The curatorial team has worked closely with the Bluhm family on this project and we are grateful to them for so generously sharing Norman's art, along with archival material and personal memories of his life and work. We extend our gratitude to the Museum's Board of Trustees, and special thanks to Linda C. Harrison, Director and CEO of The Newark Museum of Art, for lending her energy and enthusiastic support to this project.

A retrospective requires a gathering of great works, and we are indebted to the distinguished museums and private collectors that lent works to this exhibition. We also wish to thank numerous colleagues who assisted with research and image acquisition, including: Lexi Bishop at Christie's; Hollis Taggart and Debra Pesci at Hollis Taggart Gallery; Joan Washburn; Andrew Arnot at Tibor di Nagy; Adele Stroh; Kerby Smith; Nicholas Ostness at Martha Jackson Gallery Archives; Constance Lewallen; and the Archives of American Art. Thank you also to the staff of The Estate of Norman Bluhm, who, along with Nina Bluhm, were instrumental in helping us to photograph an ambitious number of paintings in the Estate.

Our colleagues at The Newark Museum of Art have been essential to the success of this project. We especially thank Timothy Wintemberg, Deputy Director for Exhibition Design, for his thoughtful collaboration and smart design of the exhibition; Richard Goodbody for so beautifully handling all the new photography required for this publication; and Andrea Ko and Emily Laverty, Registrars, who coordinated all of the photography. William Peniston, the Museum's Librarian and Archivist, provided critical support during the research stage of this project. A special thanks to U. Michael Schumacher, Director of Marketing and Public Relations and the Museum's manager of publications, for overseeing this publication with creativity and patience, and to Libby Hruska, consulting editor. We also gratefully acknowledge the contributions of Deborah Kasindorf, Vice President and Deputy Director for External Affairs, and the entire Development team.

Jay Grimm would like to thank the staff at both the Watson Library at the Metropolitan Museum of Art and the New York Public Library, especially Lyndsi Barnes, for providing extensive research assistance for this project. Thanks also to Gina Cashia, who helped gather citations for the bibliography. Finally, deep gratitude to his wife, Emily-Jane Kirwan, for her unwavering support.

Tricia Laughlin Bloom
Jay Grimm

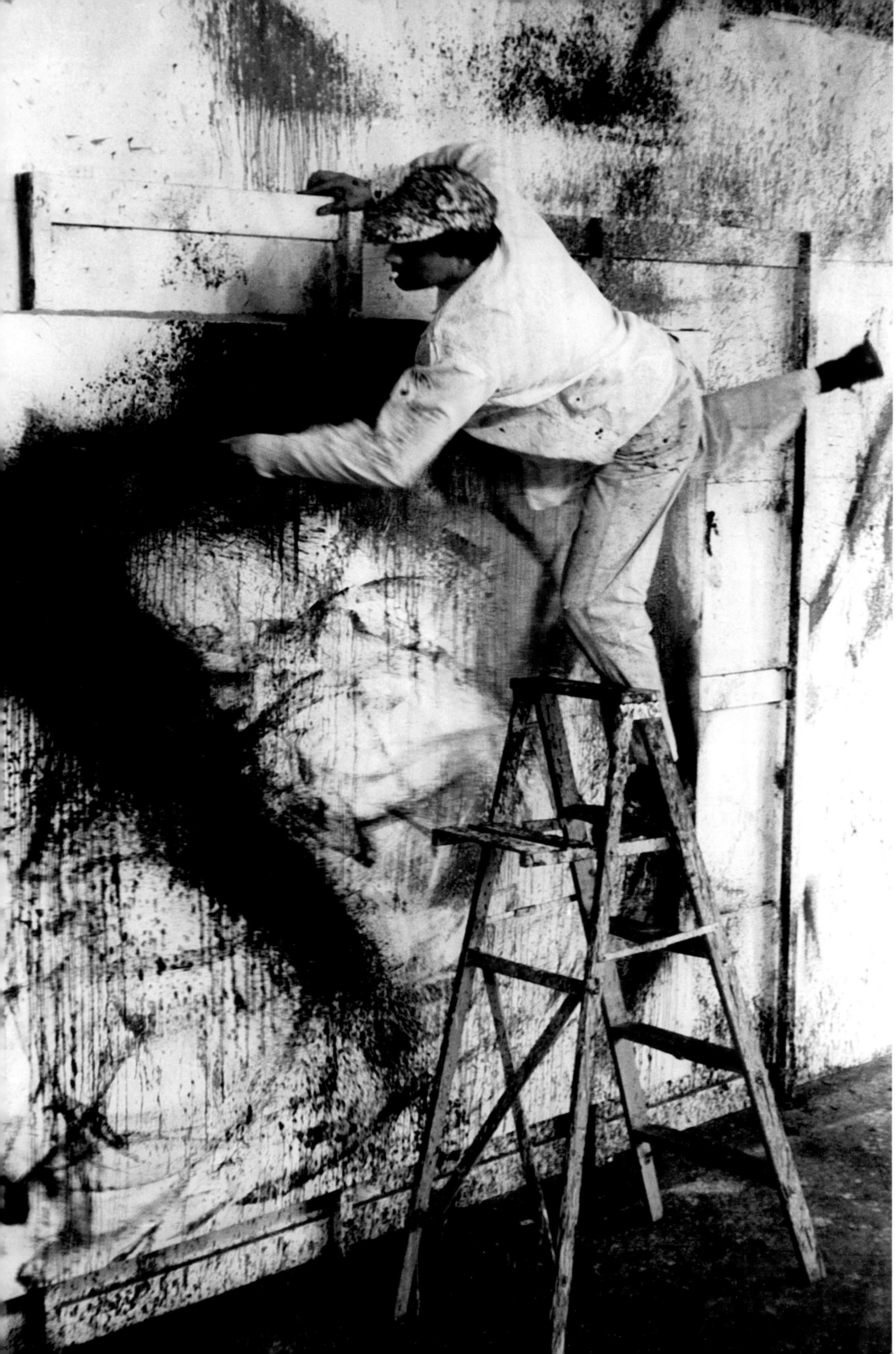

Fig. 1
Norman Bluhm works on the oversized canvas of one of his action paintings in his studio at 333 Park Avenue South, New York City, February 22, 1961. Photo by Fred W. McDarrah / Getty Images

JOY IS FOREVER THE UNKNOWN

The Art of Norman Bluhm

Jay Grimm

Fig. 2
Exhibition announcement, first solo show at Leo Castelli Gallery, October 1957, courtesy Castelli Gallery. Photo courtesy of The Estate of Norman Bluhm

In 1956 Norman Bluhm arrived in New York City, determined to establish himself in what was rapidly becoming the most important artistic center in the world (Fig. 1). Harnessing the energy of Abstract Expressionism, Bluhm quickly gained the respect of his peers and representation by an up-and-coming gallerist (Fig. 2). Having spent the previous decade immersed in the rich milieu of Paris, absorbing avant-garde ideas and studying masterpieces from numerous cultures and time periods, he came to New York well equipped to contribute to the advancement of Action Painting. Within six years, however, amid relentless change in the art world, a new set of artists and concerns that were in direct opposition to gestural abstraction dominated the critical discourse in the United States, and by the mid-1960s Abstract Expressionism no longer commanded the attention it once had. While his professional network continued to provide some support, Bluhm's lifelong commitment to gestural painting meant that he developed his career in an art world that often misunderstood his work. Despite this adversity, Bluhm persevered with great fortitude and a deep commitment to his craft, producing an oeuvre of beauty and intellectual heft that spans five decades.

Bluhm's early success and association with Abstract Expressionism helped launch his reputation, but it arguably hindered the reception of his works after the 1950s, and often continues to do so today. This exhibition—the first major monographic museum show to survey the full range of his paintings—provides an opportunity to reassess Bluhm's entire career and his stylistic evolution and to situate him not as an Abstract Expressionist but rather as a painter who seized upon aesthetic ideas new and old to create works he hoped would connect to the grand sweep of art history.

Bluhm was born in Chicago in 1920 to a striving, cultivated Jewish family.[1] His mother, Rosa Goldstein Bluhm—a trained musician from Lucca, Italy—cared for Norman and his younger brother William. Bluhm's father, Henry Bluhm, of Central European heritage, supported them as a civil engineer. Bluhm never enjoyed a warm relationship with his father, who was a harsh and difficult man. For a period in the mid-1920s, as Henry Bluhm oversaw a multiyear project in the Soviet Union, the rest of the family went to live with Bluhm's mother's family in Florence.[2] The Bluhm family moved back the United States in the late 1920s. As a teenager, Bluhm began to express his interest in art; as he took drawing classes at the Art Institute of Chicago and studied its world-class collection, his family steered him toward architecture, seeing it as the creative profession most likely to enable him to support himself. Conflicts with his father led to Bluhm leaving the family home around the age of sixteen; at about the same time, success in high school allowed Bluhm to enroll in the Armour Institute of Technology (now the Illinois Institute of Technology) in Chicago. Mies van der Rohe—the seminal Modernist architect of the Bauhaus School in Germany, who was fleeing Nazi persecution—was soon hired to lead the program and Bluhm became one of his youngest students.

Because of the profound effect of the Bauhaus on twentieth-century art, it is tempting to look for its influence on Bluhm. Certainly some of his late work, with its regular, gridded organization of space, may seem to relate to Modernism, but Bluhm never regarded Mies as inspirational. Bluhm credited Mies's pedagogical exercises with instilling in him a rigorous, disciplined intellectual approach to art-making and acknowledged the importance of the exposure to life drawing and art history he received from Mies. However, most of Bluhm's anecdotes about Mies tell how his teacher's precise methods convinced Bluhm of his own unsuitability for a career in architecture.

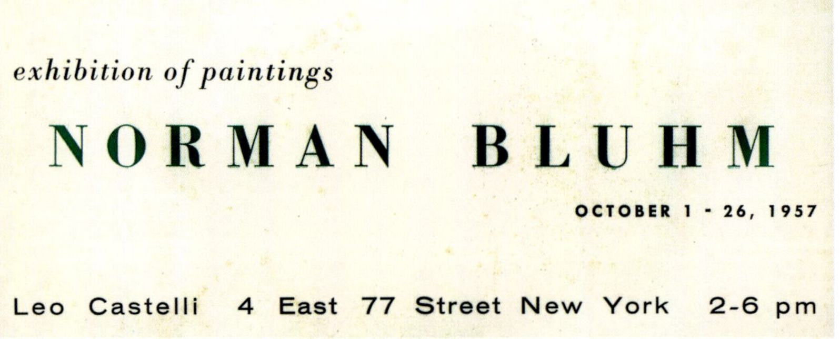
exhibition of paintings

NORMAN BLUHM

OCTOBER 1 - 26, 1957

Leo Castelli 4 East 77 Street New York 2-6 pm

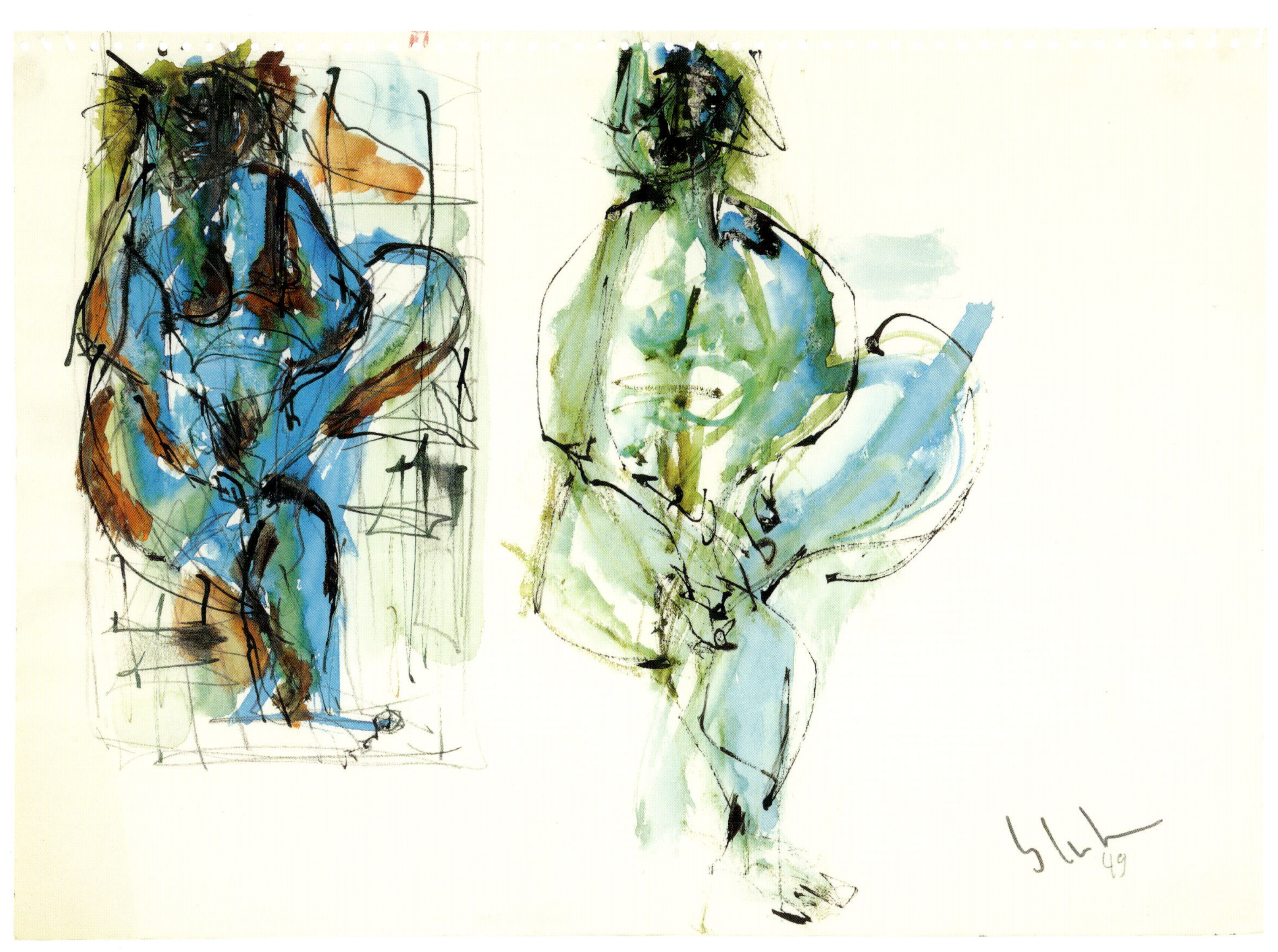

Plate 1

Untitled (*Two Seated Nudes*), 1949
Ink on paper
12 ¼ × 17 ¼ in. (31.1 × 43.8 cm)
The Estate of Norman Bluhm

Fig. 3
Claude Monet. *Waterlilies, study of water: Green Reflections*, ca. 1914–26. Oil on canvas, 78¾ × 334½ in. (200 × 850 cm). Room 1, East wall. INV20102. Musée de l'Orangerie, Paris, France. Photo Credit: © RMN-Grand Palais / Michel Urtado / Art Resource, NY

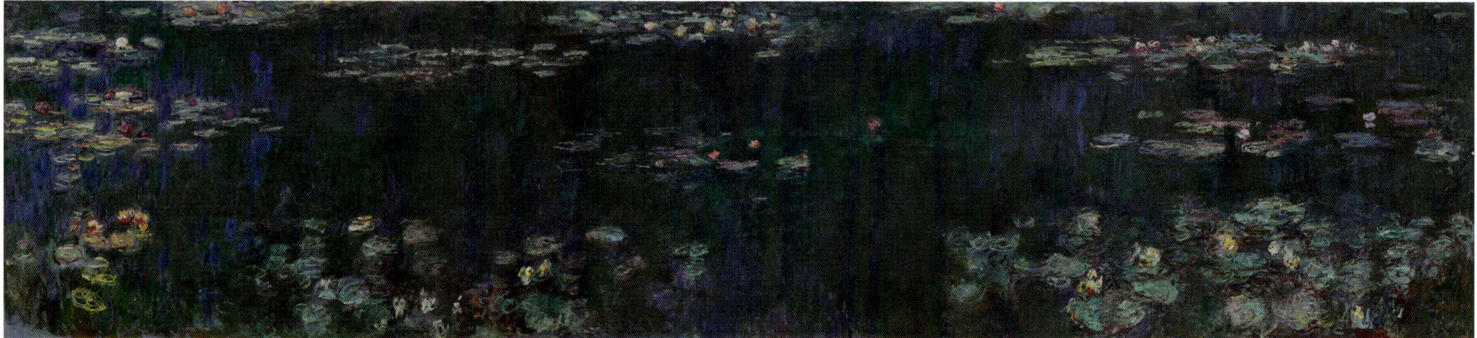

Shortly after the 1941 attack on Pearl Harbor, Bluhm and his younger brother enlisted in the United States Army Air Corps. Bluhm survived the war, but his brother was killed in action.[3] Certainly the loss of his brother was a lifelong pain that Bluhm felt keenly, and he acknowledged the trauma he experienced as a result of his own service, but Bluhm never claimed that his wartime experiences influenced his mature paintings.[4] After the war, Bluhm briefly resumed his architectural studies, but found that his heart wasn't in it. In 1946 he moved to Europe, first to Florence and then to Paris, to become a painter. The pull of Paris proved irresistible, as it has for many Americans before and since. Bluhm was drawn by what he called its "romanticism."[5] He used the term to refer to the city's central role in avant-garde painting movements, but also to signal its intellectual climate, nurtured in cafés and salons. Bluhm loved Paris for its earlier eras of towering artistic achievements, specifically the Gothic, Renaissance, and Baroque. Undoubtedly this admiration was informed by his early contact with European culture during his time in Italy as a child, as well as childhood visits to the Art Institute of Chicago with its superb collection of French painting.

With the GI Bill education benefit providing income, Bluhm studied at both the École des Beaux-Arts and the Académie de la Grande Chaumière in Paris. His choice of schools is hardly surprising, given that each had connections to the grand tradition of Western painting he so revered. The École des Beaux-Arts, more than four hundred years old, invented the traditional art curriculum, beginning with drawing from casts of classical sculptures and then, once students had attained the requisite skill, live models. The more bohemian Grande Chaumière allowed students to develop in a less formal setting, while still emphasizing drawing. Bluhm did not receive a degree from either institution, but he found his calling and began the process of becoming an artist.

As meaningful as his studies were, it was Bluhm's relationship with artist Claude Souvrain that most significantly influenced the trajectory of his life. The two met soon after Bluhm arrived in Paris, and they married in 1950. The daughter of left-wing intellectuals, Souvrain was part of elite circles within the Parisian art world; through her, Bluhm met dancers, actors, writers, poets, and artists. One of Souvrain's closest friends was Florence Loeb, whose father ran the influential Galerie Pierre, which showed canonical avant-garde artists including Pablo Picasso, Georges Braque, Joan Miró, and Alberto Giacometti, many of whom Bluhm met in person. Souvrain and Bluhm's network also included Antonin Artaud and Paul Éluard, two giants of Surrealist poetry. For Bluhm these literary connections heralded the beginning of a lifelong engagement with living poets.

At this time Bluhm also formed a close friendship with art historian Georges Duthuit and his wife, Marguerite Matisse, the daughter of Henri Matisse. Bluhm and Souvrain joined the Matisse family regularly for Sunday dinners; these meals occasionally included the master Henri Matisse himself. This remarkable connection reinforced Bluhm's admiration for Matisse's work, which would strongly influence Bluhm later in his career. Bluhm was hardly the only expatriate to join the close-knit art world of Paris after World War II. What cannot be overstated, however, is the intensity of his involvement. Unlike many Americans there, Bluhm became fluent in French and married into a local family, fully immersing himself in Parisian society.

Paris fired Bluhm's creativity. He often sketched the stained-glass windows of Notre Dame cathedral and Sainte-Chapelle, and visited the nearby village of Auvers-sur-Oise to paint outside, consciously emulating Vincent van Gogh, who had created some of his most iconic images in the surrounding fields. Bluhm copied great works of art from around the world found in Paris's encyclopedic museums to hone his technique and his eye, complementing the curriculum of his art schools with this time-honored tradition. Though Matisse always preoccupied him, Bluhm also began to look closely at nineteenth-century French landscapists Jean-Baptiste-Camille Corot, Gustave Courbet, and Claude Monet; Renaissance and Baroque painters such as Piero della Francesca and Diego Velázquez; and Byzantine and Japanese art. Bluhm was open to anything that excited his aesthetic senses, an eclecticism that persisted throughout his life and which undoubtedly contributed to his continual stylistic evolution.

From the beginning, Bluhm had a profound interest in life drawing. As can be seen in his earliest nudes (Plate 1), he developed a quirky, quivering line. Created quickly with many long continuous marks, Bluhm's lines skirt around his subject, tracing her contours and then plunging within, forming curlicues and arabesques to which he added hatching and slashes to render shadows and model form. Pulsing with energy, this idiosyncratic mark-making both describes the body before him and records time and motion.

Over the course of five decades, drawing remained the bedrock of Bluhm's art. Throughout his career, he devoted intense periods to working from female models, using the process to generate new ideas, solve aesthetic problems, and break out of creative lulls. Through constant practice, Bluhm attained such skill that he could execute intricate geometric forms freehand. Even working with a heavy, wet brush, he was able to apply paint in perfect sinuous curves and loops. The rapid assuredness of his initial line meant that he did not have to refine these passages later, allowing him to retain the original sense of spontaneous dynamism.

Also striking in Bluhm's earliest works on paper is his use of color to add dimension and drama. In *Head*, from 1949 (Plate 21), the viscous gouache flows and drips, while in *Notre Dame,* painted in 1950 (Plate 9), color is used sparingly to evoke a fleeting sense of a gloomy sky as well as the cathedral's windows. An untitled watercolor from 1952 (Plate 24) seems to describe a landscape but shows Bluhm using his flicked lines and daubed color in a much more abstract manner. It is not known if this particular work was created outdoors, but Bluhm often used the technique of *plein air* painting during his years in Paris. Bluhm, like everyone else in Paris, knew then that abstraction was taking off in America and it likely influenced him to move in a more abstract direction. However, nonobjective art had been made and exhibited in Europe since before World War I by artists such as Vasily Kandinsky (the Art Institute of Chicago acquired several Kandinsky paintings in 1931), and Bluhm specifically mentioned admiring Piet Mondrian when he was studying under Mies.[6] Monet's late *Nymphéas* paintings (Fig. 3), which Bluhm admired at the Musée de l'Orangerie, likely had as much to do with Bluhm's move as did developments in New York.[7]

As Bluhm matured, his career advanced. In 1952, when he was in his early 30s, he met the voracious collector Walter Chrysler through gallerist Pierre Loeb and sold him almost forty paintings. Despite his rootedness in the Parisian milieu, critics and collectors began grouping Bluhm with other young American expatriate artists such as Joan Mitchell and her then-partner Jean-Paul Riopelle, Paul Jenkins, and other painters who would also go on to have significant careers.[8] Bluhm's friendship with Sam Francis was particularly meaningful at that time; the two shared a studio for several years and their work from that period shows many affinities.

In 1956 Bluhm's marriage to Souvrain ended, shattering him. Broke and bereft, he decided to leave Paris and move to New York; his network now included

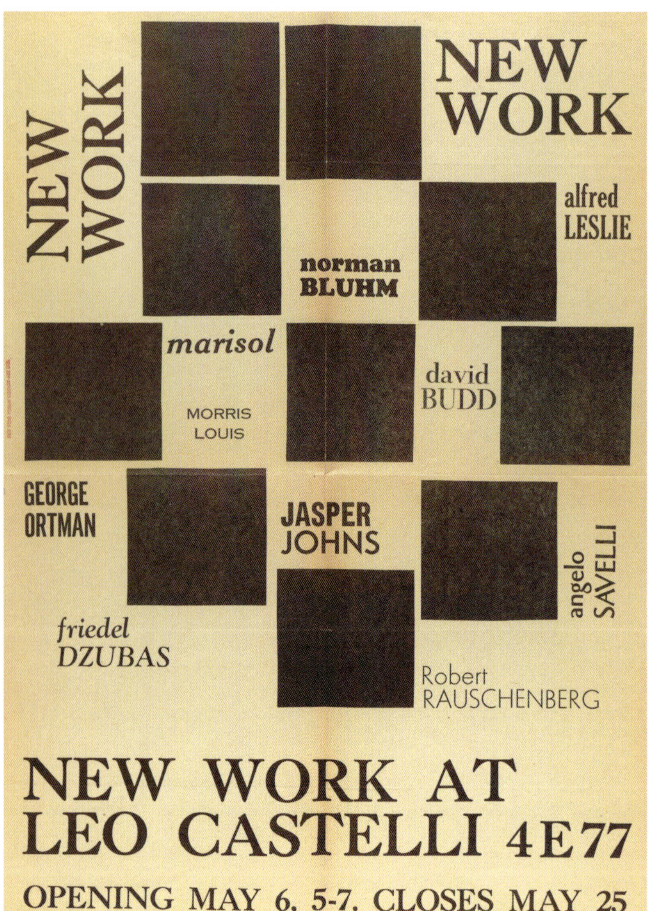

Fig. 4
Leo Castelli Gallery Group Exhibition Poster, New York, May 1957, courtesy Castelli Gallery. Photo courtesy of New York Public Library

people who could assist him, and the New York art scene had obvious appeal. With this transatlantic move, Bluhm's career blossomed. In 1957 the Leo Castelli Gallery, then a new venue for cutting-edge art, included Bluhm in a group show (Fig. 4) before giving him a solo show later that year, followed by another solo show in 1960 (Fig. 22). Between 1958 and 1961 Bluhm was also included in the Whitney Annual Exhibition, the Carnegie International, Documenta II in Kassel, Germany, and surveys at the Solomon R. Guggenheim Museum and the Walker Art Center in Minneapolis. As Bluhm's reputation grew both in New York and internationally, the critical reaction to his work was overwhelmingly positive, and, more importantly for Bluhm, his fellow artists accepted him. In New York, as had happened in Paris, Bluhm joined a lively subculture consisting of well-known artists (Fig. 5), and he became a member of The Club, an exclusive group of writers, poets, and visual artists that gathered regularly to debate and socialize. Bluhm also frequented the Cedar Tavern, the East Village bar now legendary as the meeting place for artists, poets and writers in the 1950s.

The paintings that brought Bluhm initial acclaim in New York arose from the approach he had perfected in Europe; in fact, he brought a number of such works with him from Paris to New York when he moved. His inspiration for the 1956 painting *Bleeding Rain* (Plate 2), for instance, sprang from the stained-glass windows he used to sketch in Paris, and the work of French landscape artists he revered. The downward-flowing washes, applied with vigorous gestures derived from his drawing practice, create an astonishing, intense field of red. In *Jaded Silence* (Plate 26), painted in 1957, Bluhm first laid down a ground of bright colors and then used progressively darker ones to generate a feeling of emanating light.[9] While both of these large-scale paintings are completely abstract, a horizon line fixes them as landscapes.

The Anvil (Plate 3), made a few years later, shows Bluhm's absorption of the Abstract Expressionist idiom; the entire surface of the canvas is covered with abstract marks—thick, thin, and dripping—which dispense with any reference to the natural world. From an art historical perspective, *The Anvil* is truly an "allover painting," the critical term used to describe the decentralized composition often used by the Abstract Expressionists. The creative act becomes a primary subject, and the extension of marks and gestures beyond the edge of the canvas emphatically conveys the physical process of painting. Bluhm here abandoned the use of a strong background color, emphasizing his free-floating, vigorous gestures. While both *The Anvil* and *Squall* (Plate 28) mark a significant step in Bluhm's stylistic development and a wholehearted embrace of Action Painting, it would not be correct to say that the artist had broken with his previous work. As before, veils of color created by fluid drips of paint modulate light and give a sense of depth, and Bluhm's knowledge of drawing governs the muscular strokes. In *Peacock* (Plate 4), painted in 1964, a further change takes place: Bluhm now isolates his gestures against a minimal yet powerful composition of thickly painted opposing angles. Drips and sprays from the furious paint application are used to evoke a mood and not to create space.

In 1960 Bluhm met Cary Ogle, a Smith College graduate and Fulbright Scholar who was working at the Staempfli Gallery, an established dealer on Manhattan's

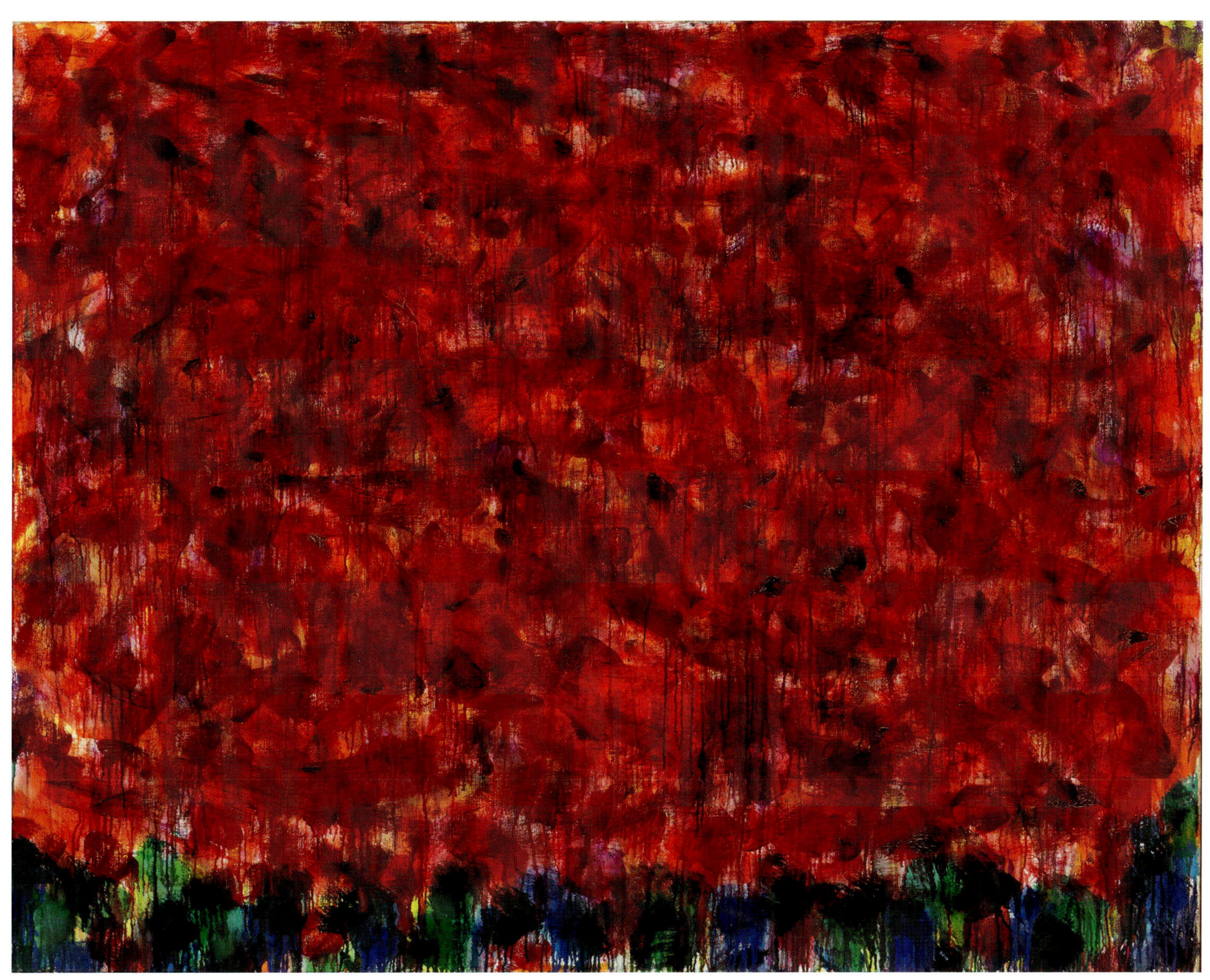

Plate 2

Bleeding Rain, 1956
Oil on canvas
51 ¼ × 64 in. (129.5 × 162.5 cm)
Herbert F. Johnson Museum of Art, Cornell University, Ithaca, New York
Gift of Katherine Komaroff Goodman *77.074.001*

Fig. 5
East Hampton, New York, 1958. From left to right: Libby Durgin, Norman Bluhm, Joan Mitchell, Michael Goldberg. Photo by Walter Silver, © Photography Collection, The New York Public Library, courtesy of The Estate of Norman Bluhm

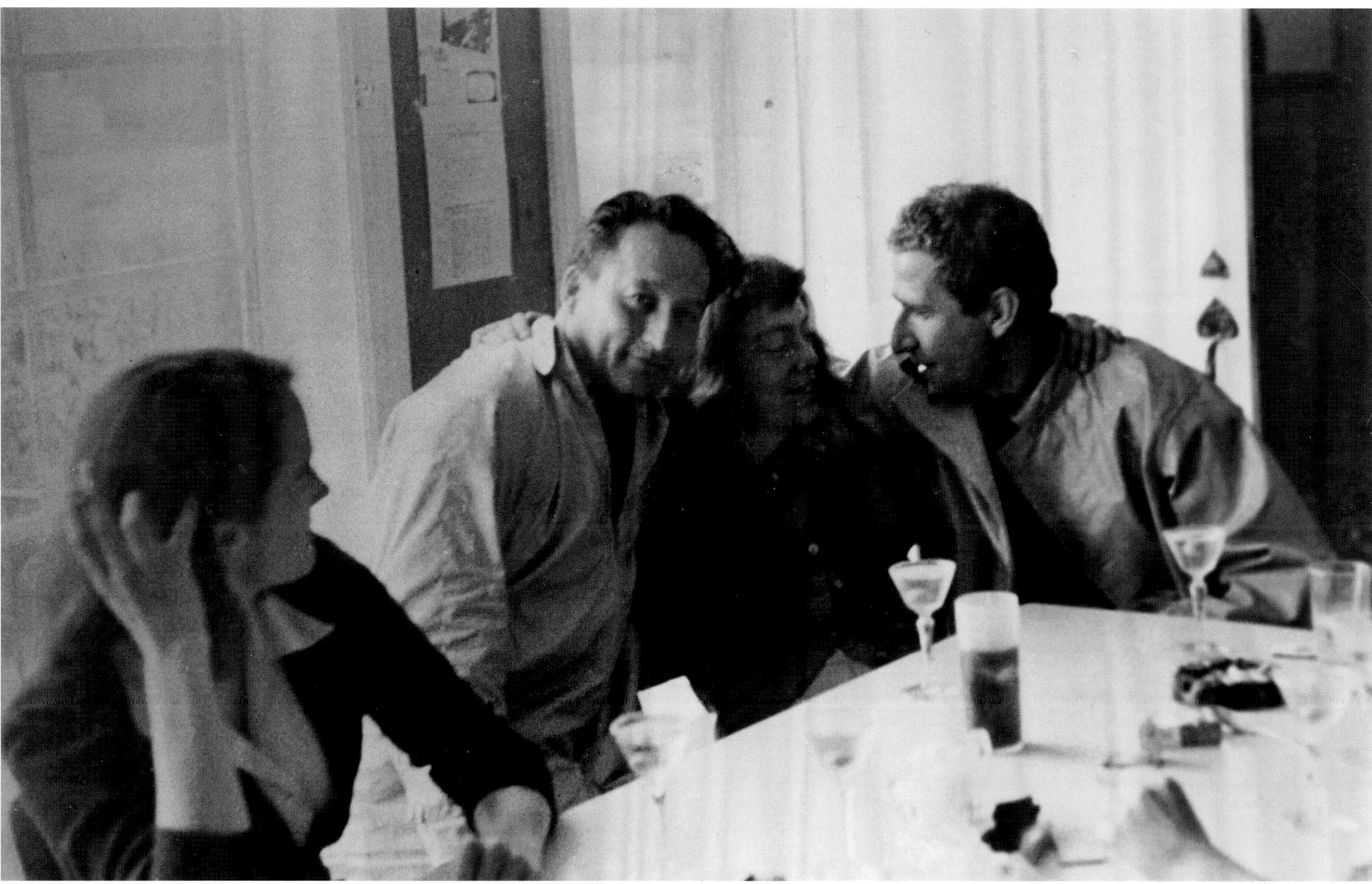

Upper East Side; the two married in 1961. Their son David was born in 1962 and daughter Nina in 1963. Though this was a time of positive personal change, it became a challenging period for Bluhm professionally. The 1960s saw a general increase in interest in contemporary art, shifting the economics of the New York art world. Rising prices spurred collectors to speculate on art and gave greater power to dealers. The emerging Pop Art movement allowed practitioners to build careers through branding and celebrity. The idea of cutting-edge art being made by a small coterie of artists in opposition to mainstream culture disappeared. Although famously gruff, Bluhm was quite gregarious and fed off of what he called the "energy" between artists in 1950s New York; the loss of this sense of community affected him greatly. The tragic death of poet and critic Frank O'Hara in 1966 was of particular significance to Bluhm; the two were close, and O'Hara was one of Bluhm's greatest champions.[10]

At the same time, by the mid-1960s, the critical tide had turned against gestural abstraction. Observers began worrying that an "academy" of Abstract Expressionism had been established, and that what once was innovative had become hackneyed.[11] The term "Second Generation" has now lost a lot of its sting, but over much of Bluhm's career it was often used as a slur to refer to Bluhm, as well as many others, such as Joan Mitchell, Michael Goldberg, and Al Held, implying that they were unoriginal imitators with nothing new to say.[12] This galled Bluhm.

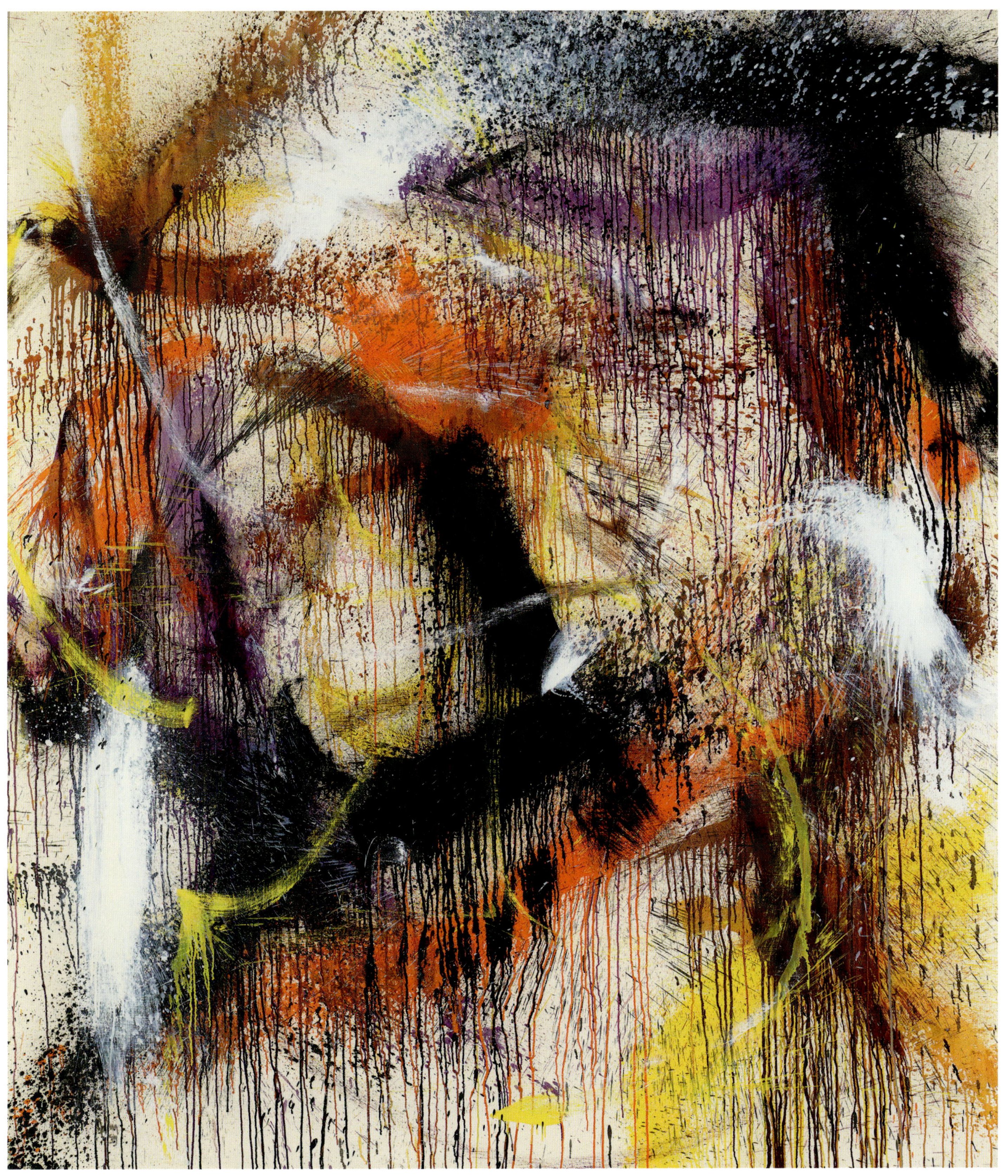

Plate 3

The Anvil, 1959
Oil on linen
84 × 72 in. (213.4 × 182.9 cm)
Whitney Museum of American Art, New York
Purchase, with funds from the Friends of the Whitney Museum of American Art *60.22*

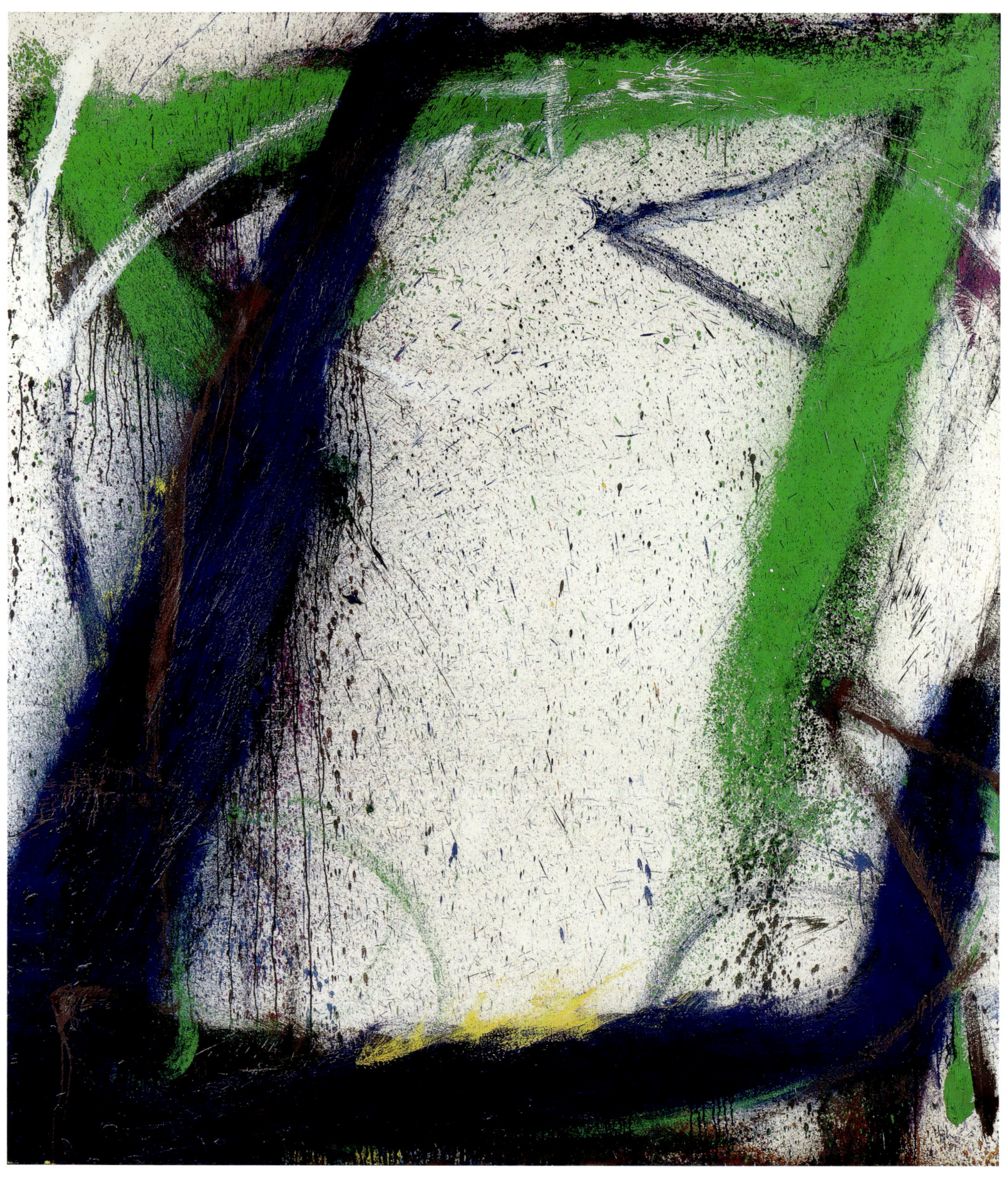

Plate 4

Peacock, 1964
Oil on canvas
90 × 78 in. (228.6 × 198 cm)
The Newark Museum of Art, New Jersey
Purchased in 1987 by the Special Acquisition Fund *87.40*

He had come to New York a fully formed artist already in his late thirties who had studied with Mies and been part of a sophisticated Parisian milieu. He had also received accolades for his mid-1950s paintings that are only tangentially Abstract Expressionist. Without a doubt, Bluhm's embrace of Abstract Expressionism in the 1950s marks a significant moment in his artistic journey, but he never aped anyone else's work, and by 1959 he had begun to move away from the style. In a 1985 interview Bluhm suggested that "Post Abstract Expressionism" would have been a better term to describe his work, indicating both his connection to the movement and his desire to move beyond it.[13] Nevertheless, the "Second Generation" label stuck and ultimately fostered a lack of understanding for Bluhm's evolving practice, which impacted his ability to exhibit and sell. Emerging artists such as Jasper Johns and Robert Rauschenberg, who worked in opposition to gestural abstraction, captured the attention of an art market that was fixated on ingrained notions of originality. Leo Castelli became very involved with these new artists and turned his attention to them. During his 1960 solo exhibition at the gallery, Bluhm became upset with Castelli when he found the dealer offering paintings by other artists to potential buyers by leaning them against his own. The relationship ended on bad terms, with Bluhm having made an enemy of a man who became one of the most influential dealers in America.[14] Bluhm's lifelong refusal to accommodate himself to the dictates of collectors and dealers persisted when flattery or simply biting his tongue might have helped advance his career.[15]

During his lifetime, Bluhm was represented by three other major New York galleries: Martha Jackson in the 1970s, Joan Washburn in the 1980s, and Ace Gallery in the 1990s, but these relationships did not endure.[16] During long stretches between New York shows, Bluhm continued to exhibit in Europe, where he always found a receptive audience. Rodolphe Stadler, an eminent dealer in Paris, held regular solo shows of Bluhm's work; Bluhm also maintained a significant presence in Italy over the years, placing numerous works in Italian collections.[17] He also had advocates in the United States: the Corcoran Gallery of Art, Washington, DC, held a one-man show in 1969, organized by James Harithas, another prominent champion of Bluhm's work; the renowned collector Joseph Hirshhorn acquired works from this exhibition. A second solo show was held at the Corcoran in 1977, this time organized by Jane Livingston. Other notable shows were held during his lifetime, such as a traveling retrospective of works on paper organized by William Salzillo at Hamilton College, Clinton, New York, and *Action/Precision: The New Direction in New York, 1955–1960*, organized by Paul Schimmel. All told, however, in comparison to other artists of his rank, relatively scant attention was paid to Bluhm, especially in his later years.

One contributing factor to this puzzling lack of exposure was Bluhm's absence from New York City. Restless by nature, he had moved his family to Paris in 1965 in an attempt to reconnect with the milieu that had been so essential to his original emergence as an artist; however, he found the situation in Paris changed and the family soon returned to New York, where they lived until 1969. Looking for a better quality of life, the Bluhms then acquired a former winery in Millbrook, ninety miles north of the city, where they lived for more than a decade. For the first time, Bluhm (a self-described "city boy") occupied a huge studio surrounded by nature. Set up in a hayloft, with a separate area for drawing, this studio enabled Bluhm to establish his own creative space apart from the politics of the New York scene, and to immerse himself in his painting. Following a subsequent move to East Hampton, Bluhm once again relocated in 1987, this time to East Wallingford, Vermont, where he renovated a farmhouse and built an expansive modern studio to accommodate the growing size of his later paintings. While there were many advantages to living and working in these more spacious environments, the physical separation and distance from the city made Bluhm's studio less accessible to dealers and collectors.

In the same way that Bluhm moved fluidly between urban and rural environments, he was not content with stasis in his studio practice. Instead he continually innovated, setting aside pictorial problems when he felt they had been solved.[18] This ongoing stylistic evolution confused many in the art world. The art market—and

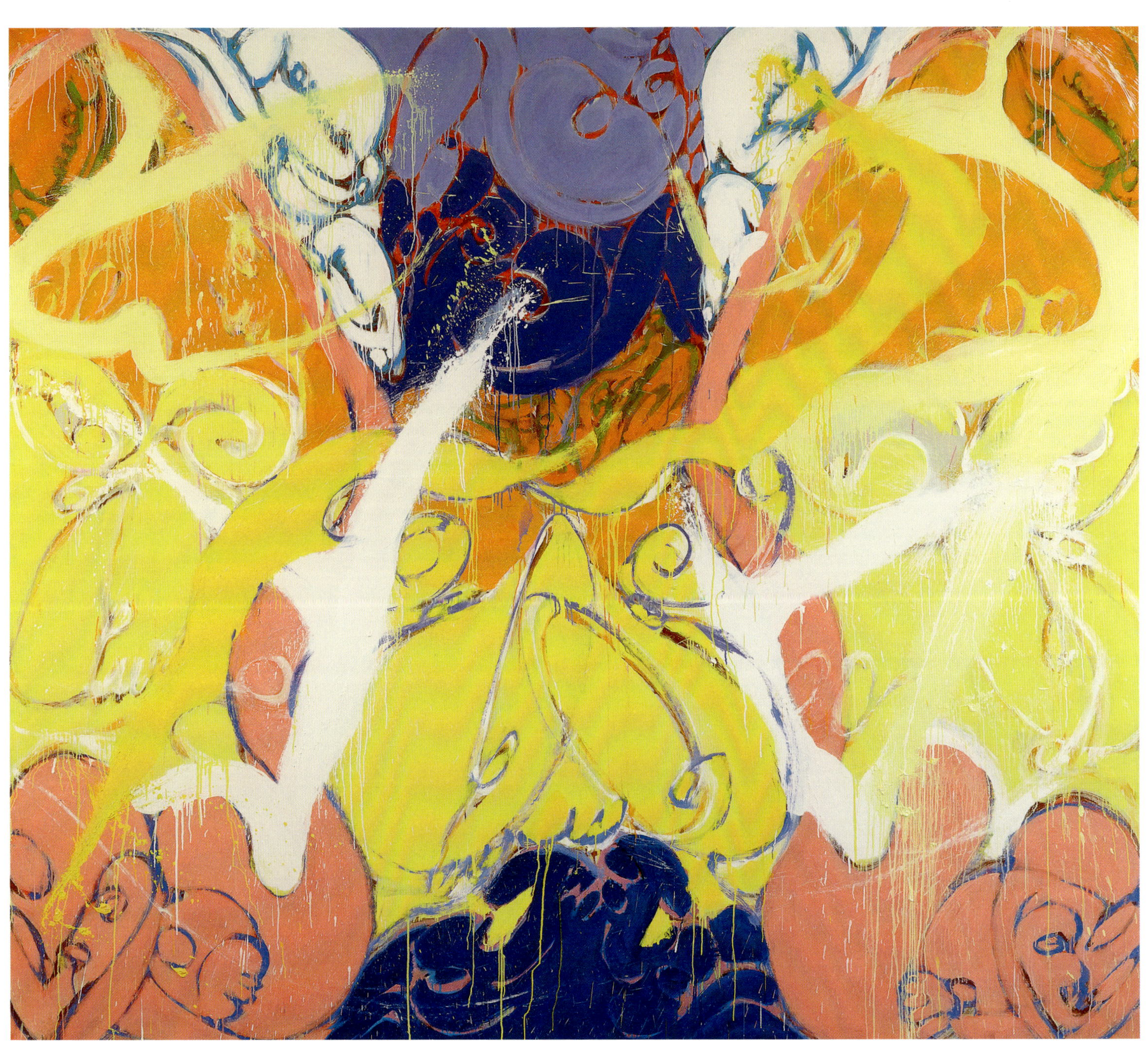

Plate 5

Pinkerton's Lady, 1986
Oil on canvas
102 × 114 in. (259 × 289.5 cm)
The Estate of Norman Bluhm

art history—privileges work that conforms to an artist's "signature" look. For Bluhm, this remains his late 1950s paintings, which for many critics and collectors effectively discounts his later output. Ironically, his involvement with Abstract Expressionism cast him out of favor in the 1960s, and then his refusal to repeat himself inhibited his reception later on. Defining Bluhm as an Abstract Expressionist overdetermines what amounts to his early production, and obscures what he achieved in his later work. While he never renounced gestural abstraction, Bluhm's innate curiosity and desire to challenge himself led him to begin mixing his recognizable active brushwork with a broader range of art historical influences and interests.

Over time, Bluhm's fascination with the figure began to inform his oils more overtly, as did his reverence for Matisse. Painted in 1967, *Theodora* (Plate 39) was his first definite move in this direction.[19] Voluptuous, pink biomorphic passages appear in much of Bluhm's output of the 1970s and 1980s, and he habitually used painting titles that invoke a female presence. Bluhm's paint application became less improvisational, more consciously controlled, and he increasingly employed a palette of purples and pastels in an ornamental manner. An unabashed sensuality pervaded his practice from the 1970s onward as well.[20] In *Rosie 1* (Plate 52) Bluhm clearly portrays a visceral enjoyment of the female form. While such eroticism is overt only in his studio drawings, many of his finished oils swing between abstraction and figuration, reveling in an ambiguity and a sense of fluid movement suggestive of carnality. Critic Barry Schwabsky noted Bluhm's "ostentatiously 'pretty' colors," which, combined with the use of curvilinear forms, "refer emphatically to the feminine," as well as Bluhm's "unreserved . . . embrace [of] the decorative".[21] In *Sooty Lady* (Plate 54), for example, Bluhm deploys his gestures and drips sparingly on top of hot yellows and flashes of violet; billowing forms created by sinuous lines intersect with elegance and frenzy, creating a sensual mood. As in many of his works from the 1970s onward, Bluhm here loosely recalls the swirling compositions of undraped cherubs and voluptuous goddesses seen in Baroque ceiling paintings, as well as the idyllic circle of linked forms, intensely emotional color, and multiple poses seen in Matisse's *La Danse* (Fig. 6). Schwabsky noted that works like *Pinkerton's Lady* (Plate 5) possess an "ecstatic androgyny" and an "objectless eroticism," as they fuse the essentially "masculine posture" of Abstract Expressionism with an overtly feminine vocabulary of color and form. Schwabsky's insight is quite useful; certainly, Bluhm's paintings of the 1970s and the 1980s revel in suggestions of the pleasures of female flesh, but the ambiguity of their imagery allows their painterly and formal properties to take precedence.

In the late 1980s, Bluhm embarked on an ambitious new direction, creating what would be his last body of work. The resulting enormous, multipanel paintings amplify many of his concerns of the previous twenty-five years, but also represent his most dramatic stylistic change. As before, the female form is the dominant motif, but now paintings like *Persephone* (Plate 74 and Fig. 7), from 1995, contain a multitude of such forms. And while Bluhm had always created wide triptychs throughout his career, the late works are uniformly massive and often grow upward, frequently ten feet high or more. The large scale enhances the effect of Bluhm's electric pastel colors. Perhaps the most startling development in the late work is his introduction of a rigid geometry. Cathedrals and stained-glass windows—important to Bluhm throughout his career—are recalled here as squares and rectangles are employed to create compartments. These niches frame gestures and forms that are more identifiably human than those in his earlier works, especially the passages that seem to depict dancing figures, or "leaping sprites."[22] Always an expert draftsman, Bluhm was able to repeat these gestures and their mirror images at will, echoing the symmetry of his gridded backgrounds. Bluhm painstakingly planned his 1990s works using preparatory drawings, following the same process as many of the earlier masters he admired.

In a 1987 interview, Bluhm reiterated his lifelong conviction that "art is all the 3,000 years that were created before me. . . . I look for the greatness I can use," and went on to say that, at that moment, he was particularly interested in the Italian Renaissance.[23] He

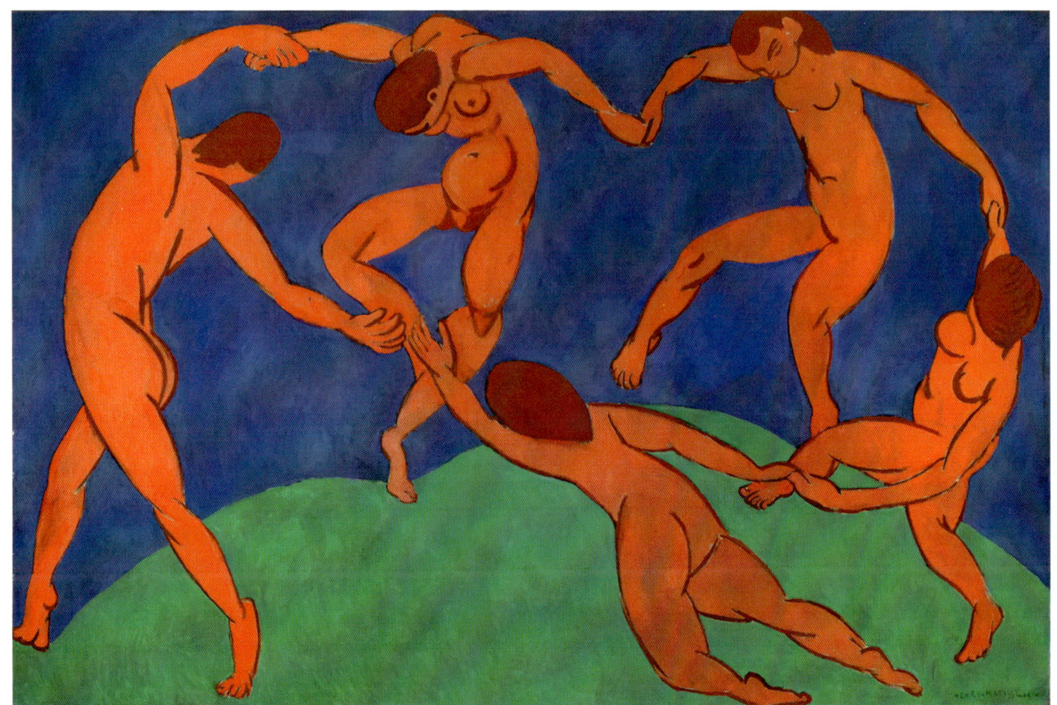

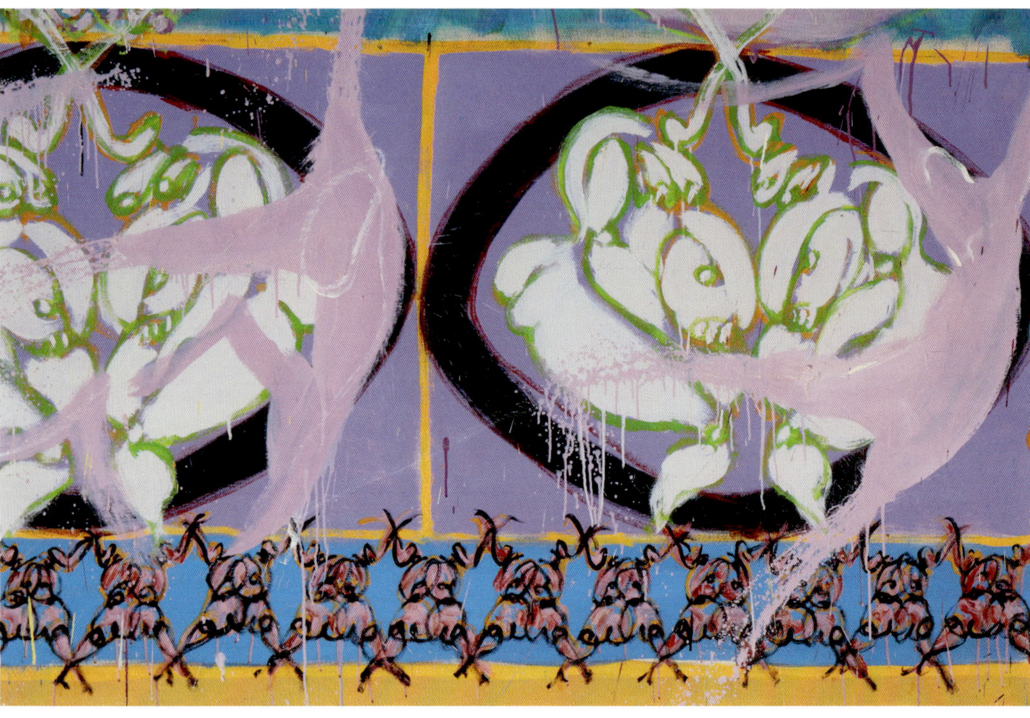

Fig. 6
Henri Matisse. *La Danse*, 1909–10. Oil on canvas, 102 ⅜ × 154 in. (260 × 391 cm). The State Hermitage Museum, St. Petersburg. Inv no. GE-9673. © 2019 Succession H. Matisse / Artists Rights Society (ARS), New York

Fig. 7
Detail of *Persephone*, 1995 (Plate 74)

Fig. 8
Piero della Francesca. *Battle between Heraclius and Chosroes*, 1452–66. Fresco, 130 × 294 in. (329 × 747 cm). San Francesco, Arezzo

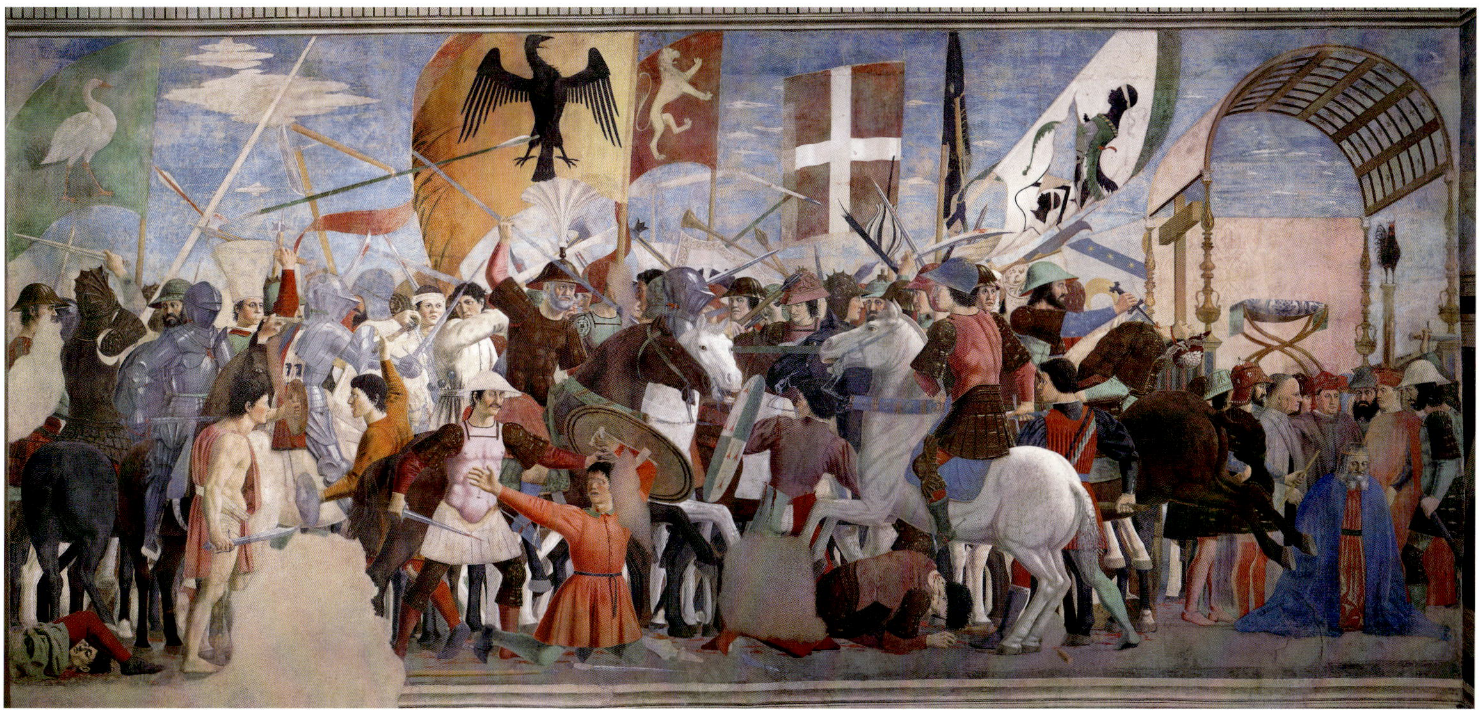

also mentioned Paolo Uccello, a key painter of the early Renaissance, in connection with these works.[24] As always, art history provided Bluhm inspiration and also affords the viewer a way into the work. A hallmark of the Italian painters was their ability to integrate large groups of figures in exalted scenes of nobility. Piero della Francesca's grandly-scaled fresco painting *Battle between Heraclius and Chosroes* (Fig. 8) uses repetition of poses and shapes to create the illusion of depth, while the structure at the right and the interlocking spears, banners, and trumpets impose harmony and add focal points to an otherwise chaotic mass of bodies in combat.[25] Through their orderly arrangement, the host of forms clustered in and around the ornamental spaces within the work give the sense that they—like the viewer—are assembled to witness an important event.

Bluhm's most perceptive critics list a dizzying number of other references to consider regarding Bluhm's late works: Tibetan mandalas; Persian carpets; Indian art; Russian icons; Japanese screen paintings; French Rococo and Italian Baroque ceiling paintings; the Venetian tradition; and more prosaic influences such as women's cosmetics and popular culture.[26] Spirituality also suffuses these paintings; this spirituality was informed by several Asian and Middle Eastern cultures, but ultimately Bluhm locates his version of the spiritual firmly within the human body. As James Harithas points out, Bluhm's late works "demonstrate the intimate connection between the erotic and the spiritual by virtue of their orgiastic intensity."[27] It would be hard to miss the obvious associations Bluhm makes between sexuality and divinity, but his vision expands beyond celebrating the life force that resides within us all. Not only is Persephone the Greek goddess of Spring, symbolizing fecundity and birth, she also spends part of every year with Hades in the underworld. Indeed, Bluhm's astonishingly inclusive late works read as depictions of Hell equally as much as they do of Heaven, and what might imply intimacy can also suggest conflict.[28] Moreover, late paintings such as *Persephone* and *Calliope's Song* (Plate 84) rely heavily on an exacting mathematical ordering of space, as do Piero della Francesca's frescoes. Piero, admired by his contemporaries as much for his skill as a mathematician as for his achievements as a fresco painter, believed that everything in the firmament could be described and understood through numbers and equations. So, too, did Bluhm seek to exalt the power of human rationality, which he saw reflected in great art from around the world and throughout time.

At the time of his death, Bluhm had completed several major works in this vein. With two notable exceptions, until the Newark Museum retrospective, these late paintings have not been exhibited.[29] Challenging in scale and subject matter, and difficult for some to reconcile with the Abstract Expressionist works so often favored within Bluhm's oeuvre, the artist knew that widespread appreciation of these late paintings would not be immediate. This did not discourage him; he expressed deep satisfaction in these works. Bluhm once described the life of the artist as "the choice of loneliness in the motion of time," noting that "joy is forever in the unknown."[30] Never one to adapt to the market or to those who didn't understand his artistic evolution, Bluhm persisted in painting as he always had, by his own instincts. Striving to unite his own vision with his diverse interest in the "greatness" that came before him, Bluhm trusted that his engagement with the vastness of art, both past and present, would be matched by the openness and imagination of viewers who would recognize in his work a love of beauty and a pure reverence for the human spirit.

Notes

1. Bluhm's birth certificate lists his birth year as 1921, but Cary Bluhm strongly suspects this document, obtained several years after his birth, is incorrect and that Norman Bluhm was in fact born in 1920. In most catalogues from the early part of his career 1920 is listed as his birth year, and in a 1969 interview, Bluhm told Paul Cummings that he was born in 1920. "Oral History Interview with Norman Bluhm," October 23–November 12, 1969, Archives of American Art, Smithsonian Institution, p. 1. An excerpt of this interview is published on pp. 29–41 in this catalogue.
2. In a 1974 interview that was broadcast nationally on PBS, Bluhm told interviewer Russell Connor that he lived in Italy for eight years as a child, but the exact time period remains unknown. *Group Portrait: Four Artists of New York State* (Cable Arts Foundation, 1974).
3. Critics often have focused on the artist's war years, relating the technical skill of flying a plane to his later proficiency with controlling his athletic gestures, for example, or speculating on how the sensation of being aloft informed his artistic approach. See Thomas Hess's untitled essay in the catalogue for Bluhm's 1965 one-man show at Anderson-Mayer Gallery, Paris; B. H. Friedman's obituary of Bluhm, "Young American," *Artforum* (April 1999): 30; and John Yau, "Drawing in Color: A Portrait of Norman Bluhm," in *Norman Bluhm: Opere su carta, 1948–1999* (Milan: Padiglione d'Arte Contemporanea, 2000), p. 17.
4. "Oral History Interview with Norman Bluhm," p. 24.
5. In numerous interviews Bluhm used the term "romantic" to refer both to his stance as an artist as well as the allure of the Parisian milieu. See, for instance, ibid., pp. 4, 6, 7, and 21. See also William Salzillo, "Conversation with the Artist," in *Norman Bluhm: Works on Paper, 1947–1987* (Clinton, N.Y.: Hamilton College, 1987), p. 8.
6. "Oral History Interview with Norman Bluhm," p. 3.
7. "I was involved in the *Nymphéas* of Monet. I was fortunate to go see them before they even opened up [the Orangerie]." Ibid., p. 24.
8. According to Bluhm, his growing alignment with American artists was met with some hostility and jealousy from his French network, which regarded the Americans as "barbaric." Ibid., p. 18.
9. Raphael Rubinstein makes this observation in "Ecstatic Meditations: Norman Bluhm's Paintings Over Five Decades," in *Norman Bluhm* (Milan: Mazzotta, 2000), p. 21. In addition to medieval stained-glass windows and Monet's late work, Rubinstein points out the importance to Bluhm of Corot and specifically his ability to give the illusion of radiating light.
10. B. H. Friedman's obituary of Bluhm, "Young American," *Artforum* (April 1999): 30. The death in 1978 of noted writer, editor, and curator Thomas Hess, another of Bluhm's close friends and supporters, was another great loss for Bluhm during this period.
11. For example, in a review of the exhibition *Abstract Expressionists and Imagists* at the Guggenheim (which included Bluhm), artist and critic Sidney Tillim wrote, "They fill, they empty, they pour, they dump. In short they are doing pretty much the same thing that they were doing yesterday and last season." *Arts* (December 1961): 42–43.
12. According to Irving Sandler, Clement Greenberg was one of the first to use this term in a 1956 talk at The Club; it gained greater use after 1960. Irving Sandler, *A Sweeper-Up After Artists: A Memoir*. New York: Thames and Hudson, 2003, pp. 231–32. Bill Berkson used the term in his complimentary piece, "Bluhm Paints a Picture," *ARTnews* (May 1963). See also William Agee's introduction to Bluhm's 1969 Corcoran Museum exhibition catalogue.
13. Stephen Westfall, "Then and Now: Six of the New York School Look Back," *Art in America* (June 1985): 115.
14. Bluhm recalled that after their split, Leo Castelli attempted to collect $9,000 that Bluhm owed the gallery from advances against sales. Bluhm stated he replied, "Leo, what would you rather have, $9,000 or your life?" George Hofmann, "Interview with Norman Bluhm," July 21, 1997, East Wallingford, Vermont. Hunter College Artists Research Group Oral History, https://huntercollegeart.org/artists-research-group/norman-bluhm/.
15. In a 1986 feature, Bluhm told Amei Wallach, "Once in a while I make attempts in the art world, I shake hands. It's difficult. People bow so much it should be a world of hunchbacks." "The Artist as Rocky: A Brawler in Paint," *Newsday*, September 2, 1984, sec. 2, p. 5.
16. Martha Jackson died in 1969; the gallery was run by her son David Anderson under her name until he closed it in the early 1980s. In 2016 Ace Gallery declared bankruptcy and the trustee overseeing the reorganization fired its owner, Doug Christmas, amid accusations of non-payment to creditors, many of whom were artists.
17. Milanese collector Alberto Ulrich, Bluhm's friend since the 1940s, was particularly supportive in Italy.
18. Bluhm said, "In order to be a creative, you have to move through the various channels of your life. If you do the same goddamn painting for fifty years, you'd be one of the most boring painters you ever met." Norman Bluhm, unpublished interview with the author, March 1992.
19. In 1987 Bluhm specifically referenced this work as the first to directly reference the figure, stating, "I was interested in closed and open forms and the way one form defeated another. The gesture around a closed form. I first saw it at the Cloisters [museum, New York]." Salzillo, "Conversation with the Artist," p. 11.
20. John Yau points out that the American discomfort with sexuality, what he calls its "repressive puritanical strain" was yet another factor that affected the reception of Bluhm's sensual abstractions. Yau, "Norman Bluhm and the Venetian Tradition," in *Norman Bluhm: Works on Paper, 1947–1987*, p. 18.
21. Barry Schwabsky, "Norman Bluhm and the Eternal Feminine," *Arts* (Summer 1986): 47.
22. Rubinstein, "Ecstatic Meditations," p. 27. Rubinstein also points out the strong relationship of these forms to Matisse's *La Danse*.
23. Salzillo, "Conversation with the Artist," p. 11.
24. Bluhm, unpublished interview with the author, March 1992.
25. During a 1987 family vacation to Tuscany, Bluhm insisted on visiting churches housing Piero della Francesca's work. Nina Bluhm, conversation with the author, April 2019.
26. See, for example, Yau, "Norman Bluhm and the Venetian Tradition"; Rubinstein, "Ecstatic Meditations," pp. 27–28; and Barry Schwabsky, "Norman Bluhm at Ace Gallery," *Artforum* (February 1995): 89–90. All three of these critics have written extensively on Bluhm.
27. James Harithas, "Norman Bluhm: Works on Paper," in *Norman Bluhm: Opere su carta, 1948–1999*, p. 12.
28. Barry Schwabsky noted that Bluhm's 1990s works "remind us that heavenly hosts and witches' sabbats are remarkably alike," and made specific reference to Bluhm's use of sinister titles for his paintings. Schwabsky, "Norman Bluhm at Ace Gallery," pp. 90–91.
29. Ace Gallery held a show of Bluhm's late works in 1994, and the Station Museum, Houston, showed numerous such works in 2007; the latter exhibition, organized by James Harithas, was an extraordinary gathering of almost all of Bluhm's work from the late 1990s, allowing them to be seen together for the first time.
30. Bluhm, quoted in Daniel Frasnay, *The Artist's World* (New York: Viking Press, 1969), n.p.

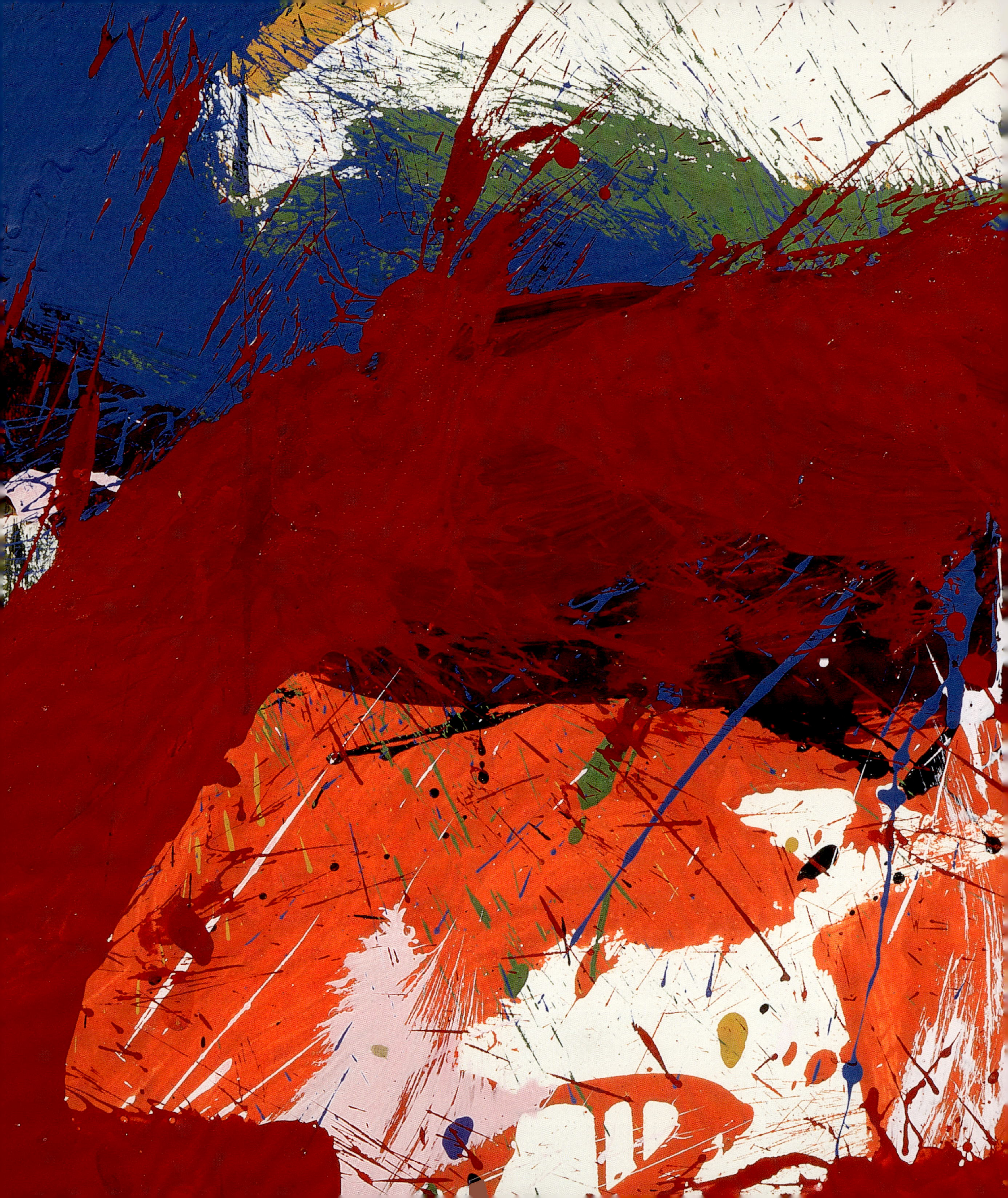

INTERVIEW WITH NORMAN BLUHM

Transcript of a Tape-Recorded Interview with Norman Bluhm by Paul Cummings at Bluhm's Studio, 333 Park Avenue South, New York City, October 23, 1969

Paul Cummings: You were born in Chicago in 1920.

Norman Bluhm: Right. I studied architecture with Mies [van der Rohe].

Do you have brothers and sisters?

I had a brother who was killed in the war. And I have a sister . . . she still lives in Chicago. I haven't seen my family in years. I don't have much to do with them. I'm what they call the bad penny. No, but to make it easier and a quicker conversation, I studied with Mies.

How did you go to that school?

I wanted to be an architect at one time in my life. I decided I wanted to go [to] what was then called the Armour Institute of Technology, which is now the Illinois Institute of Technology. I was lucky because I had a very high average in high school . . . so I got in and I studied under Mies.

What do you think started your interest in architecture?

I read books. Basically, I read books. My father was involved more in engineering. He wasn't involved in anything aesthetic. . . . [I remember, with Mies] one time we had a problem which involved a white space of a certain dimension and a black space of a lesser dimension—a big white space and a very small black line almost and then maybe just another white space. And you arranged these things in order to give a certain understanding of volume and creative space with the black against the white. It's quite a problem architecturally speaking. It's a Bauhaus idea. I worked on it; I arranged it. Mies came in. He put it up on the wall, and he looked at it. He said to me, "Ja, Herr Bluhm" (he always said "Ja, Herr Bluhm"), "very interesting, very interesting; very good. But maybe I would move this black"—and he took the little black line—"I would move this one-sixteenth of an inch." Well, in a strange kind of way I think when I paint now, especially now, or when I really become terribly involved in painting, I go to the other extremity. Because, interestingly enough, when I was in college I was painting and who was one of the first painters I painted like? It was Mondrian.

Oh, really?

Yes. Of course, with a Van Gogh kind of texture about it, real heavy. But I was involved in that whole Bauhaus world. And when I left that whole school probably the painter I became most involved in was Matisse, which was a complete reversal to another form of beauty. Even now when I go around to galleries and look at certain painters—I won't drop any names—I always say, "Well, maybe if you'd move that one-sixteenth of an inch . . . "

Yes. How long did you study there?

I was there 1936–1937—until the war. Then I came back after the war and studied again.

What happened during the war?

Oh, the war. Let's not talk about the war. We're talking about art; we're not talking about military matters. Let's just say I was in the war.

In the Air Force?

Yes. That's enough. [Getting back to my time at Armour] . . . I began to think about what I was in architecture. I felt that I didn't have any kind of individuality in architecture. And I thought, well, what am I going to end up being but a little Mies? Maybe, I'll do a Mies-type garage one day, or a Mies-type drug store; but I'd be nothing but a little Mies because I somehow didn't feel even any individual arrogance about architecture. I admired it, I loved it. I still do. I like architecture. But I felt I would never make even an interesting architect. I'm not talking about greatness or fame. I was honest enough to say—thank goodness—that I couldn't make a good architect. . . . Maybe it's romantic. But I'm a romantic. So what the hell am I going to do about it?

Fig. 9
Norman Bluhm in his studio at 333 Park Avenue South, New York City, early 1960s. Photo courtesy of The Estate of Norman Bluhm

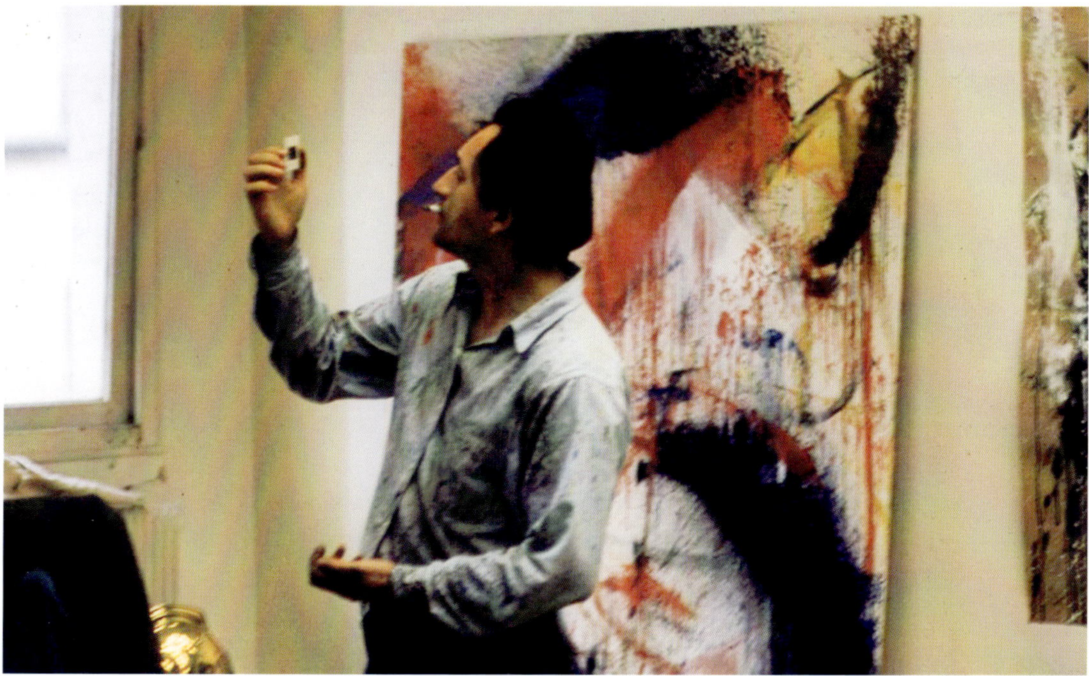

What do you think the training as an architect did for you? You know, the discipline, the organization?

Basically, what architecture did for me was to give me a totally different concept of space. I mean, taking the Bauhaus idea of what space is, and also a great idea of scale. One of the great remarks is that we always say that some people's gesture in space or in scale sometimes can be, well, let's say, twelve inches, and sometimes it can be ten feet. In an unknown way—I'm not talking about the known aspect of architecture, but the unknown—that's what it did for me: it gave me an idea of scale, how it could go outside of yourself, how you get outside of those little fingers we all have. I think it was an extremely valuable thing. And also I began to understand things in a different aesthetic kind of way.

How do you mean in a different way?

Well, a different kind of analytical interpretation of things. Do you see what I mean? Maybe it was a little corny—corny from the standpoint that it was on a certain level, a very high pitch, which was the Bauhaus idea as far as I'm concerned. It doesn't have the emotional and romantic fluctuation of, let's say, the École des Beaux-Arts, but it gives you . . . a way of looking at things in an extremely serious way. . . . I think those are the simple spiritual values that the Bauhaus—Mies—gave me. I think that they were deeper and more *unknown* to me than they are known to me.

What decided you on going to Paris?

Hell, that's quite obvious. Very simple.

The GI Bill and everything?

Well, not the GI Bill. Forget the GI Bill. Everybody of a certain period was romantically involved. I mean, in Europe we were all romantically involved. If we had a certain education we were involved in the idea of Matisse or Picasso or, going back through time, the Renaissance.

I think the great dream of every ex-GI, to use your phrase, was that kind of romanticism if he was capable of fulfilling it. . . . That's what I went there for. That was the thing I wanted to do. As to its value—well, there could be hours of discussion.

You lived there a long time?

Yes, I sure did.

About nine or ten years?

Longer than that actually, because I also went back recently with my family and lived there for another two years.

It was 1947 you were there?

Yes. Paris, well, let's see . . . I was fortunate that when I arrived in Paris I met my ex-wife and she was a part of what was known in those days as the Maison des Lettres, which was a continuation of the Groupe de Charenton. . . . The Groupe de Charenton was the group of Antonin Artaud and Roger Blin. The reason I'm mentioning this is I just heard this morning that Beckett got the Nobel Prize. So my ex-wife was involved with that whole group of people.

Who is she?

Her name is Claude Souvrain. Her best friend was a girl named Florence Loeb, who was the daughter of Pierre Loeb, of the Galerie Pierre, where Picasso showed and Miró showed. And I got into that group immediately. I was fortunate, I didn't get involved with all those GIs who sat around the Dôme [Café] looking for Hemingway or Fitzgerald or somebody to walk by. Although I was kind of mad in those days, it was of great value to me that I met all these people and I saw a lot of them. I knew Paul Éluard very well. I was telling somebody the other day a story about those days in Paris. I remember my ex-wife and I were kind of broke, I had that famous GI Bill of Rights—what was it? Seventy-five dollars a month? We weren't married; we were living in sin *à la francais*. . . . I met Picasso a number of times. To go on rapidly—I don't want to drop a thousand names—my closest friends in Europe for years were the Matisse family. Which was a weird kind of situation because I admired Matisse so much, and I became a very close friend of theirs. Of Marguerite Matisse especially, the Matisses' daughter; and Georges Duthuit, who was her husband, and their son, Claude Duthuit, the grandson of Henri Matisse. I saw those people for years and years, every day. When I had matrimonial troubles, they'd put me up for a while. I could tell thousands of stories about the Matisse family.

I was telling one the other day about my ex-wife. This is in reference to painting, which is very interesting in a strange kind of way about the École des Beaux-Arts and various art institutions of a classical nature. Matisse at one time in his life, when he was broke and young, wanted to become a professor of drawing, went to the École des Dessins and tried to become a professor. He took the test and flunked. And the reason why I know this is because my ex-wife tried to do the same thing. And we were at lunch one day at Marguerite and Georges Duthuit's. Claude broke down and was bawling like a baby, and I told them the story. So Madame Matisse laughed—you know, not terribly loud but, you know, a little smile on her face and she said to my ex-wife, "Oh, Claude, forget it; Henri tried three times and flunked every time." It was just one of those schools where you sat around and did these lousy cast drawings. I have nothing against that—I've done them myself; I think it's important to do them. But there's a certain point of perfection that any individual can't go into because then he loses his own spirit. . . . But I knew all those people. Then I got involved with the Surrealists, people like Patrick Waldberg. I knew Oscar Domínguez, who was mad. I know Max Ernst quite well, and his wife, Dorothea. I knew a lot of Surrealists, oddly enough.

How did you come to meet them? Through the poets?

Fig. 10
Norman Bluhm and Claude Souvrain in Paris, 1950s. Photo courtesy of The Estate of Norman Bluhm

Well, you know how Paris is. Paris is a café world. Or it used to be. It used to be that you met so-and-so, you'd meet so-and-so, then you were introduced to so-and-so; you met writers, poets, painters, people in the theater, people in the dance. This doesn't exist anymore. But right after the war especially, there was this period where all the art people somehow were together. . . . In the old days in the *quartier* where I lived, you know, people like Sartre and Picasso and everybody was there. If you were at least capable of going into a world of creative people you encountered them all. There wasn't this kind of standoffishness. I went to the theater all the time. I never bought a ticket in my life. They'd give you a ticket to go to see all the plays. The reason I mentioned Beckett, you know, I went to the first performance of *Waiting for Godot*. You got to know all those people and they had some sort of sympathy for what you were doing. That doesn't exist anymore in Paris.

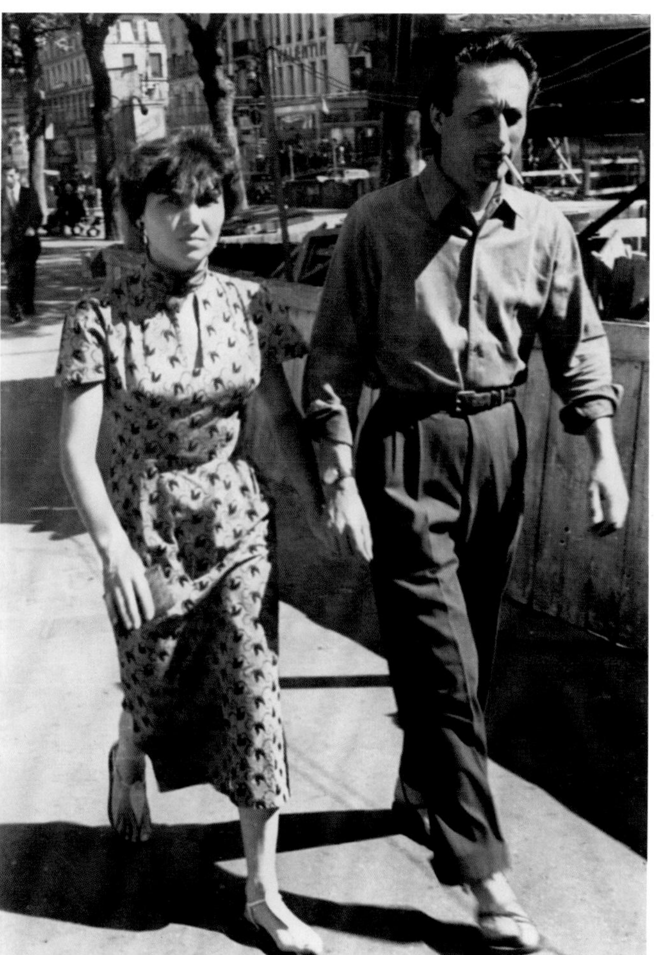

Yes. Did you get to know a lot of the Americans that were there, too?

Oh yes, sure, I knew a lot of them. Well, not a lot of them. For example, I knew Wally Reiss, I remember when "Bix" [Oscar Piagentini] was there.† There was a little group called the Gallery Eight that was formed sometime in Paris, I forget when; it was Reggie Pollack, Norman Rubington, a guy named Hugh Wysse, a fellow called John Anderson. I remember all those people. They had a little gallery which they opened up, it was called the Gallery Eight. . . . And then I knew Joan Mitchell, who is the godmother of my kids. I knew Paul Jenkins. And a lot of people I don't talk to and they don't talk to me. I could give you a long list of those.

It's interesting you seem to have gotten very involved in the French community and French life as well as with the Americans.

Much more. Well, first of all, I was married to a French woman. And although I knew a lot of them [Americans] and I saw a great deal of some of them and of course I was a very close friend of, and still am, Jean-Paul Riopelle. Of course, he's a Canadian but now he's really much more French than he is Canadian in a funny kind of way. But I associated with more French people than I did with Americans. I didn't see any reason to go to Europe to see Americans.

† Oscar Piagentini (1926–1991) went on to direct the J. L. Hudson Gallery in Detroit in the late 1960s through the early 1970s. Bluhm had a solo show there in 1971.

How did you meet the actors?

Through my ex-wife. All those people like Roger Blin all got their start out of the Maison des Lettres and the Groupe de Charenton. There was a young writer by the name of Roland Weingarten who I understand is quite a success now. As a matter of fact, he was the one who was offered the first play that made Gérard Philipe famous. He turned it down. Gérard Philipe was in that group also. . . . It's funny how you get to know all those people just by the mere fact that you associated with them. I was in a movie.

Oh, really?

That's my big success story.

What was the movie?

Orphée by Cocteau. I played a poet. That was a big moment in my life to be in the movies. Although, oddly enough, I found it terribly boring. The reason I bring this up is when you think of all the painters today who have gone into the movie scene. I find it terribly boring. Kind of a waste of time.

Over and over and over.

Yes. Shoot that same scene many times. I always recall a couple of scenes in that movie. It was shot out in the country—we used to go out in buses. There was a scene where it's supposed to look as if everybody is throwing rocks over a wall. It seems that they started to do it one day and then stopped. Cocteau no doubt paid a fabulous fortune to rent this house, but he received some insulting remarks from the owners. So the next day they were shooting that scene and he said, "I don't care if you have to throw the rocks through the windows. I want it to look right." We had some great scenes. There was one part where the scene starts—I sound like an actor but it was my only experience—it was shot at the Café des Poètes in the Place Stalingrad in Paris. There was one scene where Roger Blin was sitting on a terrace with Jean Marais—I think it was Roger Blin and Jean Marais—one little scene, and they hired this great big French guy to play the part of a cop. And he was supposed to come up and say, "Let's see your papers." Cocteau is up there, and they've got all the cameras going and this huge guy comes up and says, "*Fais voir vos papiers*," speaking in a very, very high, thin voice and Cocteau sort of screamed, "Cut!" And then he said the most marvelous thing: "One voice like mine around here is enough! Throw him out!"

I'm curious about where people went—what restaurants, what galleries?

Well, the restaurants were—what?—people went either through the tear-jerking idea of the 1920s looking for the shades of Hemingway. They went to the Dôme, they went to the Coupole, to the Café Flore, to the Deux Magots, and to Lipp. The group we were with used to go to a little place in the rue du Dragon, just a little bistro. Every little group somehow had their own little café. For example, still in Paris on Thursday nights in the café called La Palette, which is just off the rue de Seine, all those old Surrealists—by now they're probably coming in wheelchairs—but they meet there every Thursday night. It's a very European kind of thing. Everybody has their little café. Of course, when I lived in Paris I knew all the French painters. I remember friends of mine were François Arnal, César Baldaccini, the sculptor. I know Soulages very well. A Chinese fellow named Zao Wou-ki. Not all of them were good friends of mine. Zao Wou-ki was a very good friend of mine. "Wou-ki" they call him. He's a very good friend, I like him as a person. And then I used to go to galleries. I had a few experiences with galleries. I went to Pierre Loeb.

What are the galleries that you were shown with there?

I never had a one-man show until I came back here. I showed with Pierre Loeb. He had some work of mine in the early days, in the height of people like Miró, who was still in the gallery; people like that. But somehow we didn't

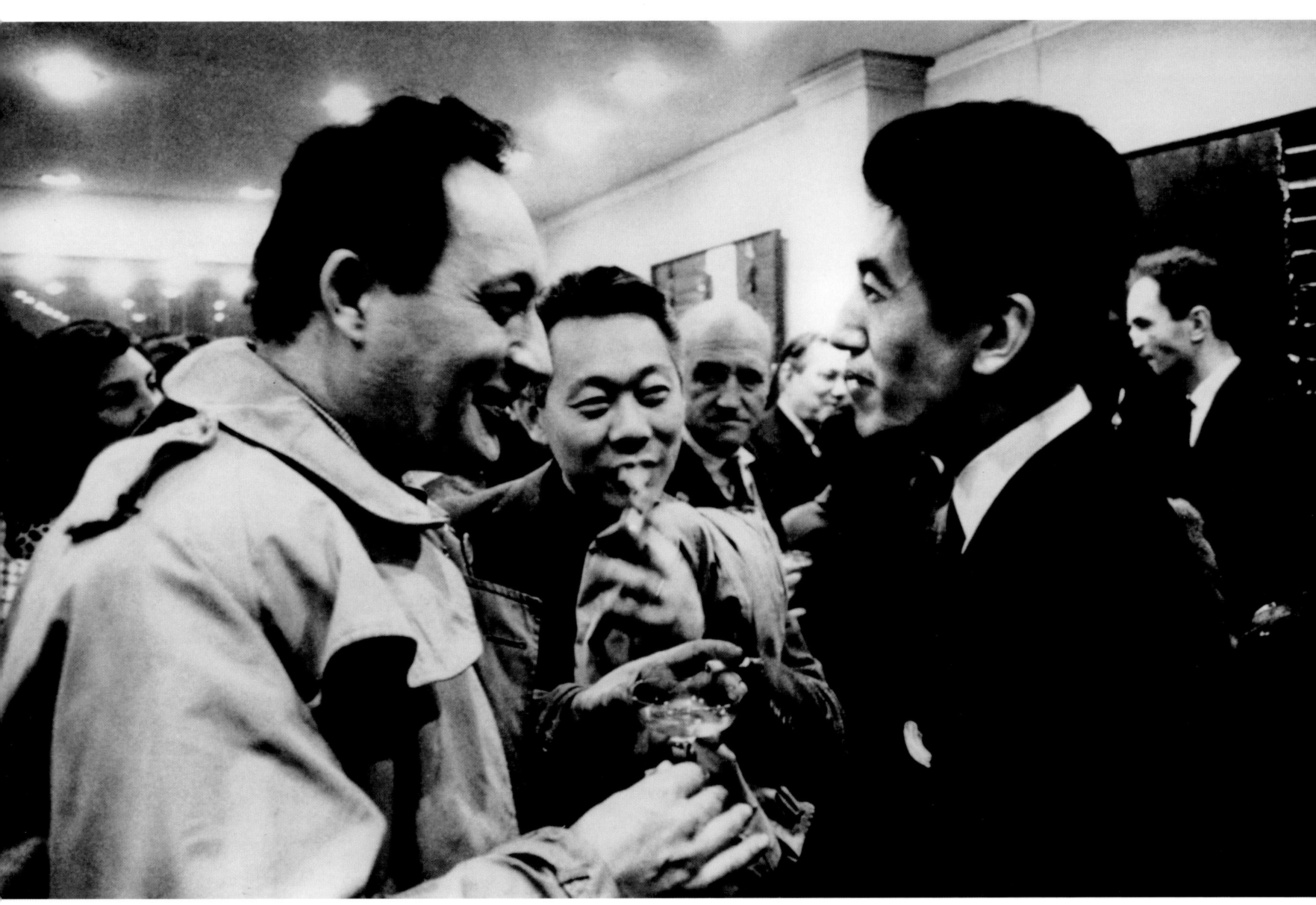

Fig. 11
Norman Bluhm, Zao Wou-ki, and Hisao Domoto, New York City, 1960s. Photo courtesy of The Estate of Norman Bluhm

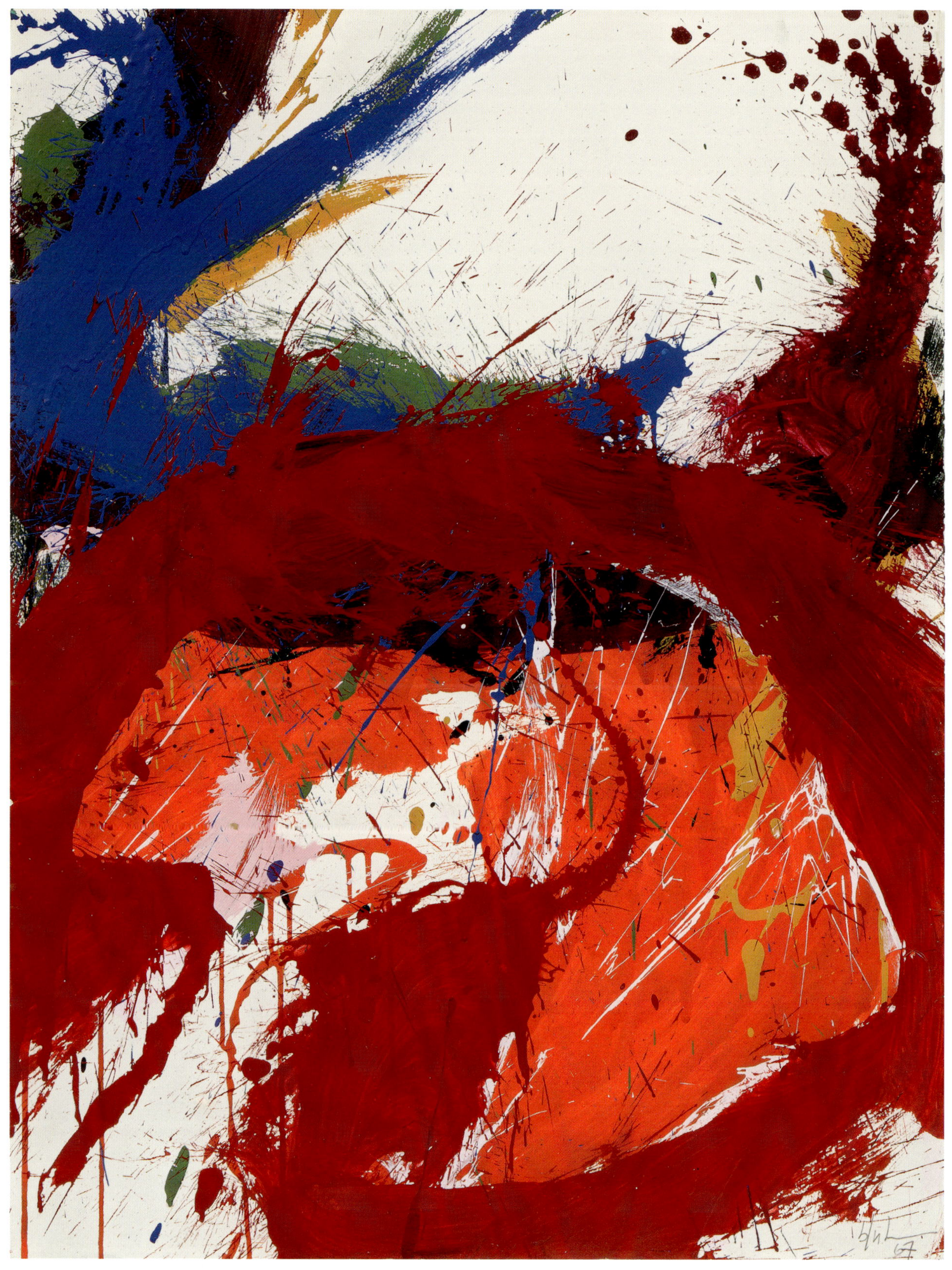

Plate 6

Study for Brizo, 1967
Acrylic on paper
30 × 22 ½ in. (76 × 57 cm)
The Estate of Norman Bluhm

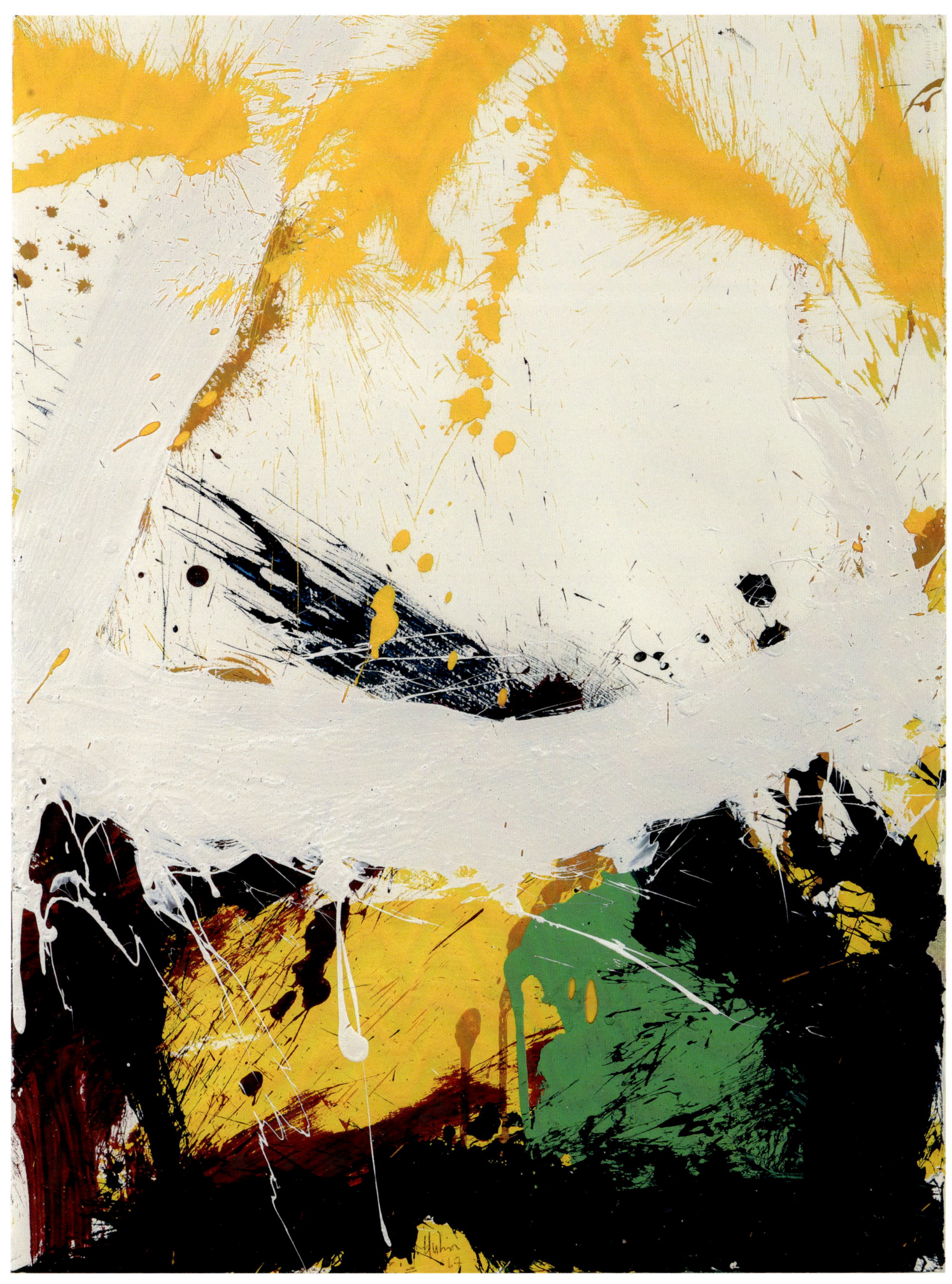

Plate 7

Untitled, 1967
Acrylic on paper
29 ½ × 23 ¼ in. (75 × 59 cm)
The Newark Museum of Art, New Jersey
Gift of Ruth Bowman, 1996 *96.6.1*

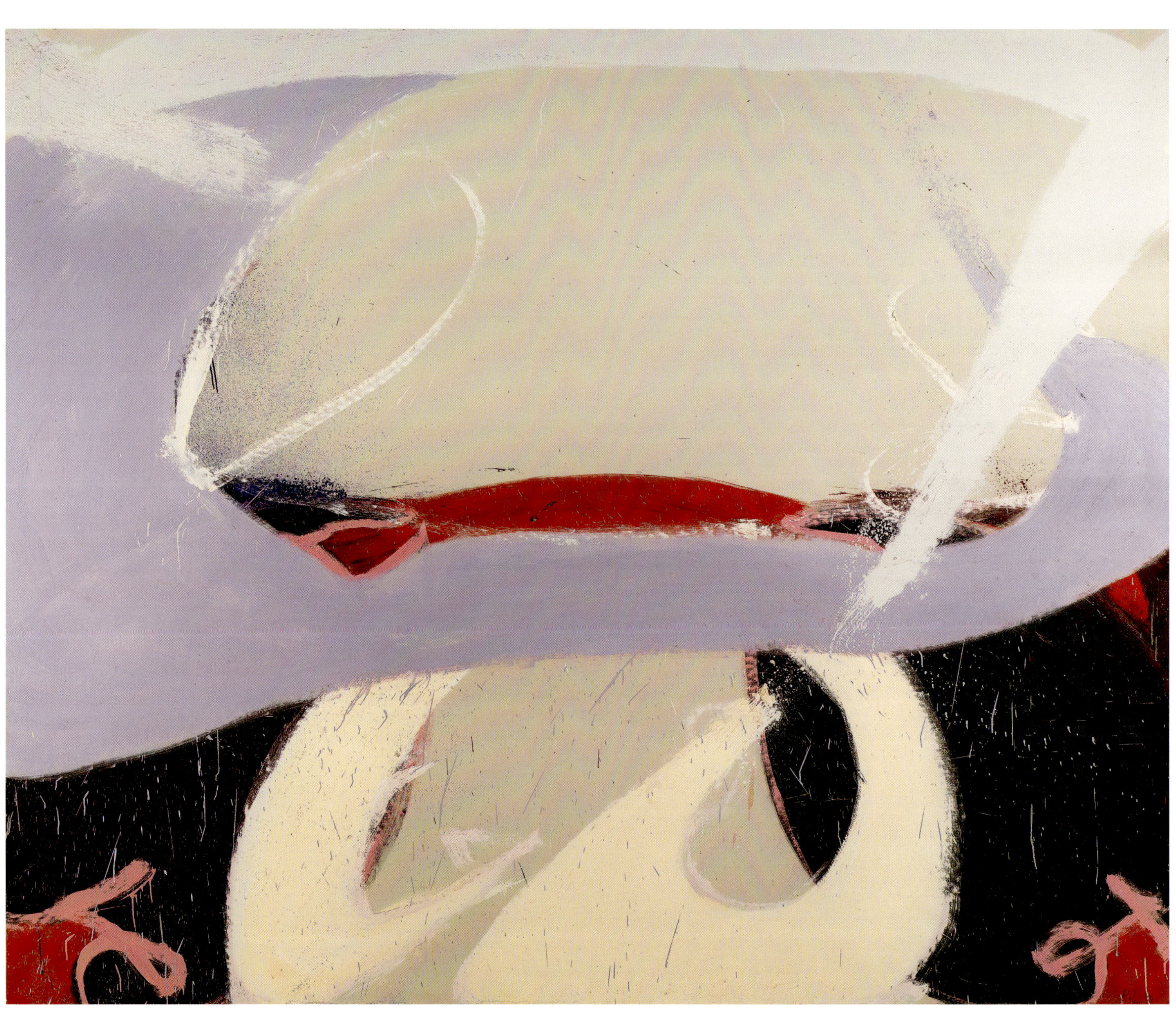

Plate 8

Erythea, 1971
Oil on canvas
96 × 114 in. (243.8 × 289.5 cm)
Smithsonian American Art Museum, Washington, DC
Gift of Mr. and Mrs. Oscar Piagentini *1974.17*

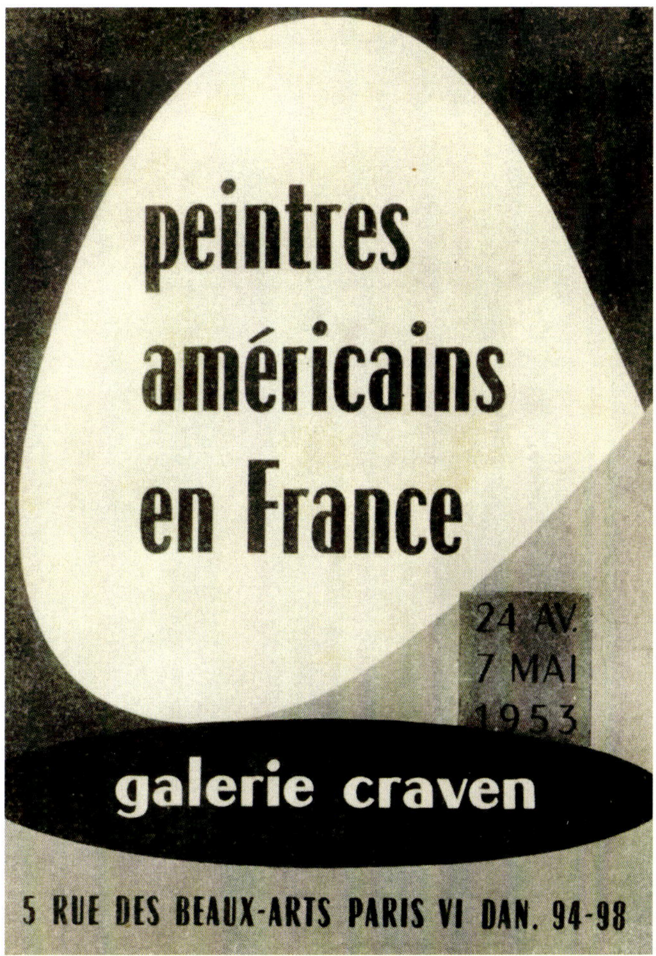

Fig. 12
Catalogue from one of Norman Bluhm's earliest Paris group exhibitions, *Peintres Américains en France*, Galerie Craven, Paris, April 24–May 7, 1953

get along. Not because of him. It was because of me. I was kind of an angry young man to put it briefly. They had these shows like "American Painters in Paris." I've even got the catalog here somewhere.

How did the French take to all these Americans coming to Paris and getting involved?

Not too well. I remember many times, especially in the late 1940s after the war—I'm talking mostly about painters—the first great expression was they always called somebody a "barbarian." I'm talking about an intellectual or aesthetic attitude . . . you know, "A bunch of barbarians". And then there was this terrible attitude, "Well, whoever heard of American painting? There's no American painting." Of course, the interesting thing is that in about 1952, when there were a few Pollocks and a few [Clyfford] Stills and a couple of paintings of Bill de Kooning shown, then suddenly there came another form of jealousy. Of course, a few Pollocks were shown before 1952 but really around 1952 this jealousy became apparent. It was just a little breath, but it began about then. From that time on until—well, I left in 1956—you slowly began to see this change about. First there was not basically anger but some sort of, "Well, what's this?" Then there was competition. Then there was anger. . . . I met Walter [Chrysler] in Paris at the time I was with Pierre Loeb. Walter was on that first big buying spree of paintings. He bought lots of Mathieus, lots of Jean-Paul Riopelle. He was buying a lot of paintings . . . I'll guess [this was in] 1952. The early '50s. I met him actually at Pierre Loeb's gallery. Pierre showed him a painting of mine. We talked for a moment. I don't recall the events exactly. Anyway, that following evening I was at a party at Robert Lebel's. . . . Robert and I were talking, and he said that Chrysler was coming over. I said, "Oh, he is?". "Yes, why don't you stick around and say hello to him?" So I waited around, we talked, I had a glass of wine. And in walked Chrysler. I think there was a painting of mine there, though I don't recall exactly. I said, "Why don't you come over to the studio?" So the following day he came over to the studio—it was some studio!—and he bought thirty-seven paintings.

That's fantastic. What did you think about him?

Oh, I thought he was marvelous! I didn't have any money. To put it lightly, I was screwed to the teeth. But when you have no money you don't care. I didn't have the courage to say no. I needed the money. Then he came back the next day and he bought, I don't know, ten more. Of course, I blew all that money in about a year. I took everybody out to dinner and things like that.

Is he a hard bargainer? Or was he in those days?

He was a cheapskate, just to be honest with you. Then he bought a big painting which I was to ship to him. He owed me about eight hundred dollars. . . . For that eight hundred dollars I had a piece of paper with me with which I was able to walk around for about a year in Paris borrowing money on that little slip of paper saying that he owed me eight hundred dollars. . . . When I landed [in New York] I called Chrysler and I said, "You owe me eight hundred

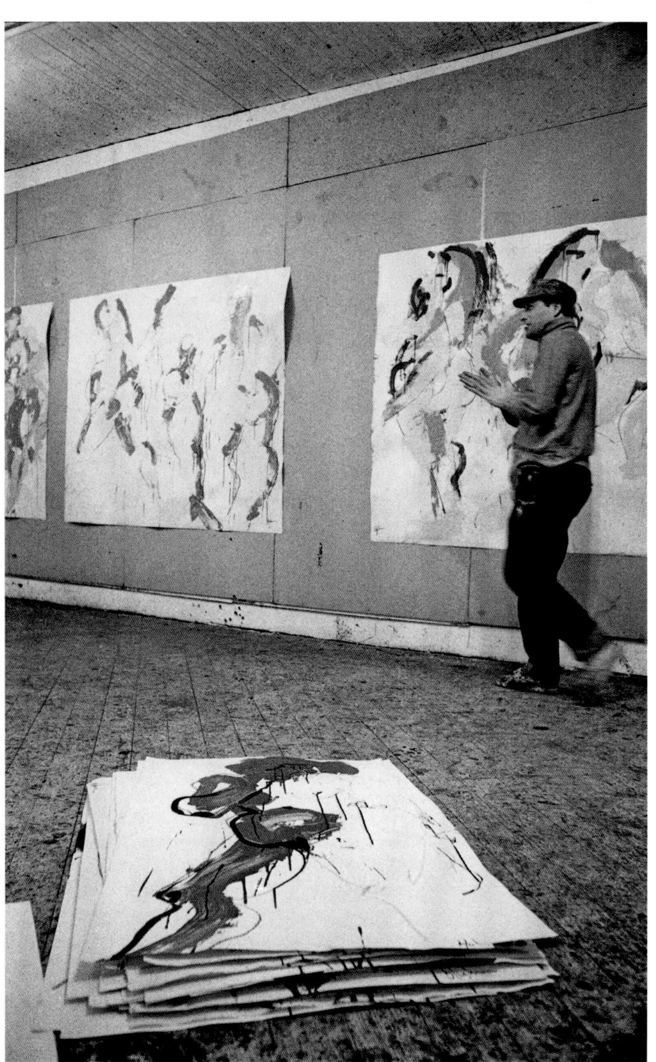

Fig. 13
Norman Bluhm with his new figure drawings from the model, New York City, 1967.
Photo by Jerry Schatzberg/Trunk Archive

bucks." He said, "It's right here. Come up and get it." That was my relationship with Walter. When I came back in 1956, he bought some more paintings. He bought from me until about . . . the last time was 1958. I moved in 1958 to this studio [on Park Avenue South] and he came up here once and we had a terrible argument. After a couple of articles came out about me, especially after Bill Berkson wrote the article "Norman Bluhm Paints a Picture," Walter said to somebody, "Norman didn't even put in the article that I'm the one who discovered him." Of course, that's the great myth of art history. Everybody wants to discover somebody. A person has no idea what he's doing; they discovered him. Since then I've never seen him. He has bought some great paintings in his lifetime. Take the Matisse *Dance*, the blue one. That was his. The *Nymphéas,* the Monet, was his. He bought some great paintings and he also bought some of the world's worst garbage.

Were you aware of what was going on here, the kind of art scene here as opposed to the one in Paris?

Yes, of course I was aware of it. But, oddly enough, I think—to get into more straight conversation—I was aware of it but at the same time I was involved in my own romantic values. It wasn't that I didn't find it extremely interesting and very fascinating, but the early paintings of mine, especially those after the war, had such Matisse overtones mostly, you know, the color tried to be very Matisse. And I remember I was kind of involved in Soutine. I liked Soutine. Why, I don't know. I liked the sort of peasant brutality about him. Basically I thought of him as a peasant. I never knew him, but I thought of him as a peasant. The emotion of the movement and torture in his work. At that time in my life I was kind of mixed up and kind of confused and kind of angry. And I liked that. Somehow it registered in me as a person. And I also was still romantically involved with Van Gogh—but no longer now. I had all these little old romantic niches that I had to somehow go through, get rid of, or whatever.

It's interesting that you had that kind of feeling towards expressionism and also towards Matisse.

They're so opposite, yes. As an individual I couldn't admit to my own self, as to my own poetic license or my own poetic values in life. I felt that I just had to be a kind of bastard. I remember I used to walk around, you know, I'd threaten to murder anybody—I don't mean to a criminal extent—but I just walked around with not a chip on my shoulder, but something. And I was involved with all these different people. But at the same time, I became very involved in Oriental things. I don't know how the hell that ever happened. But I got involved in Japanese drawing, things like that. . . . Of course, maybe I got it from Van Gogh or from Cézanne. Everybody in the Impressionist period was terribly involved in the Oriental idea. . . . But somehow I got over that period of being involved with Soutine and, as I said, with Van Gogh. And then oddly enough, I became terribly involved—and I'm not talking about the pictorial thing, I'm talking about the beauty and what it meant to me in feeling—I became very involved in Corot and Courbet. I always tell a story about how I once went to the Orangerie—there was a big Courbet show. I remember I went with Georges Duthuit. We were walking through looking at Courbets and I saw a little *paysage*, a little seascape; it was beautiful. I broke down crying just looking at it. Somehow I became very involved and I started to paint landscapes, very Impressionistic landscapes, except bigger. I was very involved in Courbet. I remember once talking with Giacometti, who loved and was a great admirer of Courbet. He thought those snow scenes of Courbet were the most beautiful things he had ever seen. And I was very involved in the idea of the earth, you know, that Courbet was able to paint the crystal, the light of the rocks. And the certain transparencies of Corot.

Did you do large canvases then?

No. First of all, I never had enough money to do big paintings . . . In the first place, what are you involved in in France? I mean you're involved in a kind of old Beaux-Arts dimension, you know, *vingt figure* or the *trente paysage*, or the *quarante marine*†† . . . I remember one time I was sitting with a group of old painters at the Select [Brasserie in Montparnasse]. We were talking. One of them, an old guy who I knew was kind of still carrying the load of Cézanne on his back, said to me he'd like to see what I was doing. So he came up to my studio. I had painted a nude because I've always been involved in nudes. Every year I do a series of nude drawings. I like to do them.

Still?

Yes, still. Every year I do just a few, maybe ten, fifteen . . . I never painted very big until, let's say, I sold all those paintings to Chrysler. Then I had some money and I started to paint like two meters by three meters, three meters by four meters. I really went wild with dimension . . . I recall that the last figurative paintings I did . . . they were very large, they were a little bit like Matisse's *Red Studio* . . . [and] throughout that period, I always painted one painting where there was always one element of death . . . I remember that for a long time that every painting had a skull of some form . . . or I painted a cemetery.

I'm curious about the landscapes. Were they drawn from real landscape studies?

Yes. I used to have one of those portable easels that you carry on your back. And I used to go out to the Bois de Sèvres or out to Fontainebleau and, wherever I went, I used to do these big landscapes. I didn't paint the trees or anything like that—just big green things.

Were they related to specific places?

I was involved in the *Nymphéas* of Monet. I was fortunate to go see them before they even opened up the whole thing, which they had been working on for years. Maybe that's where I got the idea of doing these large landscapes.

Were these directly done on canvas? Or did you make sketches?

They were done directly on canvas. Then I began to do them in the studio. But for the first group I carried a canvas right out there. I had heard all those great stories about Monet, how he used to nail these big canvases right up to the tree and how he painted—you know, very funny tales whether they're true or just hearsay. That's what I did for a long time. They were actually landscapes, but there was always the moment where that kind of cemetery idea walked in somehow. The linear motion of a cemetery. For example, if you try to do a rectangle a hundred times and you just do that rapid and rapid and rapid and rapid. Those are very interesting things. I never really thought about them until this moment. Well, I have thought about it. It's something that I must have been involved in for a long, long time. I think it's all postwar mental evaluations about death and images of death. And somehow you can't shake them. It takes you a long time before you can look at a bright flower, so to speak. I kept this up for a long, long time. I did the same thing. But at the same time, I always did a few nudes.

Excerpt from "Oral History Interview with Norman Bluhm," October 23–November 12, 1969. Archives of American Art, Smithsonian Institution.

†† Standard canvas sizes used for specific painting genres from the 19th through the mid-20th century

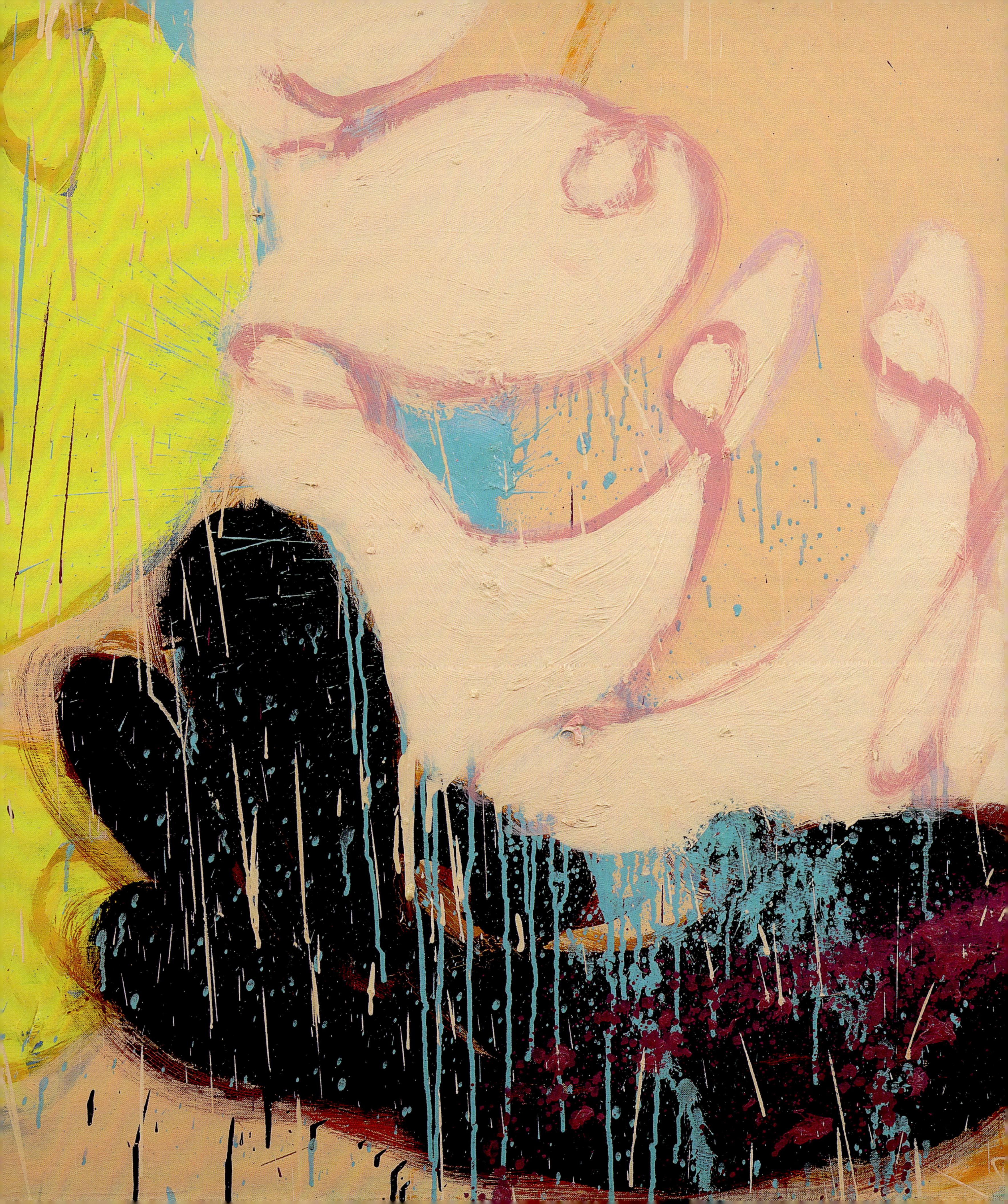

A MAN CREATES HIS OWN SPACE

Norman Bluhm's Iconography

Tricia Laughlin Bloom

Norman Bluhm self-identified as a romantic, and his passion for the expressive potential of paint is evident throughout his production, which spans more than fifty years. Bluhm had a remarkable ability to convey his own physical energy as well as his interest in the world of things—bodies, buildings, light, art history—through abstract forms and fields of color that seem to move and bristle with life. "A man creates his own space"—the poet and critic Bill Berkson noted that this was one of Bluhm's favorite phrases.[1] Certainly Bluhm created his own space in the sense of taking a solitary path, trusting his own instincts rather than the trends of the art world. But there is also the unusual vibrancy of the pictorial spaces he created. Despite a penchant for narrative and literary subjects he assigned to his abstract compositions, Bluhm's painterly paintings are classic explorations of the medium—art about art, and about the act of creating.

Sometimes razor sharp and sometimes lush and layered, looking at Bluhm's brushwork and stylistic shifts over time one sees an artist moving confidently between stereotypically masculine abstract forms—slicing, angular, hierarchical—and feminine ones—curving and interlacing. Both his palette and the titles he assigned to many of his works from the late 1960s onward associate strongly with women, often referencing decorative and applied art traditions that were coded as feminine for most of the twentieth century. Although Bluhm was a part of the New York School, also known as Abstract Expressionism, in the late 1950s, his approach of combining gestural abstraction with references to ornamental design and global art history put him at odds with the critical culture of late modernism in New York. Rather than settling on a signature style in the 1950s or '60s, Bluhm continued to push his painting in new directions, swinging between the poles of total abstraction and figuration and back again.

Bluhm's retelling of an experience from his time as an architecture student reveals an early flash of the single-mindedness and self-awareness that led him down a path that was often against the current:

> One day I did a drawing, and I was screwing around, and I was feeling a little corny, and I started to draw some nudes dancing around the building. I had messed up the drawing, and I was drawing these nudes dancing around, and Mies [van der Rohe] walked in and he saw this. "What are you doing here, Herr Bluhm?" I said, "Oh, I'm ruining a drawing. So I just thought I would draw a few nudes dancing around enjoying themselves." And he said to me, "When we are going to draw nudes, I will tell you when to draw nudes." So I just kind of closed the door, and one morning I walked in and I just looked at the place like, what am I doing here? . . . So I started packing. Everybody said, "What are you doing?" I said, "I quit, I'm leaving." And I walked out.[2]

This story reveals much of what comes to fruition in Bluhm's later production: a measured respect for order (he describes his rebellious act as "ruining" a drawing, after all); a focus on the human form and all of the poetry, chaos, and art history associated with the figure; and a sense of humor. The light manner in which he answers Mies's question (or as he recalled answering it) points to the pleasure that Bluhm took in bringing high and low together and balancing the seriousness of Modernism with some levity.

Although his break with the study of architecture was definitive, Bluhm's interest in historical buildings shows up in his early work in Paris, such as Notre Dame (Plate 9). While this impressionistic watercolor is conventional in terms of subject matter, the treatment of space is collapsed, disregarding the laws of gravity and spatial order as if he had captured the monumental structure from multiple vantage points. Bluhm's emphasis in this painting is on the stained-glass windows, the place in Gothic architecture reserved for luminous color. Combining abstraction with ornament and treating color as an animate force are two aesthetic strategies that run throughout the entirety of Bluhm's production. By the end of the 1950s, such direct references to the observable world became absorbed into abstract compositions, as in *Stained Glass Landscape #10* (Plate 10). Here Bluhm

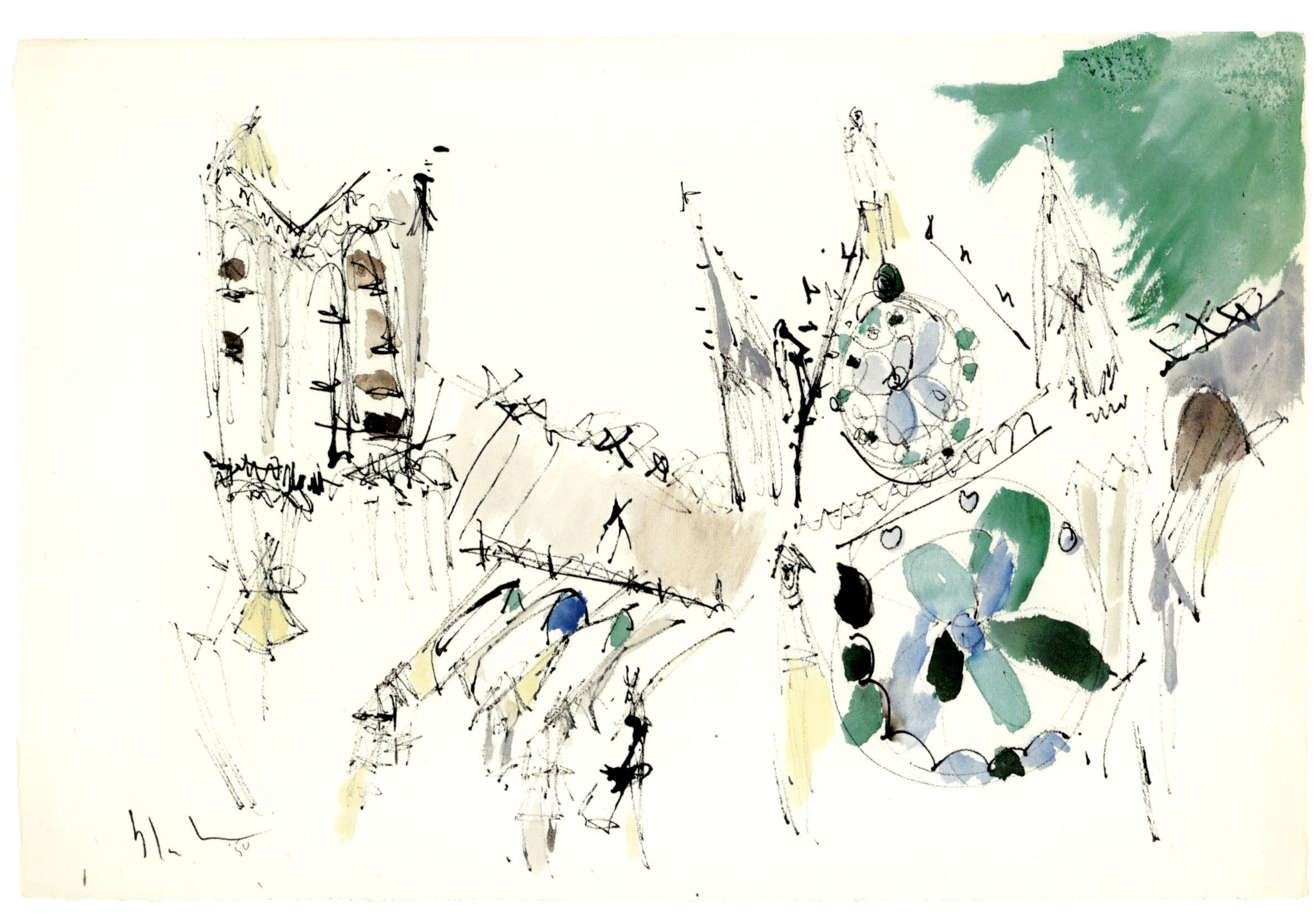

Plate 9

Notre Dame, 1950
Ink and watercolor on paper
15 × 22 in. (38 × 56 cm)
The Estate of Norman Bluhm

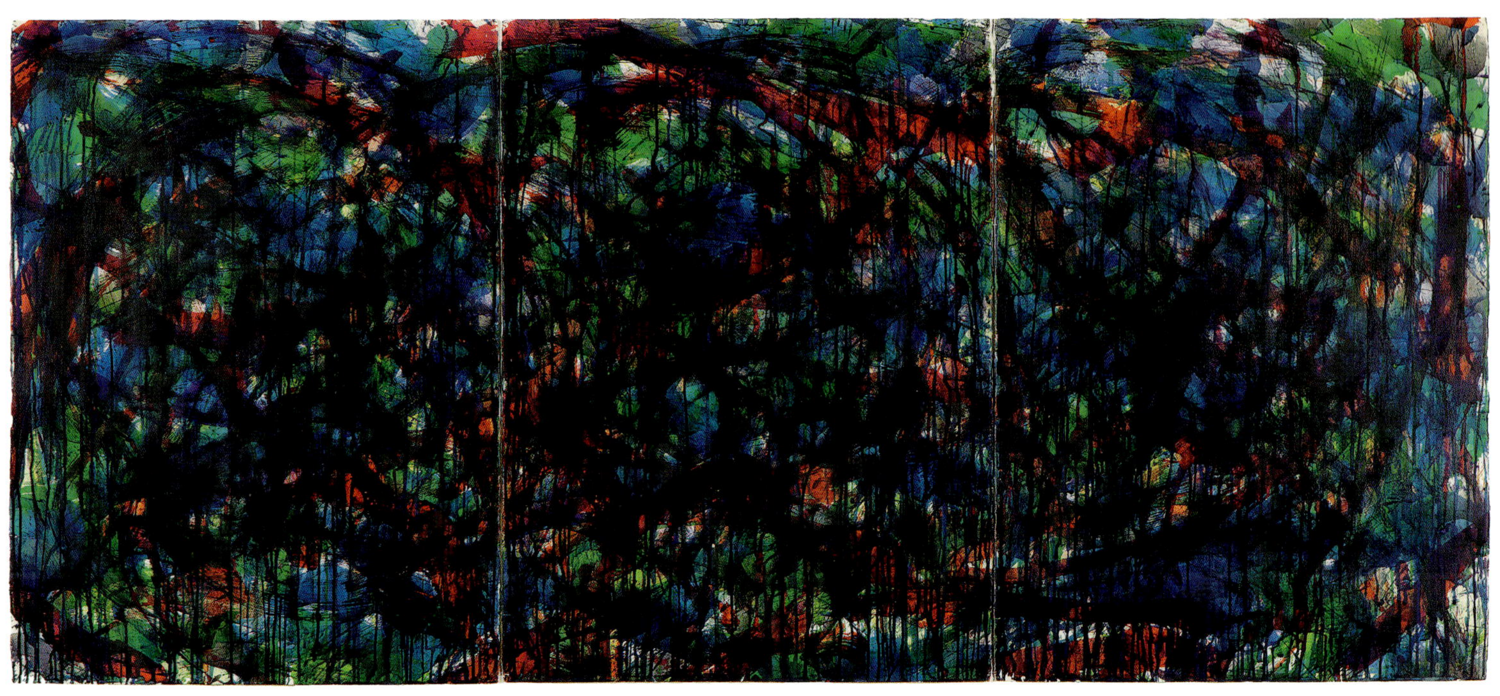

Plate 10

Stained Glass Landscape #10, 1957
Watercolor on paper
Triptych, 30 × 66 in. (76 × 167.6 cm) overall
Private collection

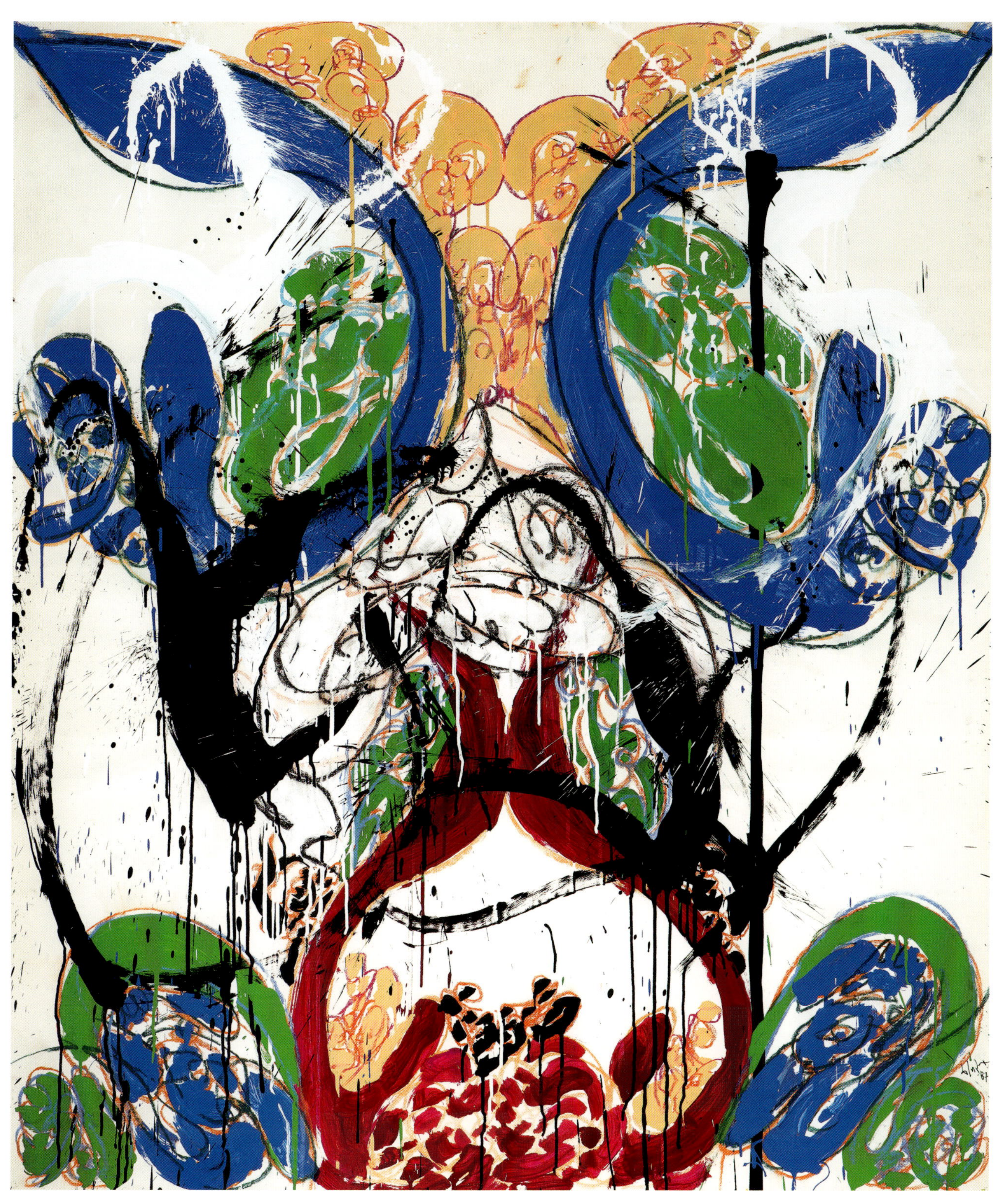

Plate 11

Fresco #15, 1987
Acrylic and pastel on paper
60 × 50 in. (152.5 × 127 cm)
The Estate of Norman Bluhm

evokes the chromatic intensity of stained glass by applying watercolor in layers of varied brushwork, using an allover composition that extends across three panels.

Bluhm's affinity for ornamental structure and for playing with the boundaries between painting and applied art is showcased in a work such as *Fresco #15* (Plate 11), one of a series of approximately twenty-four large-scale works on paper. At first glance the works in this series resemble stylized floral motifs in ancient Roman or Italian Renaissance frescoes, but they also flirt with a resemblance to wallpaper and textile design. It is worth noting that Clement Greenberg, the leading critic of American postwar art, wrote in 1957 that "decoration is the specter that haunts modernist painting," by which he meant that abstract easel painting must avoid looking too much like the less rigorous, more ordinary fields of pattern and color found in wallpaper and other decorative patterns.[3] If the decorative was taboo in the context of American avant-garde art as defined by Greenberg, Bluhm's embrace of ornamental design was at least in part a refutation of such proscriptive thinking.

In each of the works in the *Fresco* series, a symmetrical, orderly composition is turned into a space for exploration, with an overlay of loose, dripping brushstrokes in black that resemble abstracted bodies in motion or calligraphy. This kind of slippage between painting and writing reflects the significant role that language and literature played in Bluhm's life and studio practice. While Bluhm downplayed the idea that he had an interest in directly communicating with viewers through his paintings, a gestural mark can function quite effectively as a kind of handwriting or signature, both releasing and capturing the physical and emotional energy of the painter in a concrete way.[4] Rather than using a thick impasto, Bluhm worked with very wet paint, allowing for a quick application and, when he wanted it, a controlled line not unlike a calligrapher's marks made with ink.[5]

The interplay between image and word has a long history in global art history, from ancient hieroglyphs and the glyphic marks of Asian and Arabic characters to modern graffiti. Bluhm seemed to enjoy exploring the reach between these diverse sources along with referencing both grandiose and more everyday literary forms. The highly physical application of spray paint in street art (specifically tagging, in which the artist's signature becomes a graphic image beyond its function as written word) may have resonated with Bluhm as a kind of parallel to his own studio practice, where visual and written expressions often intersected.[6]

Bluhm was also an avid reader with broad interdisciplinary interests, including classical and contemporary poetry. Just as he had immersed himself in the literary circles of Paris, so Bluhm found himself closely involved with a number of the leading poets of his generation in New York. To cite just one example, his work was featured on the cover of issue no. 7 of *Yugen*, a Beat poetry journal founded in Greenwich Village in the late 1950s by LeRoi Jones and Hettie Cohen (Fig. 14).[7] Also not incidentally, some of his closest friends were poets with whom he collaborated in the studio. In 1959 Bluhm and Frank O'Hara together created a series of twenty-seven poem-paintings, combining O'Hara's handwritten texts with Bluhm's abstract imagery. This performative collaboration was informal and open to chance; the two alternated between writing and painting, while listening to Prokofiev and conversing, using ink and gouache and the brown packing paper Bluhm had tacked to the walls of his studio.[8] In *It's Raining* (Plate 31) Bluhm's feathery, dripping, explosive brushwork overlays O'Hara's handwritten text, the cursive script blending with the abstract forms in a kind of spontaneous conversation between word and image.[9]

In a studio session in the 1980s with the poet and critic John Yau, a painting and writing collaboration was again spontaneous and informal, with either artist or poet beginning and the other responding. In *Sam Spade Haiku #1* (Plate 12) Bluhm's robust and yet sketch-like figures have an especially animated quality, no doubt due to the quick pace of the back-and-forth process. The black lines overlaying Bluhm's fleshy figures are meandering and unfinished, and they seem to converse directly with Yau's loosely rendered handwritten text nearby.

This expressive but controlled line is related to some of the painting Bluhm was doing in the 1960s on a larger scale, evidence of a stylistic doubling back

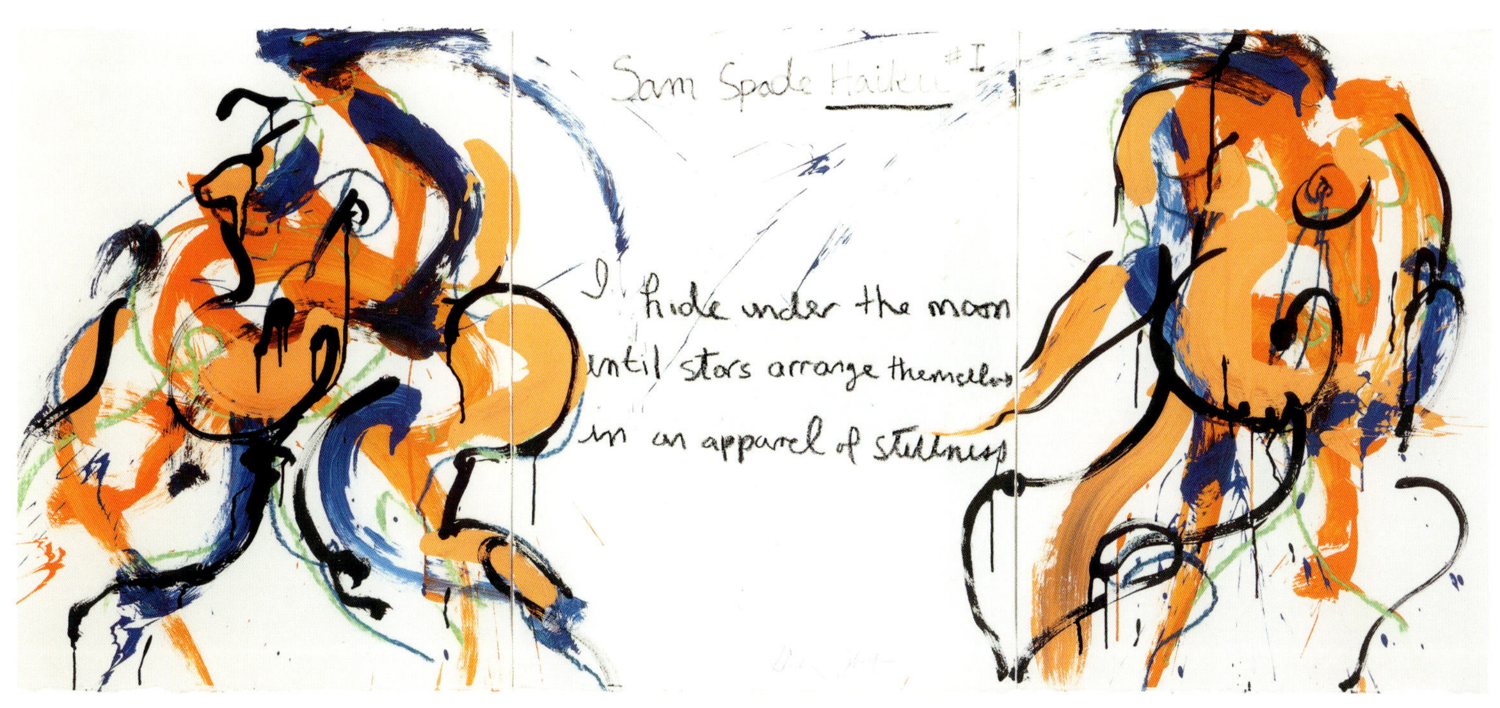

Plate 12

Norman Bluhm and John Yau
Sam Spade Haiku #1, 1987
Acrylic, ink, and pastel on paper
26 ¼ × 59 ¾ in. (66.7 × 152 cm)
The Estate of Norman Bluhm

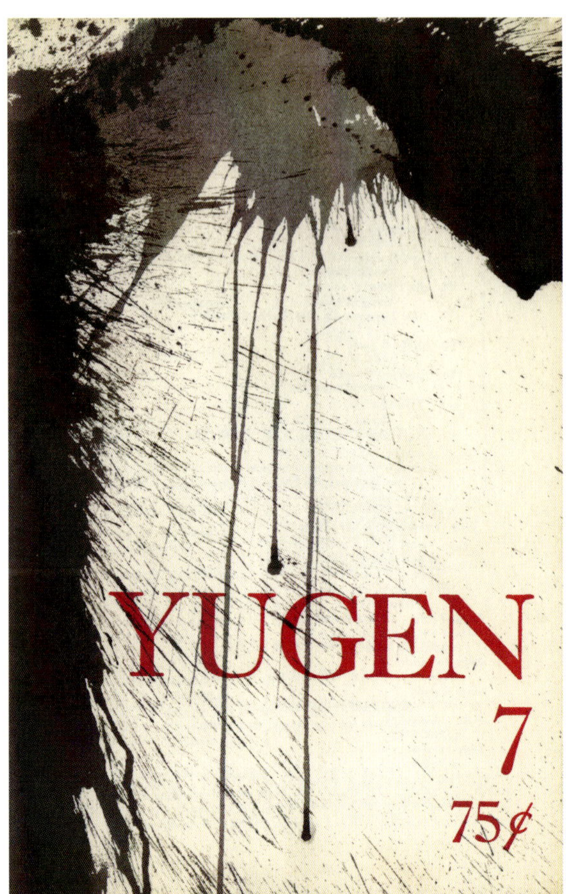

Fig. 14
Norman Bluhm. Cover for *Yugen*, no. 7 (1961)

while pushing forward that he seems to have practiced throughout his career. *Chariot* (Plate 13), an open and spontaneously rendered composition, is heroic in scale and in its sprawling landscape orientation. Rapidly painted forms stretch over the edges of three vertical panels; curving tendrils in black and yellow in the outer panels bring a sense of lightness and upward movement to the girder-like, angular composition. The use of a multipanel format to represent a single unified painting, first used by Bluhm in the mid-1950s, became a common practice for him beginning in the late 1950s. As Raphael Rubinstein has noted:

> The advent of multipanel canvases in Bluhm's work marks a break with the pictorial practice of the preceding generation [of Abstract Expressionists]. . . . While Bluhm recalls that his triptychs were partly the result of necessity—it was the only way he could paint that large and still manage to get the canvases out of his studio—this dividing of the painting support, a format which would later be taken up by countless other painters, helped drive a thin wedge . . . in the prevailing assumptions about how to make a painting, and also, perhaps, into modernist assumptions of wholeness.[10]

Chinese and Japanese screen paintings, in which an otherwise united landscape extends across multiple vertical panels in a horizontal structure (Fig. 15), informed Bluhm's approach to mural painting. In a 1992 interview he emphasized the impact that Asian art had on him.[11] The triptych format of the even earlier, modestly scaled *Stained Glass Landscape #10* is evidence that a multipanel approach was an early aesthetic choice, not merely a practicality. The influence of Asian art is especially evident in *Chariot*, where the suggestion of calligraphy is also strong.

In addition to his engagement with decorative and applied art, Bluhm further distanced himself from the mainstream of late modernism by moving fluidly between abstraction and figuration. After having gained critical attention for classic action paintings in a forceful and fully abstract style, in the late 1960s Bluhm began painting biomorphic abstract compositions in a pointedly feminine palette, and then more clearly figural forms in the 1980s and '90s. Bluhm noted that in the late 1960s his practice of regularly painting from live nude models started to influence his abstract canvases in a new way.[12] *Theodora* (Plate 39) emerged as the first in a long line of heroically scaled abstract canvases named for queens, infamous and legendary women (from the biblical Salome to the more contemporary "Pinkerton's Lady" [Plate 5], a reference to Kate Warne [1833–1866], the first female detective in the United States), prostitutes, nymphs, and other icons of womanhood. With titles drawn largely from classical

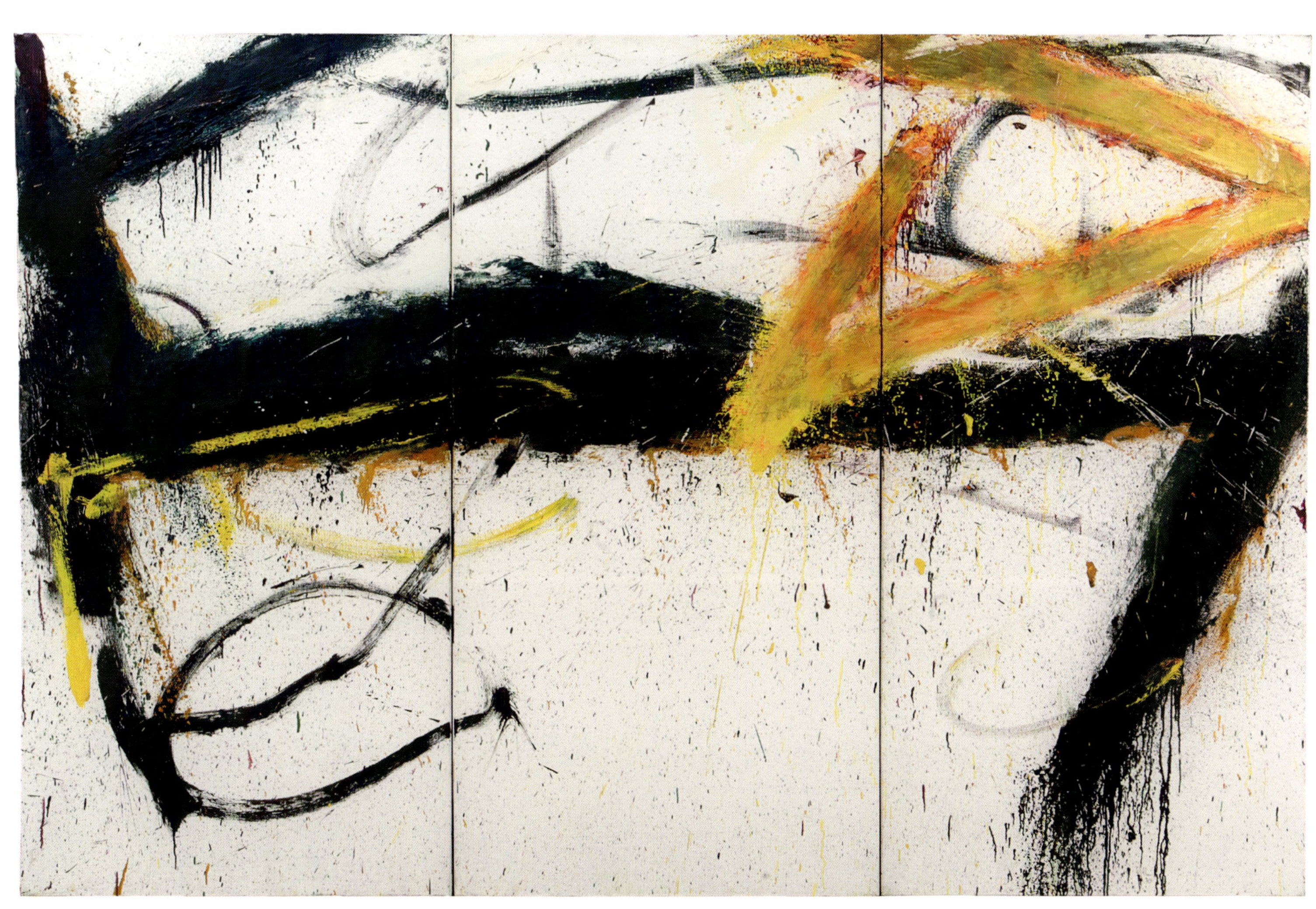

Plate 13

Chariot, 1965
Oil on canvas
Triptych, 77 × 114 in. (195 × 289.5 cm) overall
Foundation for Modern and Contemporary Art CRT –
on loan at the GAM – Civic Gallery of Modern and Contemporary Art, Turin, Italy

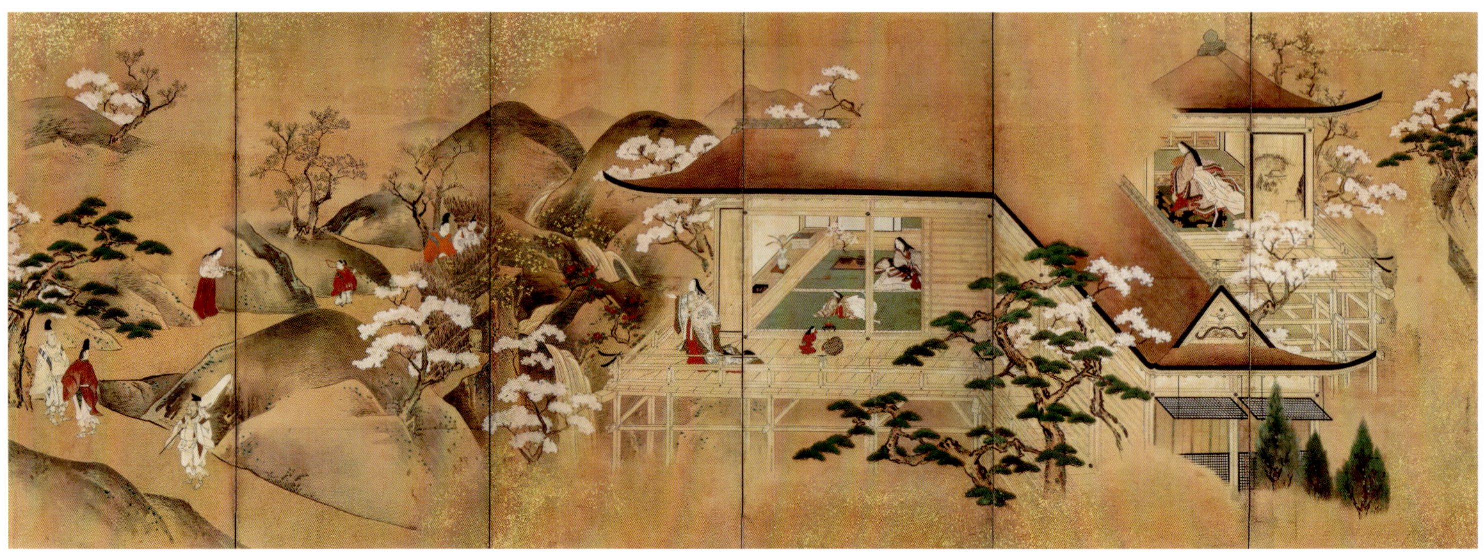

Fig. 15
Iwasa Teiun. *Scenes from the Tale of Genji* (*Genji Monogatari*), 1716–35. Pair of six-panel folding screens. Ink, pigment, and gold leaf on paper, 51 × 138⅜ in. (129.5 × 352 cm). The Newark Museum of Art, New Jersey. Purchase 1963 Wallace M. Scudder Bequest Fund *63.11A, B*

mythology and art history, works like *Dido* (Plate 14) evoke the female body in an indirect, barely discernible way. Avoiding anatomical referents for the most part, *Dido* captures a fleshy physicality and dynamic sense of movement. The irregular curving forms extending beyond the edge of the canvas and the layers of brushwork—from wet and dripping to feathery and light—are a record of the skill and bravado of Bluhm's physical act of painting at this scale. *Dido* is nine feet tall by ten feet wide, and, like all of Bluhm's large-scale works, was painted on a vertical surface, with the canvas on the studio wall rather than on the floor (Fig. 16). The palette is Bluhm's own, with flashes of fuchsia and lavender that recall cosmetics, clothing, and body parts in motion. The arabesque lines and highly keyed colors are also reminiscent of Henri Matisse's lyrical expressionist style (Fig. 17).

The affinities between Matisse and Bluhm have been widely noted, from their shared love of decoration and applied art to their overlapping interests in myth and exotic female subjects.[13] While both artists painted countless images of women, Bluhm's choice to represent the female nude in purely abstract terms was wholly his own, and his activation of strong narrative content with the titles he assigned these abstract works set up a unique dynamic in terms of viewers' expectations and experiences. In the absence of representational details, the pleasure of looking at the female subject in Bluhm's work is replaced by an immersive sensory experience of undulating line and color.

Comparing Bluhm's *Philomela* (Plate 15) with Matisse's *A Faun Accosting a Nymph* (Fig. 18), for instance, we see in Matisse's print amorous bodies intertwined—or more to the point, the implication of a rape.[14] Rape was a common subject in classical mythology, as well as in modern art. The figures in Matisse's print are so abstracted that the nymph's right leg seems detached from the rest of her body, and yet the suggestion of a violent sexual encounter is made matter-of-fact and presentable. By contrast, Bluhm's painting is fully abstract and does not allude in a direct way to the gruesome story of Philomela, a princess of Athens who in Greek

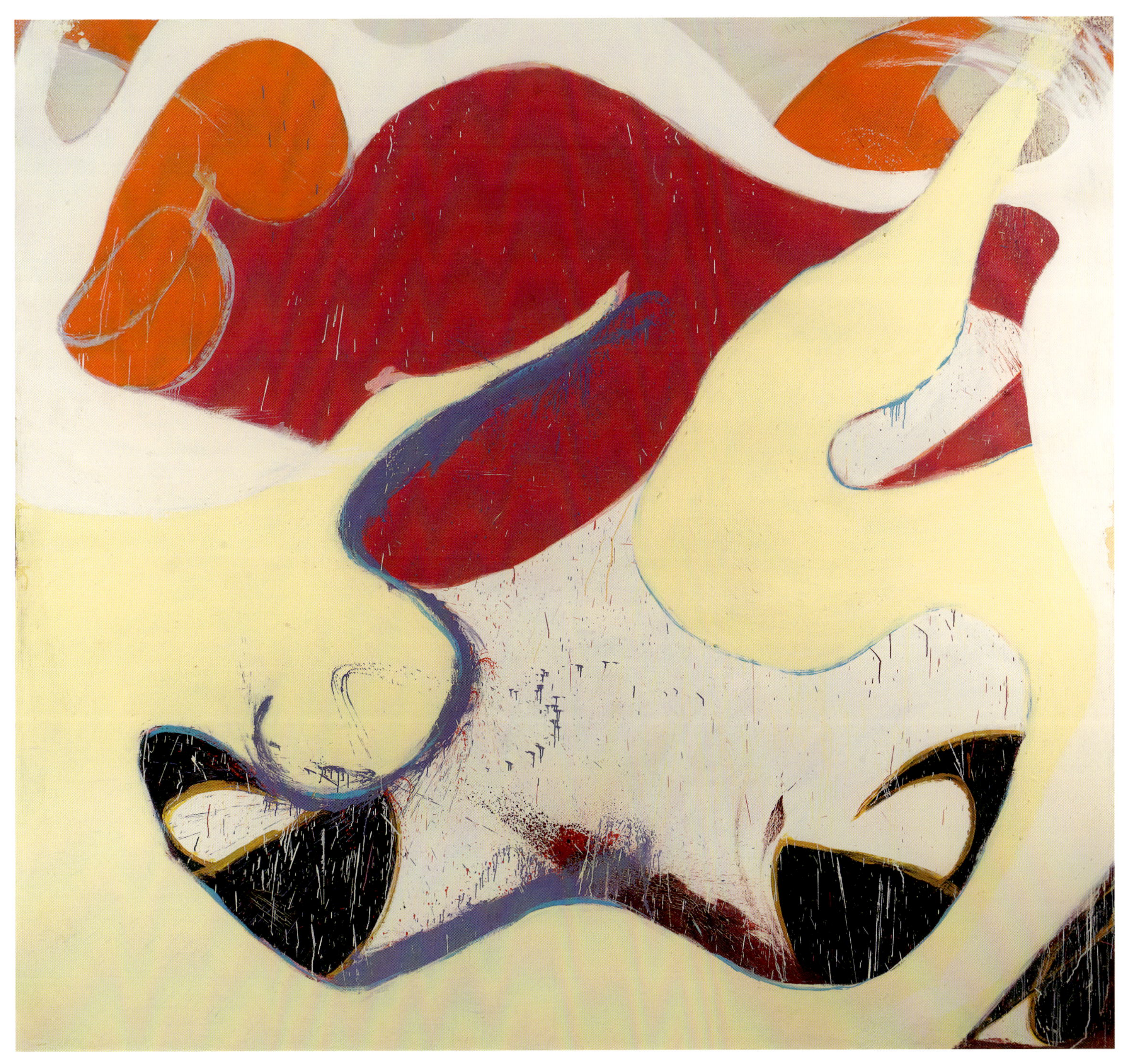

Plate 14

Dido, 1973
Oil on canvas
112 × 120 in. (284.5 × 305 cm)
Smithsonian American Art Museum, Washington, DC
Gift of Mr. and Mrs. David K. Anderson, Martha Jackson Memorial Collection *1980.137.5*

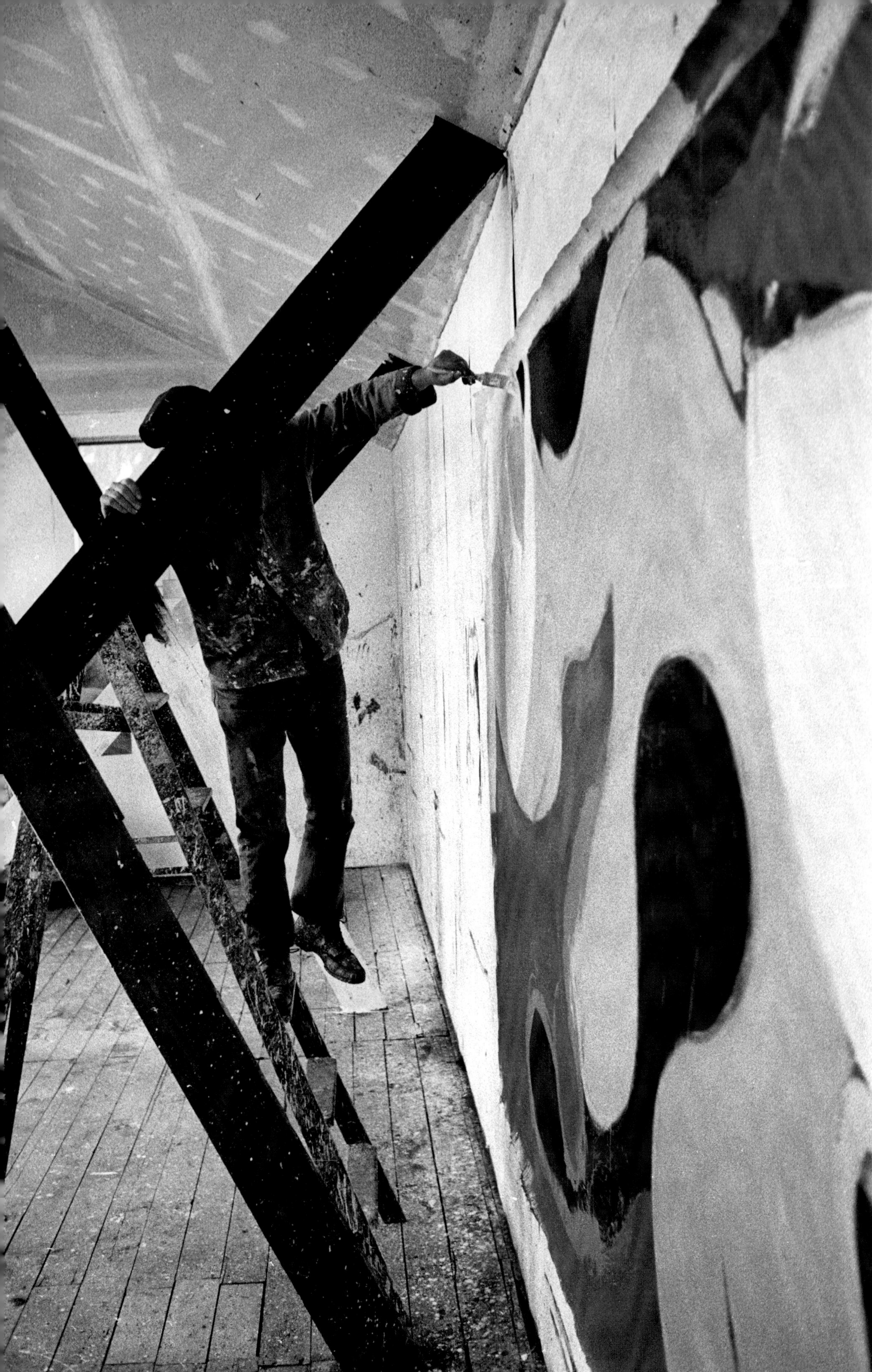

Fig. 16
Norman Bluhm in his studio, 1973. Photo by Kerby C. Smith

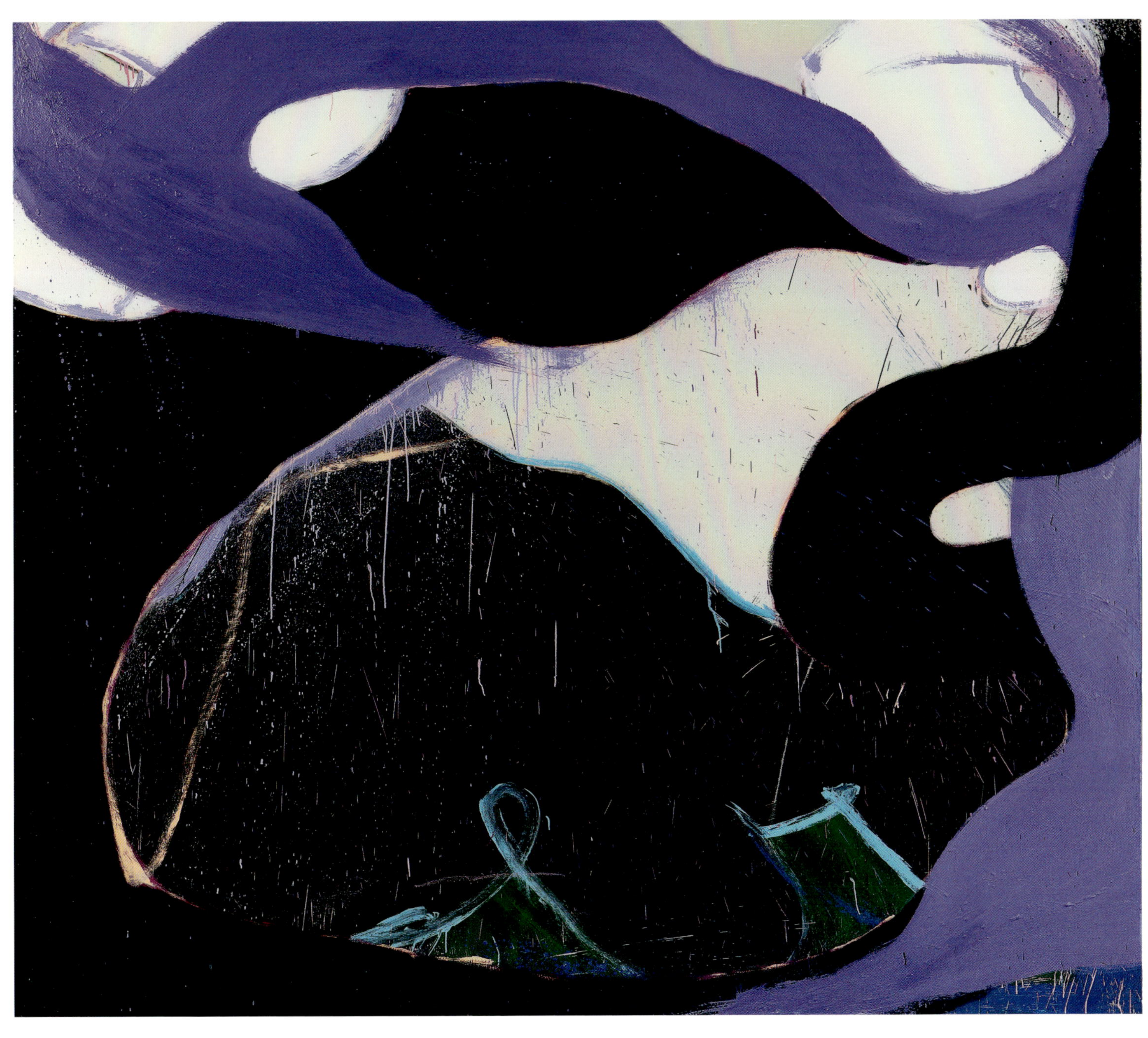

Plate 15

Philomela, 1972
Oil on canvas
96 × 108 in. (244 × 274.5 cm)
The Estate of Norman Bluhm

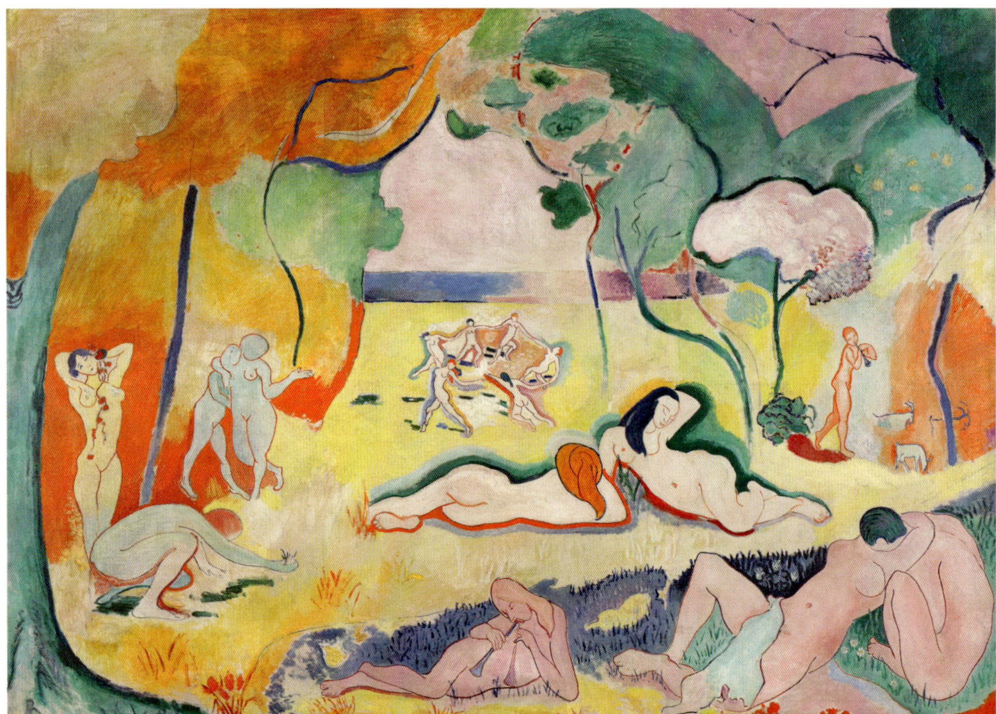

Fig. 17
Henri Matisse. *Le Bonheur de Vivre* (*The Joy of Life*), 1905–06. Oil on canvas, 69 ½ × 94 ¾ in. (176.5 × 240.7 cm). The Barnes Foundation, Philadelphia, BF719. Image courtesy The Barnes Foundation. © 2019 Succession H. Matisse / Artists Rights Society (ARS), New York

mythology was twice raped by Tereus, her brother-in-law, and who, when she threatened to tell, had her tongue cut out. Instead of signaling any of this violence, *Philomela*, like many of Bluhm's canvases, works on a sensory level, with lyrical expanses of lush color. The sinuous forms convey slow growth and rapid movement at the same time—through long, careful brushstrokes alongside the rush of physical activity signaled by the splattered paint. The precise mood is intense but unspecified, allowing for a range of interpretations. As John Yau has noted, "Bluhm's use of color is both uncategorizable and unrivaled . . . through drawing in color Bluhm was able to bring in close proximity states of soaring ecstasy and bottomless regions of immense sorrow."[15] The close proximity of ecstasy and sorrow is a poetic concept, and one that resonates with Bluhm's own comments on the existential loneliness of a painter.[16]

Without trying to retroactively cast Bluhm as a feminist, one can still read his many abstract paintings titled after powerful historical and mythological figures as a typology in praise of women. At times Bluhm was very clear about explaining his sources, yet he left the meaning of much of his work intentionally open-ended. He often titled his works after they were completed; in some cases, he allowed others to suggest titles, revealing an openness to collaboration and chance that relates to his practice of creating poem-paintings with friends. Nevertheless, in assigning historical and mythical women's names to his larger-than-life-sized abstractions, Bluhm knowingly aligned these works with female narratives, whether they are stories of erotic intrigue or power or abjection. In terms of their dominating scale and dazzling chromatic effects, these works are more valorizing than anything else. This post-feminist reading of Bluhm's female subjects is supported by his biography. Some of his closest friends were powerful and unconventional women, including Elaine de Kooning, Lee Krasner, and Joan Mitchell. His thirty-eight years of marriage with Cary Bluhm (Fig. 19), an unusually strong and independent woman, is further evidence of Bluhm's strength of character when it came to respecting women.

In bringing gendered associations to his abstract paintings, Bluhm also seems to have enjoyed blurring and disrupting conventional associations of masculinity and femininity. In works such as *Pygmalion* (Plate 16), for instance, pinkish fields of organic matter converge over a deep blue ground visible in the side panels. These amorphous forms are suggestive of microscopic organic life, with the buoyant energy of something like flagella or sea life. The sinuous curves of the twisting horizontal composition resemble a reclining nude Bluhm painted in 1979 (Plate 17), the same year he painted *Pygmalion*. Although this rough correspondence may be accidental or incidental, it underscores how Bluhm's ongoing figural studies may have fueled the evolution of his abstract imagery.

Like many of the mythical characters Bluhm used for his titles, Pygmalion is a story of transmogrification,

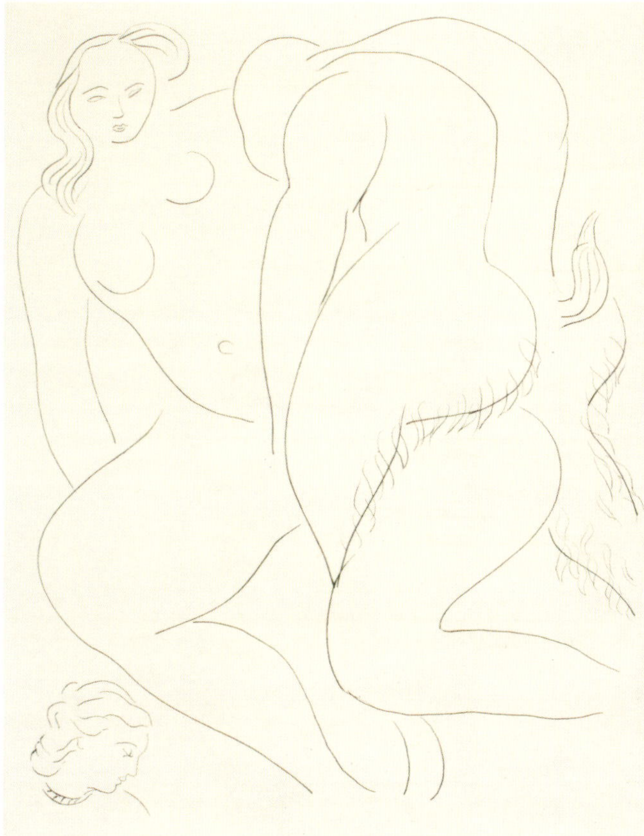

Fig. 18
Henri Matisse. *A Faun Accosting a Nymph (with Etched "Remarque" of a Woman's Head)*, 1930–32. Etching 13 × 9 13⁄16 in. (33 × 25 cm). From *Poésies de Stéphane Mallarmé*, illustrated by Matisse and published by Skira in 1932. Philadelphia Museum of Art, Philadelphia. Gift of Mrs. W. Averell Hamman, 1952, *1952-87-1q*. © 2019 Succession H. Matisse / Artists Rights Society (ARS), New York

popularized in Ovid's epic poem *Metamorphoses*. Pygmalion was a sculptor who created a statue of a woman, whom he named Galatea (Greek for "she who is milky white"); Pygmalion then fell in love with Galatea, and Venus decided to bring his beloved to life. The animate-seeming mass of undulating forms in Bluhm's painting, in which the lush, unmistakably organic matter unfurls across three enormous canvases in a tumult, may call to mind Galatea's transformation from cold stone to human flesh, or Pygmalion's original act of creation, or something else entirely.[17]

In contrast to the sprawling organic structure of *Pygmalion*, in his late work Bluhm brought a quasi-architectural structure to his paintings. Many of his late works are organized around a geometric framework, modeled on medieval and Renaissance altarpieces and stressing a kind of mathematical humanism. An untitled ink drawing from 1994 (Plate 18), one of several studies for *Persephone* (see Plates 75, 76, and 77), captures the spirit of this partial return to order in Bluhm's late oeuvre. The drawing is a geometric grid made up of eight squares set within a loose framework of twenty-four smaller squares, with human and floral forms loosely rendered throughout the grid. In the two top central panels, Bluhm sketched a pair of figures standing with arms and legs splayed. Rendered freehand in a style that is both controlled and highly animated, these two figures resemble Leonardo da Vinci's *Vitruvian Man* or a Rorschach test.

A late triptych titled *Eye of Salonica* (Plate 19) suggests a god's-eye view on the three thousand years of history that Bluhm carried into his art, and seems to bristle with an animistic or pantheistic spirituality.[18] Here a mood of ritual, cosmic dance is enacted across three panels, in front of an ornamental structure that recalls both architecture and the marginalia that decorate medieval illuminated manuscripts. The tendrils of the two groups of abstract, alien-looking figures in the outer panels reach toward the network of forms in the center panel, as if stretching across a vast expanse. In the center panel a generative burst of organic matter and light spills outward, with leaping figures that seem poised at the invisible boundary of the picture plane, as if about to enter the viewer's space. Named for the northern Greek city of Thessaloniki—a multi-ethnic metropolis with a complex and violent history as a crossroads of Muslim, Jewish, and Christian cultures—*Eye of Salonica* feels transhistorical and transcultural, with a sense of both centrifugal and centripetal movement across the three panels.

Throughout the 1990s paintings, Bluhm's abstracted bodies bursting out of the limits of their orderly niches seem to celebrate the triumph of life over rules and containment. In a 1987 interview Bluhm said, "I want to make a kind of religious painting, to surround the form with gesture, repeat the form, and push the figure up out of space, like in religious painting. I'd like to get to that source and make it more grandiose."[19] Bluhm's language is poetic and mythic—"surround the form with a gesture, repeat the form, and push the figure up out of space"—and at the same time it reads like a fairly accurate description of his approach to painting.

Bluhm's nearly lifelong practice was to paint at the full extension of his physical body and his creative capacity, to push the limits of what he could express in paint. He also often spoke of a desire to reach beyond himself, to "get outside of those little fingers we have."[20] These physical and metaphysical aspirations seem to

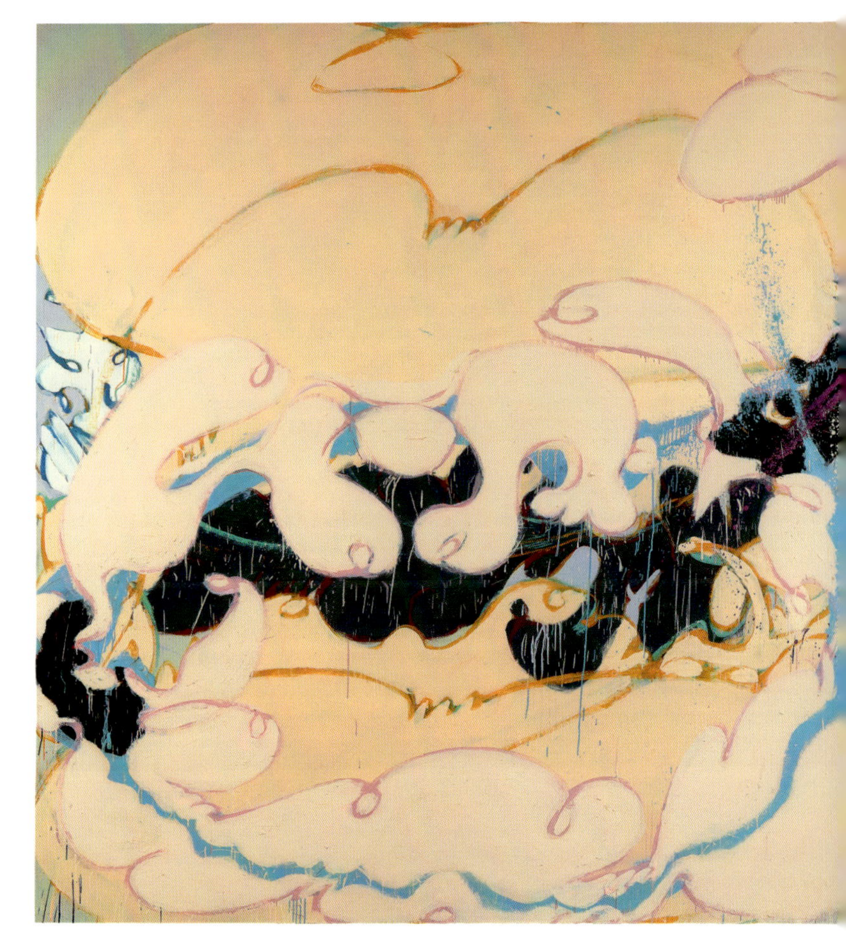

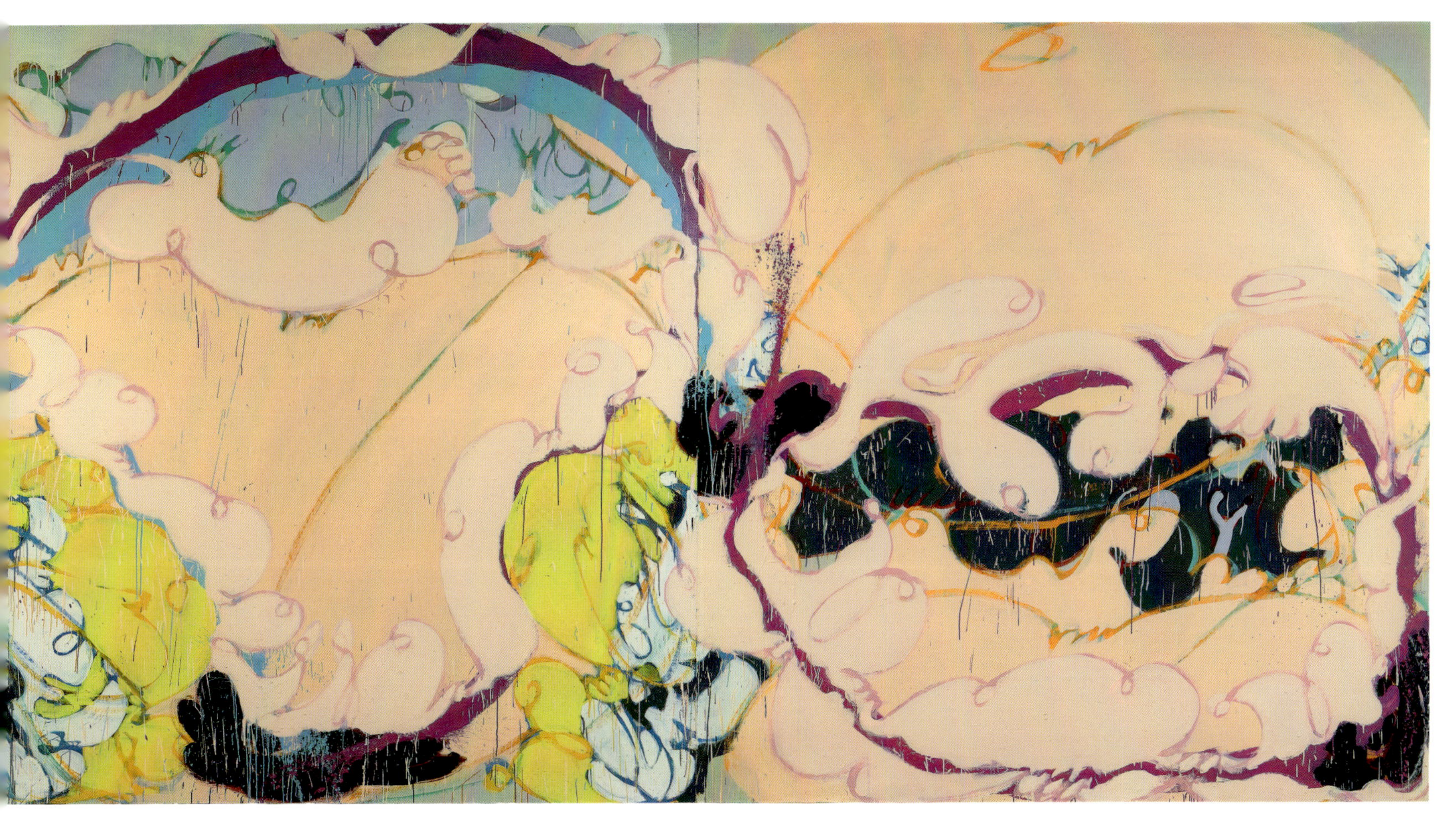

Plate 16

Pygmalion, 1979
Oil on canvas
Triptych, 108 × 306 in. (274.5 × 777 cm) overall
The Estate of Norman Bluhm

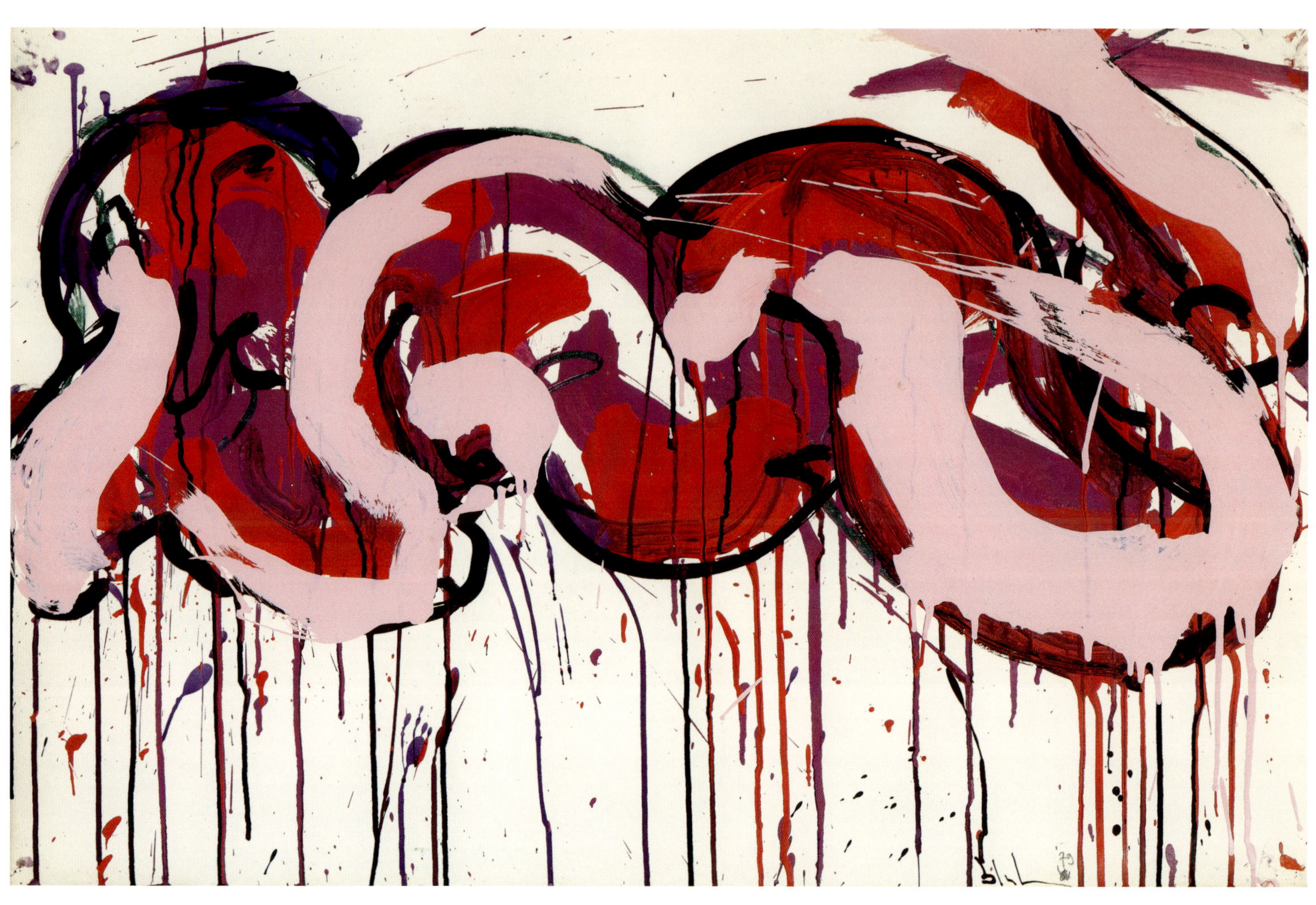

Plate 17

Nude, 1979
Acrylic, ink, and pastel on paper
24 × 36 in. (61 × 91.5 cm)
The Estate of Norman Bluhm

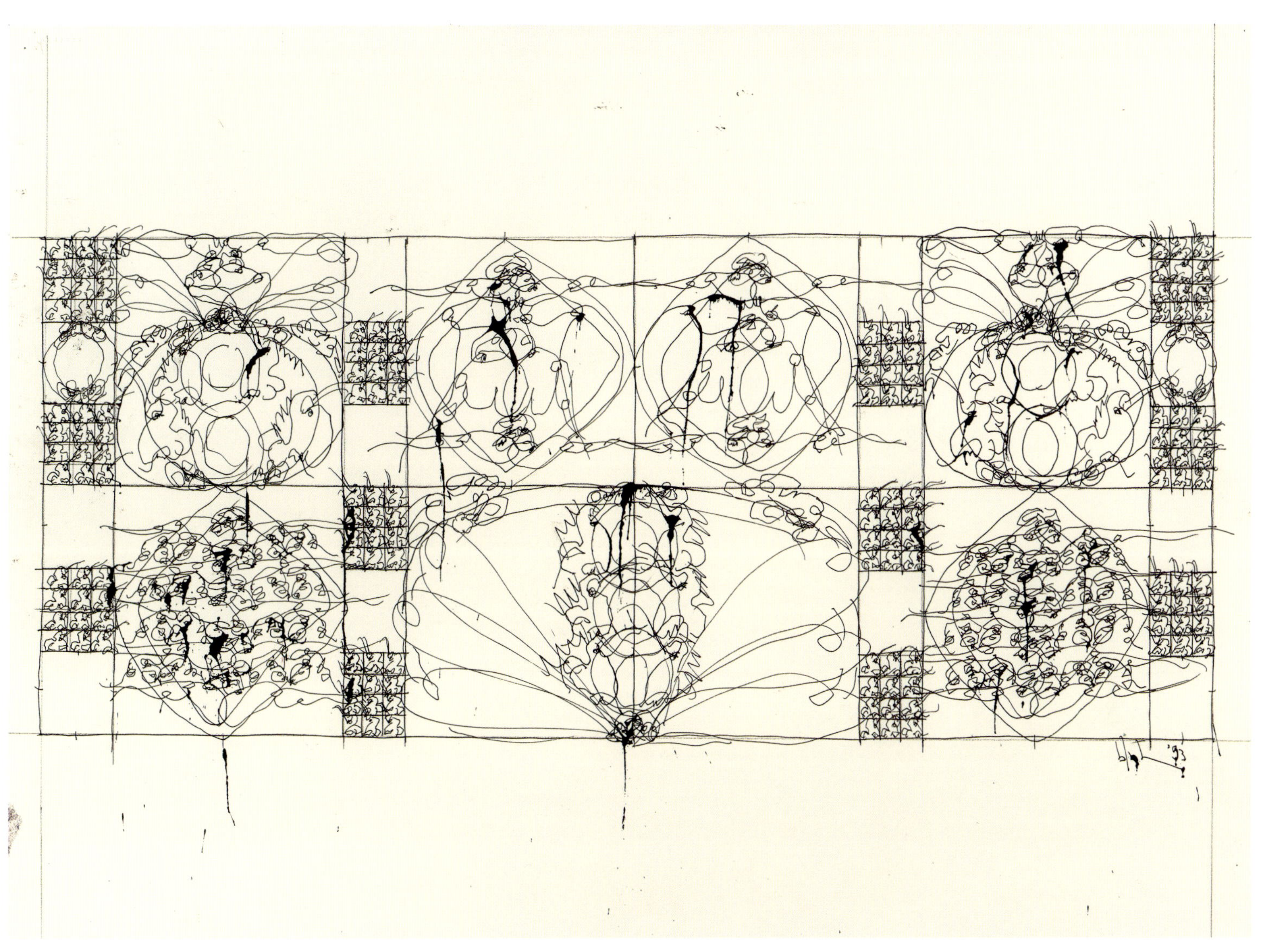

Plate 18

Untitled, 1994
Ink on paper
22 × 30 in. (56 × 76 cm)
The Estate of Norman Bluhm

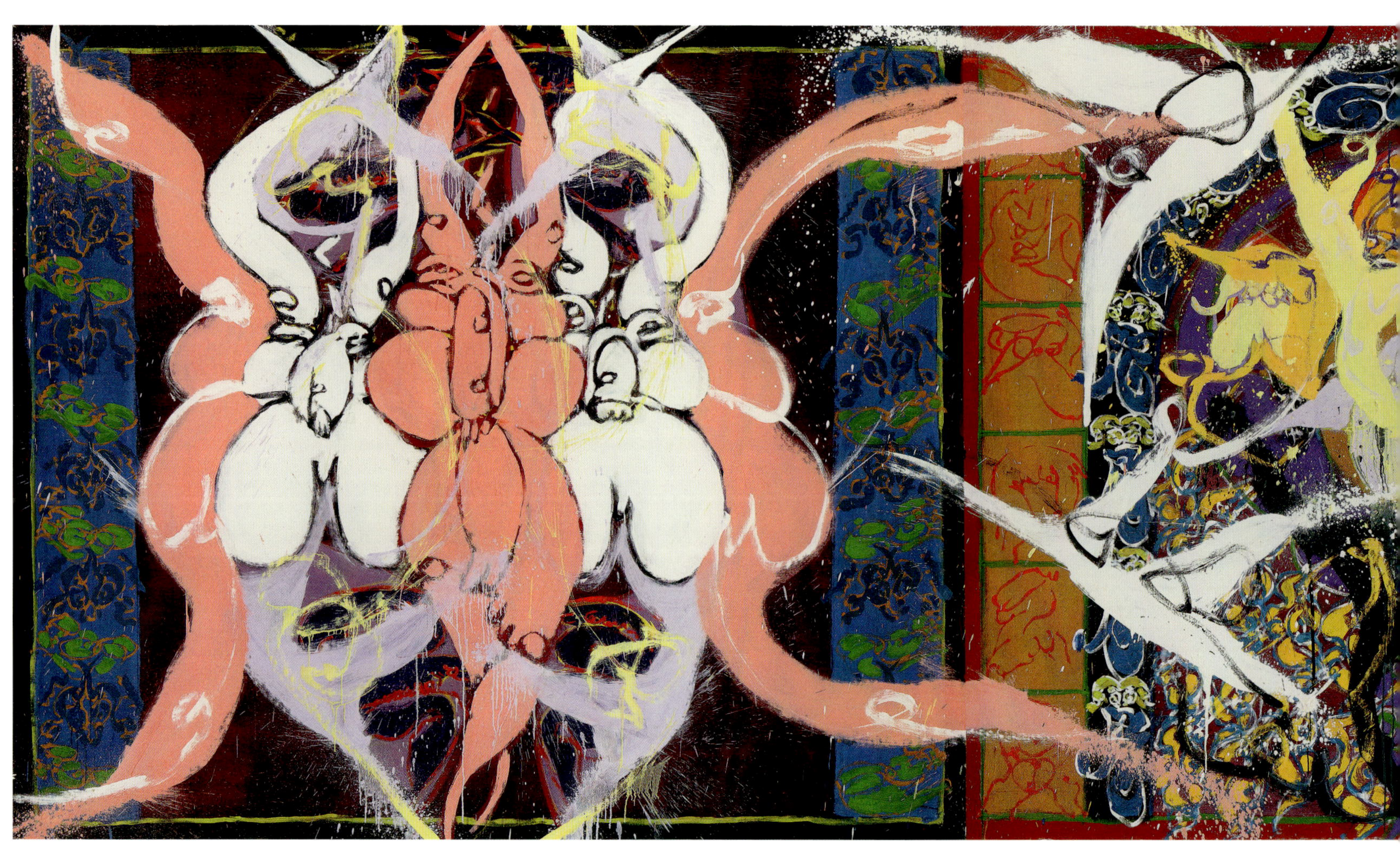

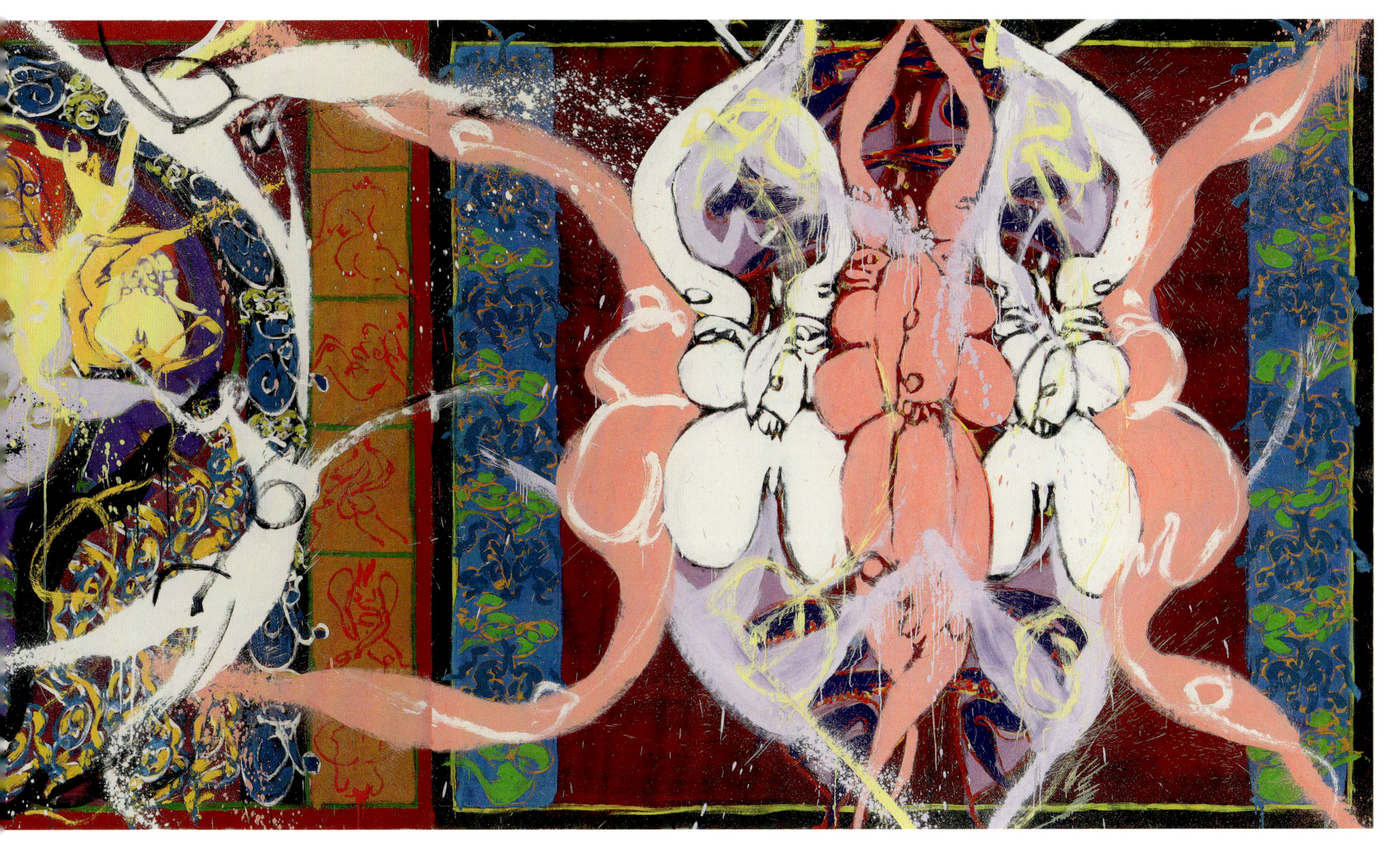

Plate 19

Eye of Salonica, 1998
Oil on canvas
Triptych, 72 × 252 in. (183 × 640 cm) overall
The Estate of Norman Bluhm

Fig. 19
Norman and Cary Bluhm with Tony Smith's sculpture *81 and More*, 1971, at The Museum of Modern Art, New York, c. 1971. Photo courtesy of The Estate of Norman Bluhm. © Tony Smith Estate / Artists Rights Society (ARS), New York

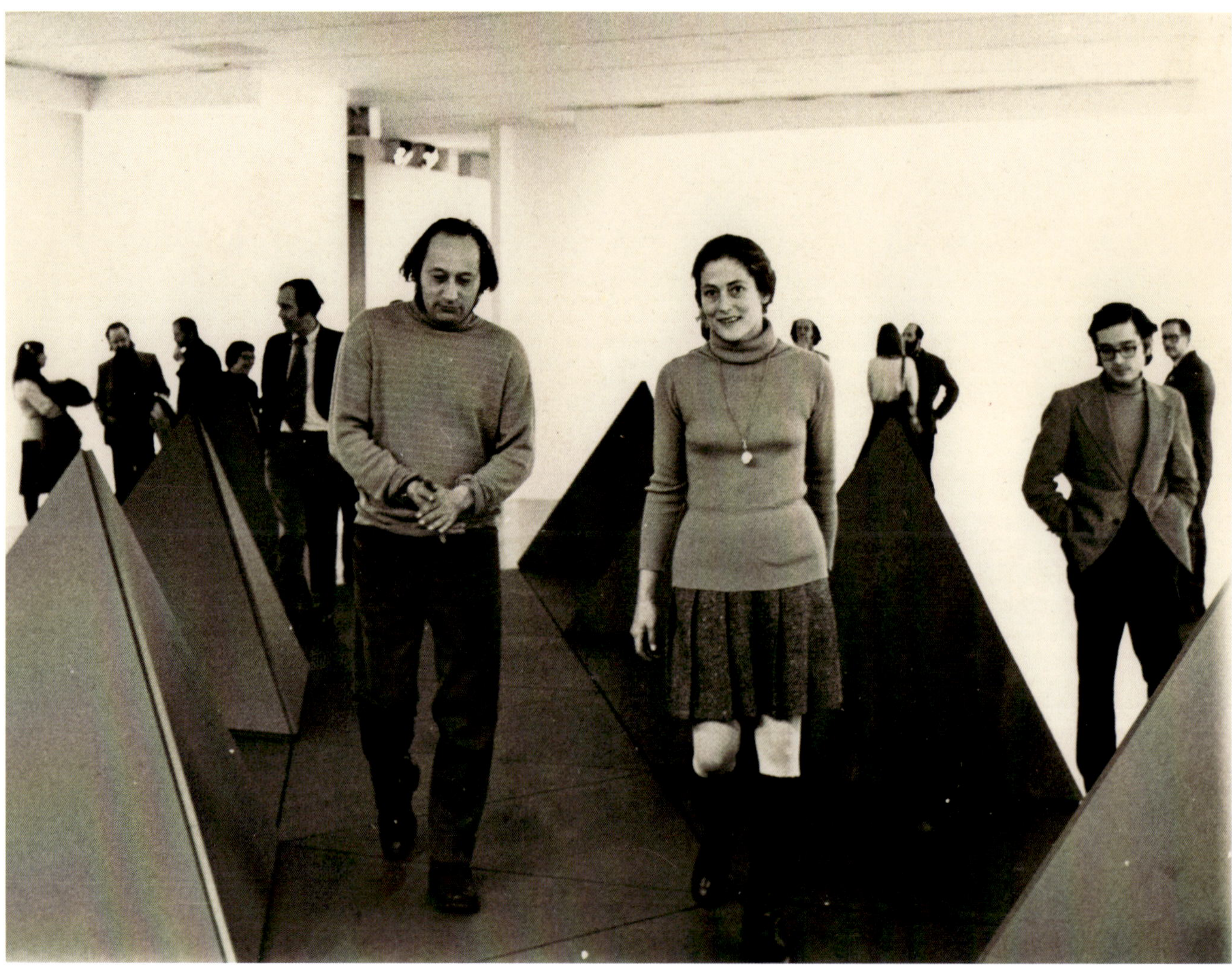

have been achieved in his paintings from the late 1990s, which have a tantric quality, as if he were striving to express abstractly a kind of hieroglyphics of universal human experiences—dancing, worshiping, strutting, pulsing, combusting. Iconographically and formally these late paintings are the most ambitious and encyclopedic works of Bluhm's production. The monumental polyptych *Cappella Ignota* (Plate 79), for instance, displays a writhing, glowing field of biomorphic forms moving in and around a structure that resembles a church or temple, a tapestry or an altar. Teeming environments unto themselves, these late multipanel works reflect all of the energy and formal experimentation of Bluhm's five decades of painting, gathered into grand compositions pointedly referencing religious art and architecture. As he did throughout his production, Bluhm pushed ornamental pattern and abstract gestures to their expressive limits in his late works. The result is a triumphant documentation of the act painting by a painter at the height of his career.

Notes

1. " 'Nothing could be farther from Mies van der Rohe,' says a fellow painter, 'than Bluhm's work'—but the influence of Mies's insistence on a ruggedly individual art and *Gestaltung* is easily detected in such a phrase of Bluhm's as 'A man creates his own space.' " William Berkson, "Bluhm Paints a Picture," *Art News* (May 1963): 40.
2. George Hofmann, "Interview with Norman Bluhm," Artists Research Group, Hunter College Oral History Project, July 21, 1997, https://huntercollegeart.org/artists-research-group/norman-bluhm/.
3. Clement Greenberg, "Milton Avery" (1957), in *The Collected Essays and Criticism*, vol. 4, *Modernism with a Vengeance, 1957–1969,* ed. John O'Brien (Chicago: University of Chicago Press, 1994), p. 43.
4. In an interview with Paul Cummings, Bluhm replied to the question, "Do you think that your painting has been involved with a method of communication, a way of talking to people?" by stating, "I think if you go through life as an artist and you can get ten people that really like your paintings you've succeeded. Just ten people. I think it's very hard to communicate." "Oral History Interview with Norman Bluhm," October 23–November 12, 1969, Archives of American Art, Smithsonian Institution, p. 30.
5. Pointing out the influence of Japanese ink painters on his work in the 1950s, Bluhm stated: "I got involved in Japanese drawing, things like that. . . . I knew a lot of Japanese people and I got involved in their ideas, ink and how to use it." Ibid., p. 21.
6. Evidence that Bluhm did not mind associating his painting practice with graffiti lies in his participation in the exhibition *Aesthetics of Graffiti*, organized by Rolando Castellon at the San Francisco Museum of Modern Art in 1978. See also the related catalogue, *Aesthetics of Graffiti* (San Francisco: San Francisco Museum of Modern Art, 1978).
7. The same issue also includes one of Bluhm and O'Hara's poem-paintings, with Bluhm's characteristic vigorous brushwork swooping across the page alongside O'Hara's handwritten text reading, "no I don't feel very haiku today." *Yugen*, no. 7 (1961): 64.
8. "Frank and I were sitting around in the studio talking, and I believe Prokofiev's 'Piano Sonata for Left Hand' was on the radio. We were talking about music. We both liked a lot of the same things, especially late 19th and early 20th century piano music and opera. . . . Frank and I often went to the opera together, along with Tom Hess . . . we also used to go to the Five Spot and other jazz clubs together. At any rate I was talking about the Prokofiev, I don't remember what I said but to illustrate my point I took a brush and went up to the paper and made a gesture. And just like that Frank got up and wrote something, 'Bust,' or something like that. It was open and quick and we were talking, what we did was part of our conversation." Interview with Norman Bluhm, "26 Things at Once: Bluhm on O'Hara, the Poem Paintings, and the Art Scene," *Lingo*, no. 7 (1997): 11.
9. Bluhm made a gift of twenty-two of the works in this series to New York University; one is in the Metropolitan Museum of Art, New York; another is in the collection of The Estate of Norman Bluhm; and one the artist gave to LeRoi Jones and is no longer extant. Ibid., p. 12.
10. Raphael Rubinstein, "Ecstatic Meditations: Norman Bluhm's Paintings Over Five Decades," in *Norman Bluhm* (Milan: Mazzotta, 2000), p. 22.
11. "I showed those paintings from the '70s, those great big form paintings and somebody said to me, 'Where did you get these ideas?' I said, well basically the real idea, if you want to know where it came from, it came from looking at Chinese paintings in the Freer Gallery in Washington." Norman Bluhm, unpublished interview with Jay Grimm, March 1992, p. 33.
12. "By 1967 I began to do a lot of nude drawing. . . . I began to insert the nude form into the pictures. It became obvious in a painting I did in 1967 called *Theodora*." Bluhm, quoted in William Salzillo, "Conversation with the Artist," in *Norman Bluhm: Works on Paper, 1947–1987* (Clinton, N.Y.: Hamilton College, 1987), p. 11.
13. In addition to Bluhm's self-professed acknowledgment of Matisse's influence on his work, other scholars have noted this connection. See, for instance, John Yau, "Drawing in Color: A portrait of Norman Bluhm," in *Norman Bluhm: Works on Paper* (Milan: Commune di Milano, 2000), p. 15; and Rubinstein, "Ecstatic Meditations," p. 27.
14. Matisse's work is from a series of prints illustrating Stéphane Mallarmé's poem *The Afternoon of Faun-Eclogue*.
15. Yau, "Drawing in Color: A Portrait of Norman Bluhm (1991–1999)," in *Norman Bluhm: Works on Paper*, p. 15.
16. "As far as I'm concerned a painter basically—although he can appear to be extremely cheerful and comical and be a great bon vivant, he can be many, many things, but that's all the exterior surface—I think basically an artist, and if we look through history most artists find out that it's a terribly lonely life. It's lonely. You do it yourself. Nobody else can do it for you." "Oral History Interview with Norman Bluhm," pp. 60, 61.
17. Raphael Rubinstein has observed that the forms in *Pygmalion* simultaneously suggest sea foam, bulging flesh, and sperm, and allude to the Birth of Venus. Rubinstein, "Ecstatic Meditations," p. 25.
18. "Art is all the 3,000 years that were created before me." Bluhm, quoted in Salzillo, "Conversation with the Artist," p. 11.
19. Ibid., p. 12.
20. "Some people's gesture in space or in scale sometimes can be—well, let's say, twelve inches, and sometimes it can be ten feet. . . . I'm not talking about the known aspect of architecture, but the unknown . . . it gave me an idea of scale, how it could go outside of yourself, how you get outside of those little fingers we all have." "Oral History Interview with Norman Bluhm," p. 3.

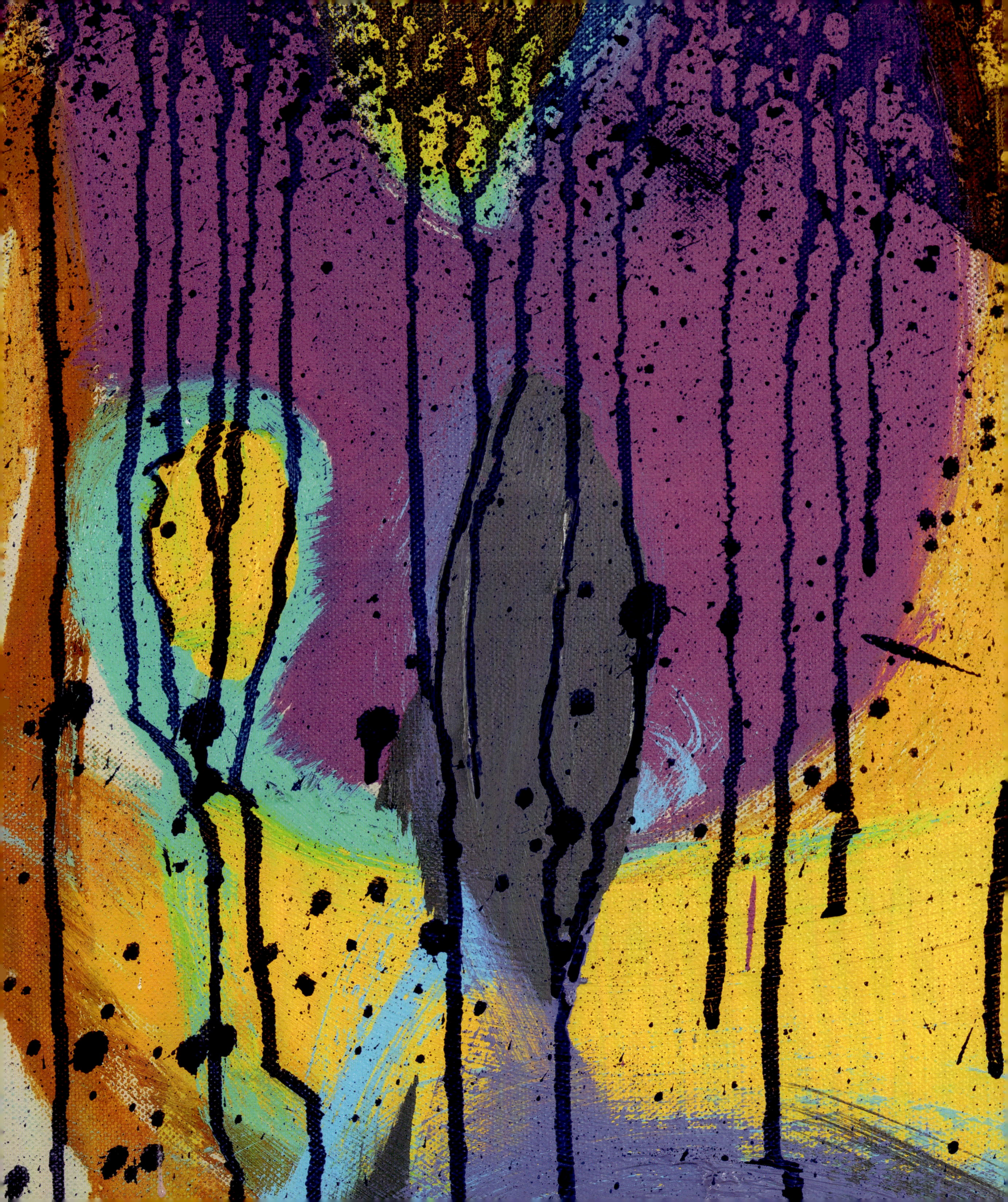

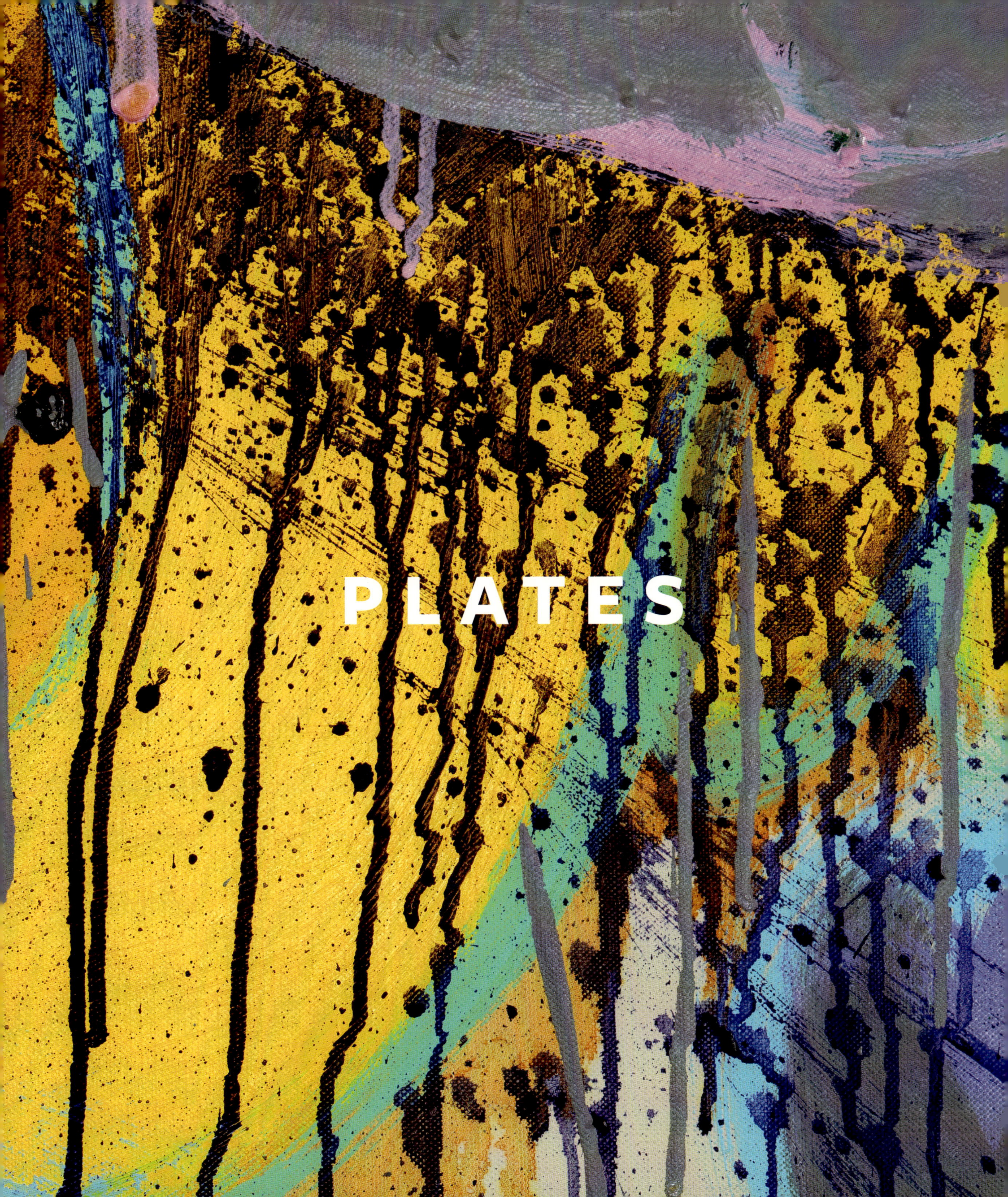

PLATES

Fig. 20
Norman Bluhm in the apartment of Michel Robinet, Paris, 1947. Photo courtesy of The Estate of Norman Bluhm

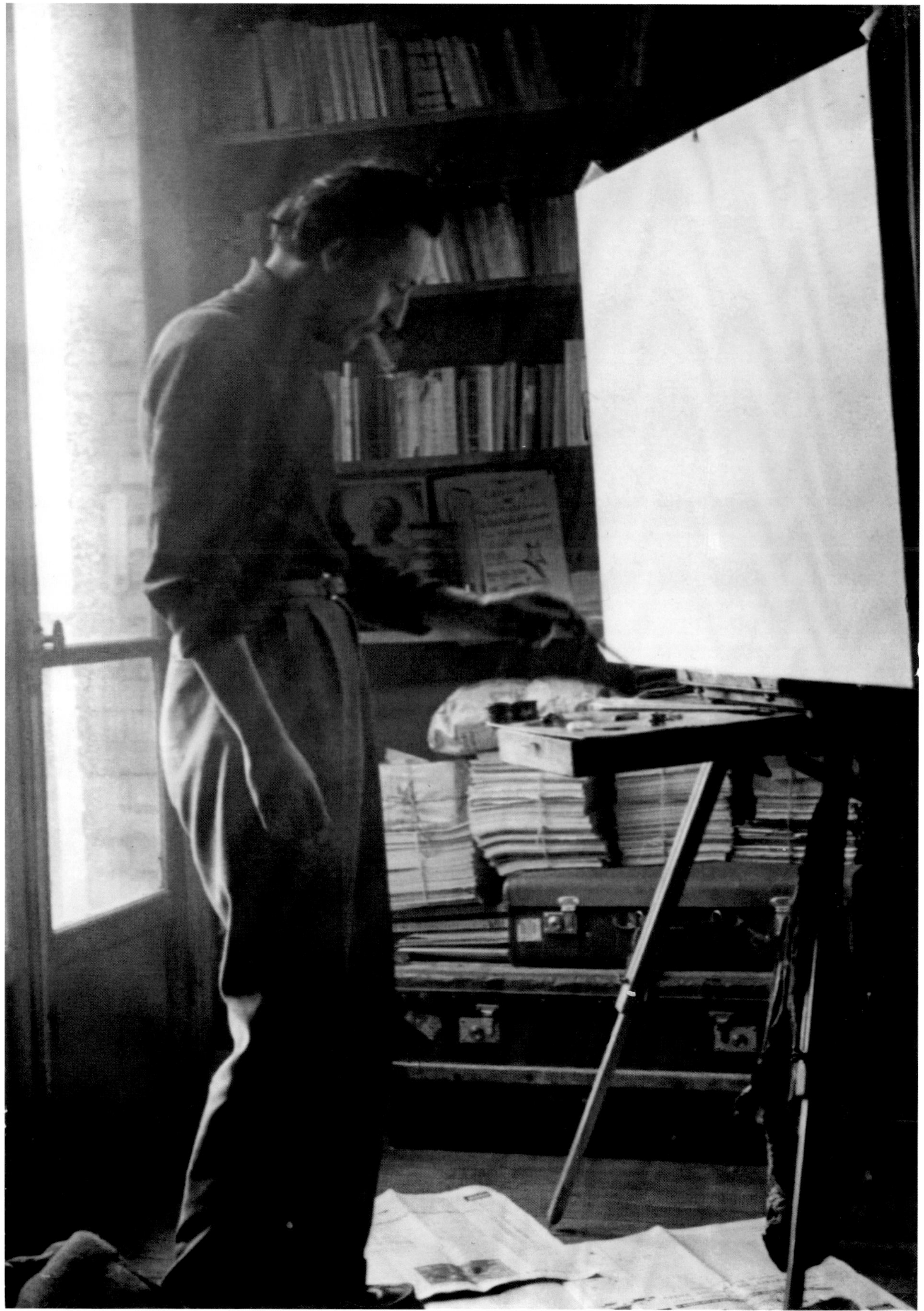

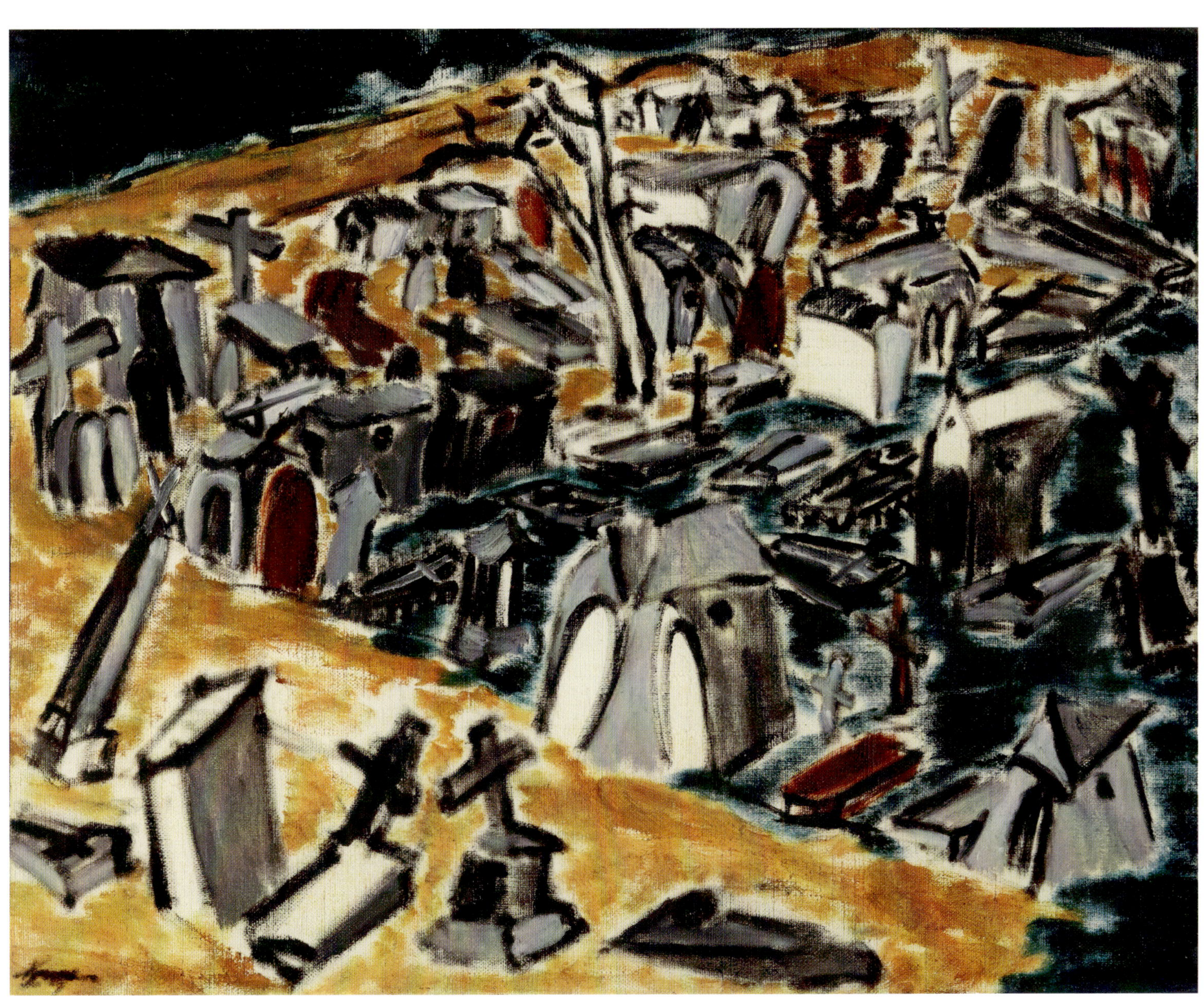

Plate 20

Cimetière de Montparnasse, 1947
Oil on canvas
32 ½ × 39 ½ in. (82.5 × 100.3 cm)
The Estate of Norman Bluhm

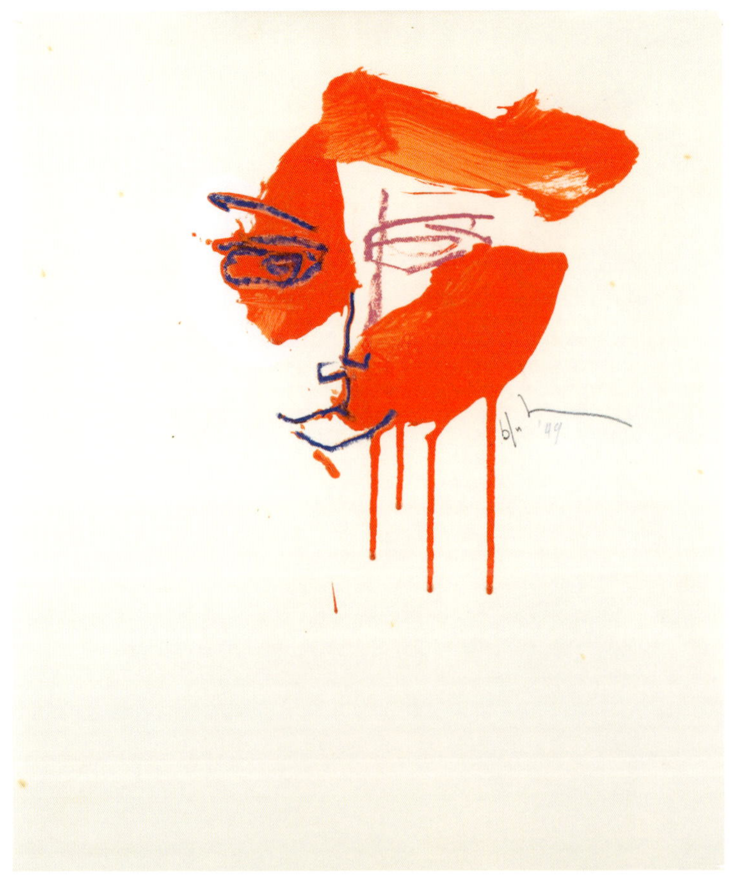

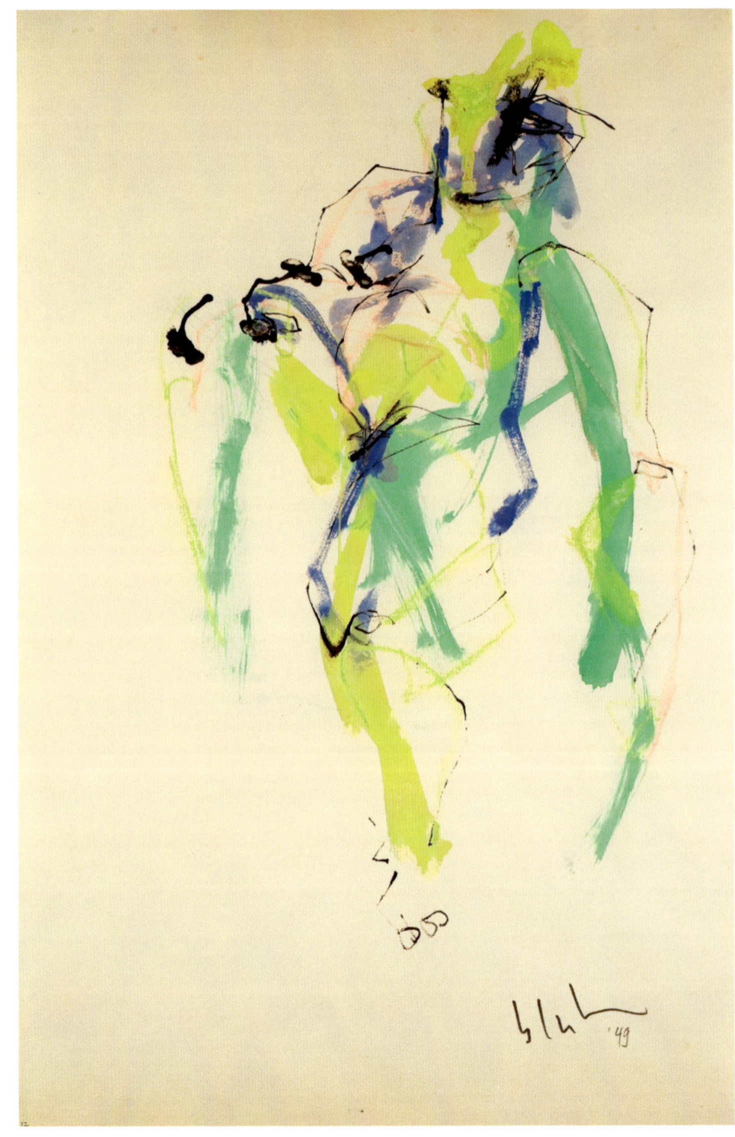

Plate 21

Head, 1949
Gouache and pastel on paper
16 ¾ × 14 in. (42.5 × 35.5 cm)
The Estate of Norman Bluhm

Plate 22

Nu, 1949
Ink and watercolor on paper
20 × 12 ½ in. (51 × 31.8 cm)
The Estate of Norman Bluhm

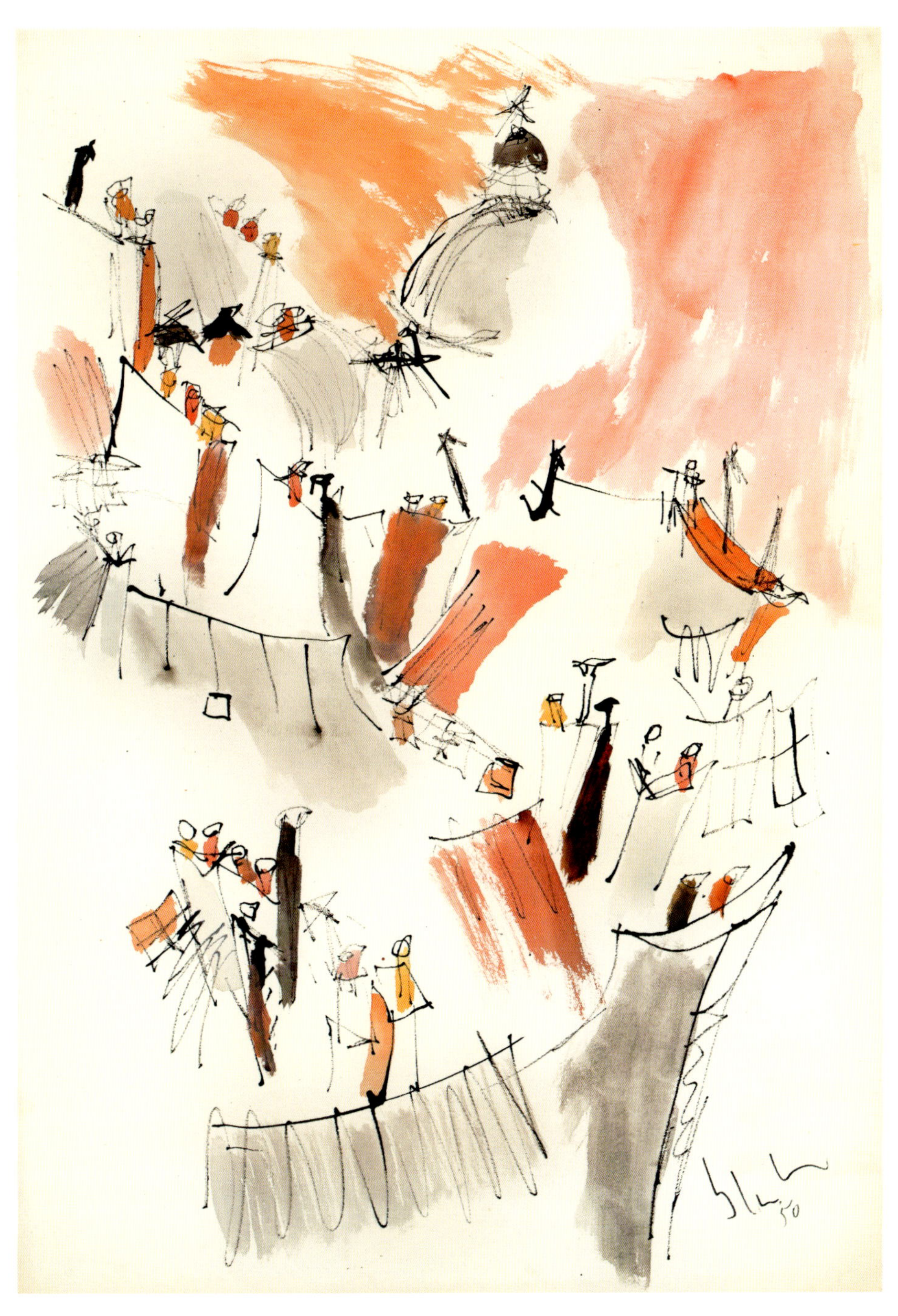

Plate 23

Rooftops, 1950
Ink and watercolor on paper
22 × 15 in. (56 × 38 cm)
The Estate of Norman Bluhm

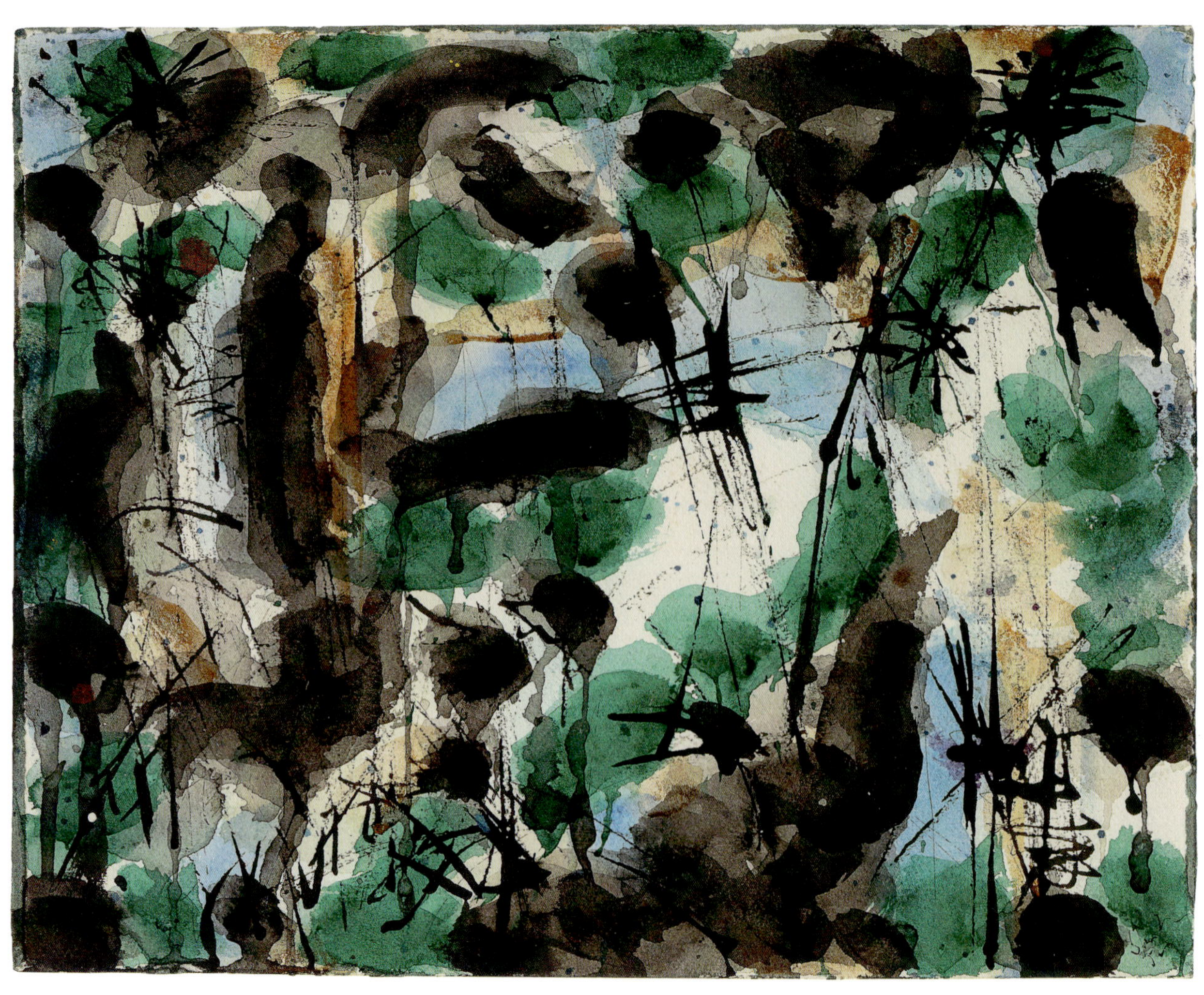

Plate 24

Untitled, 1952
Ink and watercolor on paper
8 ½ × 10 ½ in. (21.6 × 26.7 cm)
The Estate of Norman Bluhm

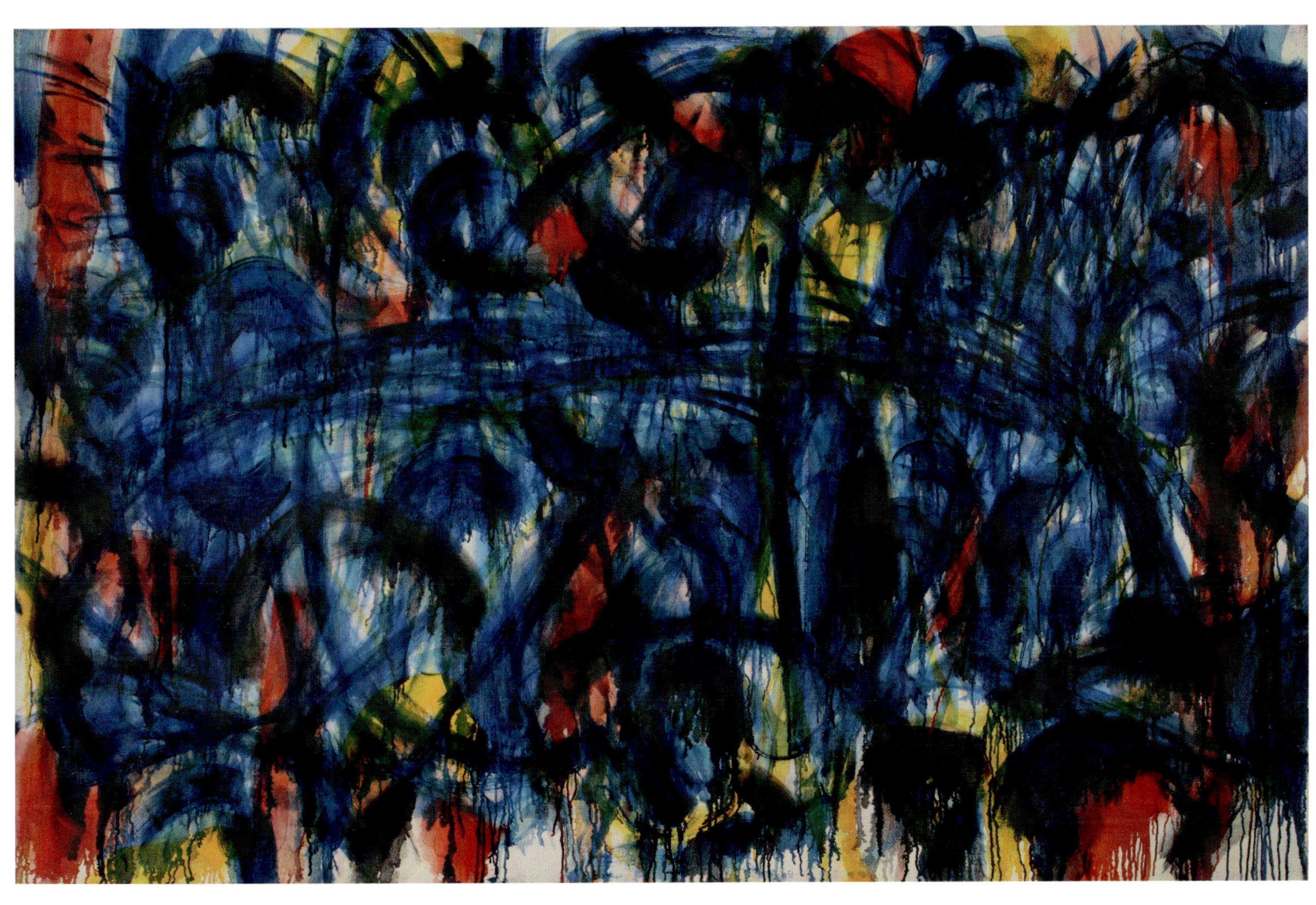

Plate 25

Untitled, 1954
Oil on canvas
50 × 78 in. (127 × 198 cm)
Collection of Sandy Gross and Anne Conaway

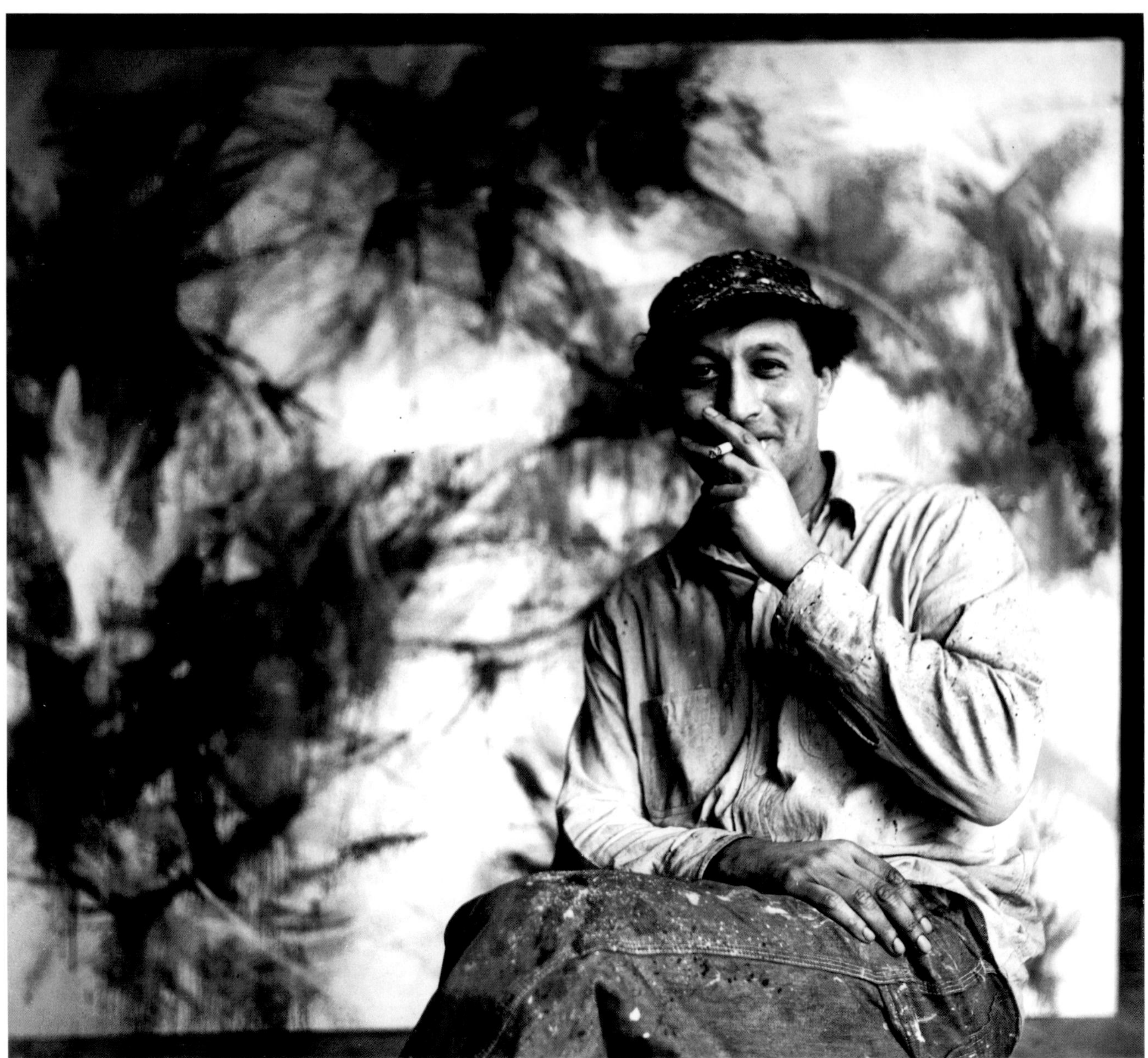

Fig. 21
Norman Bluhm in his studio, 333 Park Avenue South, New York City, 1958. Photo by George Moffett – Lensgroup, courtesy of The Estate of Norman Bluhm

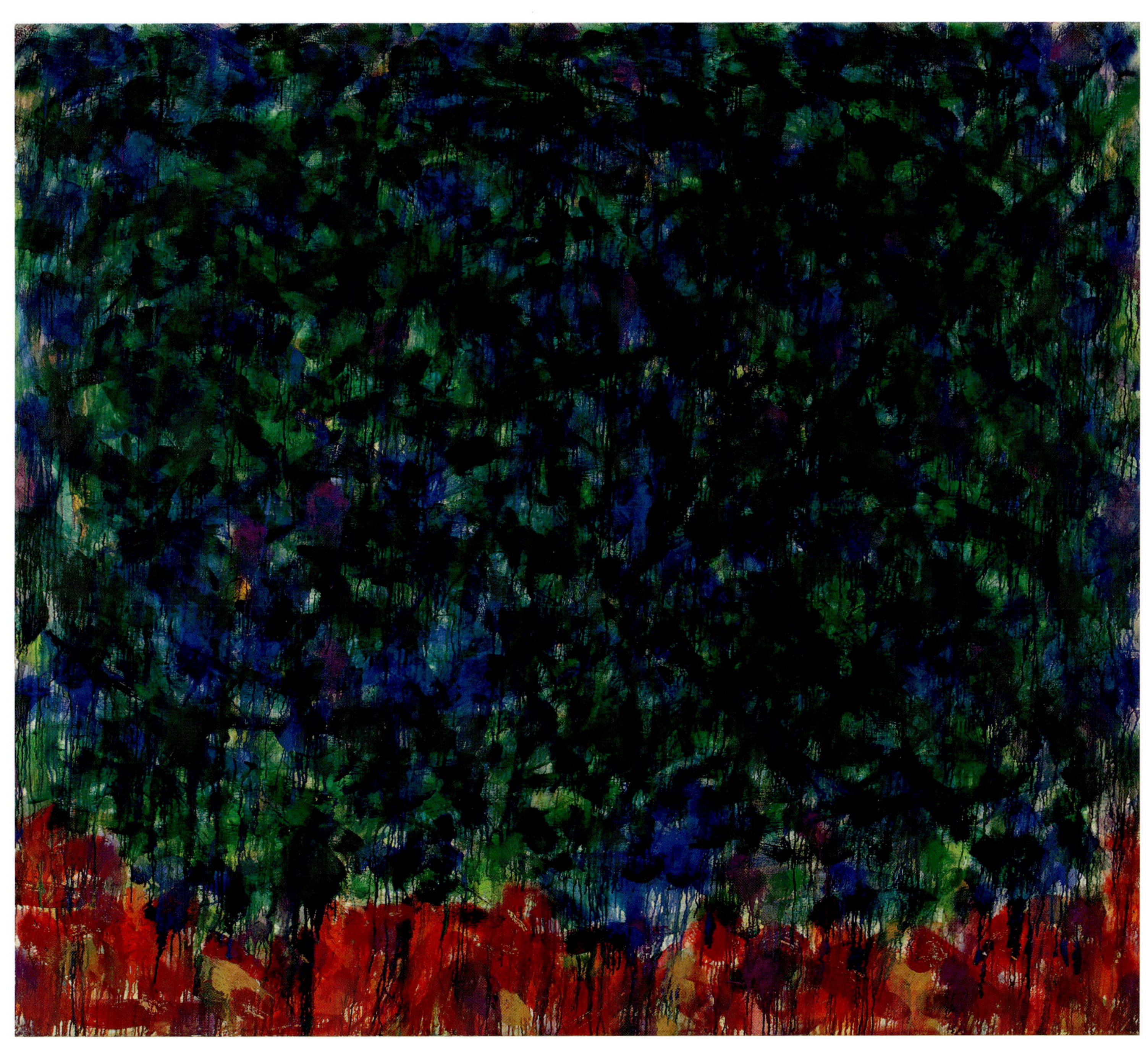

Plate 26

Jaded Silence, 1957
Oil on canvas
72 × 80 in. (183 × 203 cm)
Worcester Art Museum, Massachusetts, The Judith Rothschild Foundation, the Austin S. Garver Fund, and gift of The Estate of Norman Bluhm

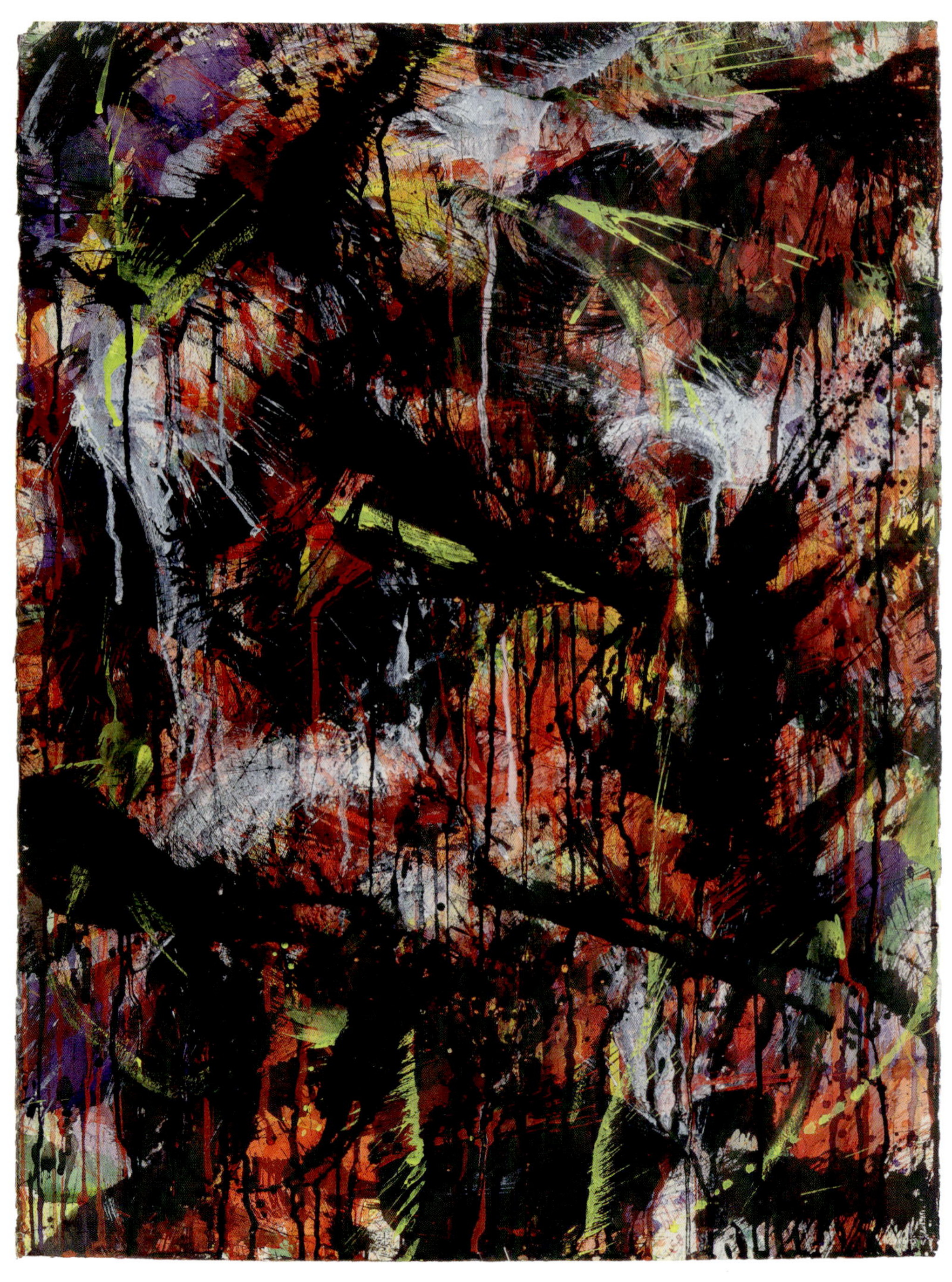

Plate 27

Study for Clouds of Magellan, 1958
Watercolor on paper
30 × 22 in. (76 × 56 cm)
The Estate of Norman Bluhm

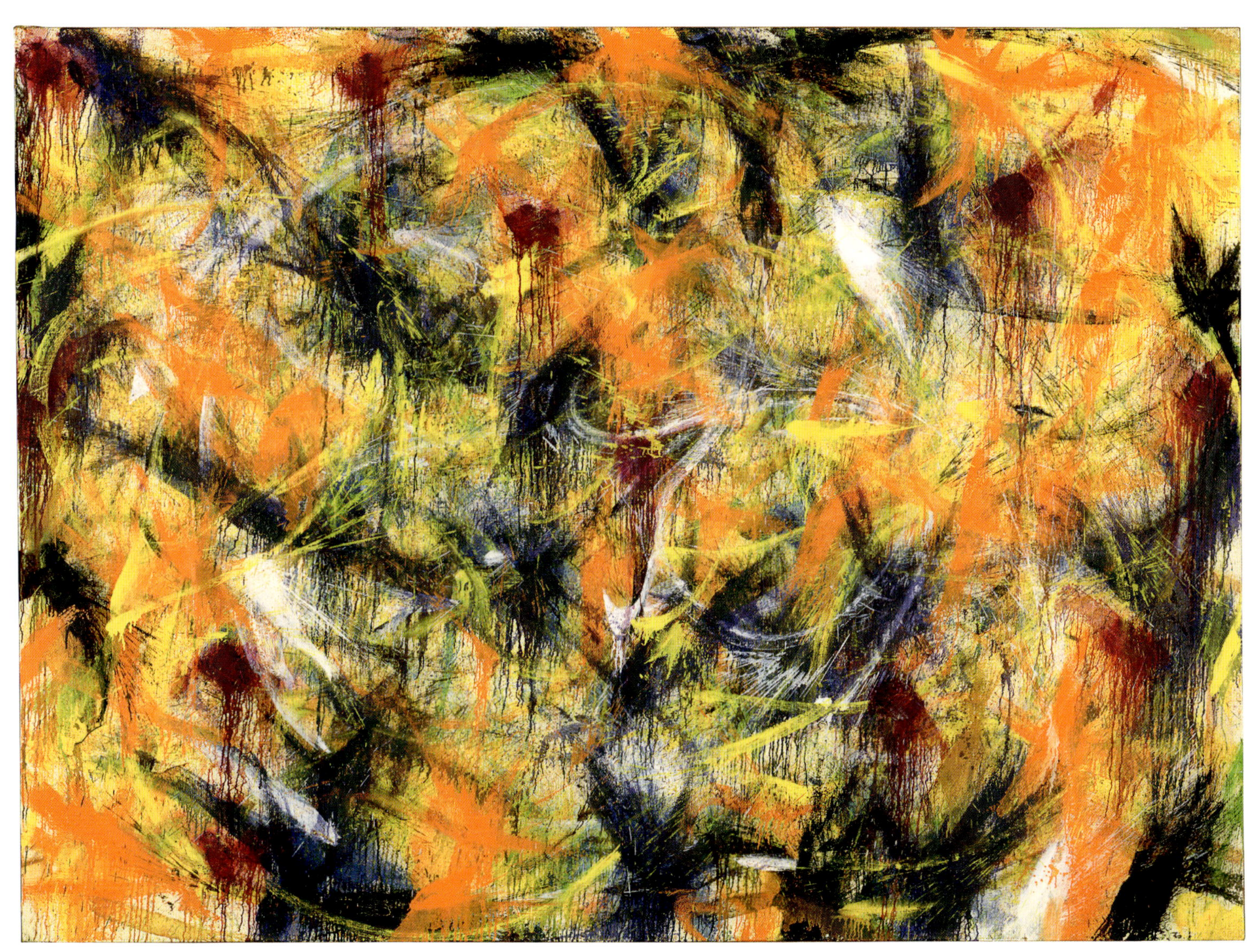

Plate 28

Squall, 1958
Oil on canvas
72 × 96 in. (183 × 244 cm)
Collection of the Neuberger Museum of Art, Purchase College,
State University of New York *1970.02.04*

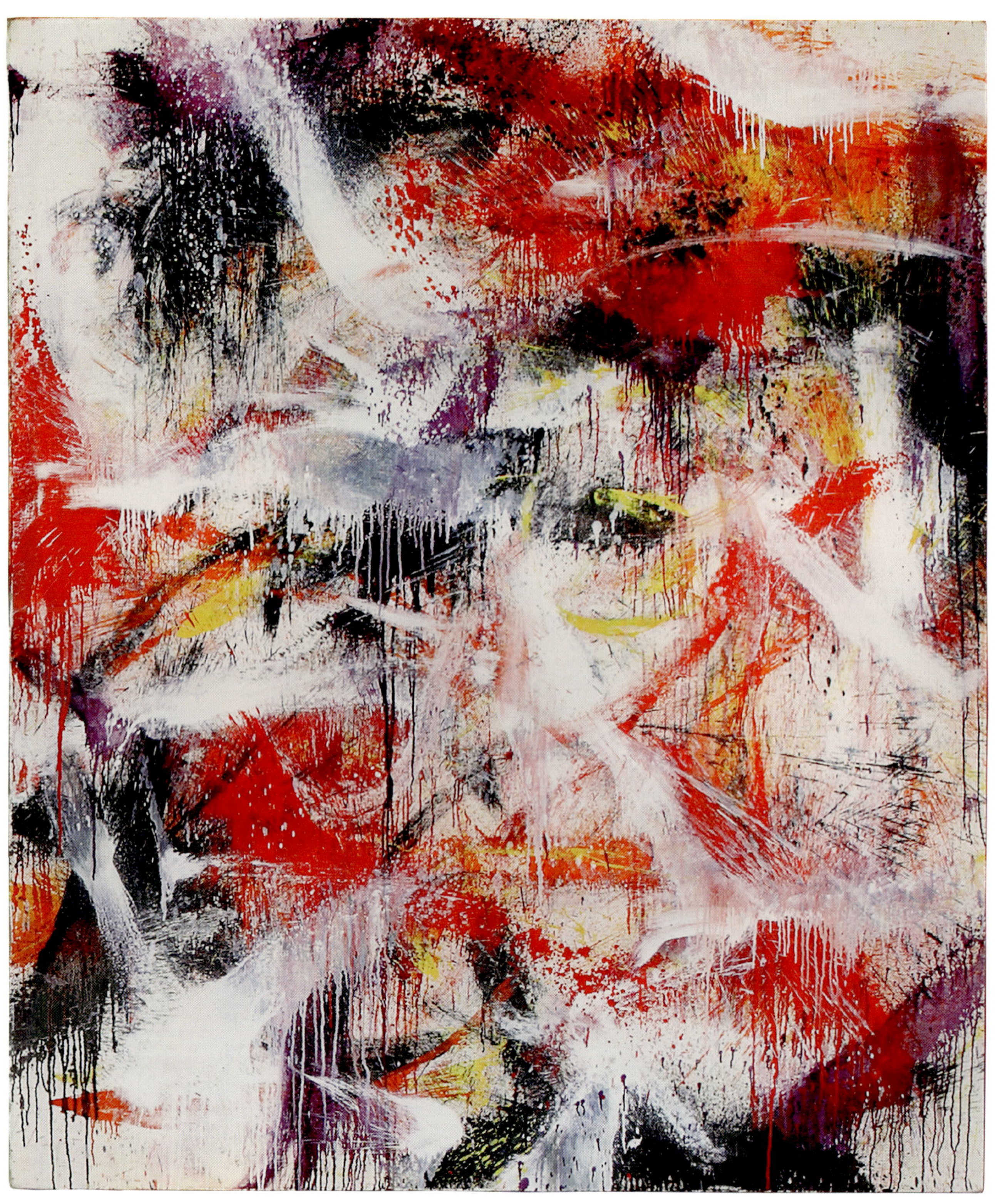

Plate 29

Open Red, 1959
Oil on canvas
72 × 60 in. (183 × 152 cm)
Collection of the Estate of Tom Armstrong

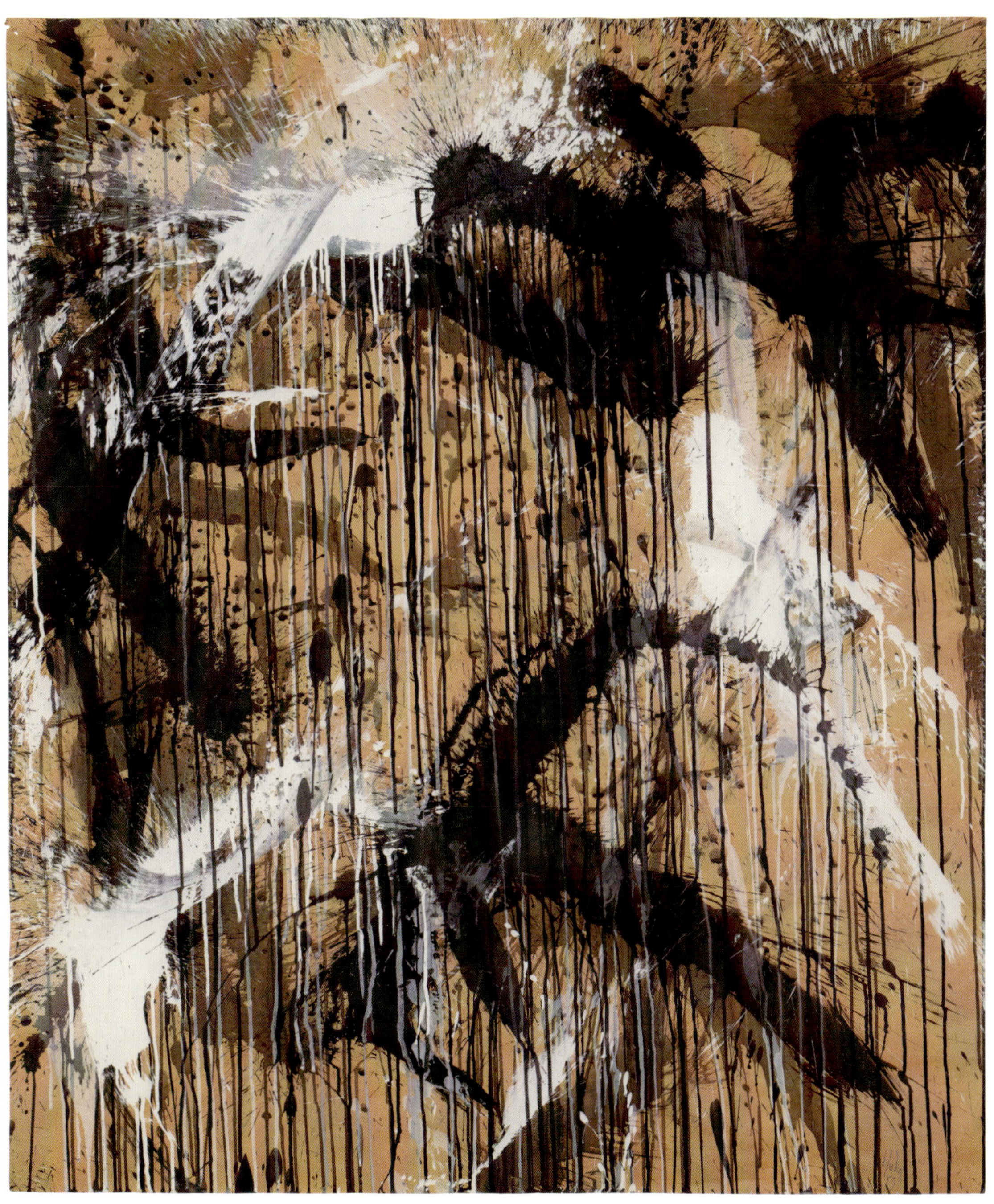

Plate 30

Untitled, 1959
Ink and gouache on brown paper
47 ½ × 39 ½ in. (120.6 × 100.3 cm)
Metropolitan Museum of Art, New York
Purchased by Longview Foundation Inc., in memory of Audrey Stern Hess, 1977 *77.368*

“Frank and I were sitting around in the studio talking, and I believe Prokofiev’s ‘Piano Sonata for Left Hand’ was on the radio. We were talking about music. We both liked a lot of the same things, especially late 19th- and early 20th-century piano music and opera. . . . Frank and I often went to the opera together, along with Tom Hess. . . . We also used to go to the Five Spot and other jazz clubs together. At any rate, I was talking about the Prokofiev—I don’t remember what I said, but to illustrate my point I took a brush and went up to the paper and made a gesture. And, just like that, Frank got up and wrote something, ‘Bust,’ or something like that. It was open and quick and we were talking, what we did was part of our conversation.”

Interview with Norman Bluhm, “26 Things at Once: Bluhm on O’Hara, the Poem Paintings, and the Art Scene,” *Lingo*, no. 7 (1997): 11.

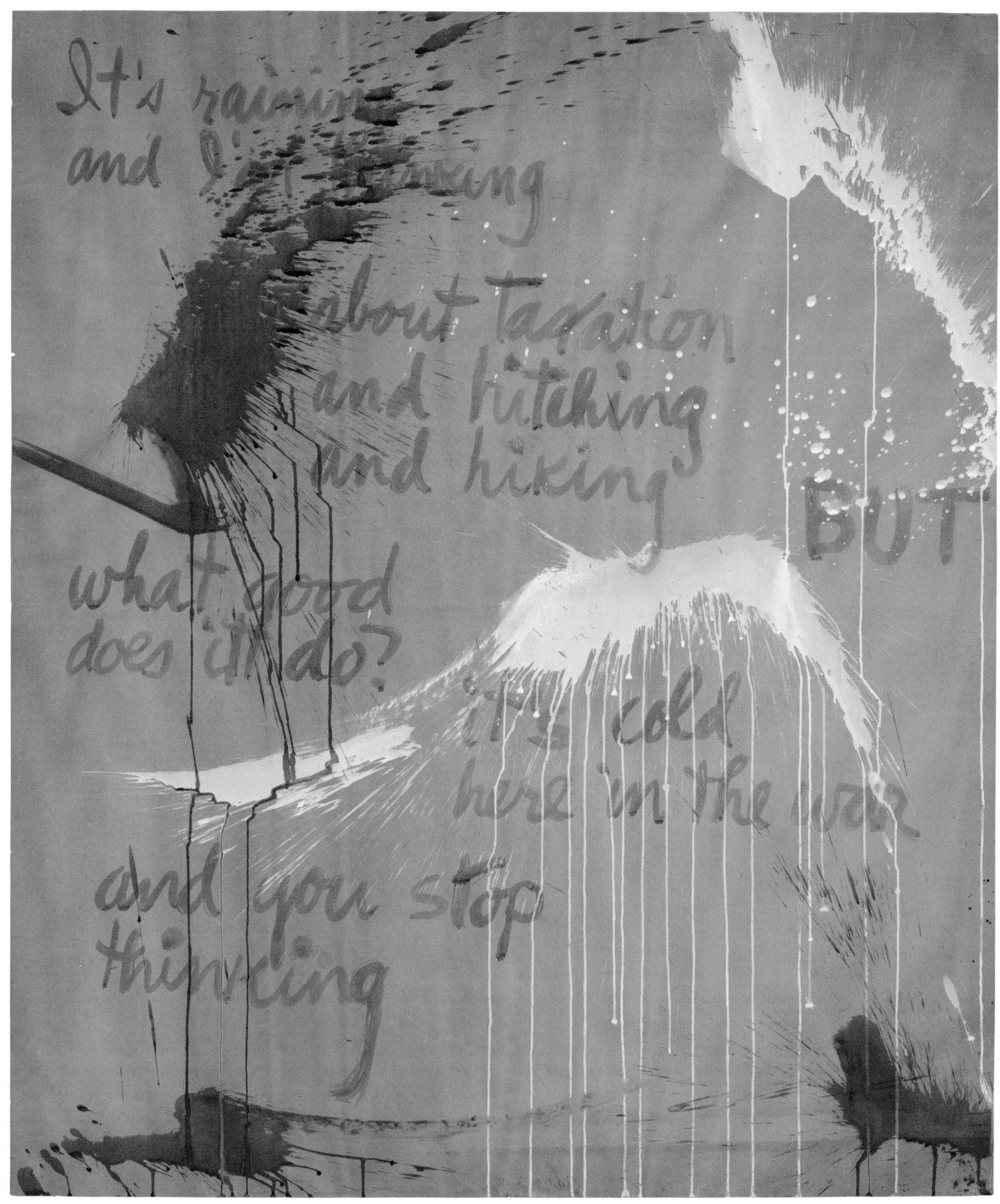

Plate 31

Norman Bluhm and Frank O'Hara
It's Raining, 1959
Ink and gouache on brown paper
48 × 40 in. (122 × 102 cm)
Metropolitan Museum of Art, New York
Gift of Mr. and Mrs. Norman Bluhm, 1984 *84.333*

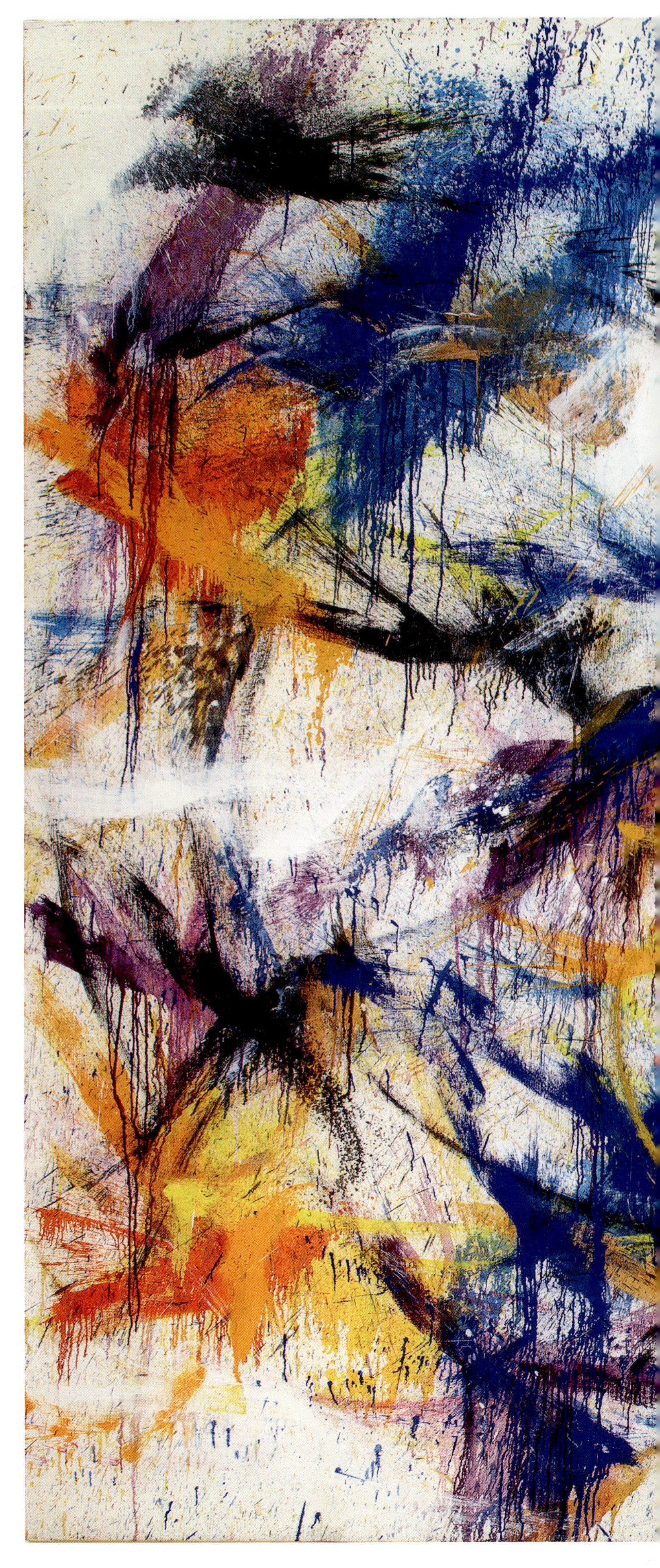

Plate 32

Time 3:30, 1959
Oil on canvas
Triptych, 96 × 126 in. (244 × 320 cm) overall
The Clark Family Collection

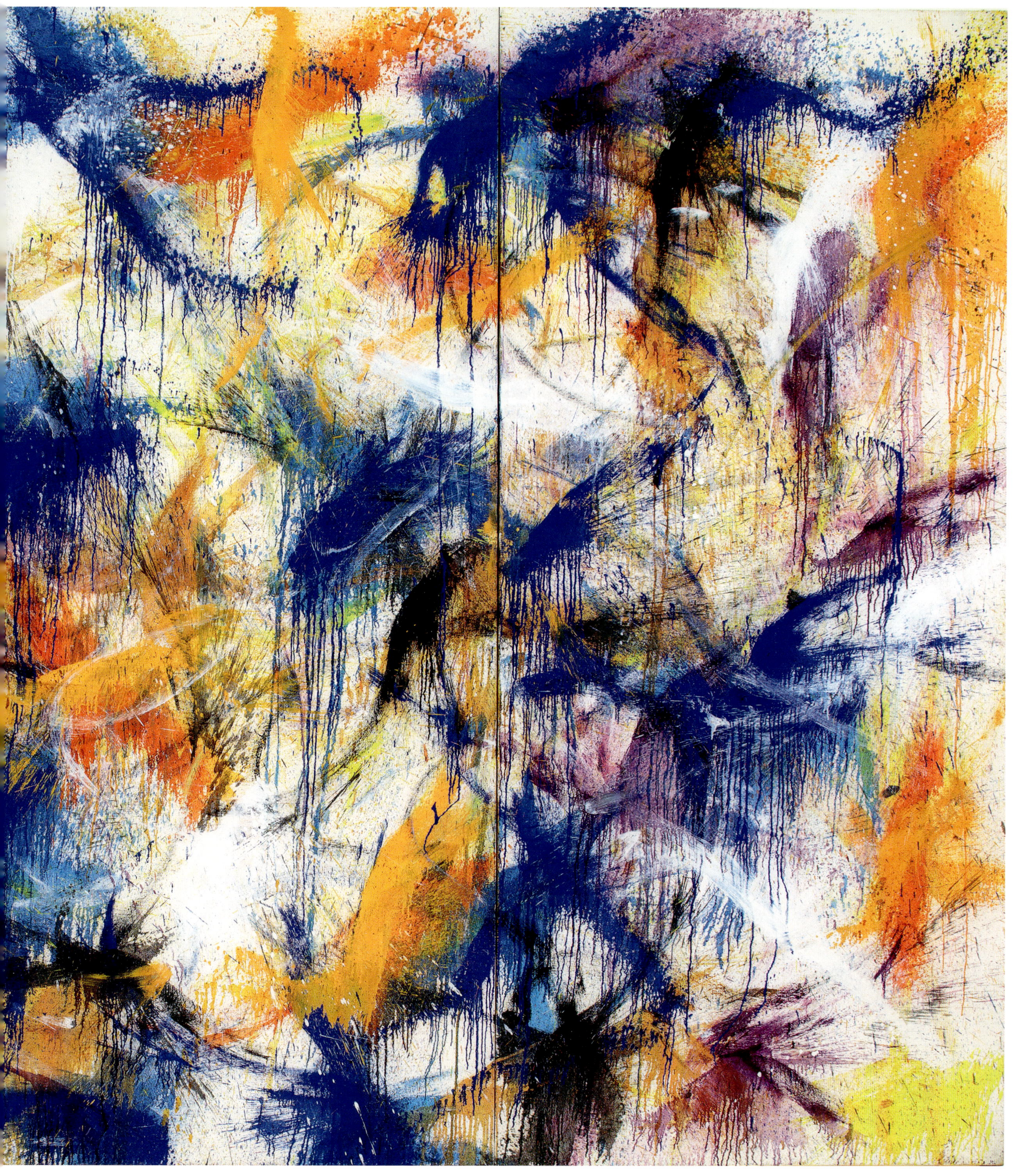

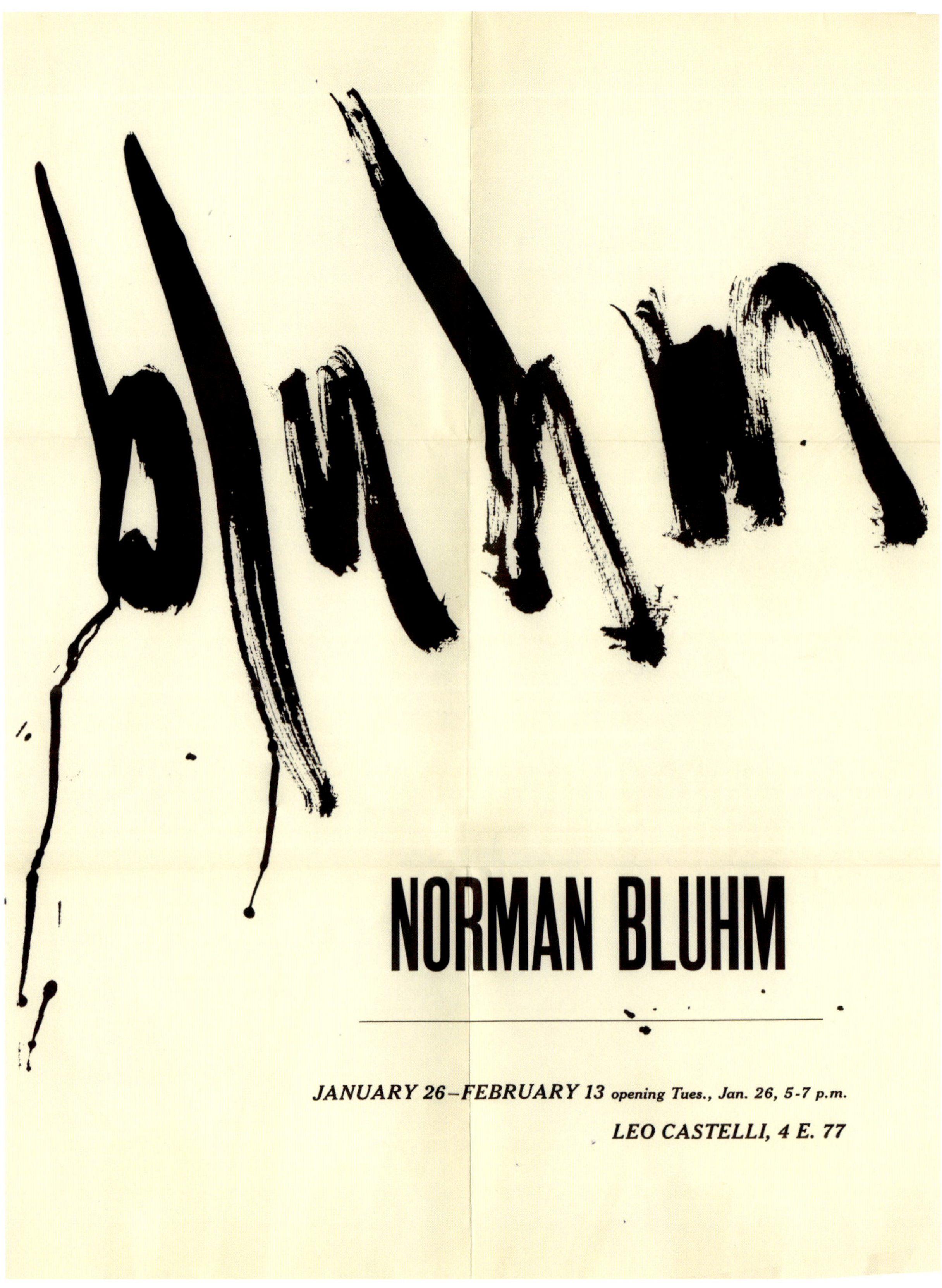

Fig. 22
Leo Castelli Gallery, Solo Exhibition Poster, New York, January 26–February 13, 1960. Courtesy of The Estate of Norman Bluhm

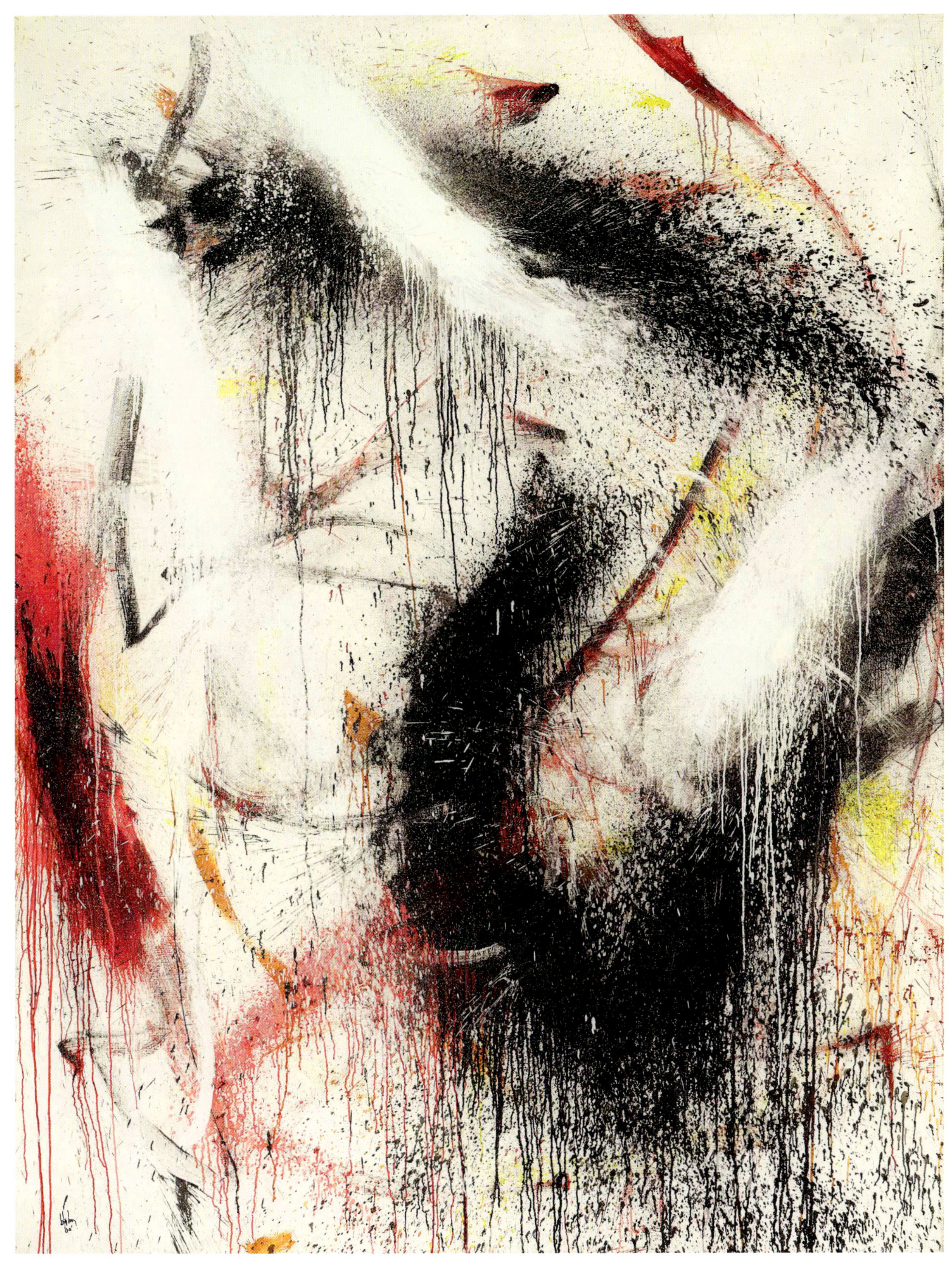

Plate 33

Ghost Town, 1960
Oil on canvas
96 ½ × 72 ¼ in. (245 × 183.5 cm)
Private collection

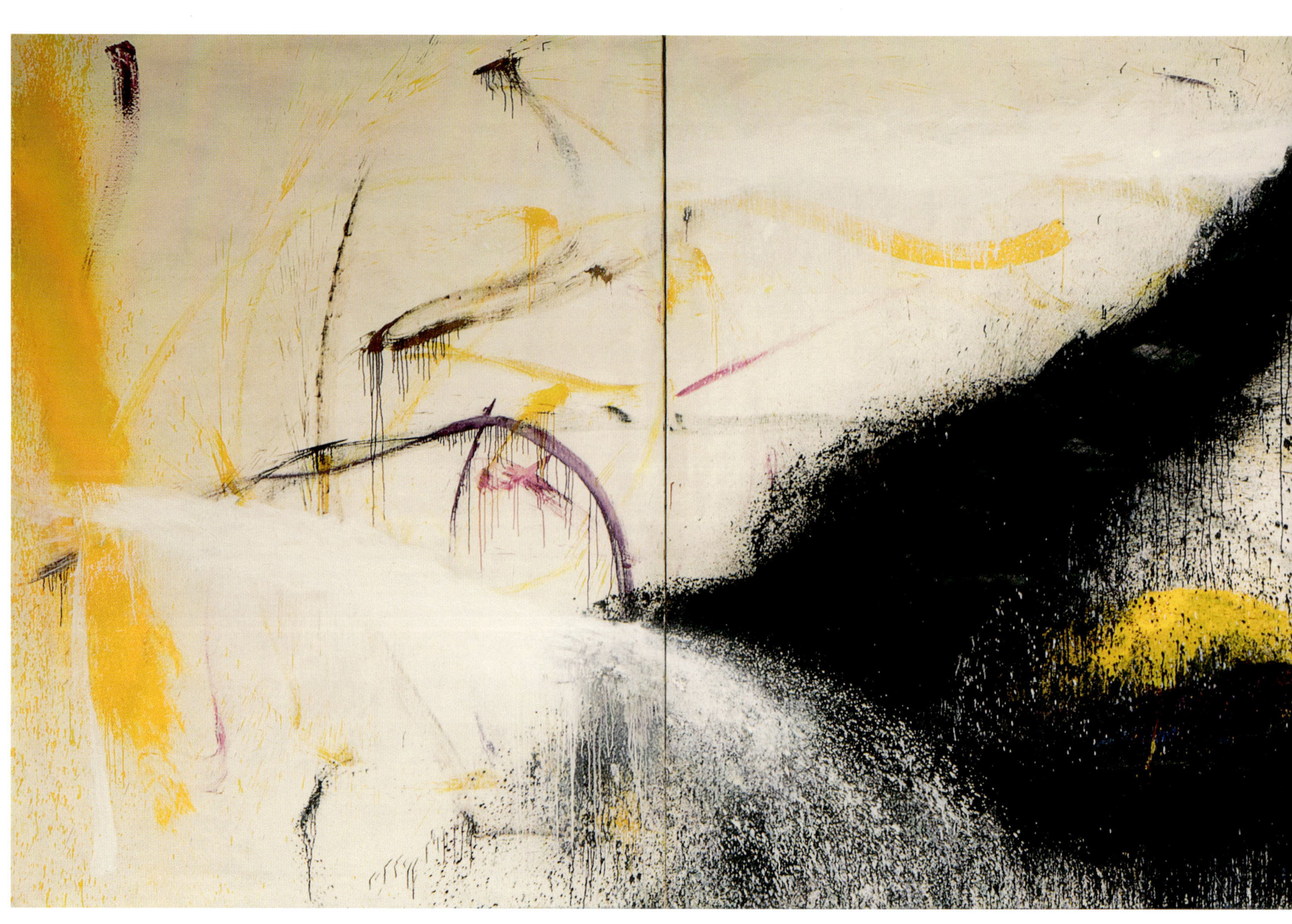

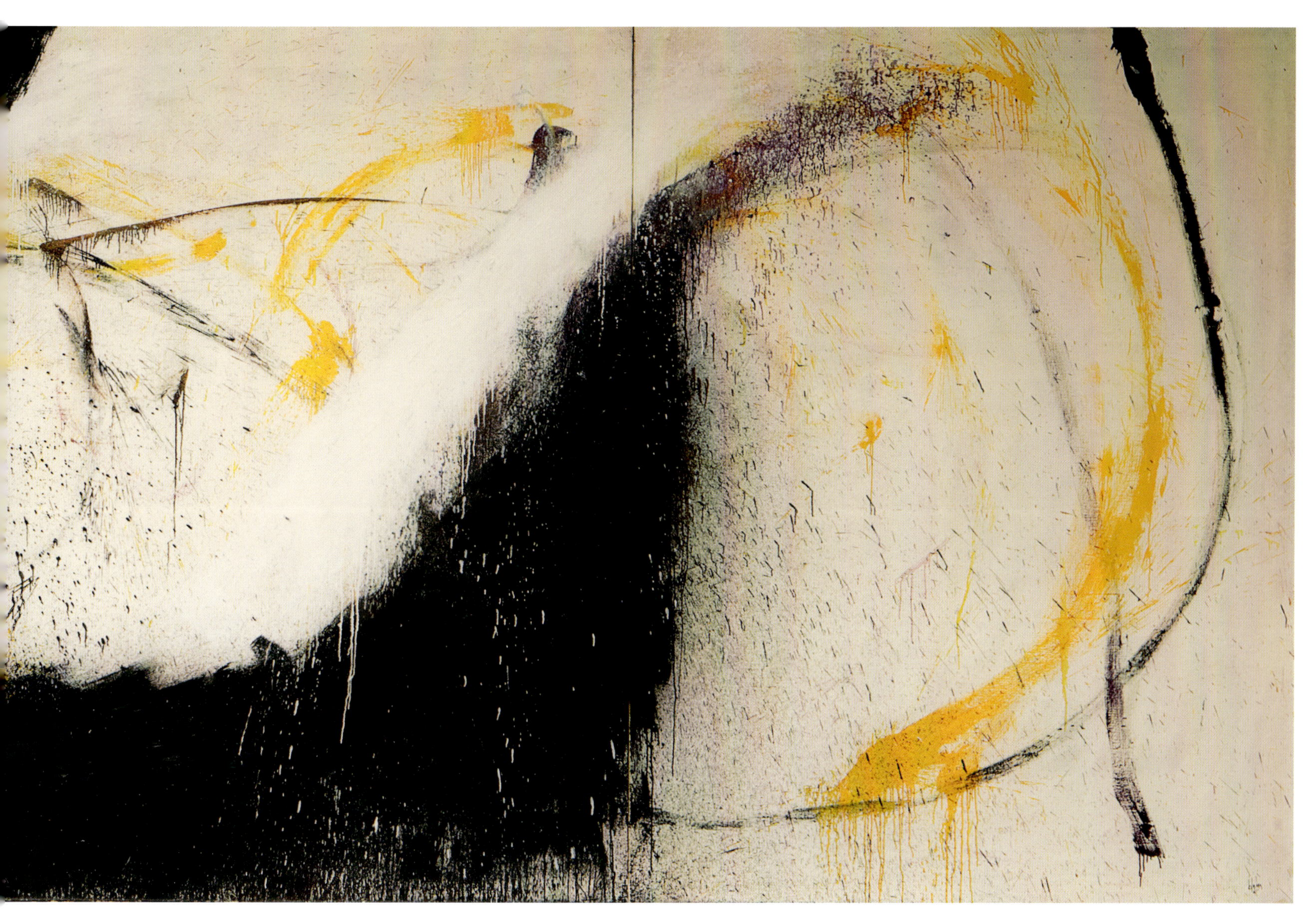

Plate 34

Oz, 1961
Oil on canvas
Four panels, 96 × 288 in. (244 × 731.5 cm) overall
David Owsley Museum of Art, Ball State University, Muncie, Indiana *L2018.016.000a-d*
On loan from The Estate of Norman Bluhm

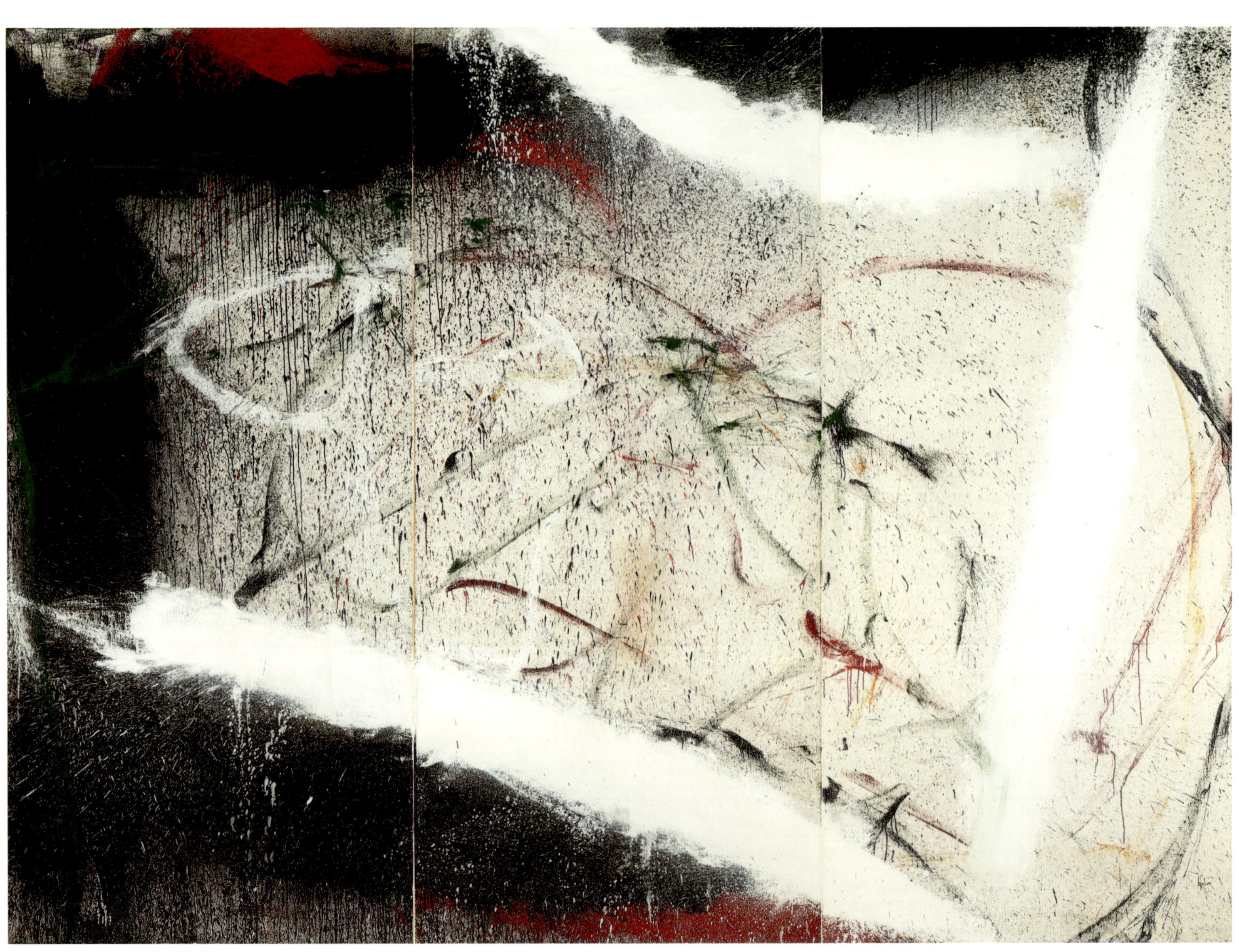

Plate 35

Flight 114, 1961
Oil on canvas
108 × 144 in. (274.3 × 366 cm)
The Estate of Norman Bluhm

Flight 114 "For Norman Bluhm"

The effervescent death
surrounded by sneaks
the arboretum remembered
            standing by the architecture
            of a time laden with noise
eating   the sky messy with dots
            the dots messy with smog
in   An airplane passes a cloud
            in your raincoat and gloves
            a tear swept back from your cheek

"My backstage life"
"It's today that I love you"
"under time's dandruff"
Connais-tu Monsieur Reverdy
ce brave à la lampe noire
and you enjoy it yourself
Têtes vides
Cœurs nus

An error was made on the flame
pero mi amor busca pura
locura de brisa y trino
We are loafing under time's asbestos

For the accident will not happen
and someone else comes dangerously near
as over the mountain a pump is pumping
and your heart is yawning in the smoke

". . . it is apparently later than we think
and me not out of Barcelona yet! I expect to
arrive in Paris Wednesday or sooner
if possible. Why don't you leave
your address with Joan Mitchell
so I'll know where you are. The
Pont Royal is full—who knows
where we'll all be on Coronation
Day? See you soon . . ."

Your face emerging from my eyes
Sunlight leans on the pillows

I don't believe what you believe
but I believe you when you say it

            A weather sped past the blocks
            In the coffee-colored dawn
            factory whistles, yawns, jets . . .

                        a drip on the sill
            an interesting cloud in your eyes.

I was just about to call you
when you called, sighing
the weather didn't matter
There was sugar left over
from the coffee   "Sugar"
We melted into the grey
yellow bronze pot of traffic
There will no longer be
any perspective to Park Avenue
Bronze hides the sky
from our eyes although our eyes
are in it, drifting along
now that everything has left
as if we had not had to wish it

Bill Berkson
December 27, 1961

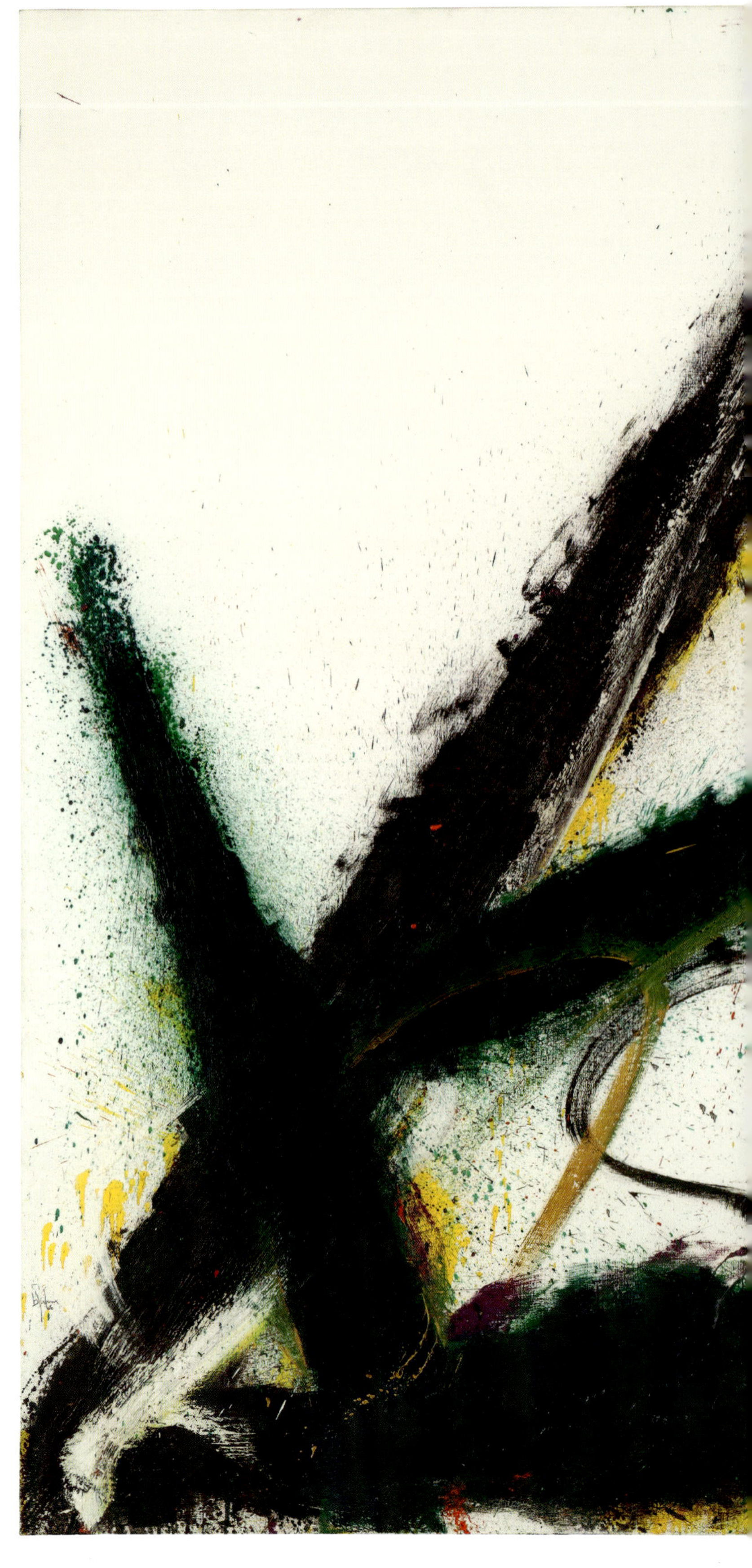

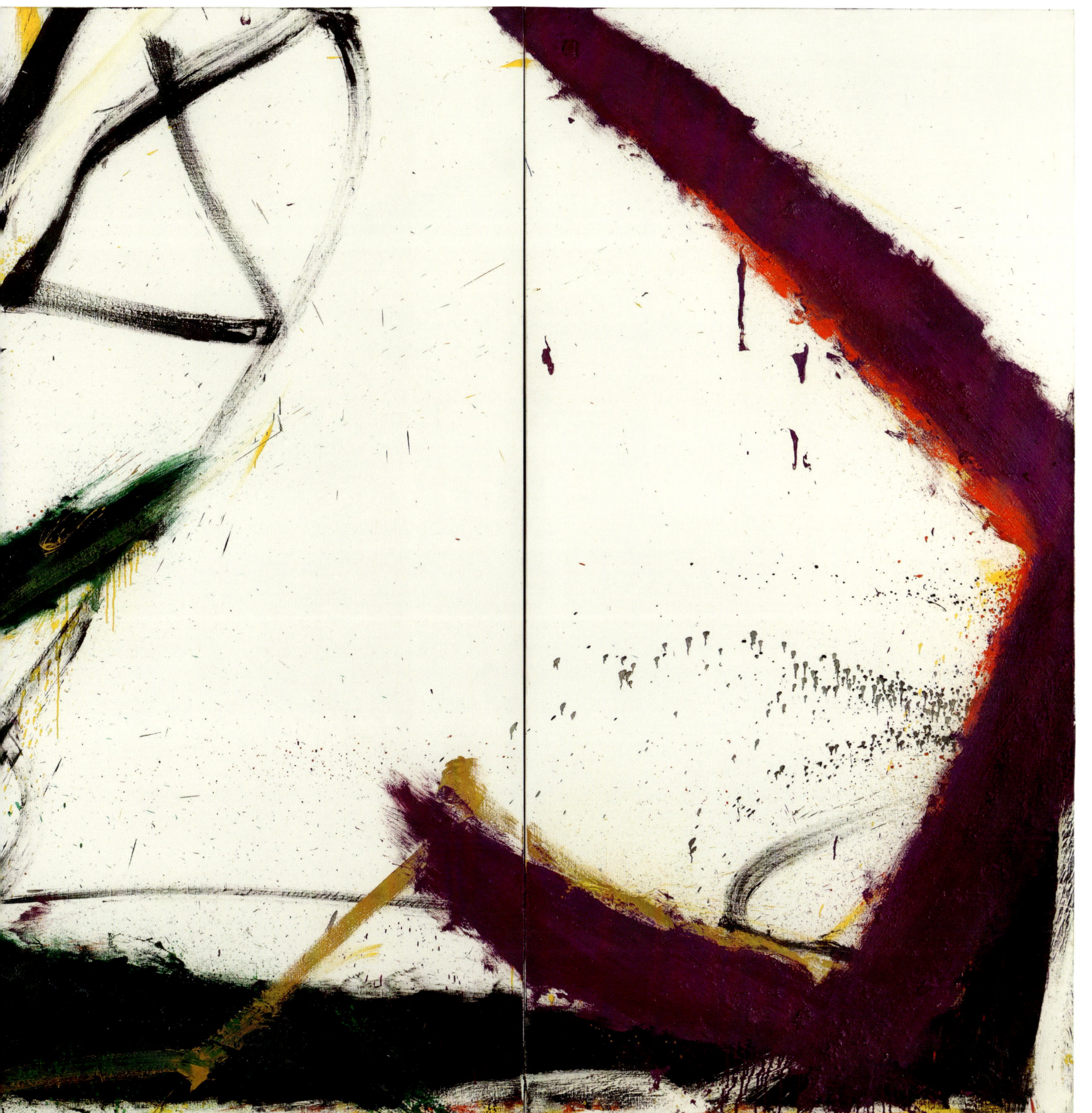

Plate 36

Himalayas, 1966
Oil on canvas
Triptych, 72 × 108 in. (183 × 274.3 cm) overall
Courtesy of Manny Silverman Gallery, Los Angeles, Graham Shay Gallery, New York, and The Estate of Norman Bluhm

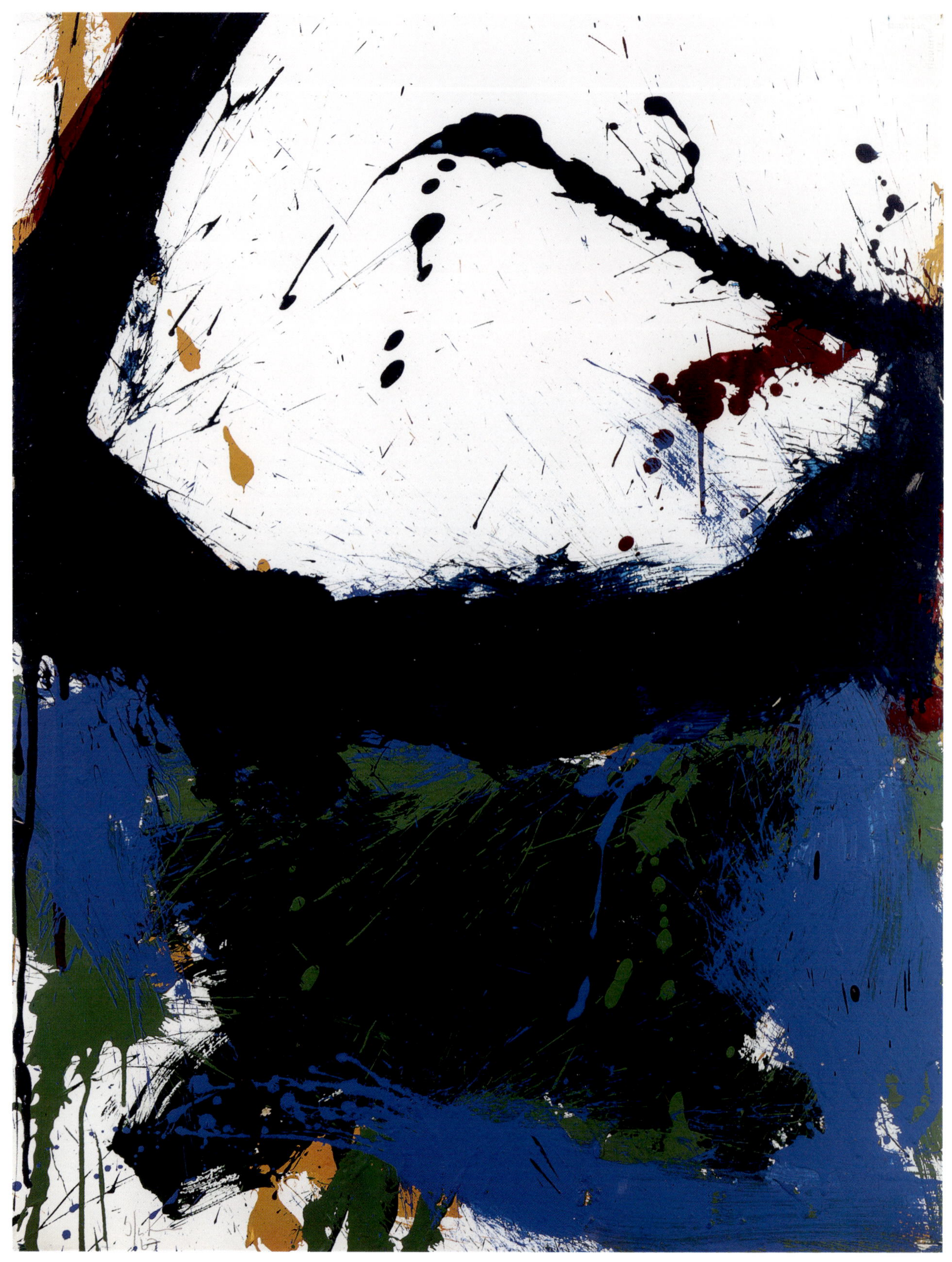

Plate 37

Untitled, 1967
Acrylic and ink on paper
30 × 22 ½ in. (76 × 57 cm)
The Estate of Norman Bluhm

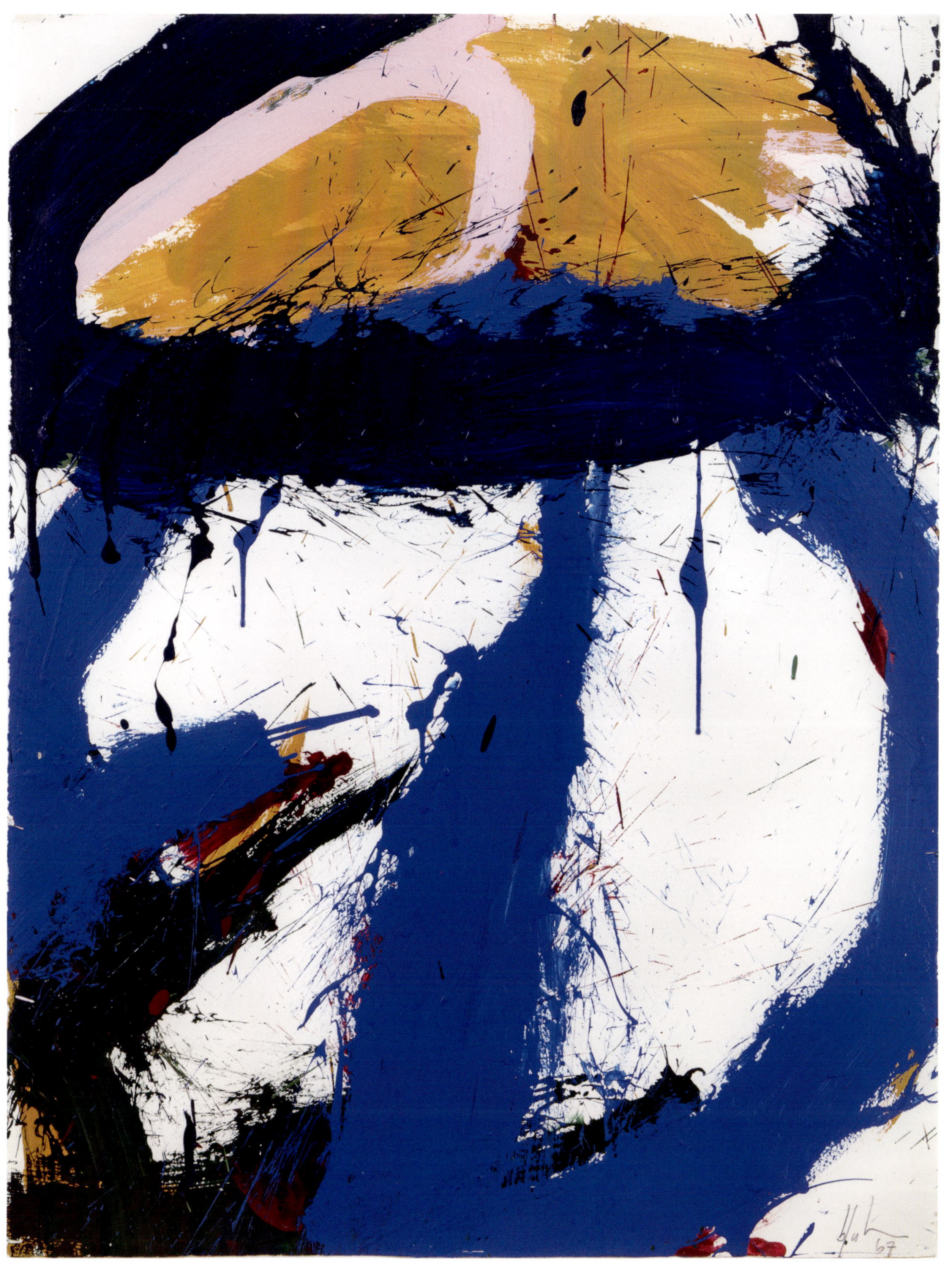

Plate 38

Untitled, Study for Isaac Commenus, 1967
Acrylic on paper
30 × 22 ½ in. (76 × 57 cm)
The Estate of Norman Bluhm

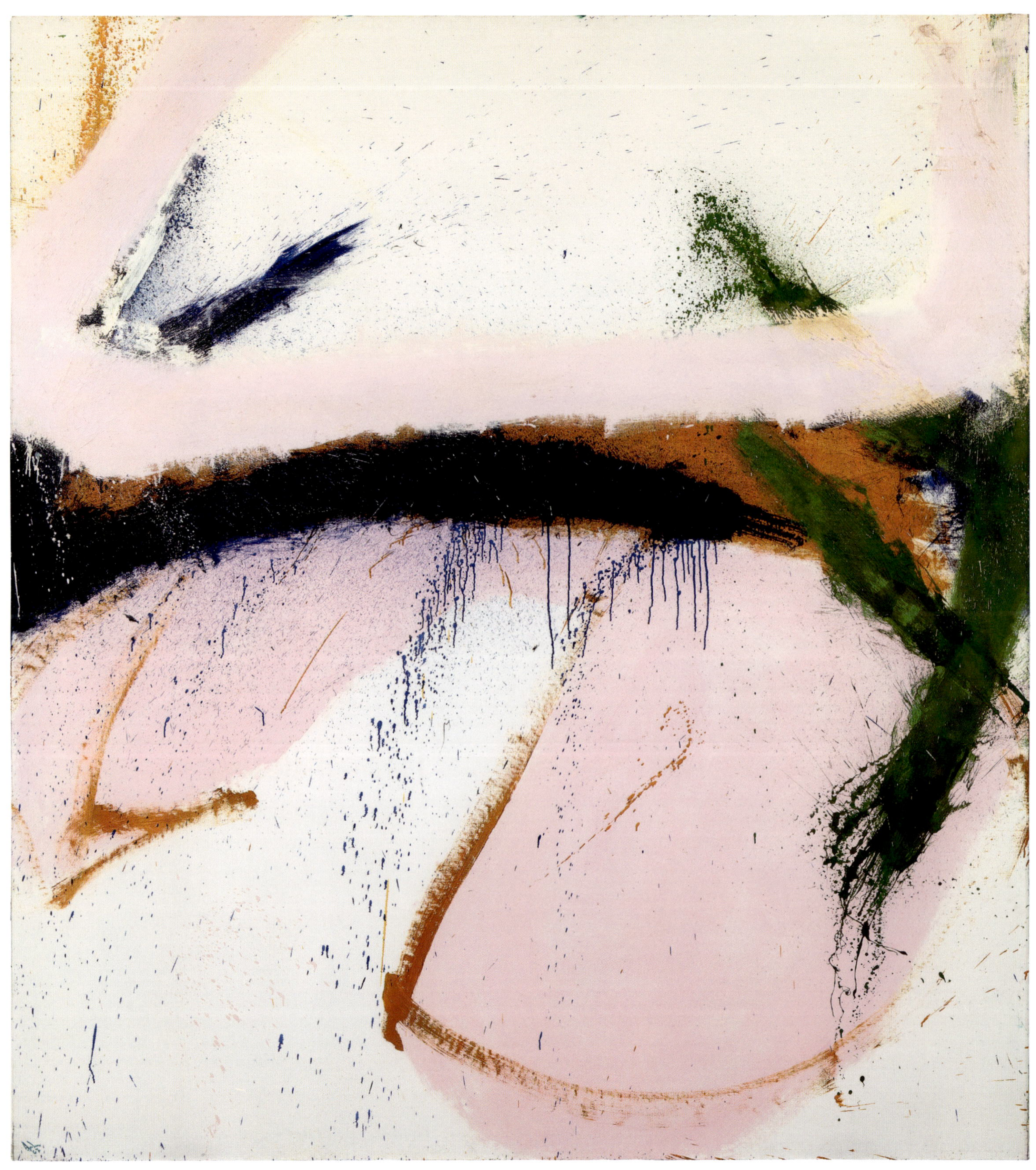

Plate 39

Theodora, 1967
Oil on canvas
90 × 80 in. (228.6 × 203 cm)
The Estate of Norman Bluhm

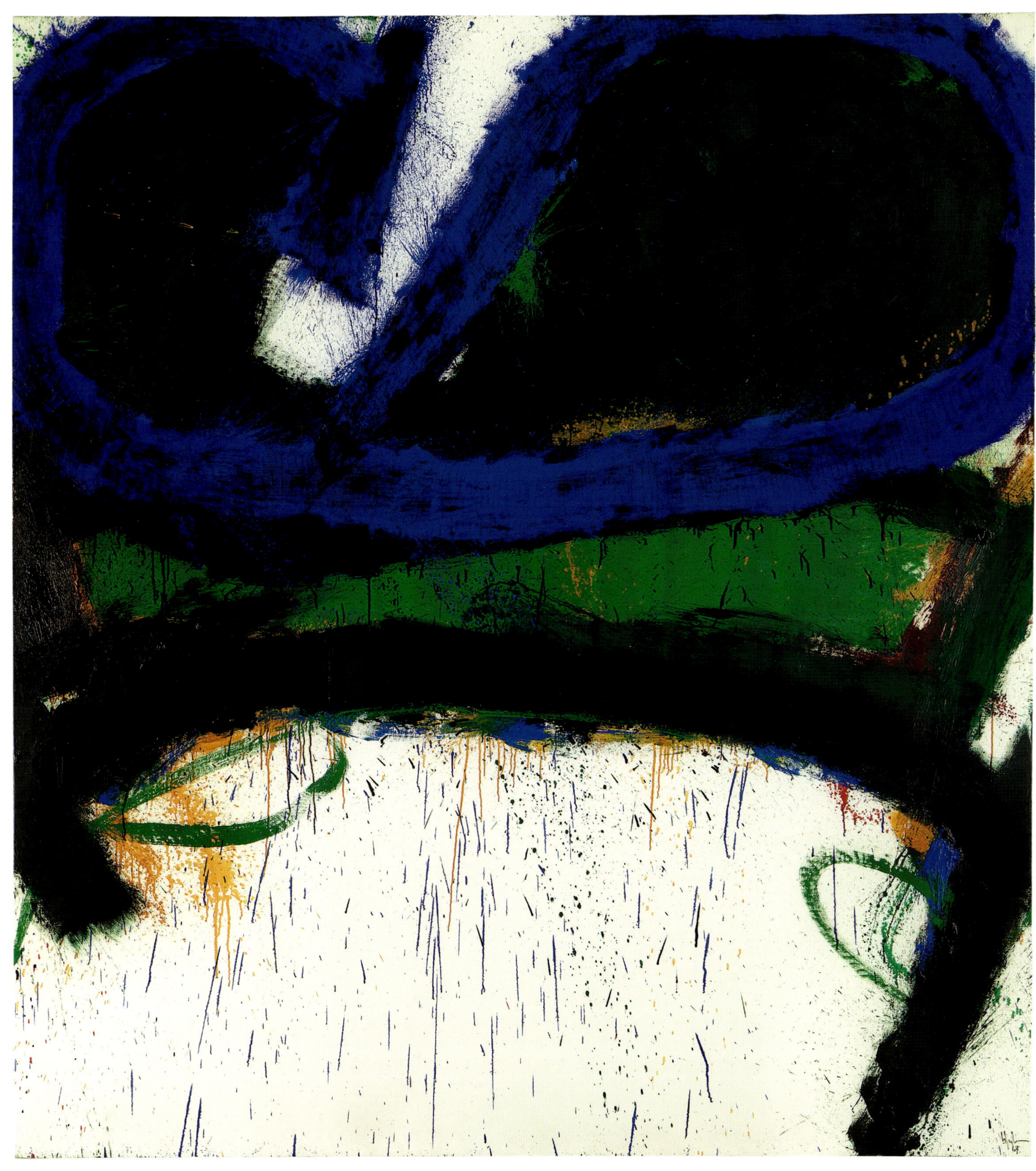

Plate 40

Bulgaroctonus, 1967
Oil on canvas
90 × 80 in. (228.6 × 203 cm)
The Estate of Norman Bluhm

Fig. 23
Norman Bluhm, Millbrook, New York, 1973.
Photo by Kerby C. Smith, courtesy of
The Estate of Norman Bluhm

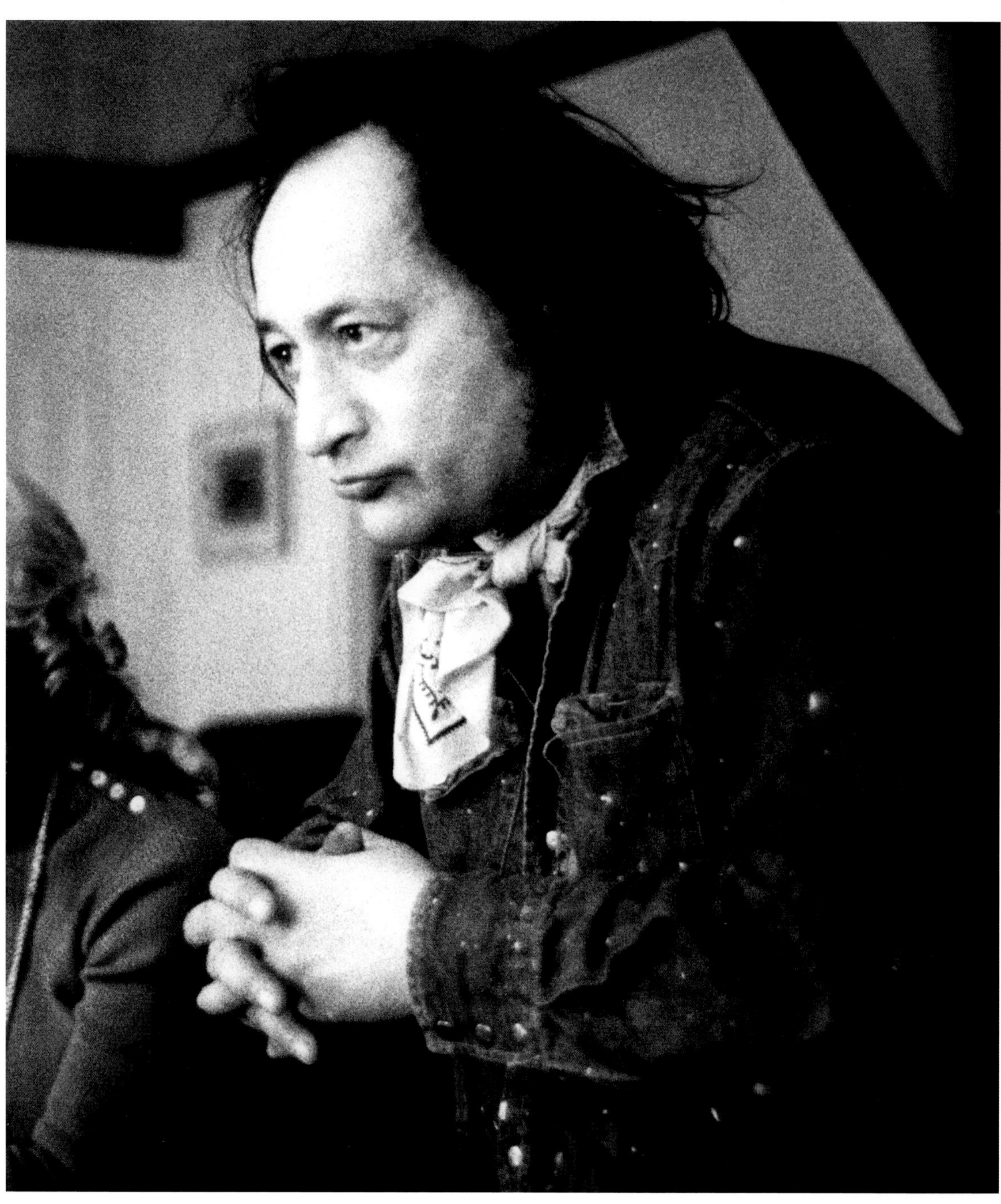

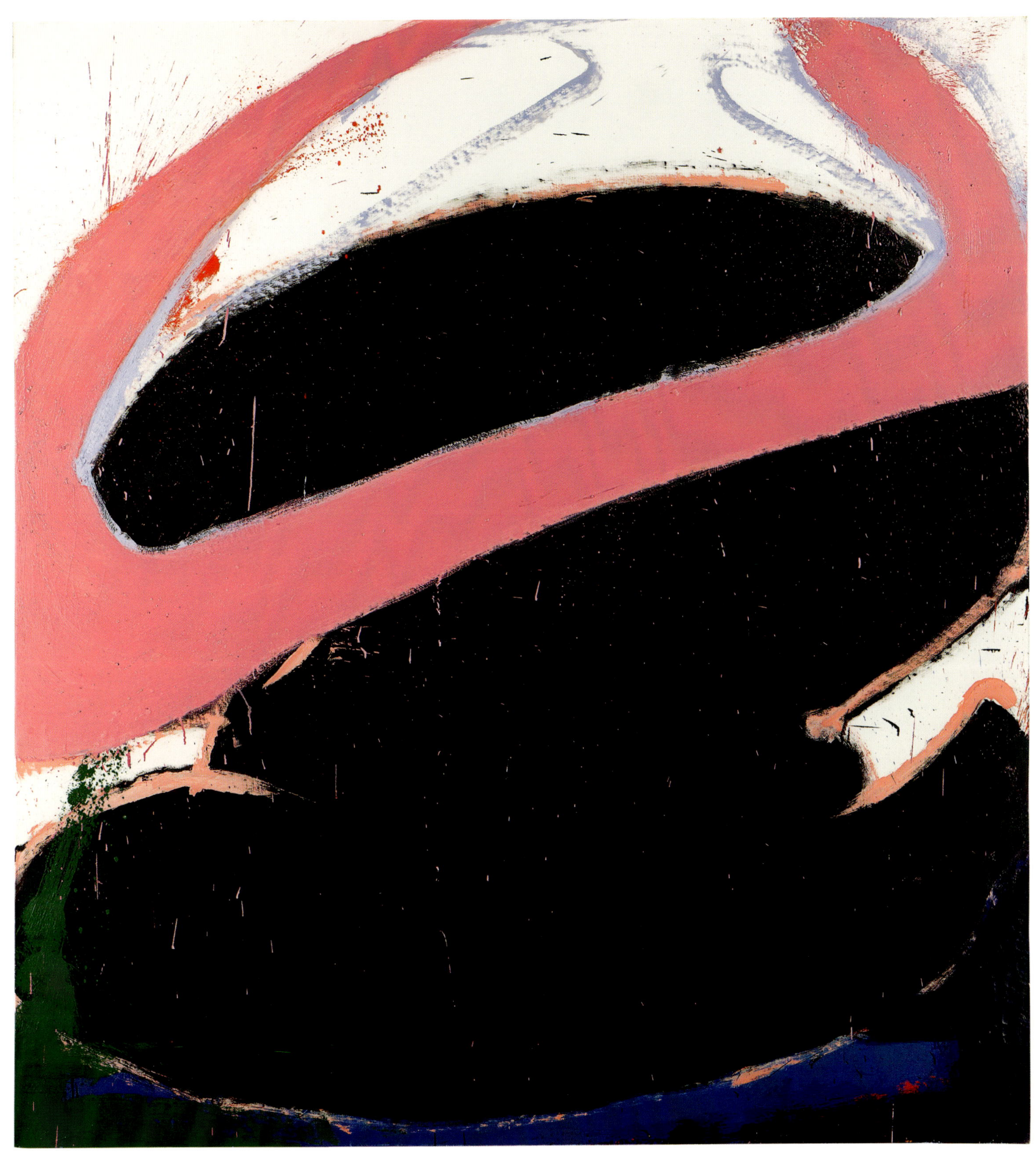

Plate 41

Opis, 1970
Oil on canvas
85 × 76 in. (216 × 193 cm)
The Estate of Norman Bluhm

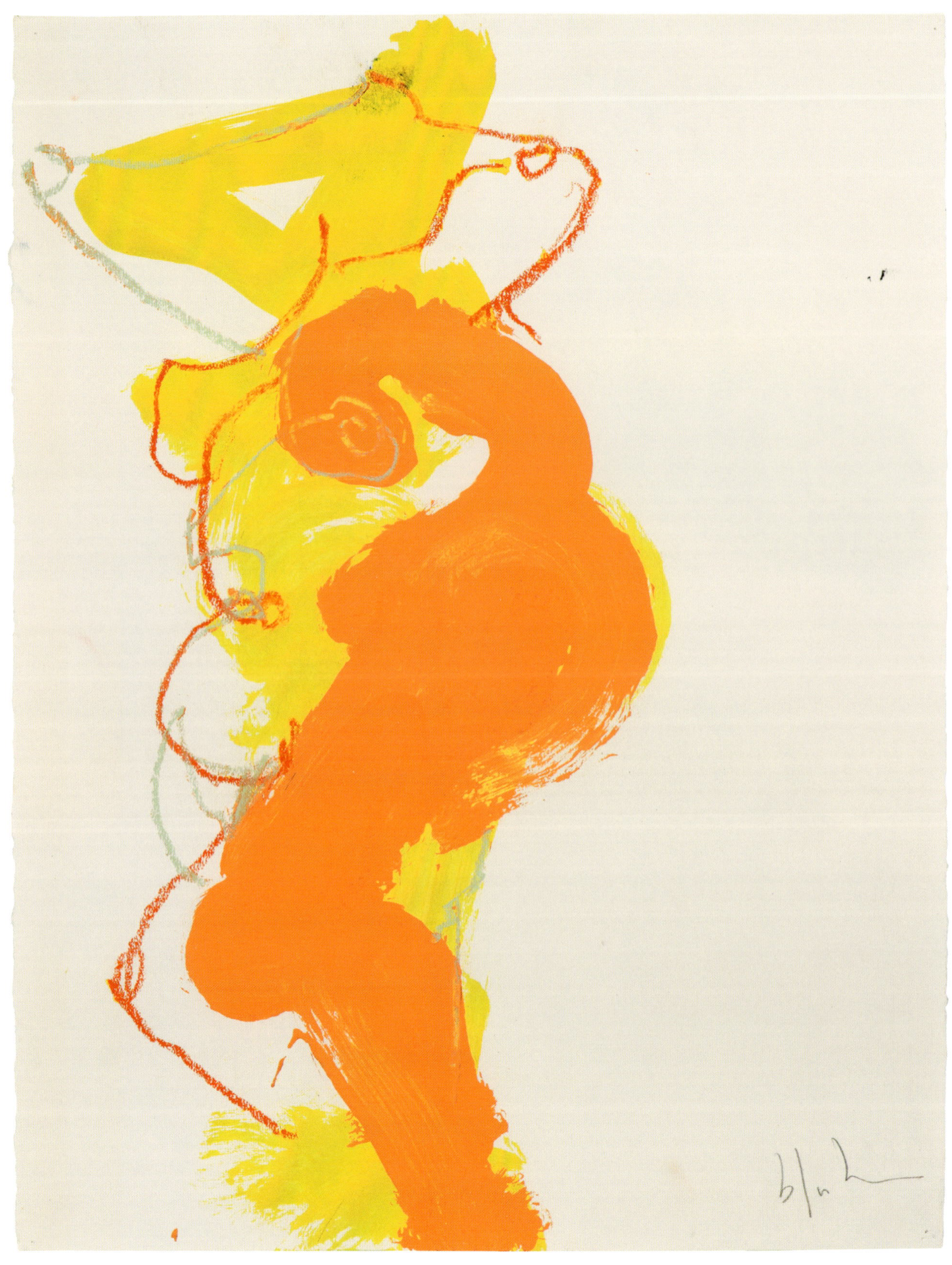

Plate 42

Nude, 1970s
Acrylic and pastel on paper
24 × 18 in. (61 × 46 cm)
The Estate of Norman Bluhm

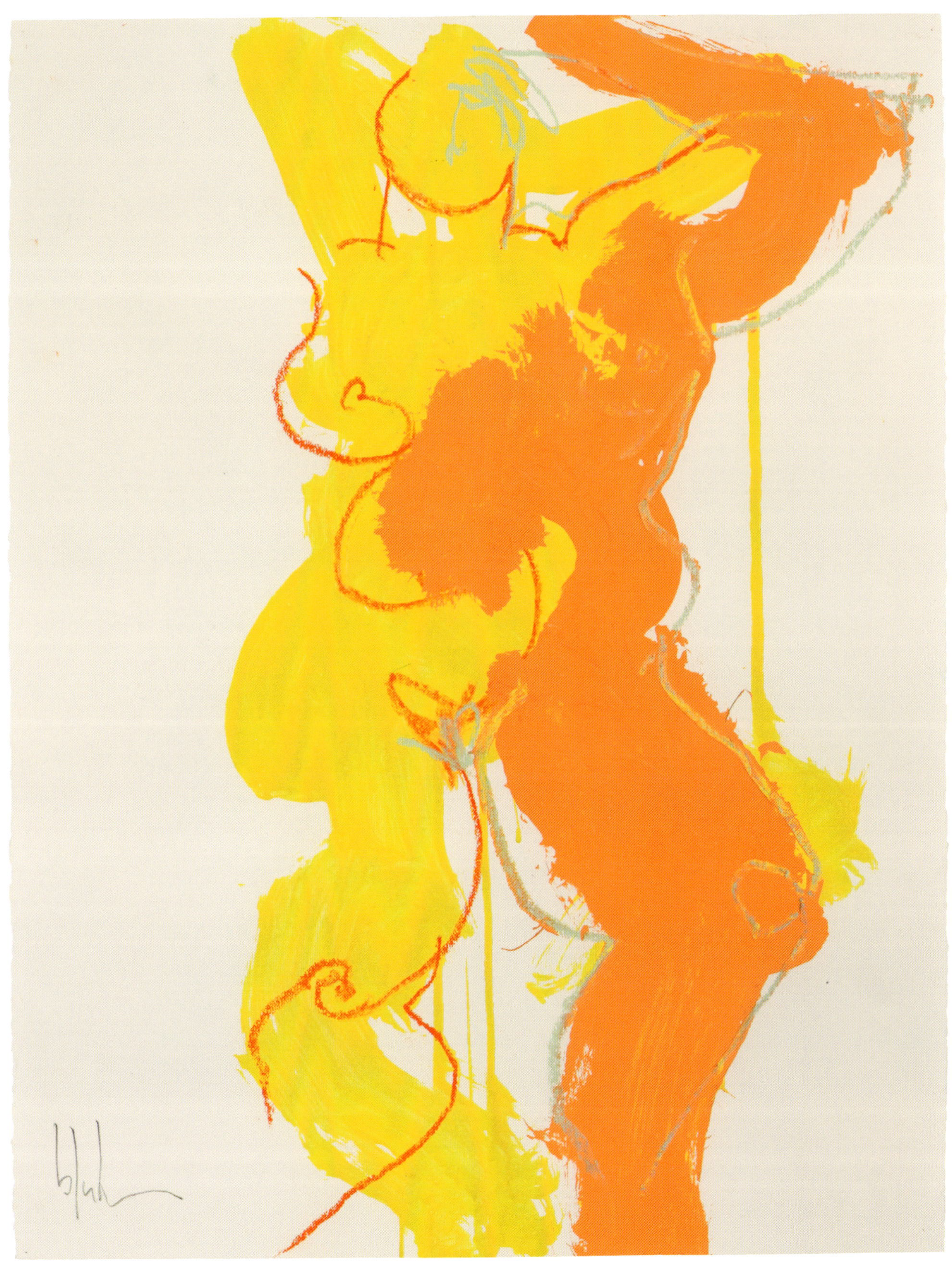

Plate 43

Nude, 1970s
Acrylic and pastel on paper
24 × 18 in. (61 × 46 cm)
The Estate of Norman Bluhm

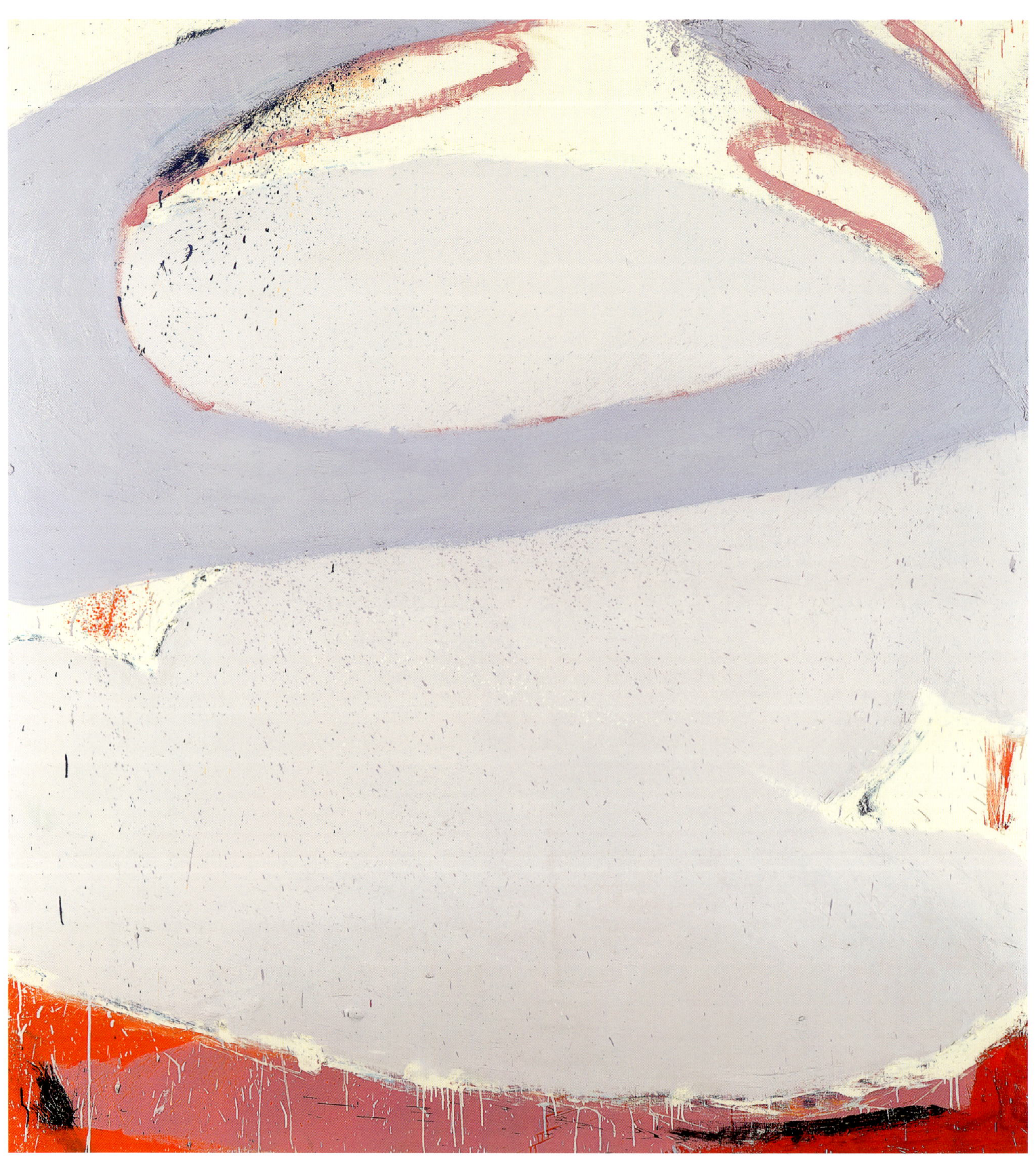

Plate 44

Niobe, 1970
Oil on canvas
82 × 74 in. (208.3 × 188 cm)
The Estate of Norman Bluhm

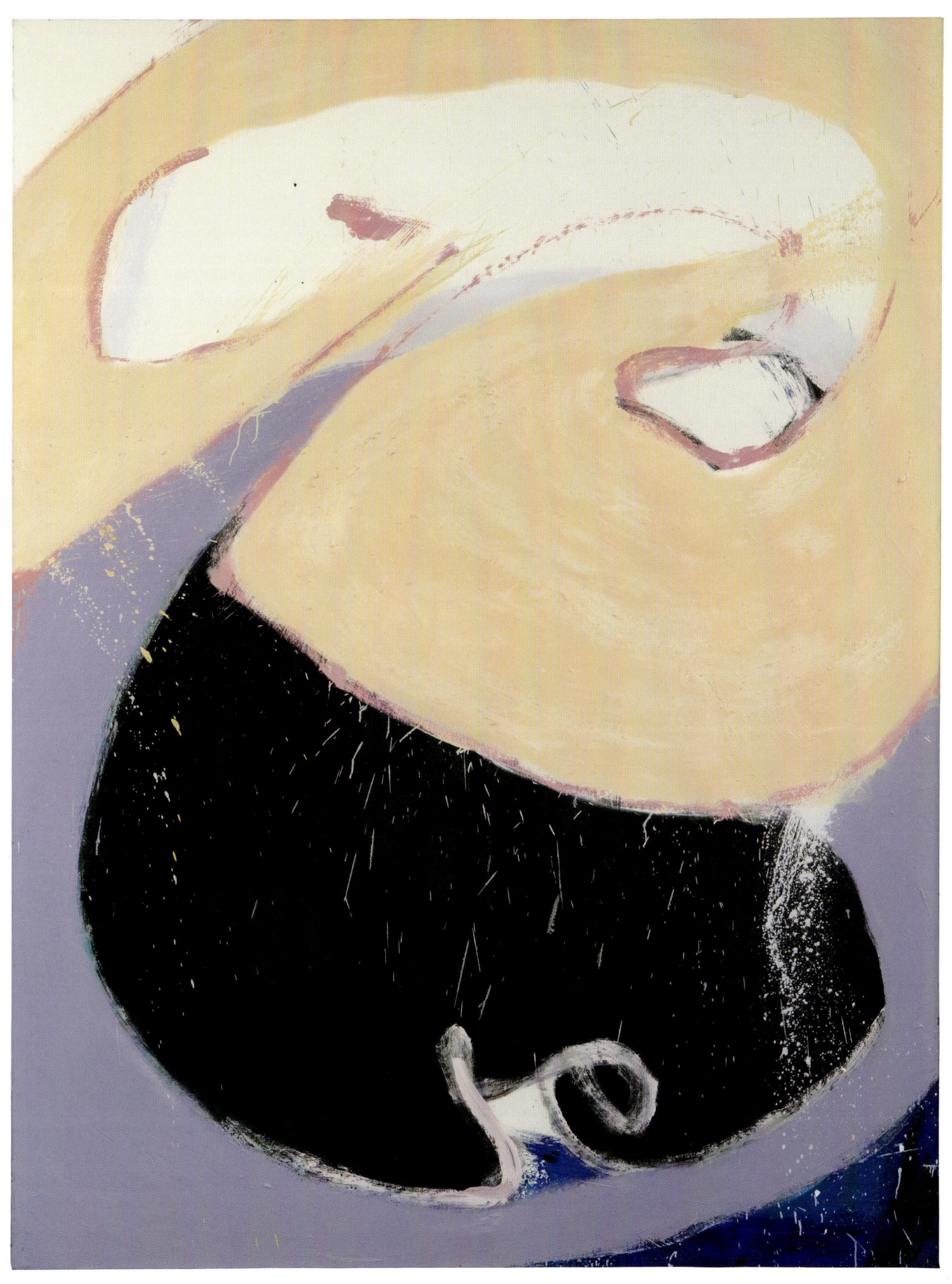

Plate 45

Arethusa, 1971
Oil on canvas
96 × 72 in. (245 × 183.5 cm)
The Estate of Norman Bluhm

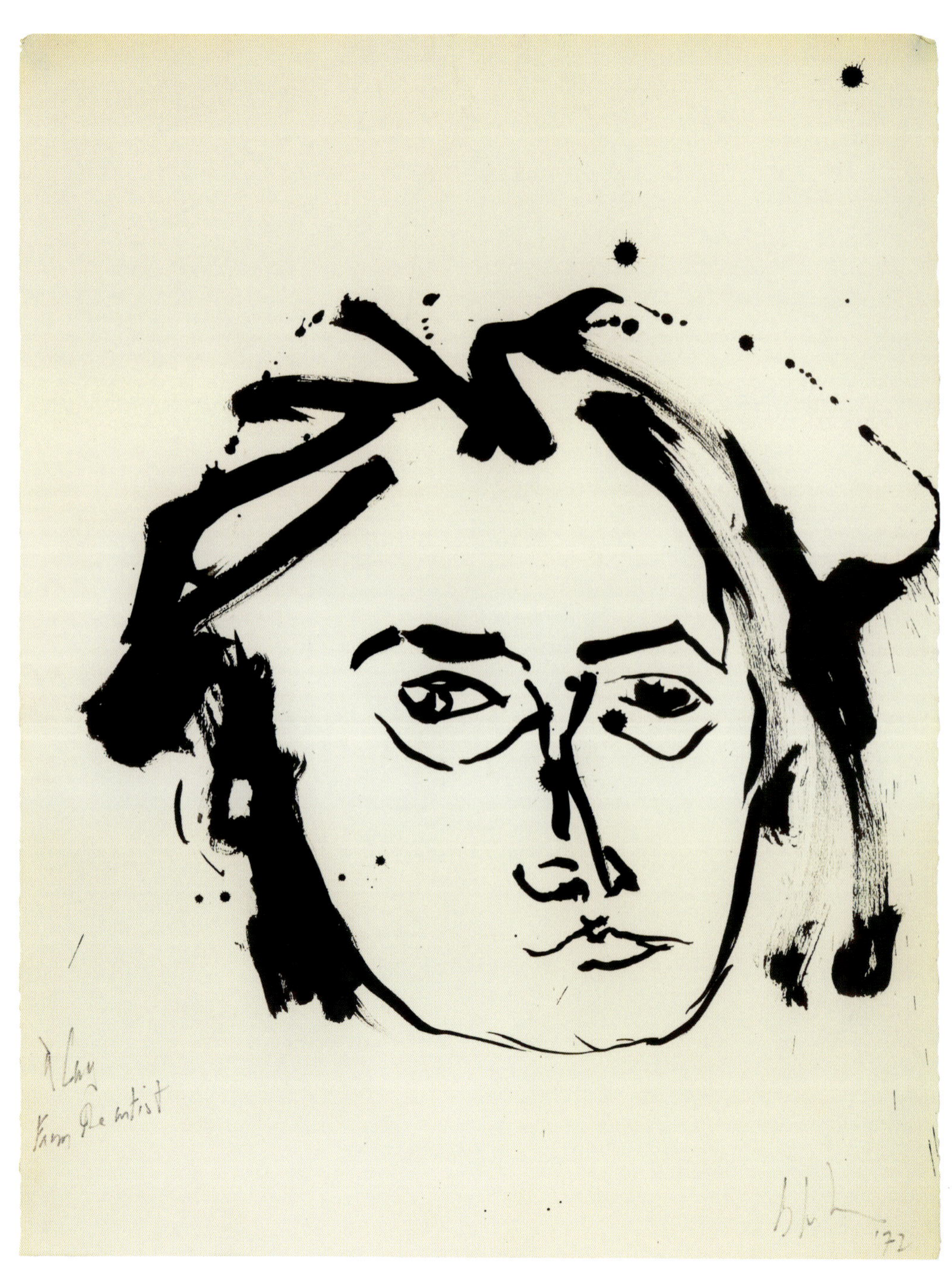

Plate 46

Self Portrait, 1972
Ink on paper
24 × 18 in. (61 × 46 cm)
The Estate of Norman Bluhm

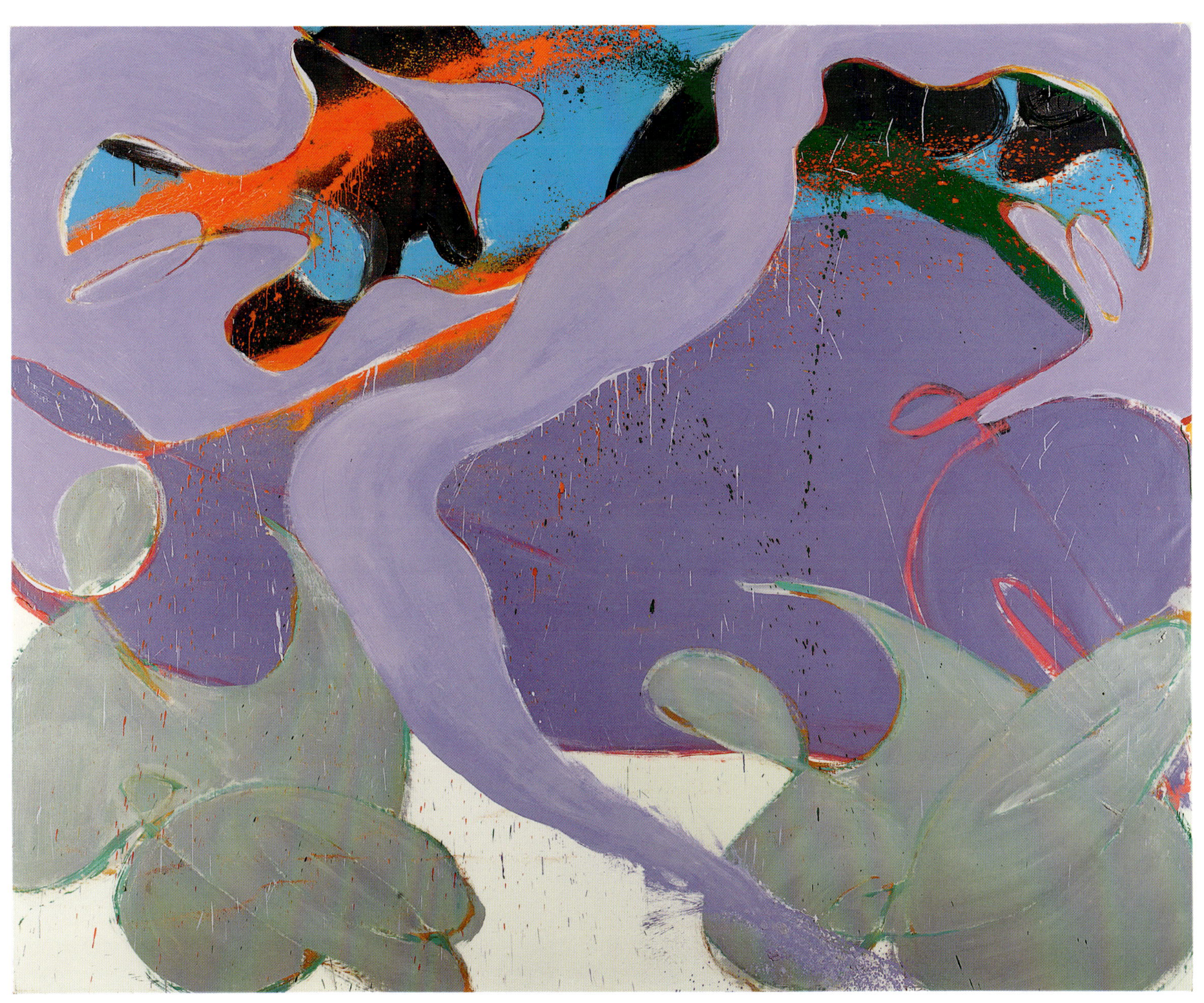

Plate 47

Henri Did It, 1974
Oil on canvas
96 × 116 in. (244 × 295 cm)
The Estate of Norman Bluhm

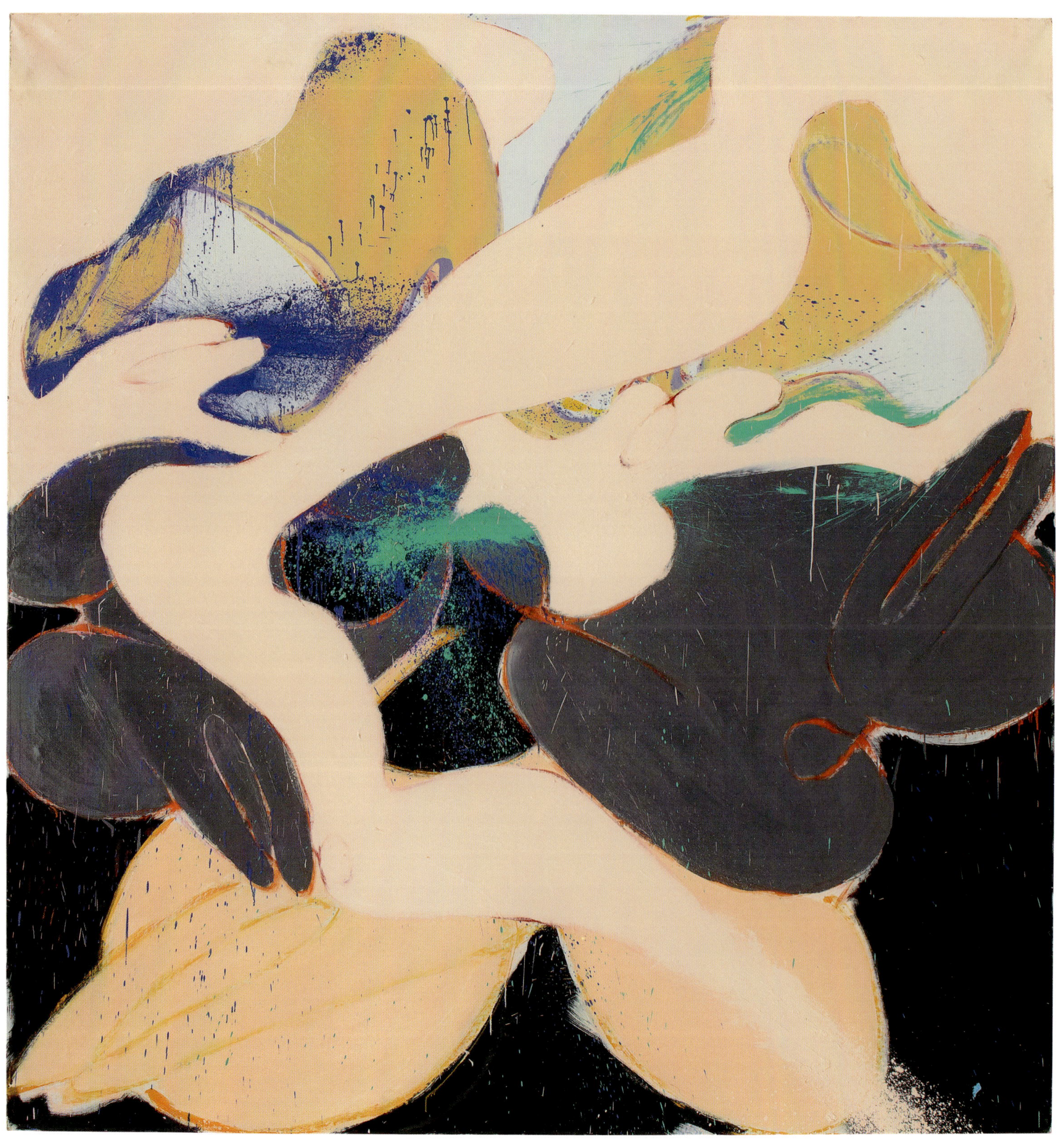

Plate 48

Ripe Summer, 1974
Oil on canvas
116 × 108 in. (295 × 274.3 cm)
The Estate of Norman Bluhm

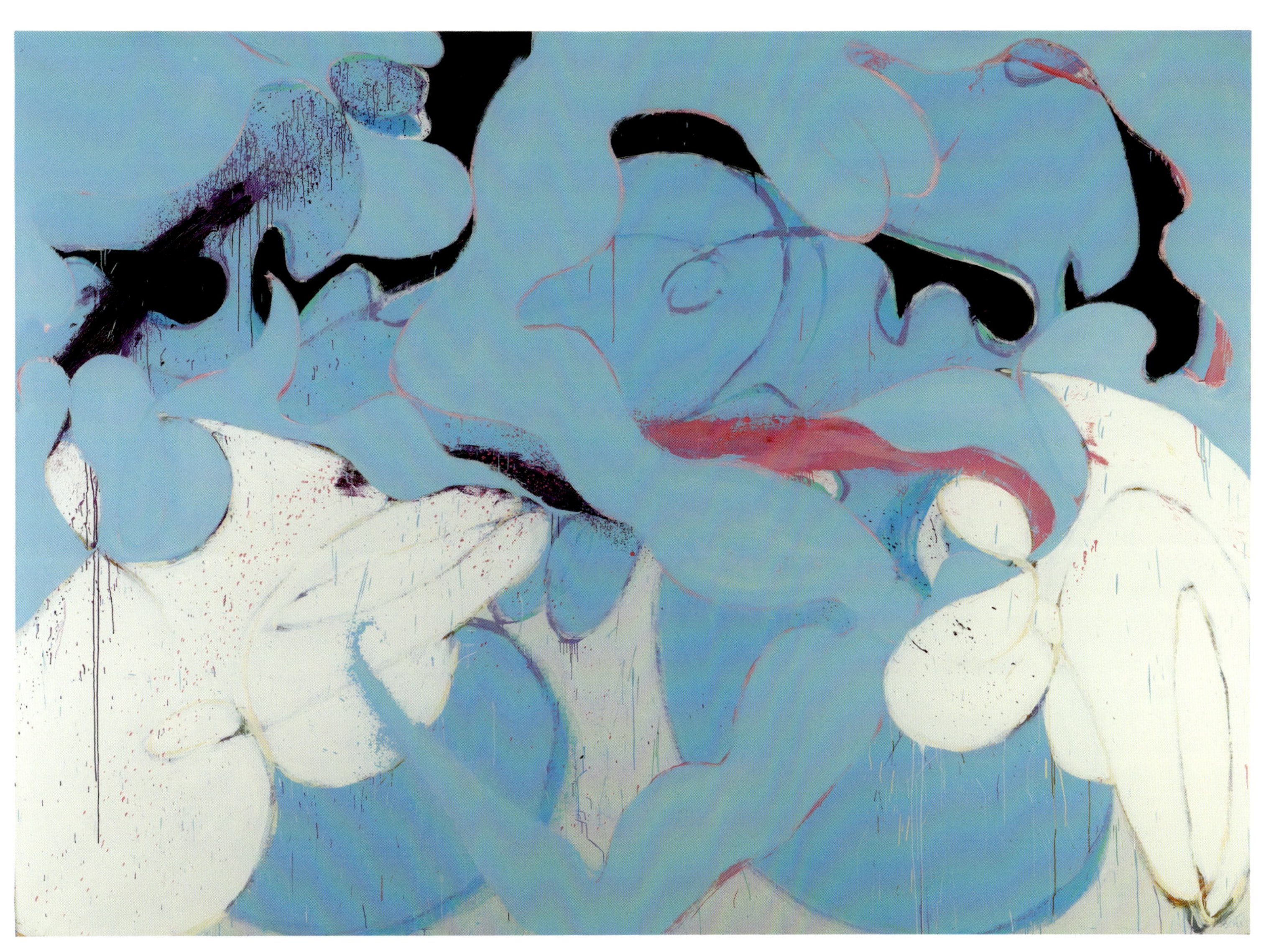

Plate 49

Neptune's Orgy, 1975
Oil on canvas
102 × 144 in. (259 × 366 cm)
The Estate of Norman Bluhm

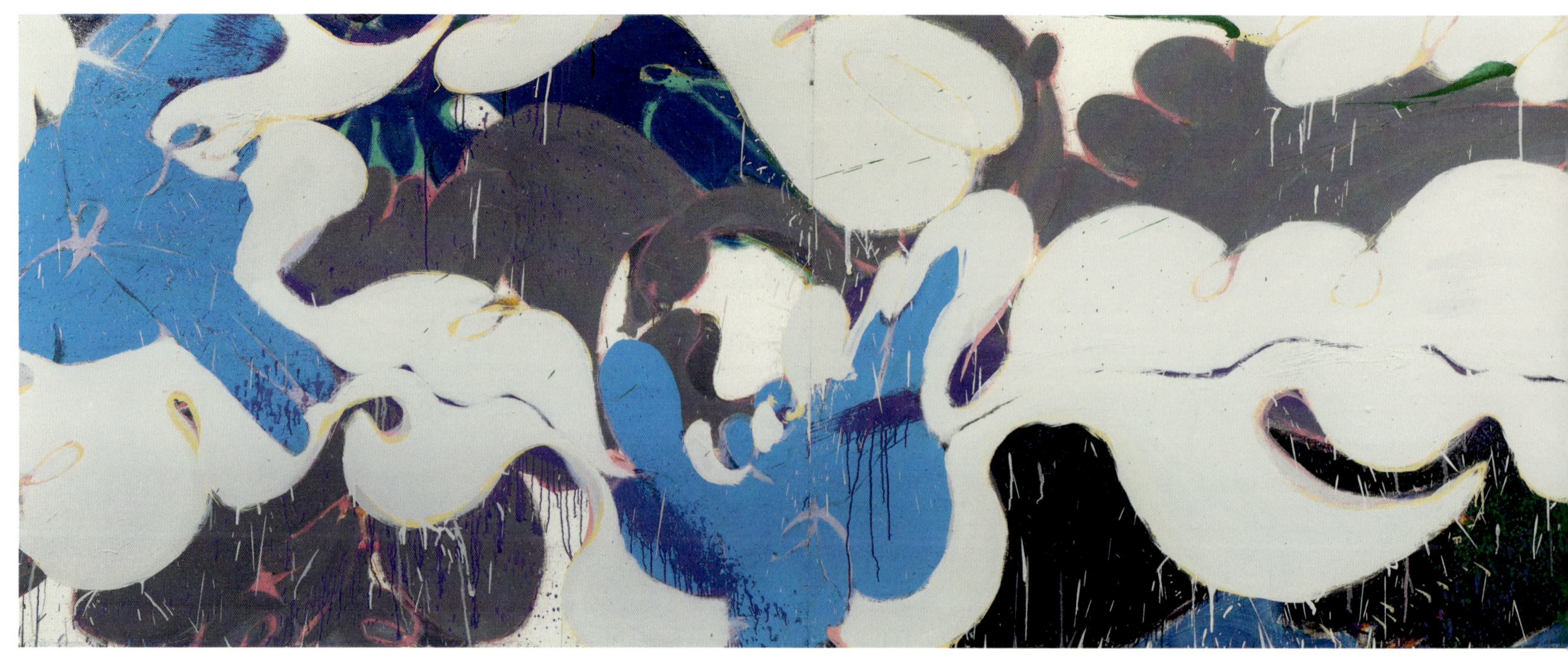

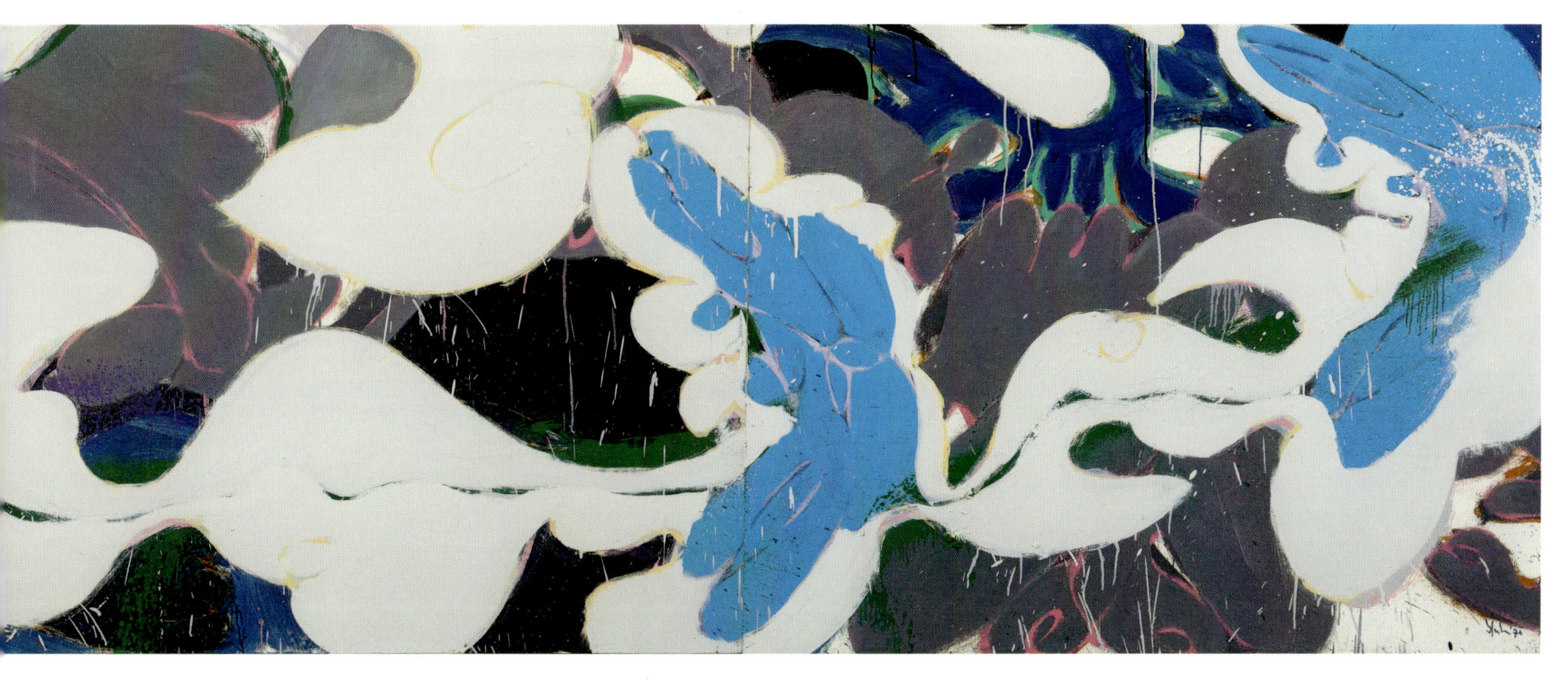

Plate 50

Untitled, Studies in Blue, White, Gray, 1975
Oil on canvas
Four panels, 48 × 240 in. (122 × 609.6 cm) overall
The Estate of Norman Bluhm

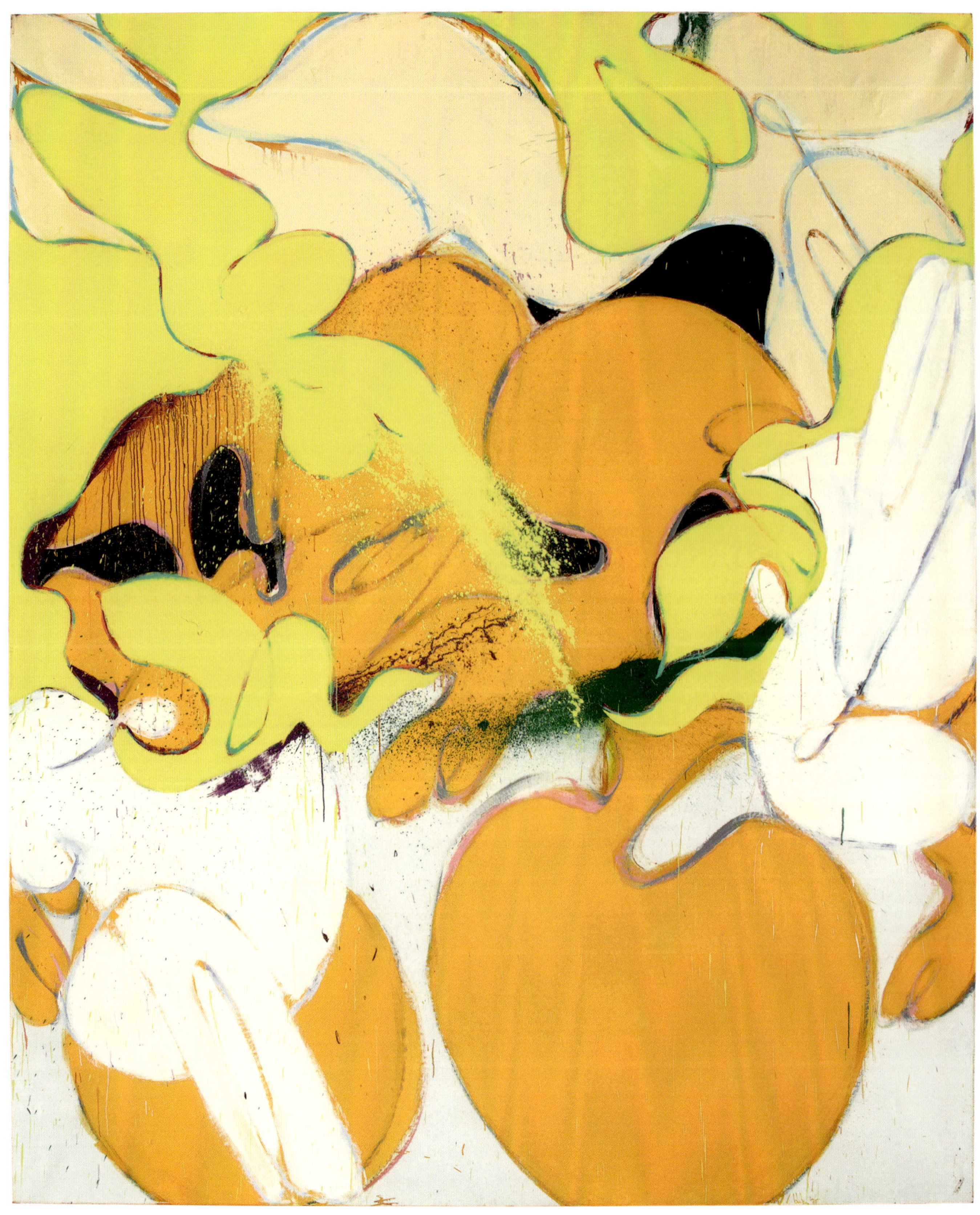

Plate 51

Yellow Hooker, 1975
Oil on canvas
144 × 116 in. (366 × 295 cm)
The Estate of Norman Bluhm

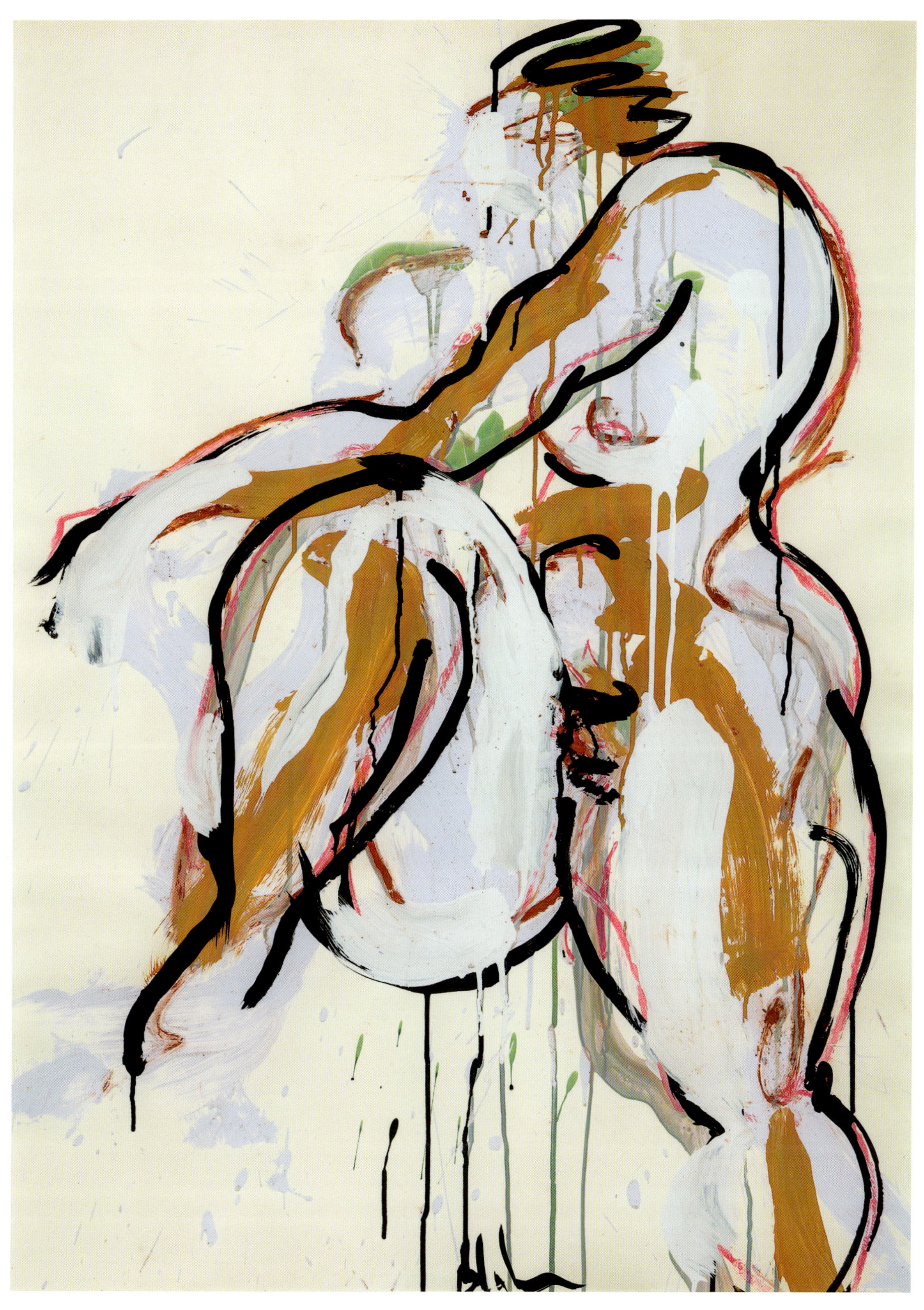

Plate 52

Rosie 1, 1977
Acrylic and pastel on paper
42 × 32 in. (106.7 × 81.3 cm)
The Estate of Norman Bluhm

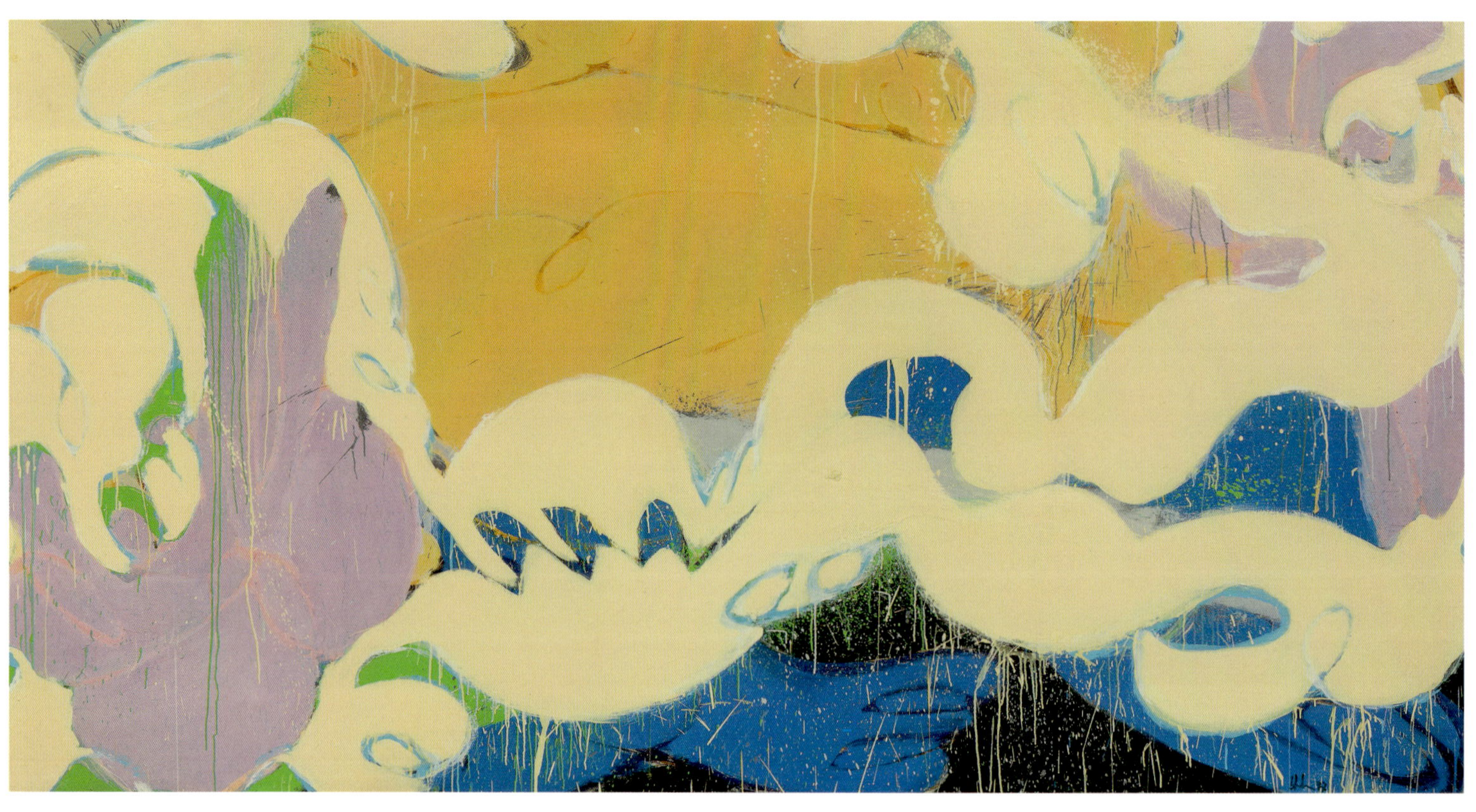

Plate 53

Milkmaid, 1977
Oil on canvas
60 × 113 in. (152.4 × 287 cm)
The Estate of Norman Bluhm

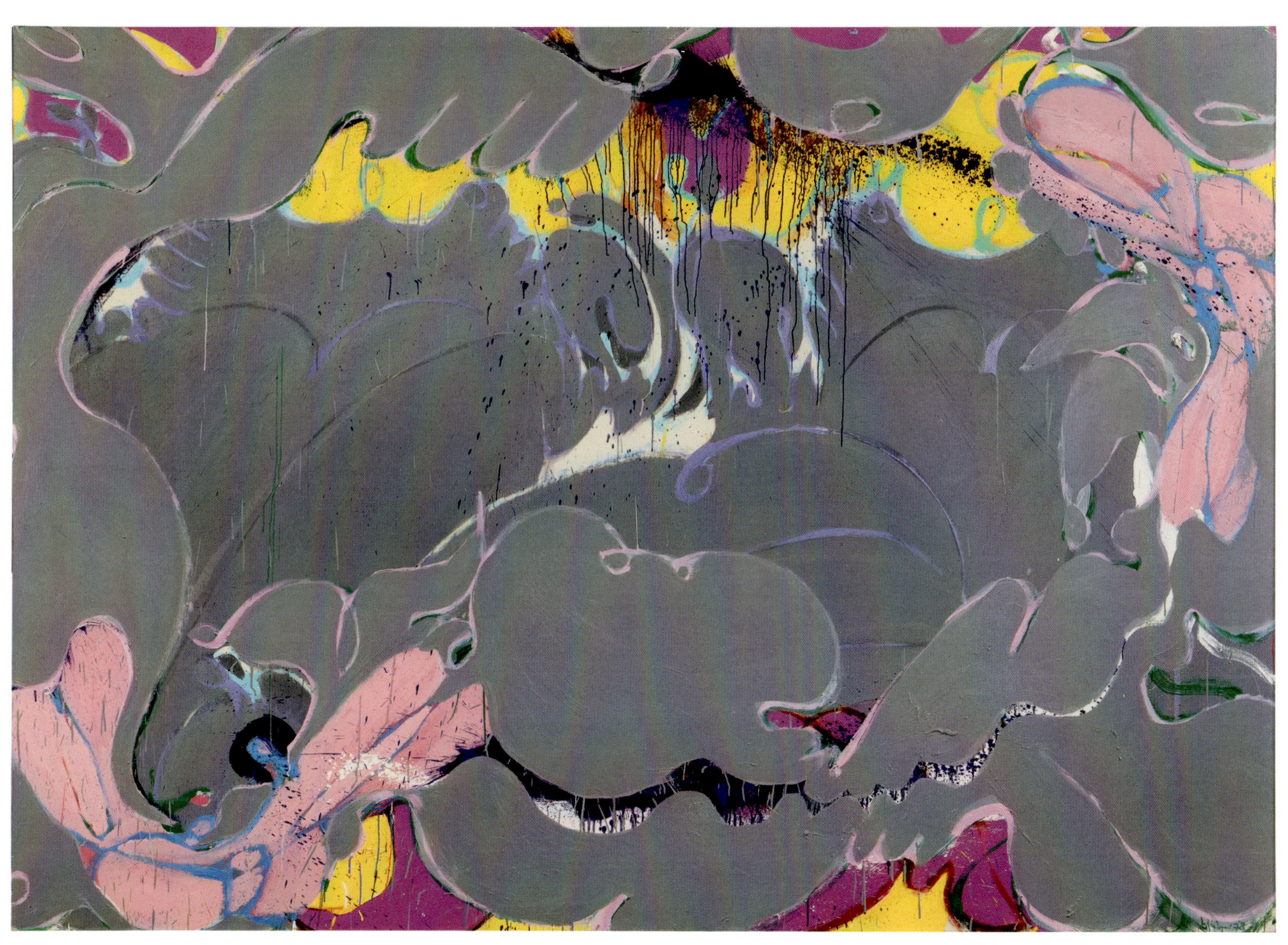

Plate 54

Sooty Lady, 1978
Oil on canvas
76 × 106 in. (193 × 269.2 cm)
The Estate of Norman Bluhm

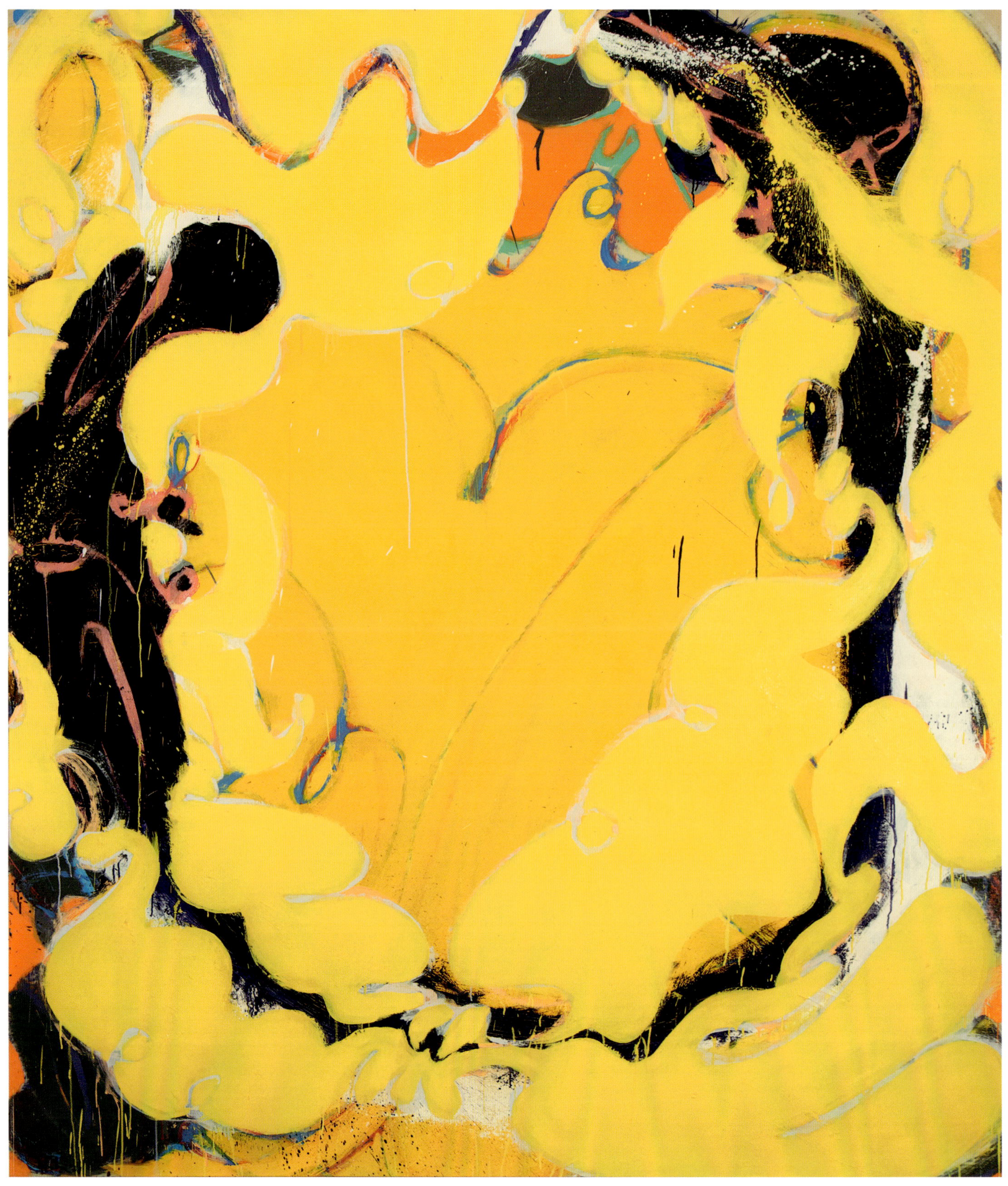

Plate 55

Golden Flaxen Maiden, 1978
Oil on canvas
89 × 76 in. (226 × 193 cm)
Collection of Mr. Anthony Scotto

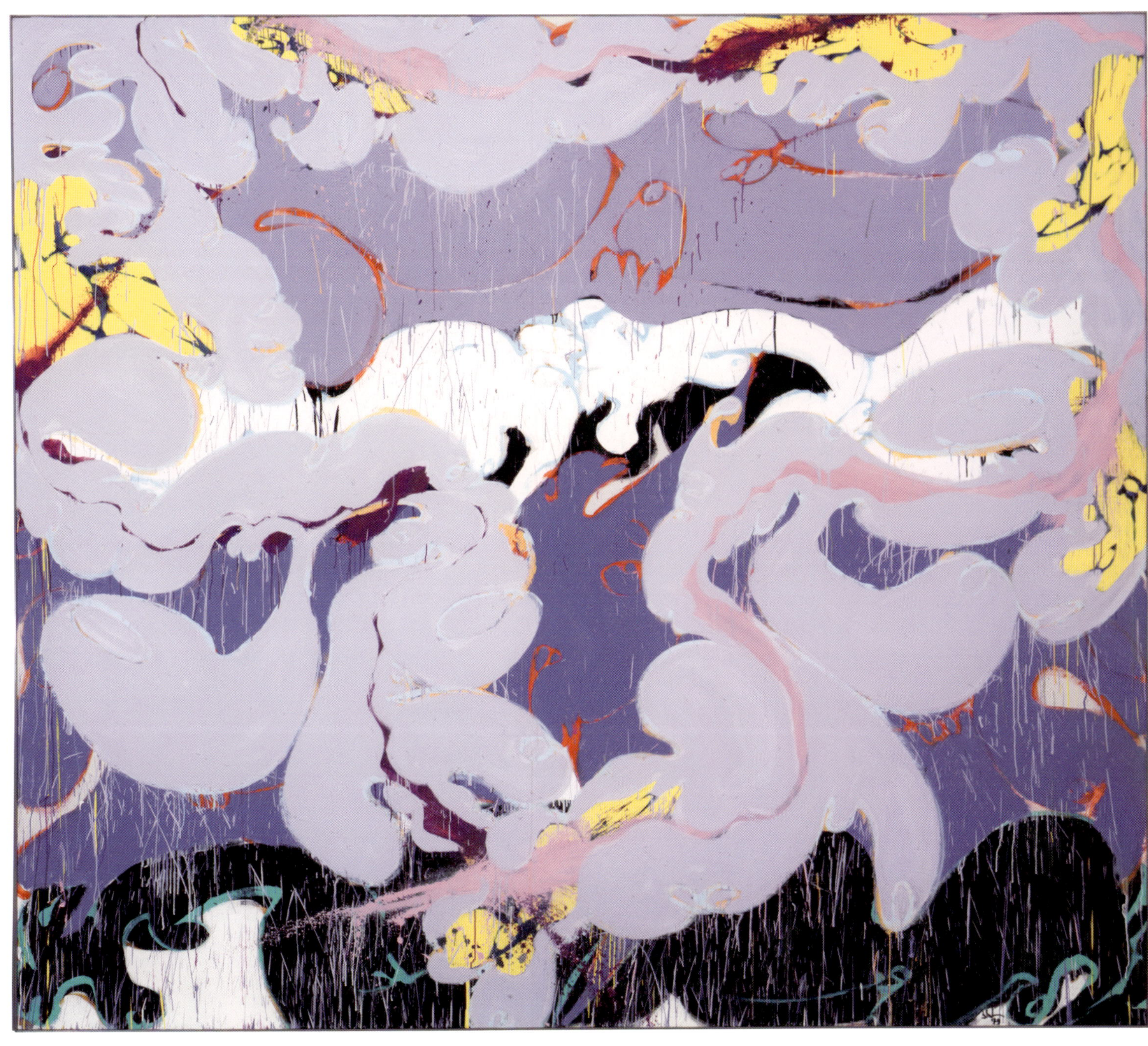

Plate 56

Romulus and Remus, 1979
Oil on canvas
102 × 114 in. (259 × 289.5 cm)
The Butler Institute of American Art, Youngstown, Ohio
Gift of The Estate of Norman Bluhm, 2001

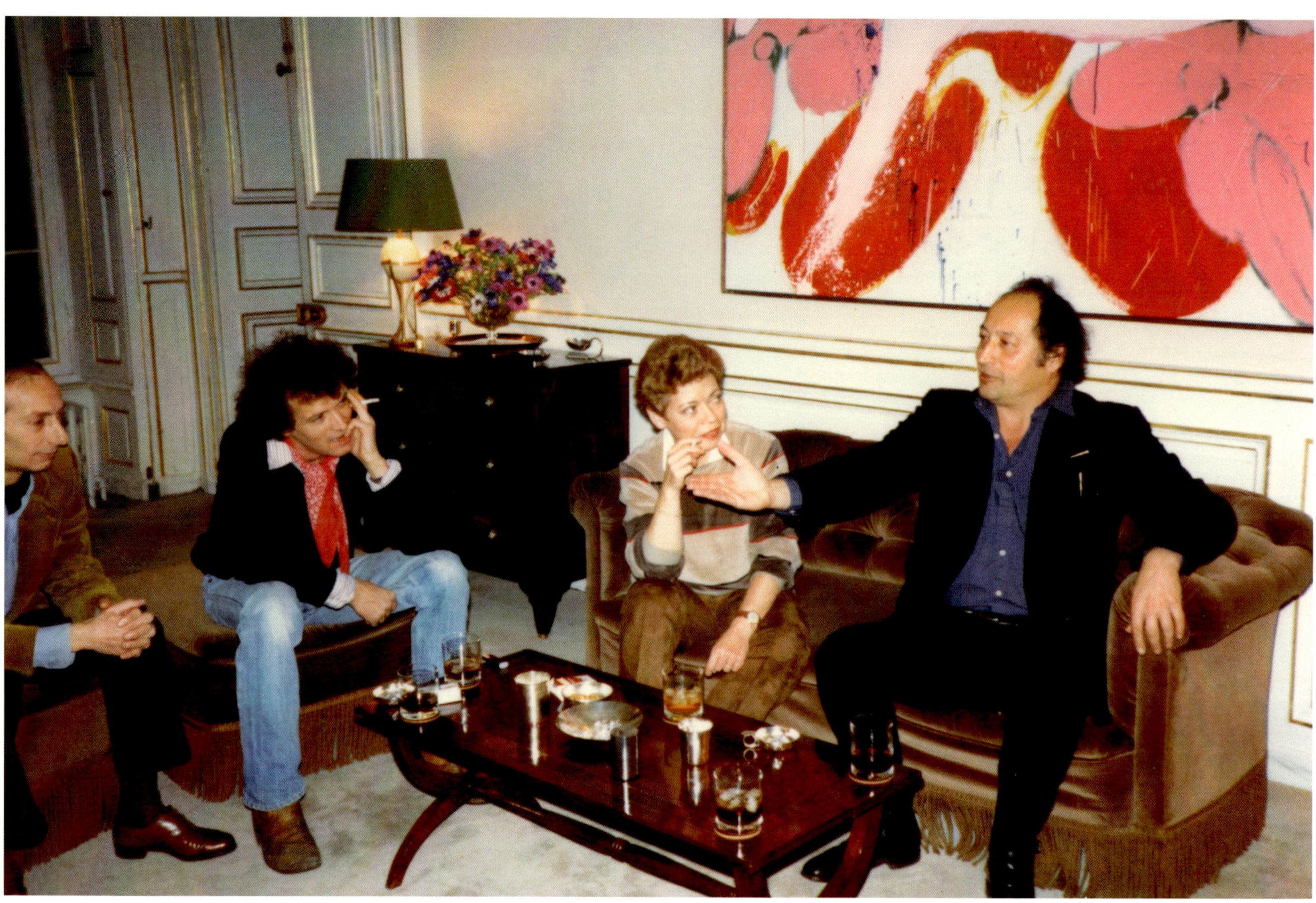

Fig. 24
Norman Bluhm at Rodolphe Stadler's Paris apartment in the 1980s, with Marcel and Jacqueline Cohen; *Manto,* 1970, is in the background. Photo courtesy of The Estate of Norman Bluhm

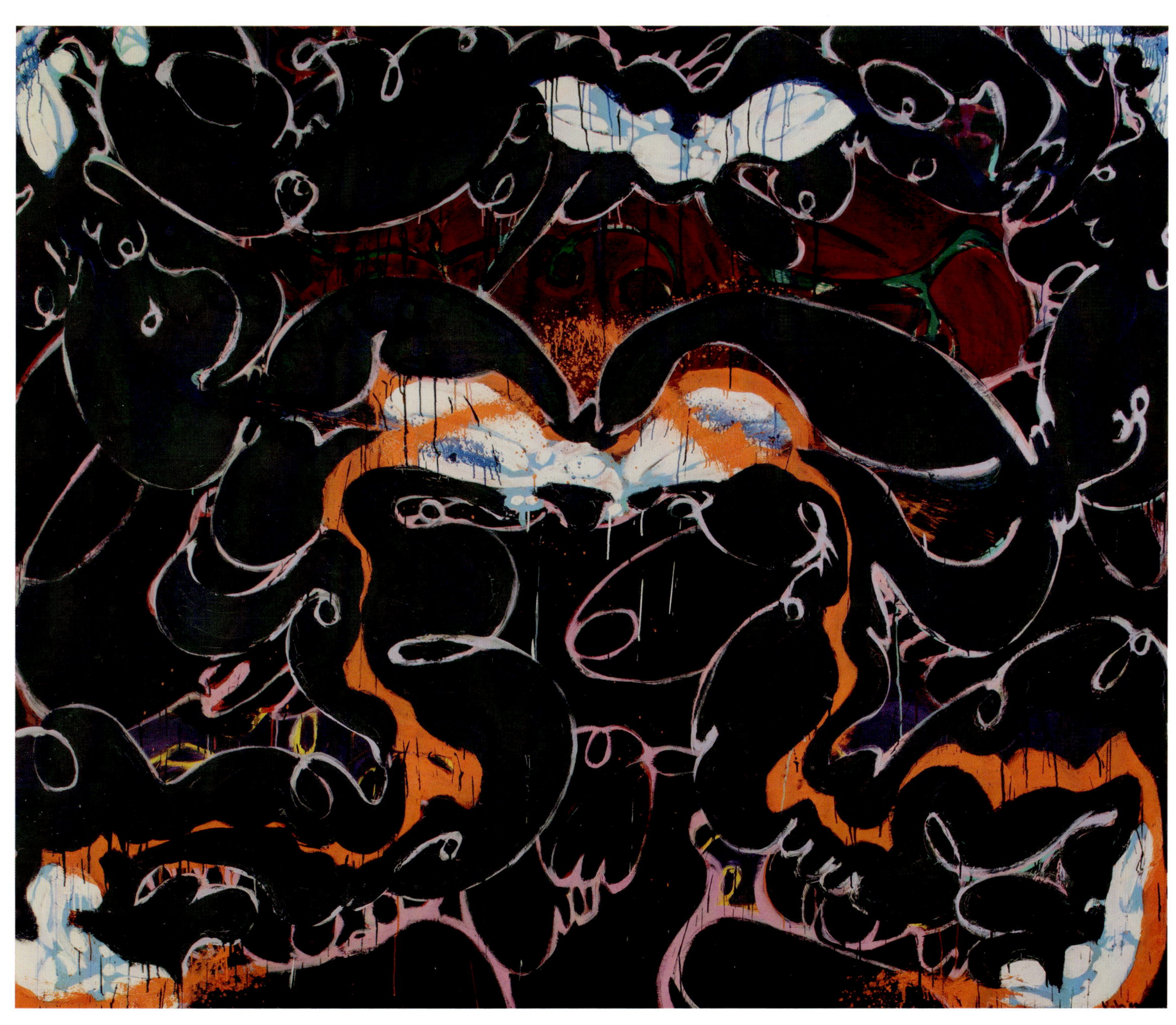

Plate 57

Silent Vamp, 1980
Oil on canvas
76 × 89 in. (193 × 226 cm)
Private collection

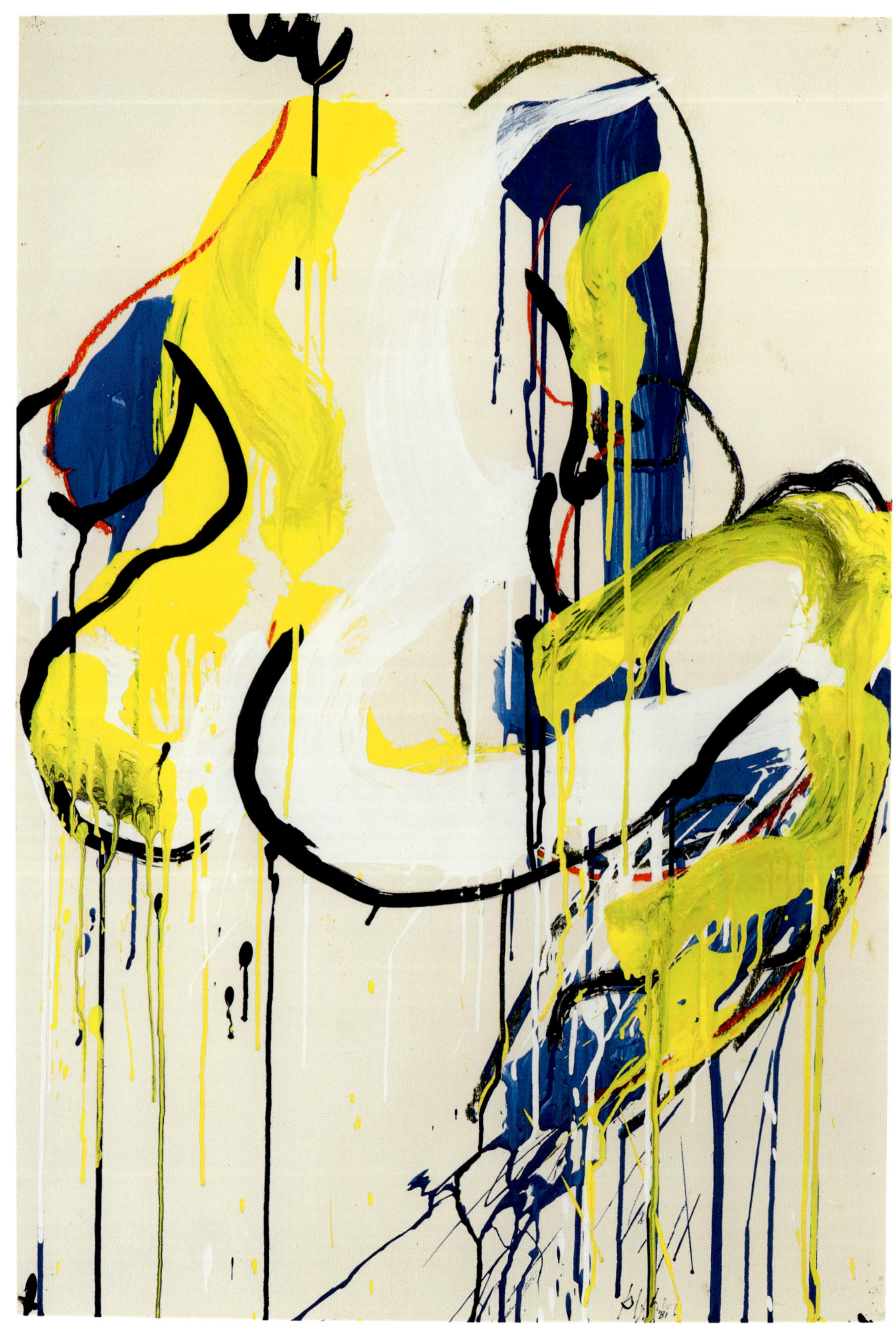

Plate 58

Nude, 1981
Acrylic, ink, and pastel on paper
36 × 24 in. (91.4 × 61 cm)
The Estate of Norman Bluhm

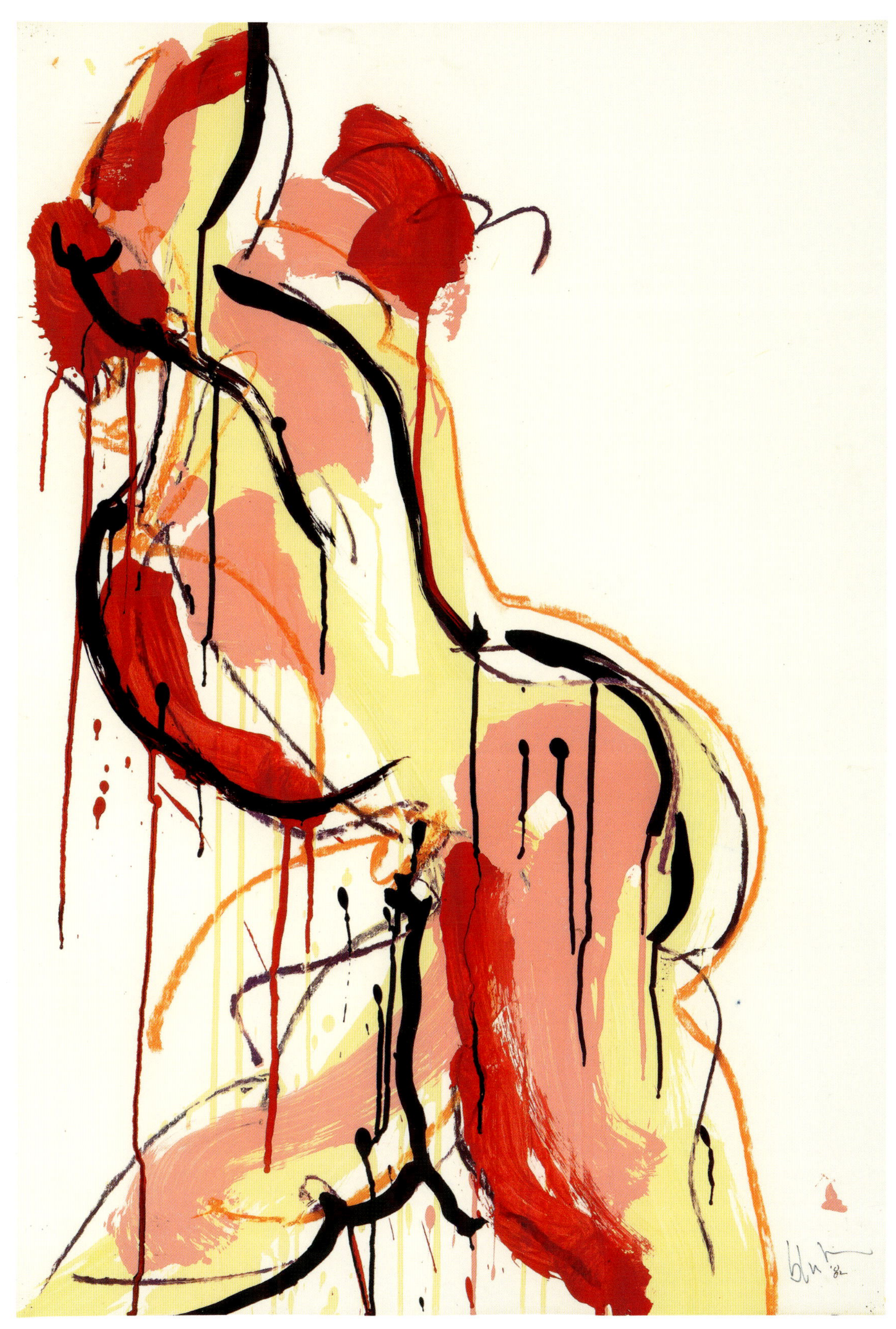

Plate 59

Nude, 1982
Acrylic, ink, and pastel on paper
36 × 24 in. (91.4 × 61 cm)
The Estate of Norman Bluhm

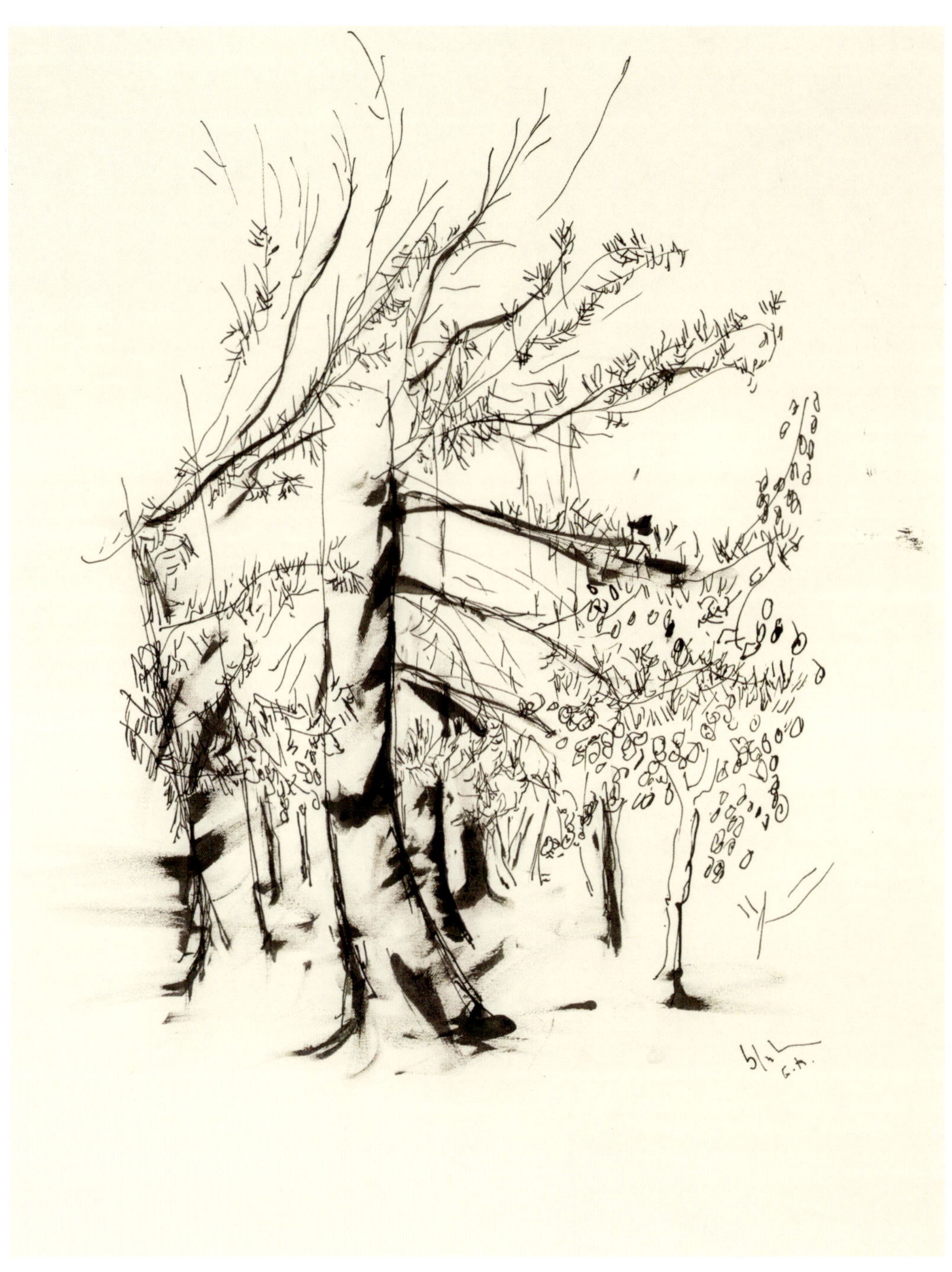

Plate 60

Trees, 1983
Ink on paper
24 × 18 in. (61 × 46 cm)
The Estate of Norman Bluhm

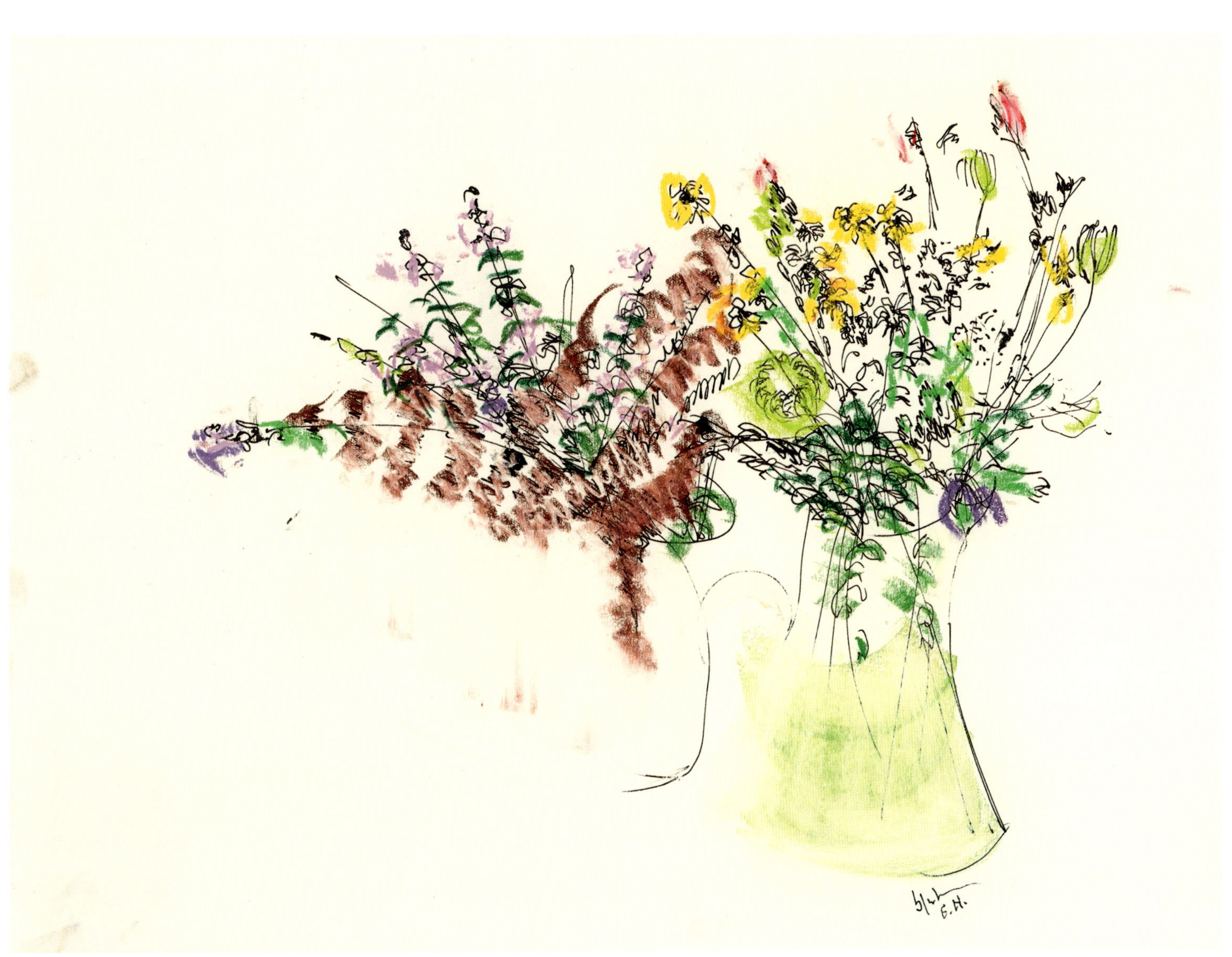

Plate 61

Two Vases with Flowers, 1983
Ink and pastel on paper
18 × 24 in. (46 × 61 cm)
The Estate of Norman Bluhm

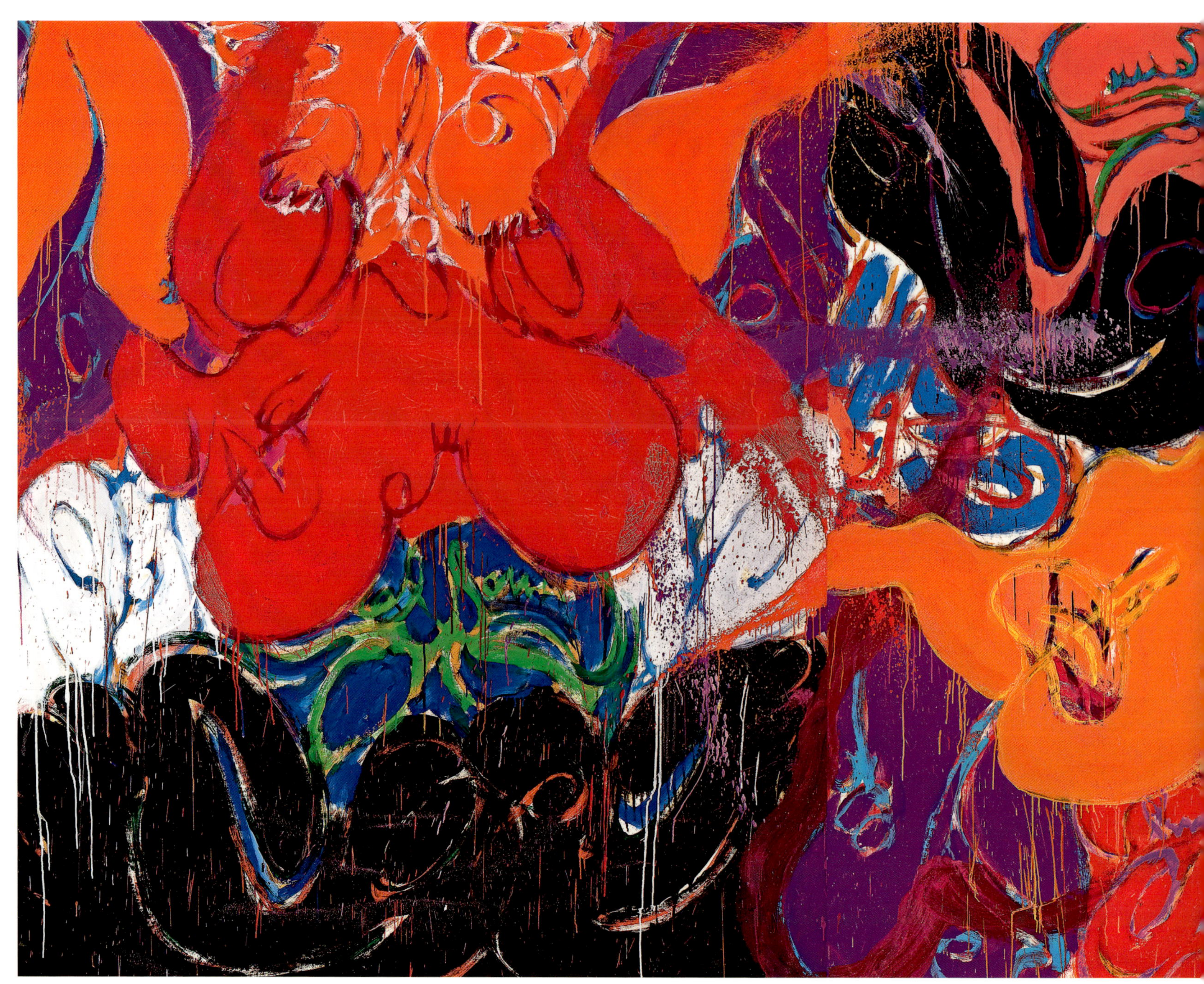

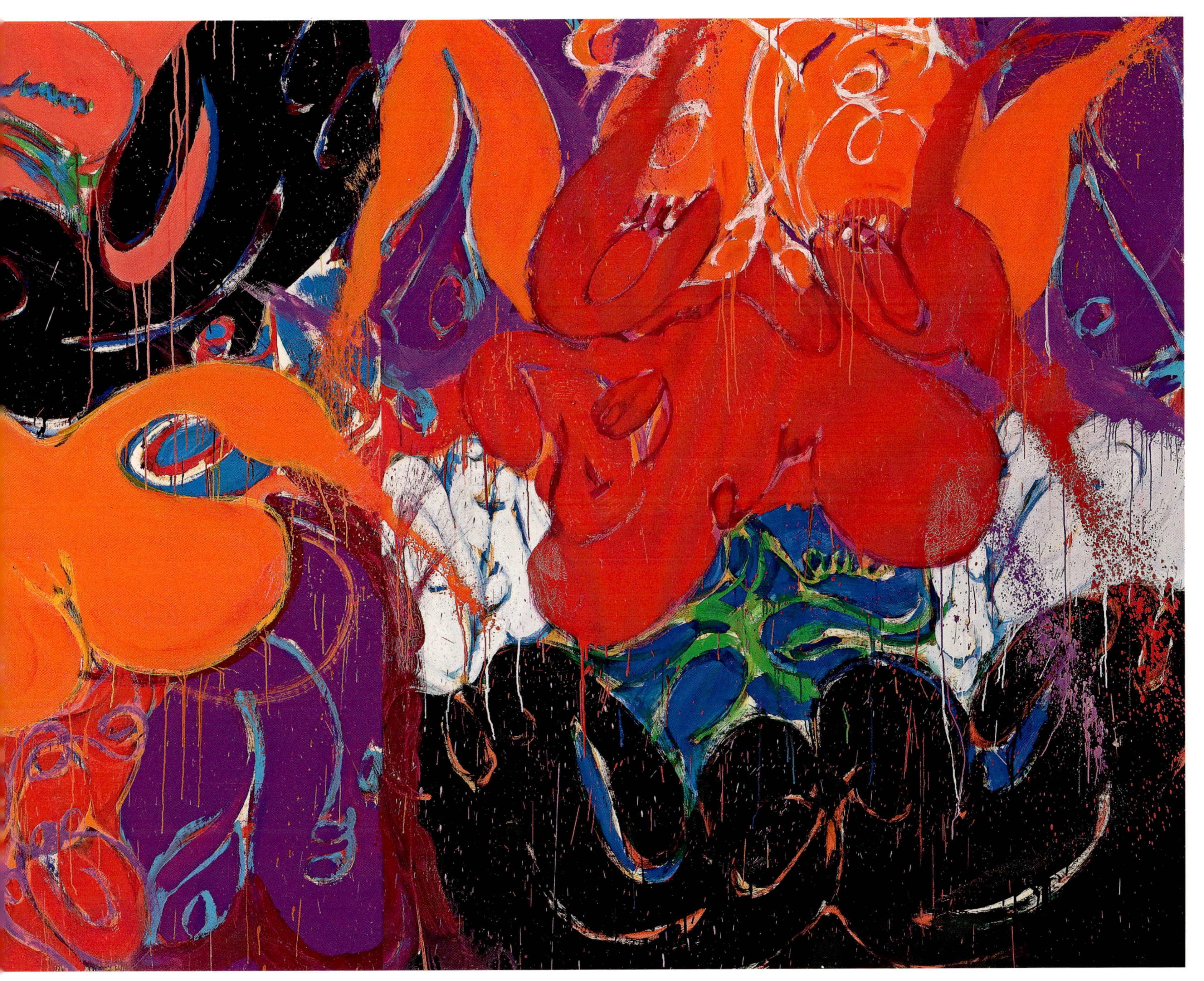

Plate 62

Dante's Promenade, 1984
Oil on canvas
Triptych, 84 × 216 in. (213.4 × 549 cm) overall
The Estate of Norman Bluhm

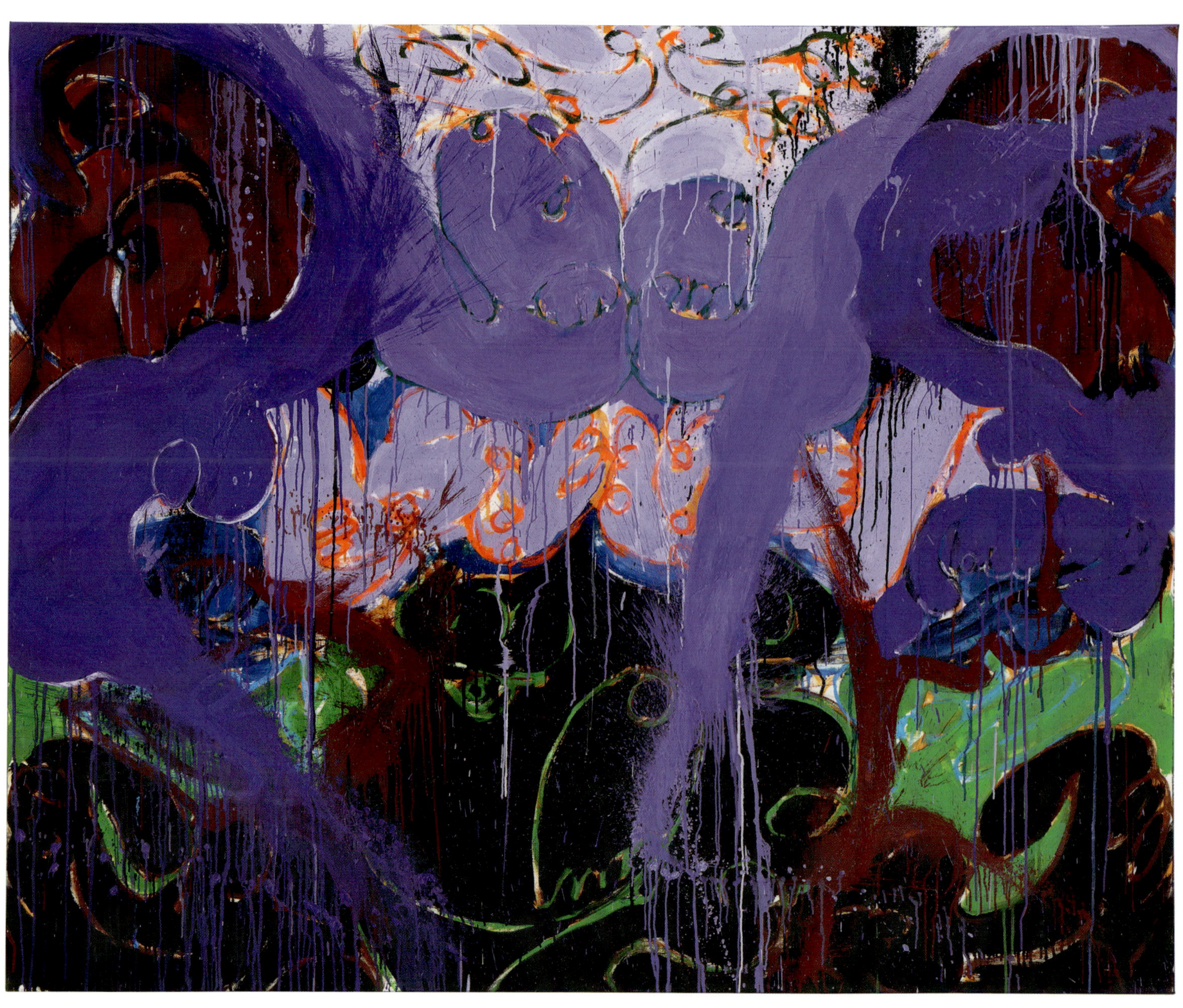

Plate 63

Amazon Dream, 1985
Oil on canvas
60 × 72 in. (152.4 × 183 cm)
The Estate of Norman Bluhm

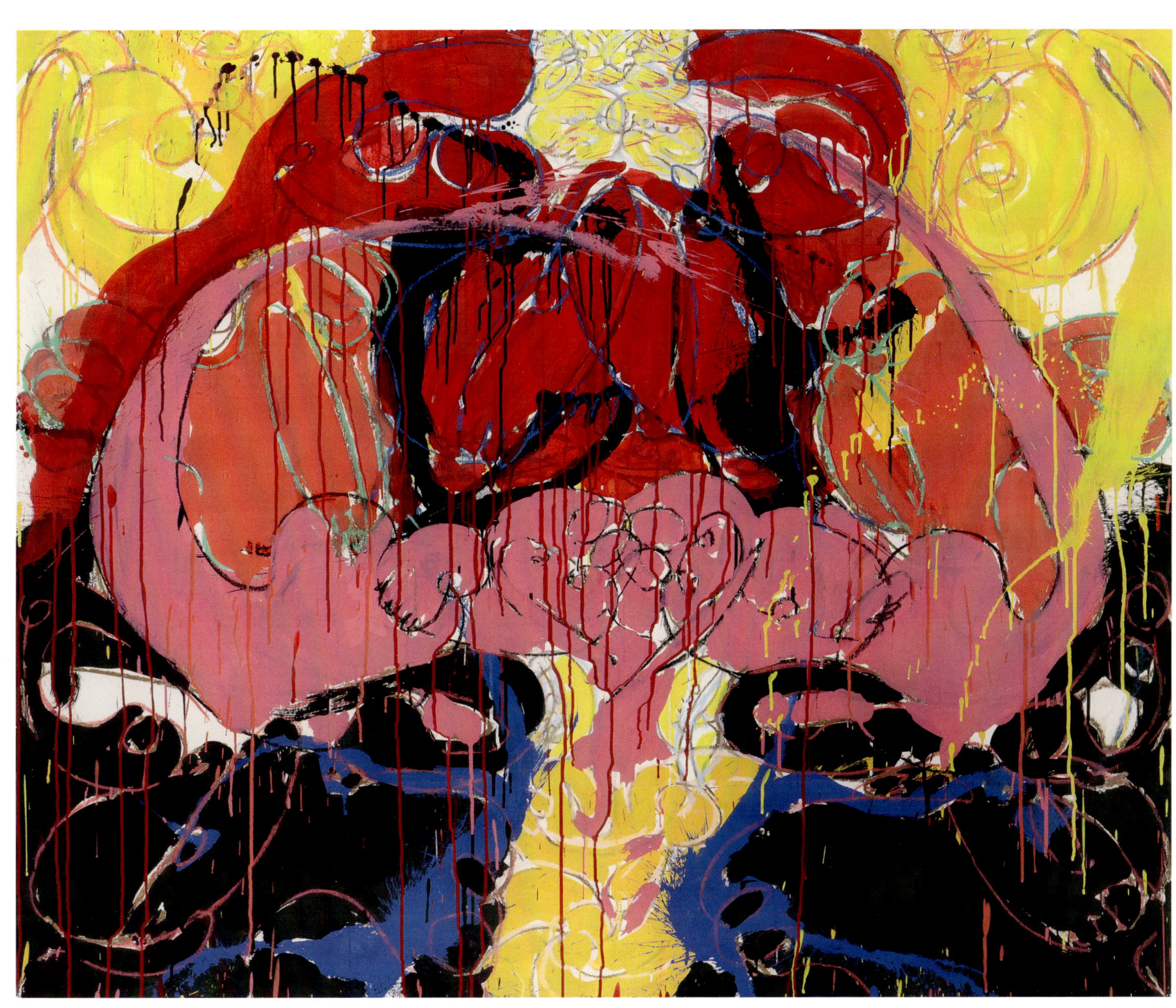

Plate 64

Drawing #7, 1985
Acrylic and pastel on paper
49 ½ × 60 in. (125.7 × 152.4 cm)
The Estate of Norman Bluhm

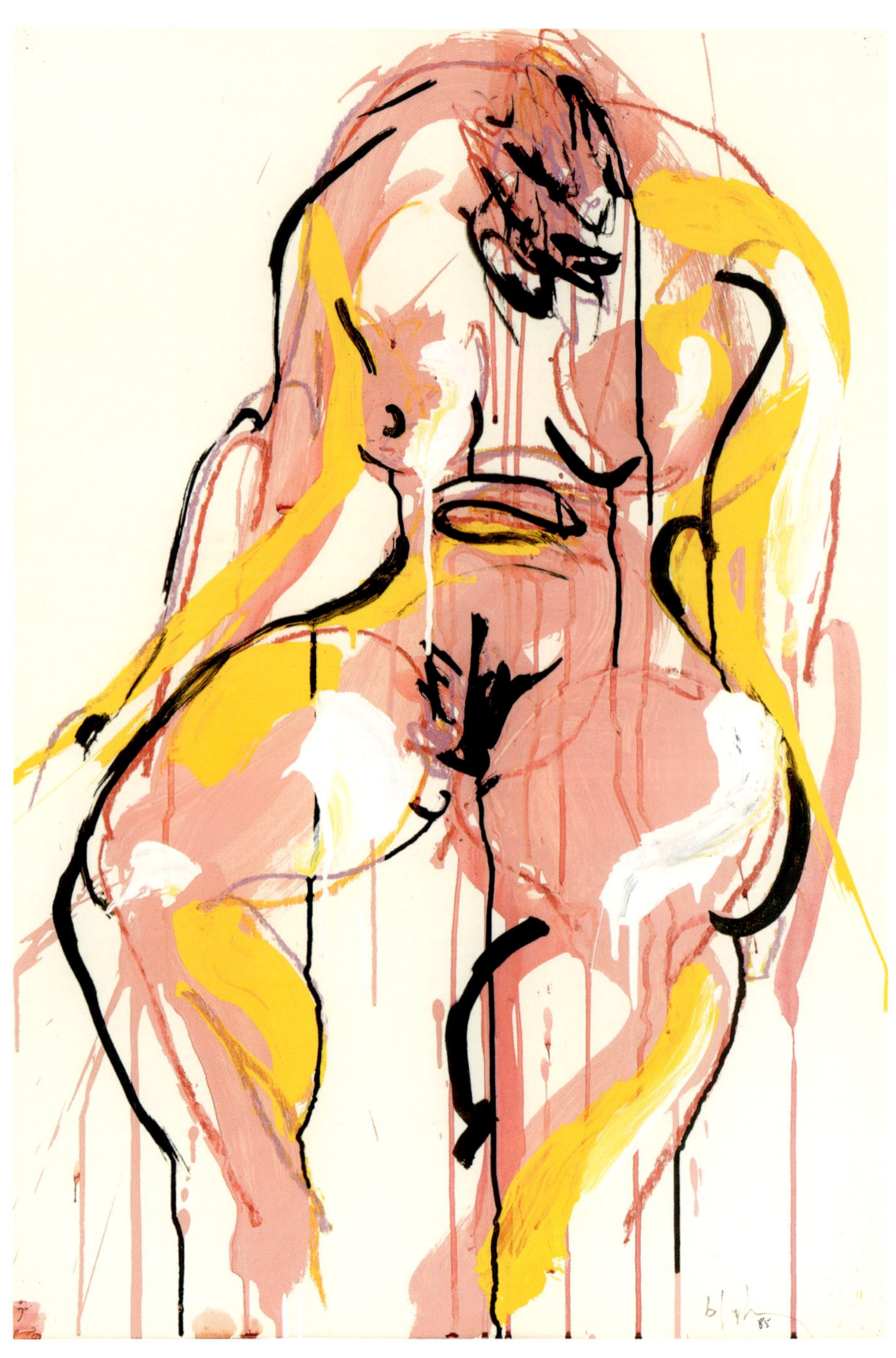

Plate 65

Nude, 1985
Acrylic, ink, and pastel on paper
36 × 24 in. (91.4 × 61 cm)
The Estate of Norman Bluhm

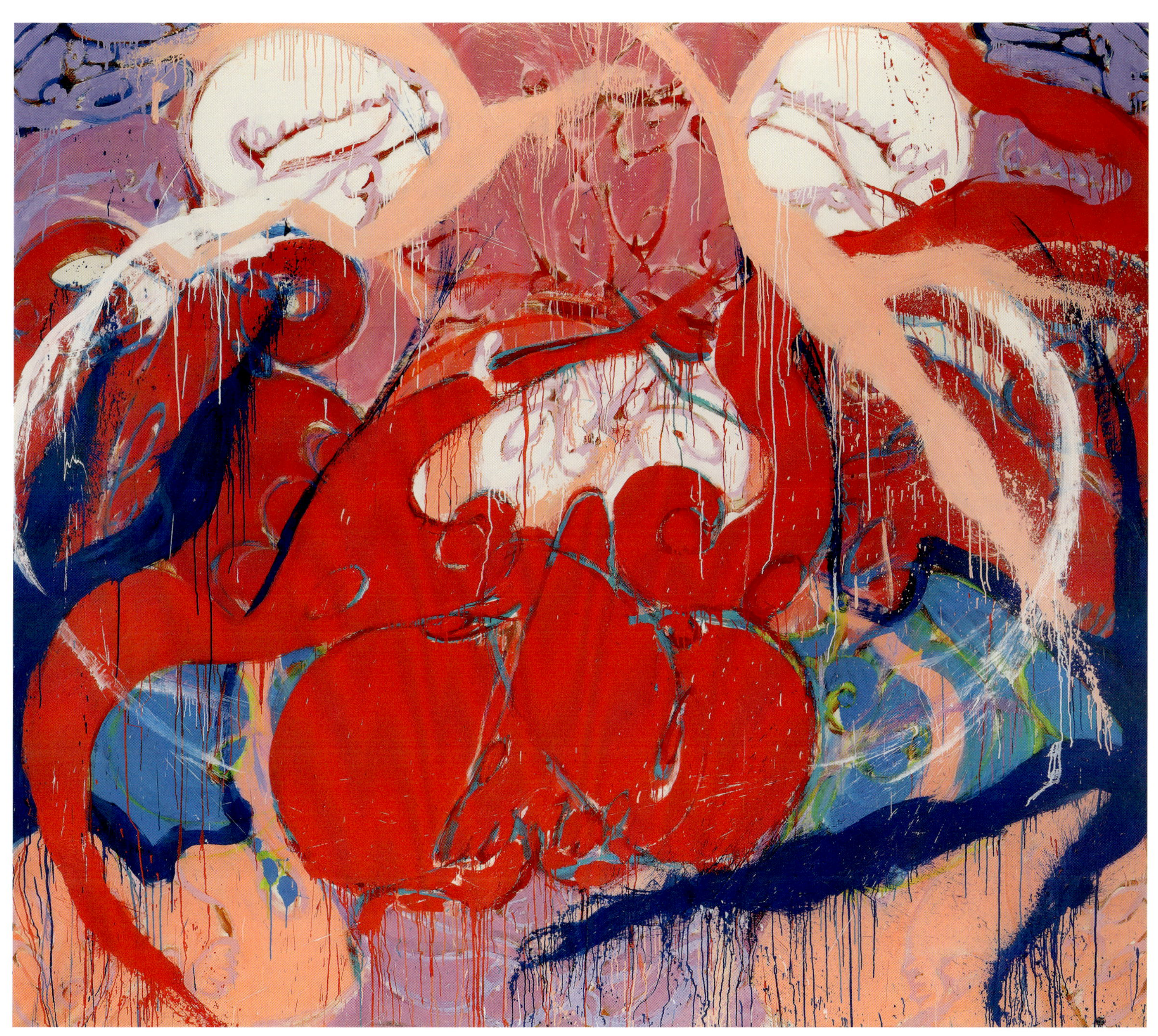

Plate 66

Dutchess of Cayenne, 1986
Oil on canvas
96 × 108 in. (244 × 274.3 cm)
The Estate of Norman Bluhm

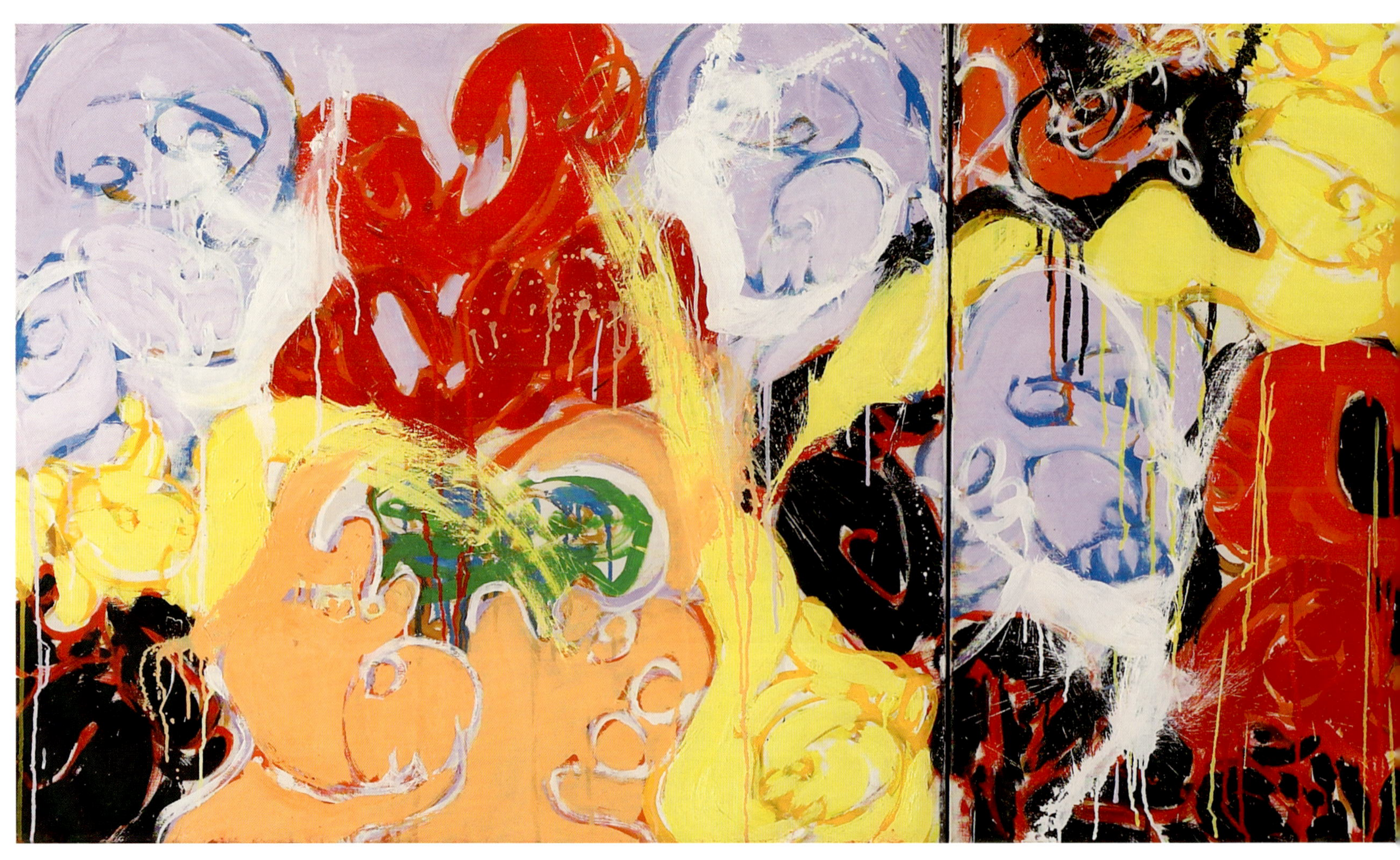

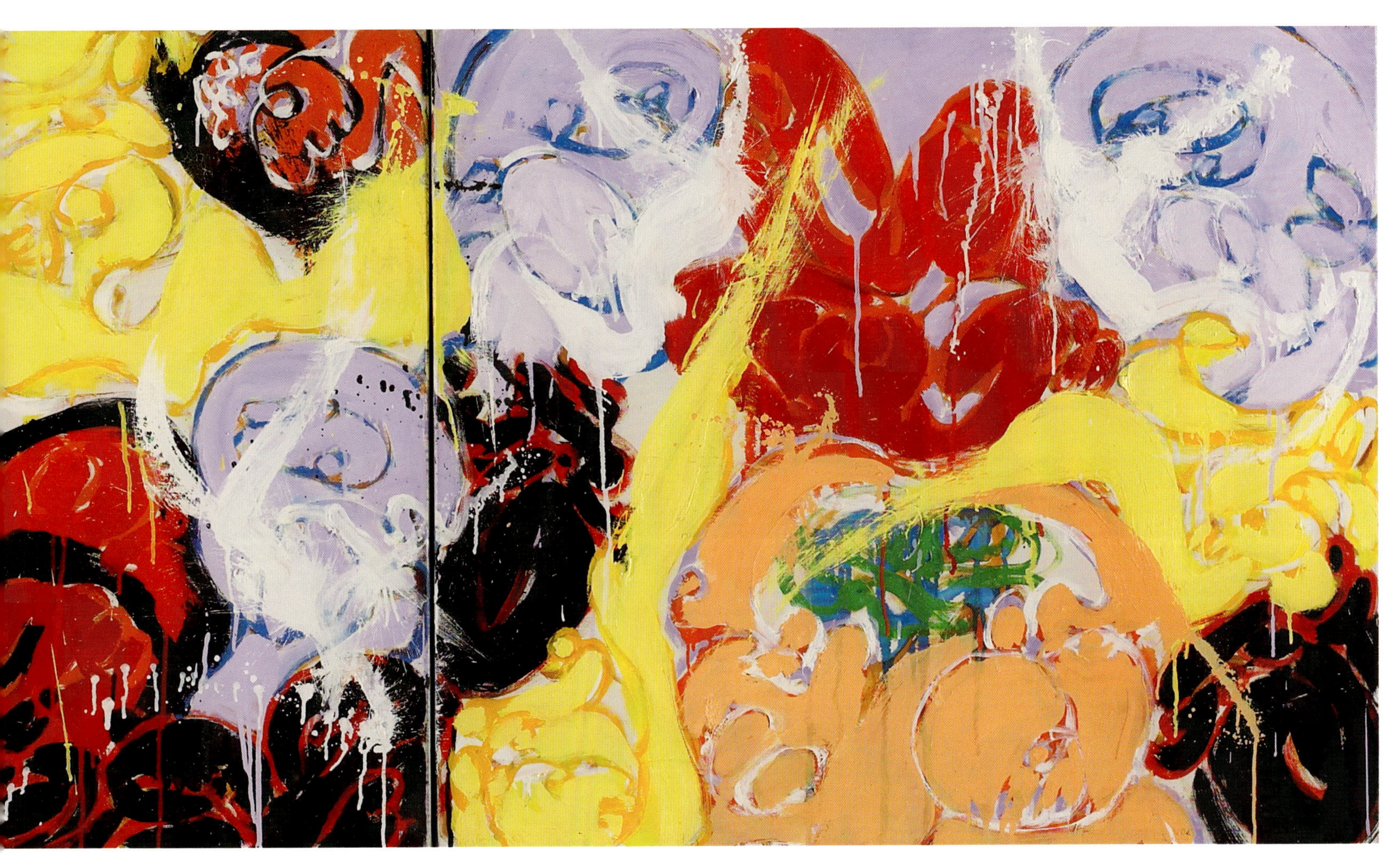

Plate 67

Dante's Fantasy, 1985–86
Oil on canvas
Triptych, 28 ⅛ × 96 ⅜ in. (71.4 × 244.8 cm) overall
Museum of Contemporary Art, Los Angeles
Gift of Larry and Susan Marx *2004.35*

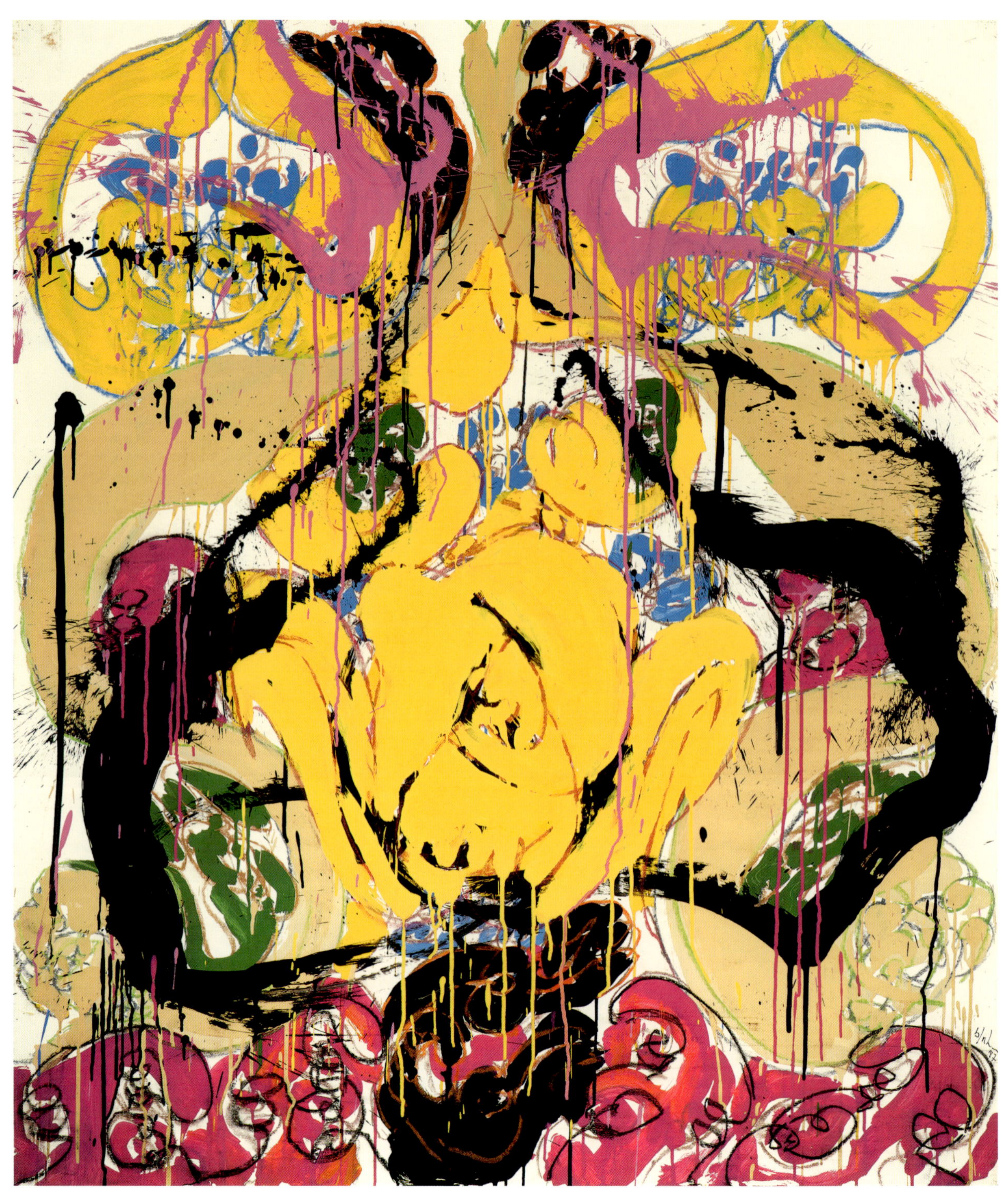

Plate 68

Fresco #13, 1987
Acrylic and pastel on paper
60 × 50 in. (152.4 × 127 cm)
The Estate of Norman Bluhm

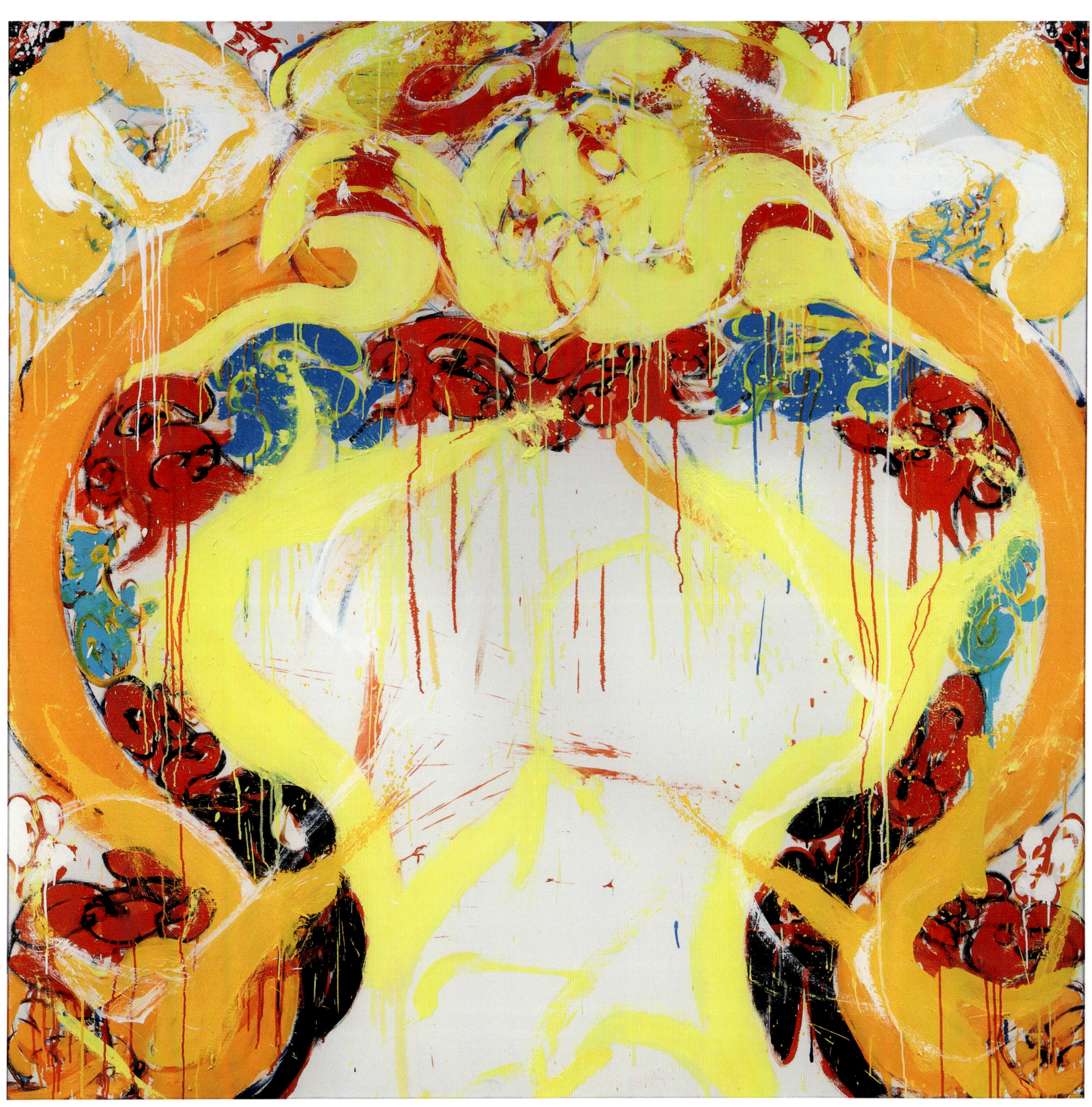

Plate 69

Aegean Angel, 1988
Oil on canvas
66 × 66 in. (167.6 × 167.6 cm)
The Estate of Norman Bluhm

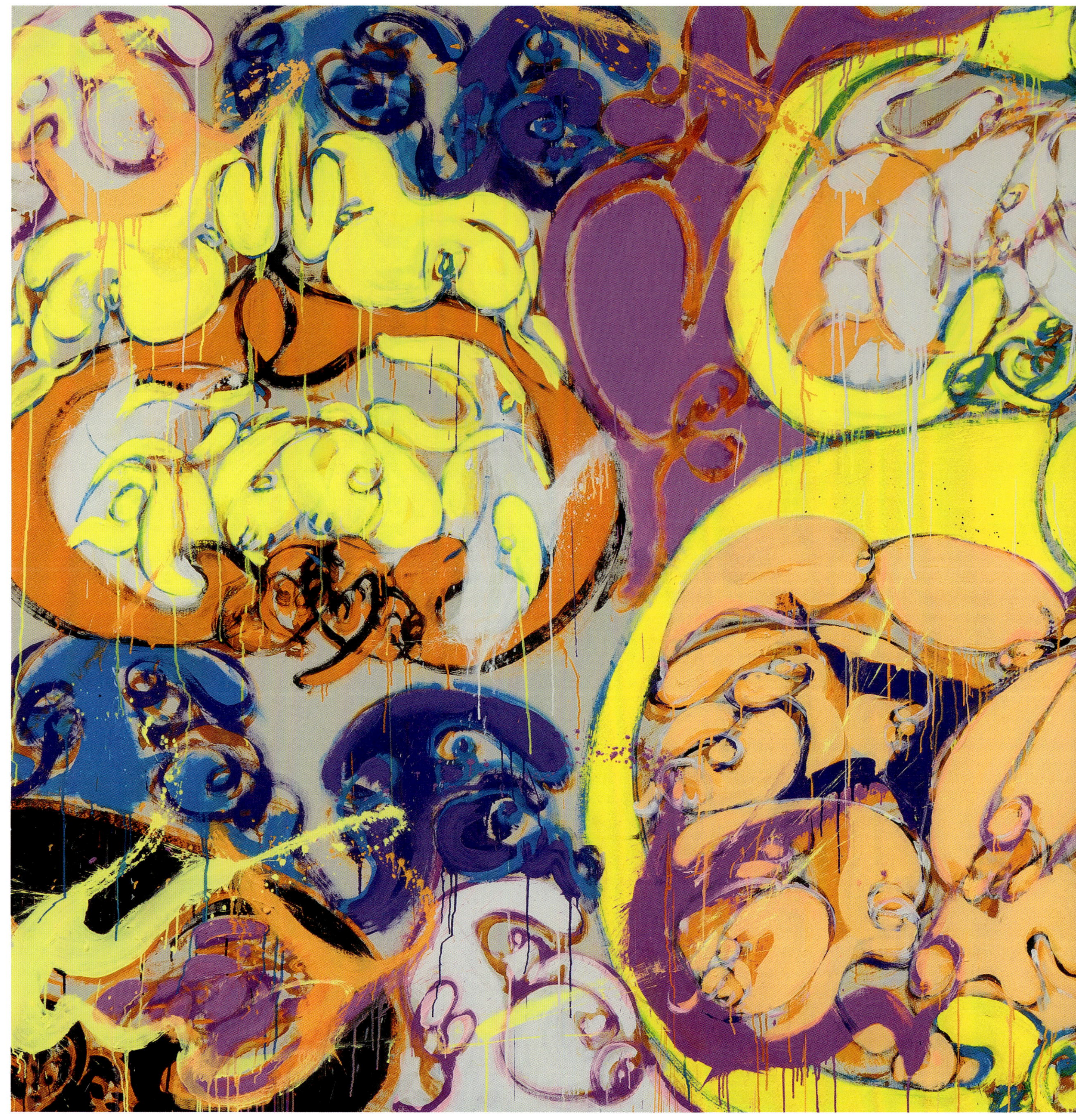

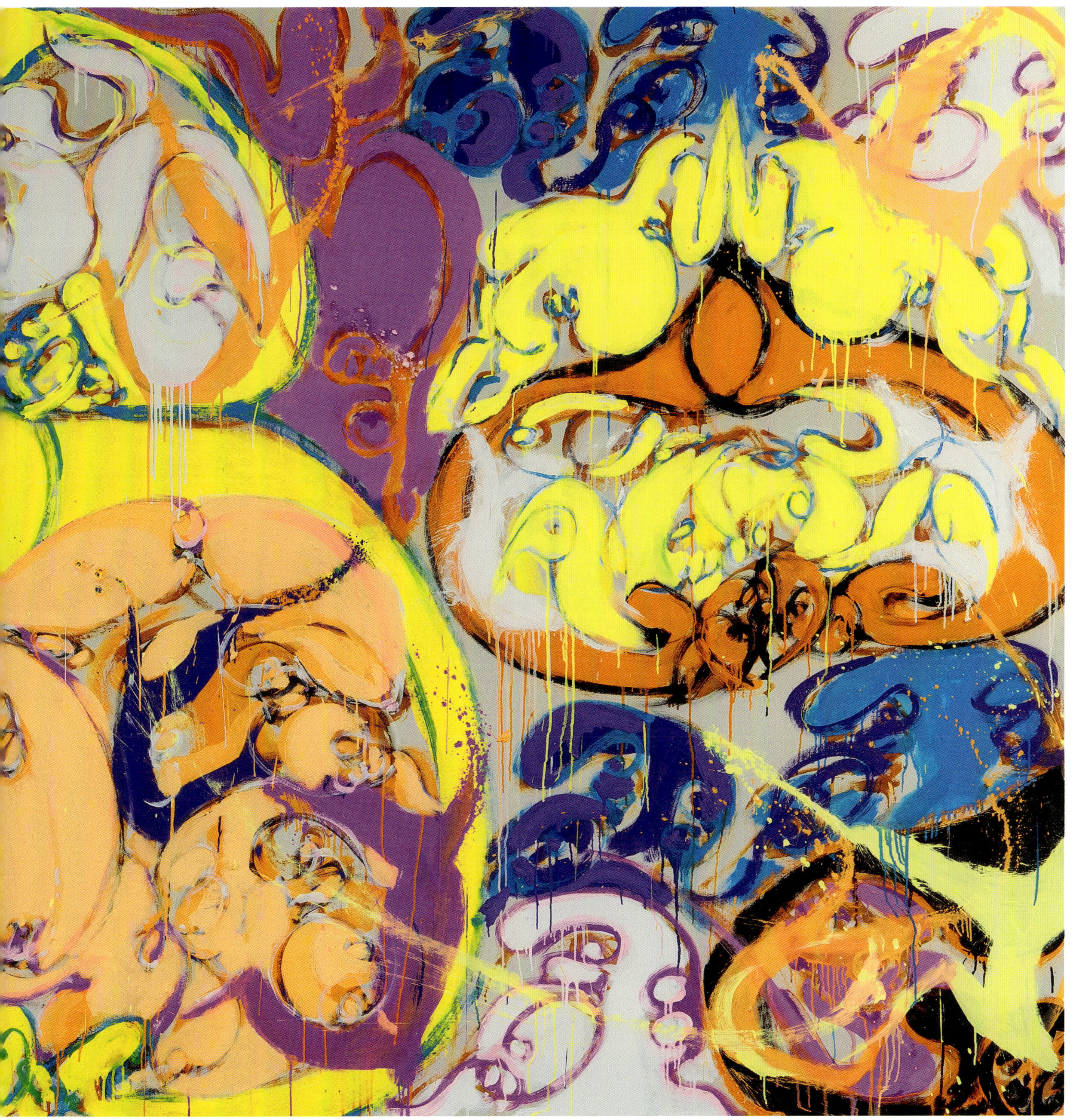

Plate 70

Reine de Provence, 1989
Oil on canvas
72 × 144 in. (183 × 365.7 cm)
The Estate of Norman Bluhm

“The choice of art in the life of man is, without a doubt, the life of loneliness in the motion of time, in so far as loneliness or remoteness is but the effort of man to touch that which is beyond the reach of his fingers. His life in relationship to his family, friends, etc. is the key to a different door than to that of his studio. How many nights do I, upon returning home in the evening, try to open the door to the apartment with the studio key! How many hours are spent like a strange lion in a cage, marching up and down in silence only to find my own reach limited to my outstretched arms! Nevertheless there are no tears: even though one lives on the edge of the glass, joy is forever the unknown.”

Norman Bluhm, quoted in *Daniel Frasnay: The Artist’s World* (New York: A Studio Book/The Viking Press, 1969), n.p.

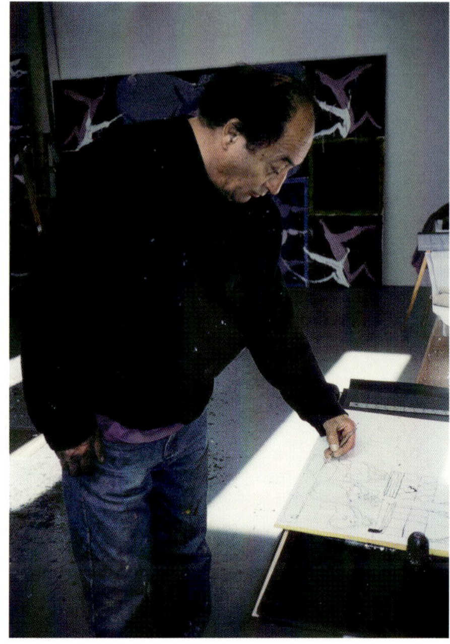

Fig. 25
Norman Bluhm drawing in his Vermont studio, c.1990.
Photo by Cary Bluhm

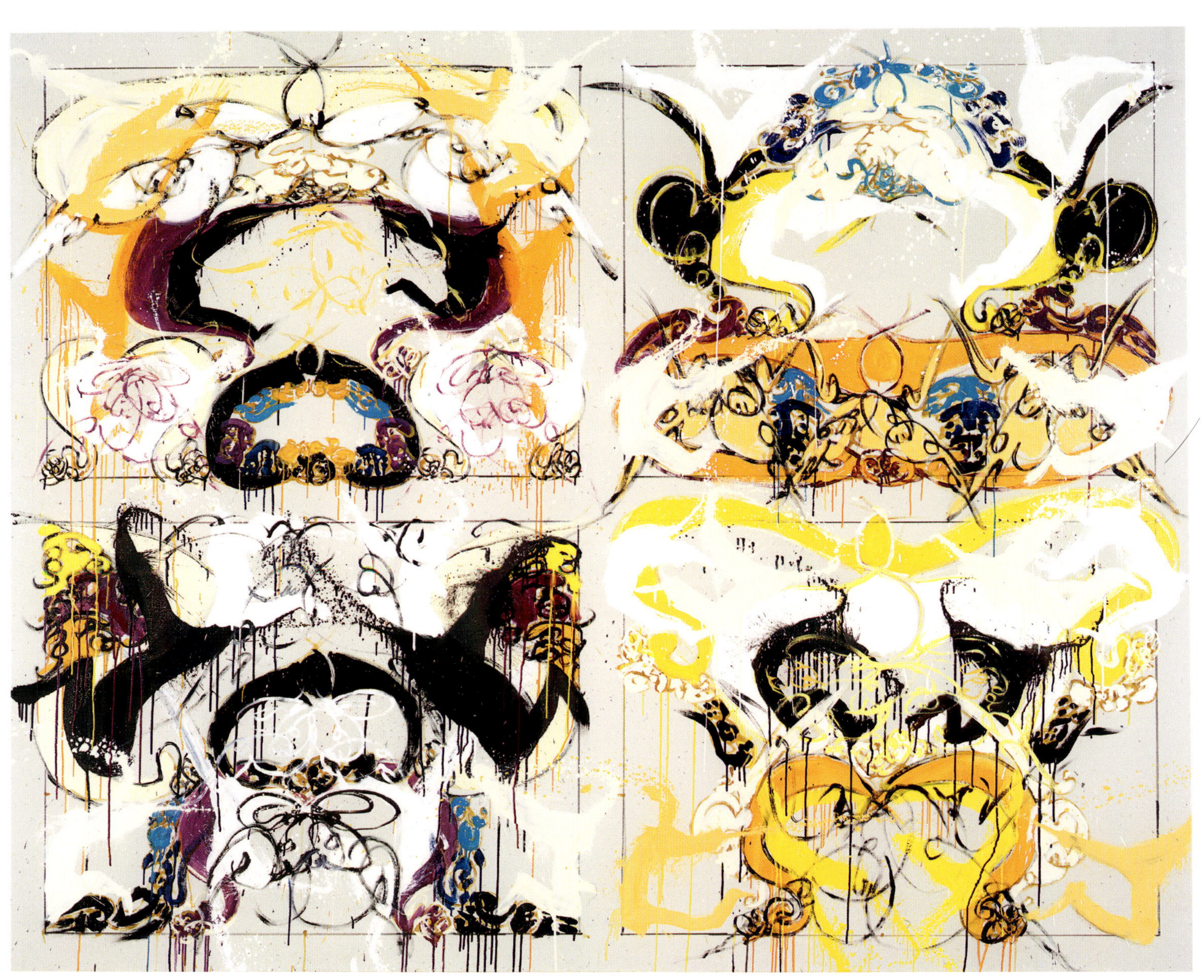

Plate 71

Gnostic Moment, 1990
Oil on canvas
77 × 96 3/8 in. (195.6 × 244.8 cm)
The Estate of Norman Bluhm

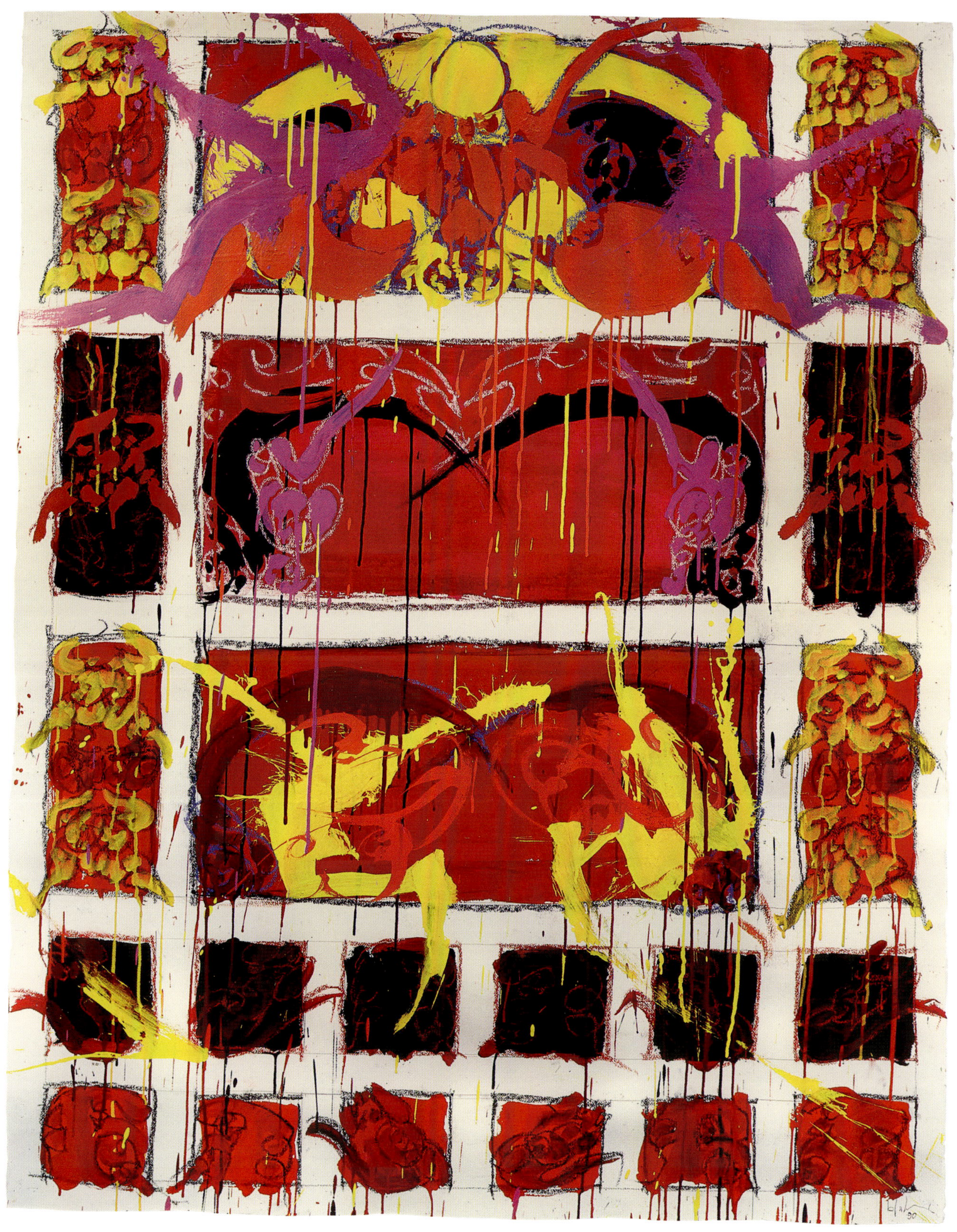

Plate 72

Study II, 1990
Acrylic and pastel on paper
58 × 44¾ in. (147.3 × 113.7 cm)
The Estate of Norman Bluhm

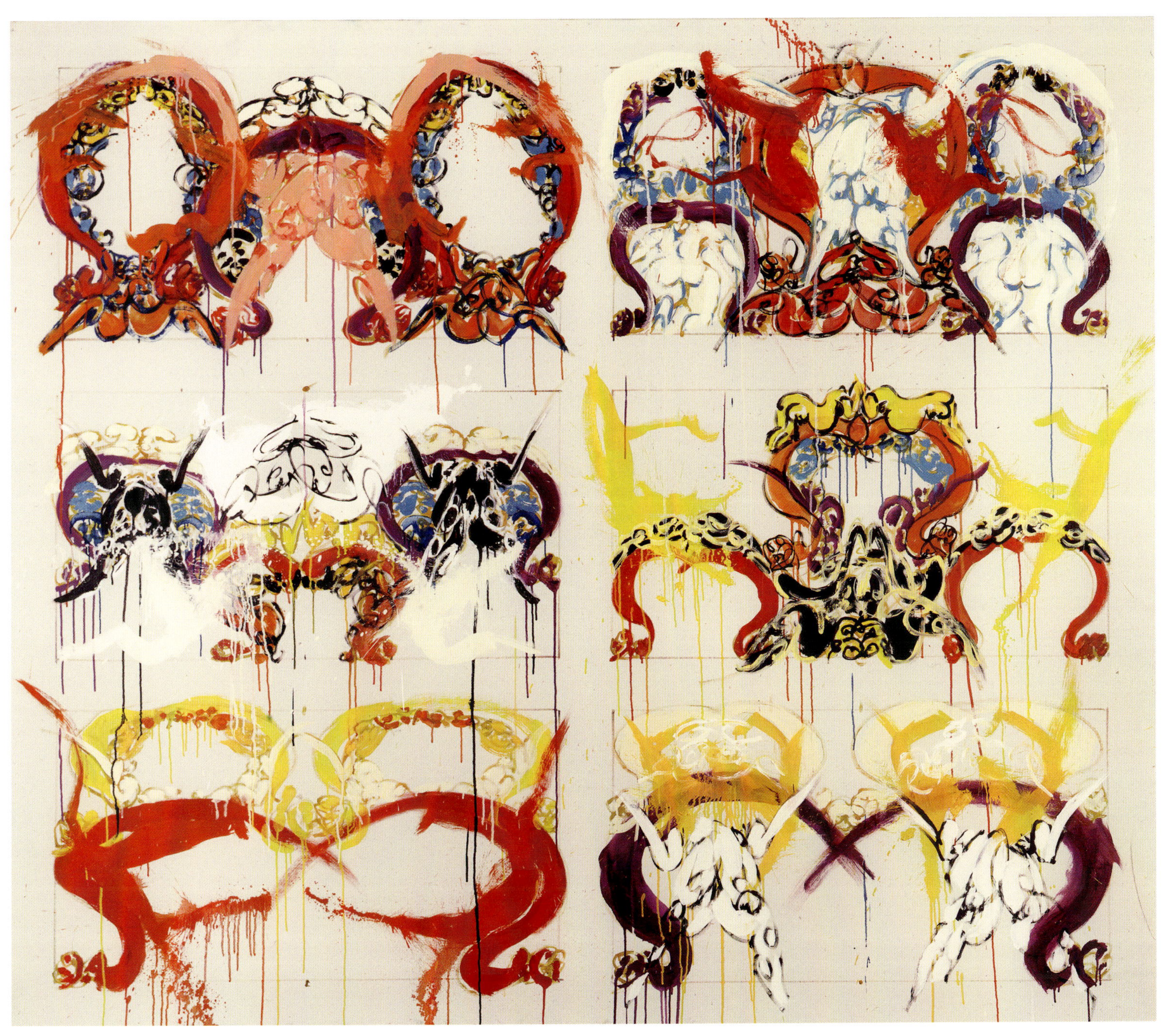

Plate 73

Medieval Doors, 1990
Oil on canvas
70 × 80 in. (178 × 203 cm)
The Estate of Norman Bluhm

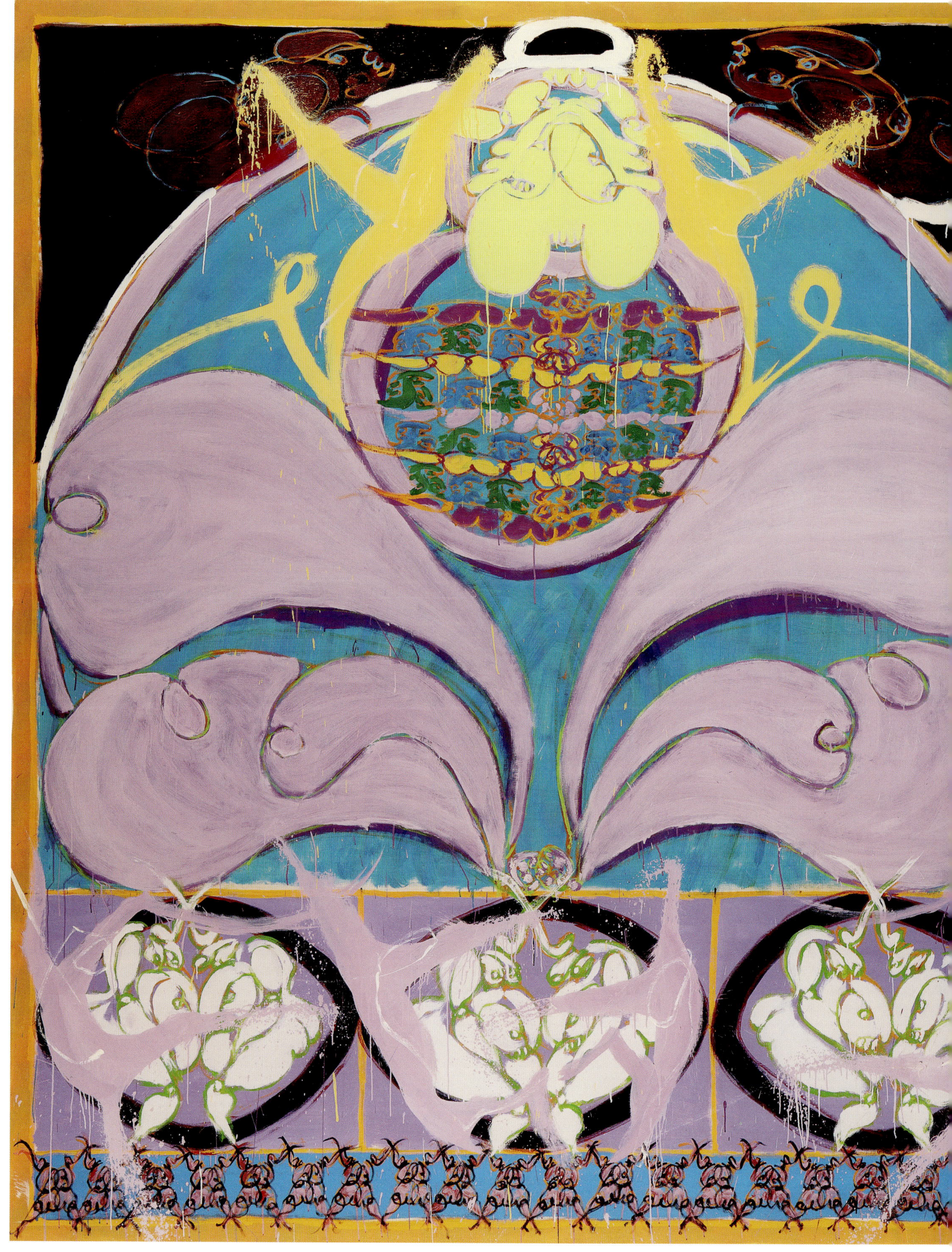

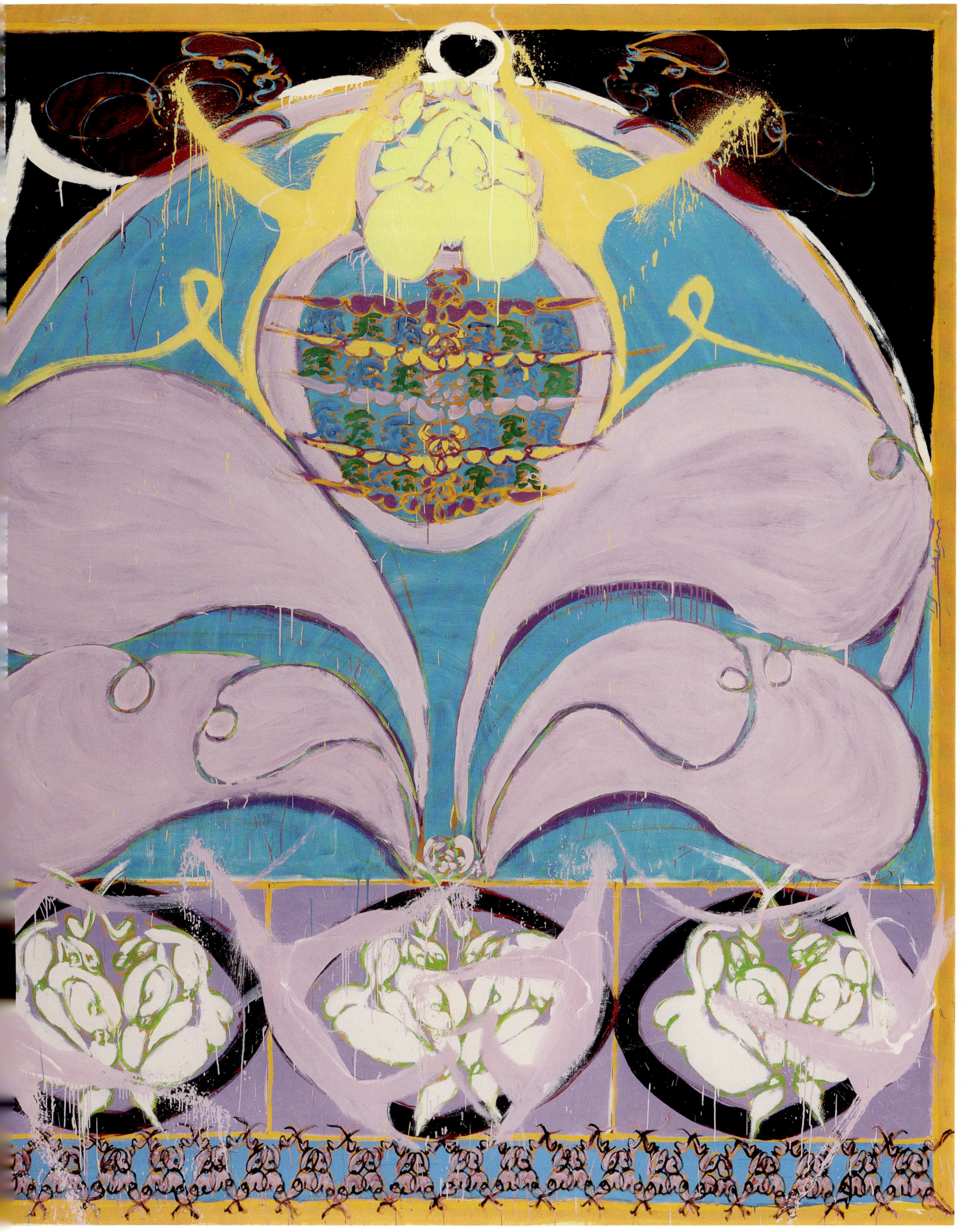

Plate 74

Persephone, 1995
Oil on canvas
Triptych, 120 × 300 in. (305 × 762 cm) overall
The Estate of Norman Bluhm

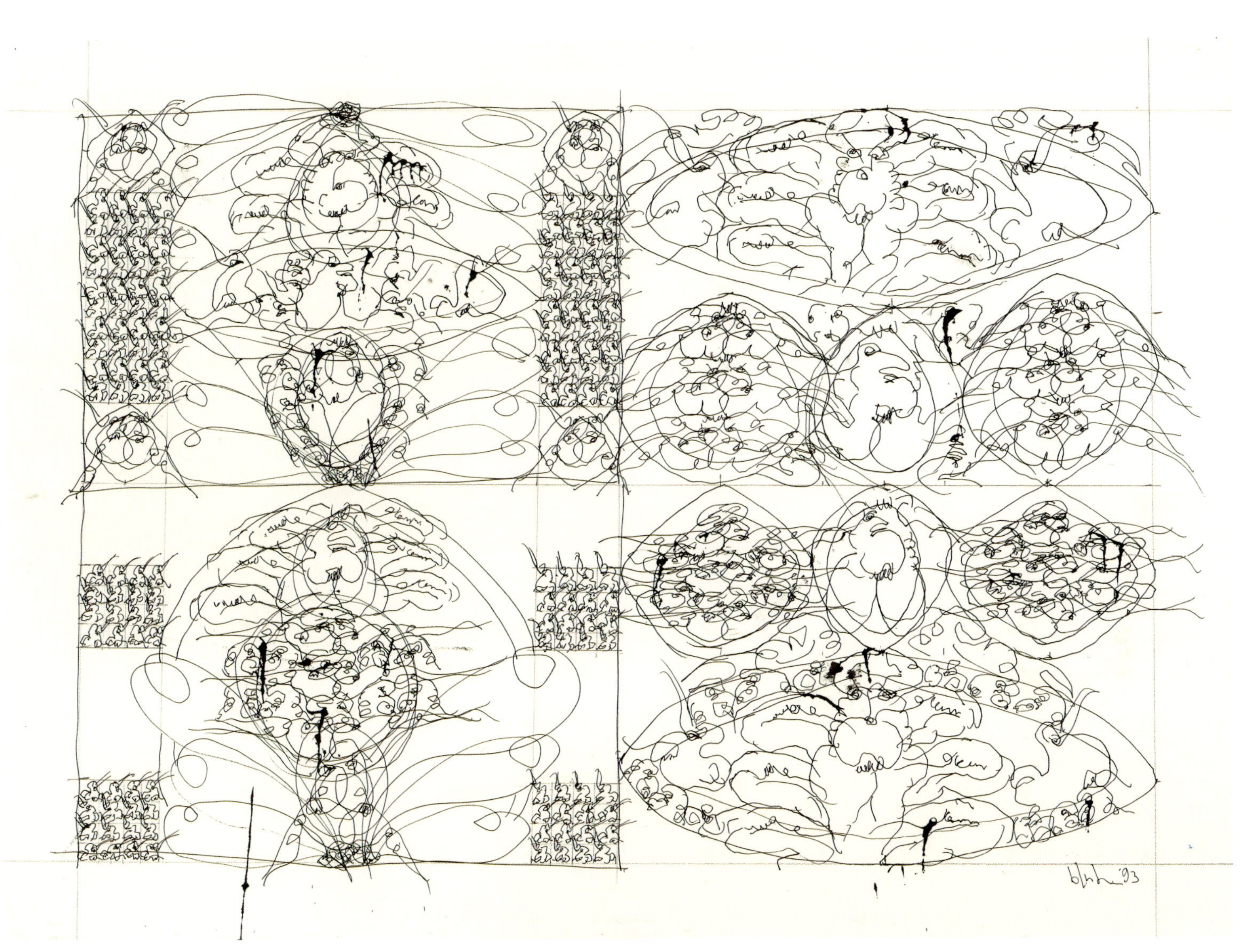

Plate 75

Untitled, 1994
Ink on paper
22 × 30 in. (56 × 76.2 cm)
The Estate of Norman Bluhm

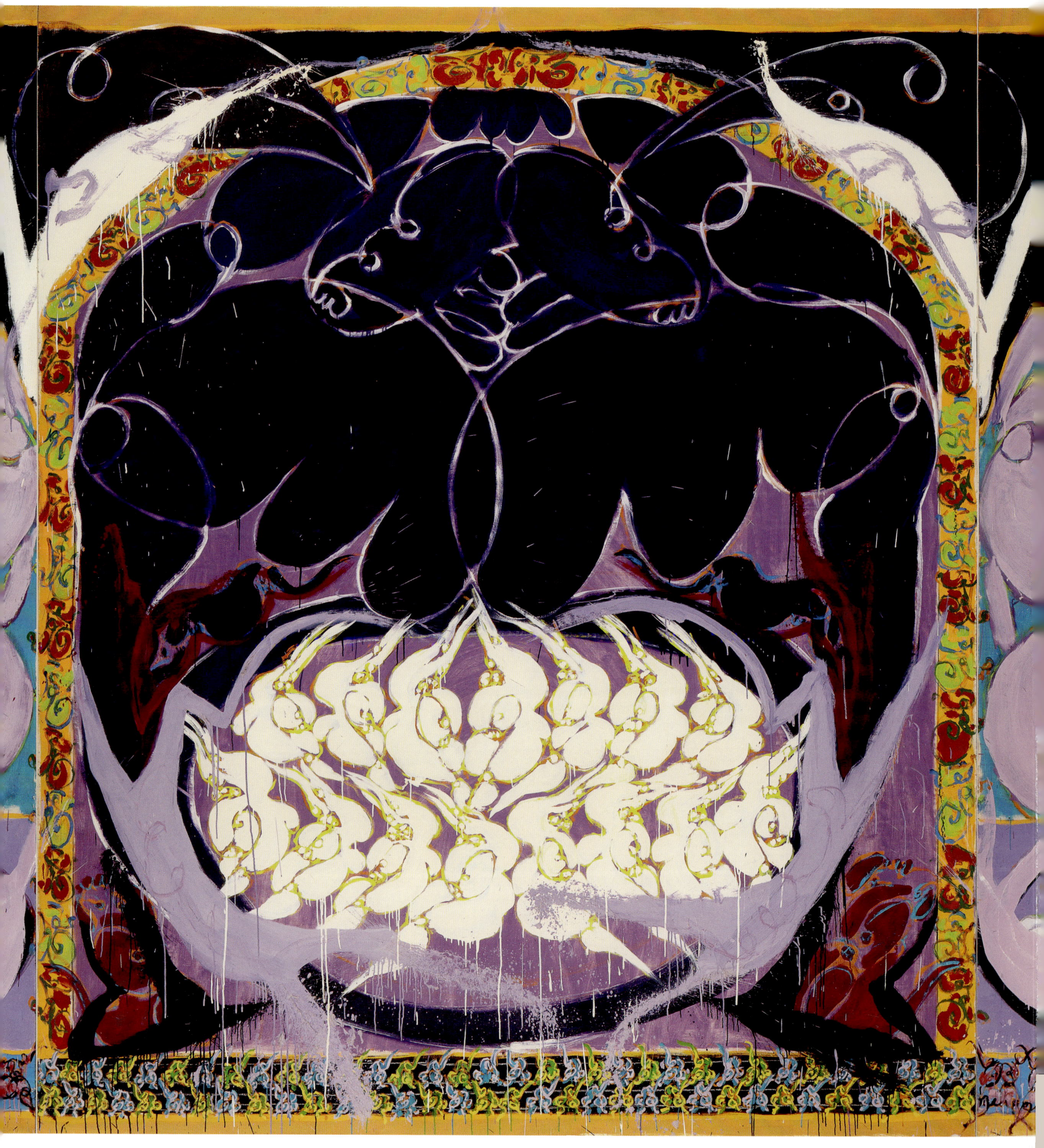

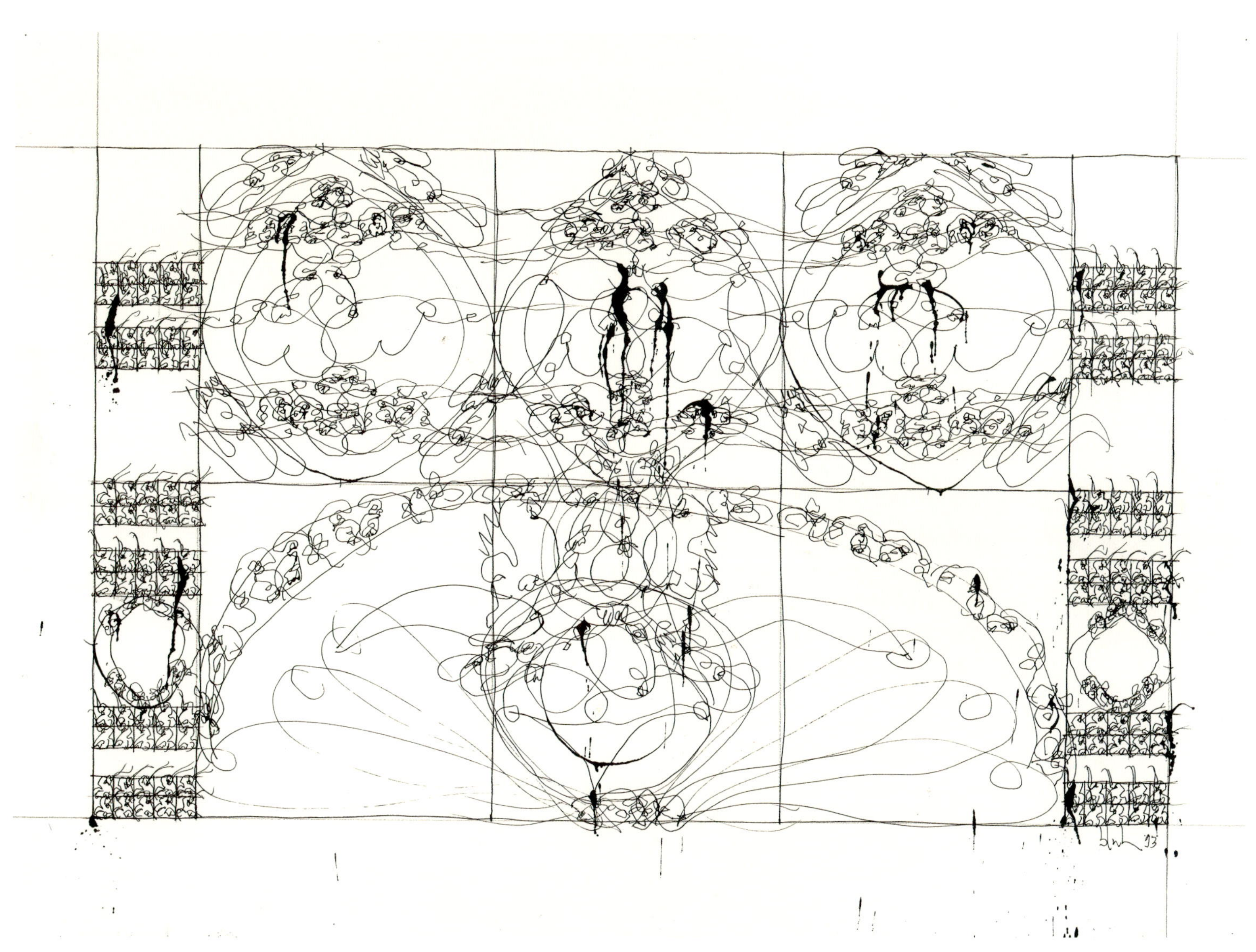

Plate 76

Untitled, 1994
Ink on paper
22 × 30 in. (56 × 76.2 cm)
The Estate of Norman Bluhm

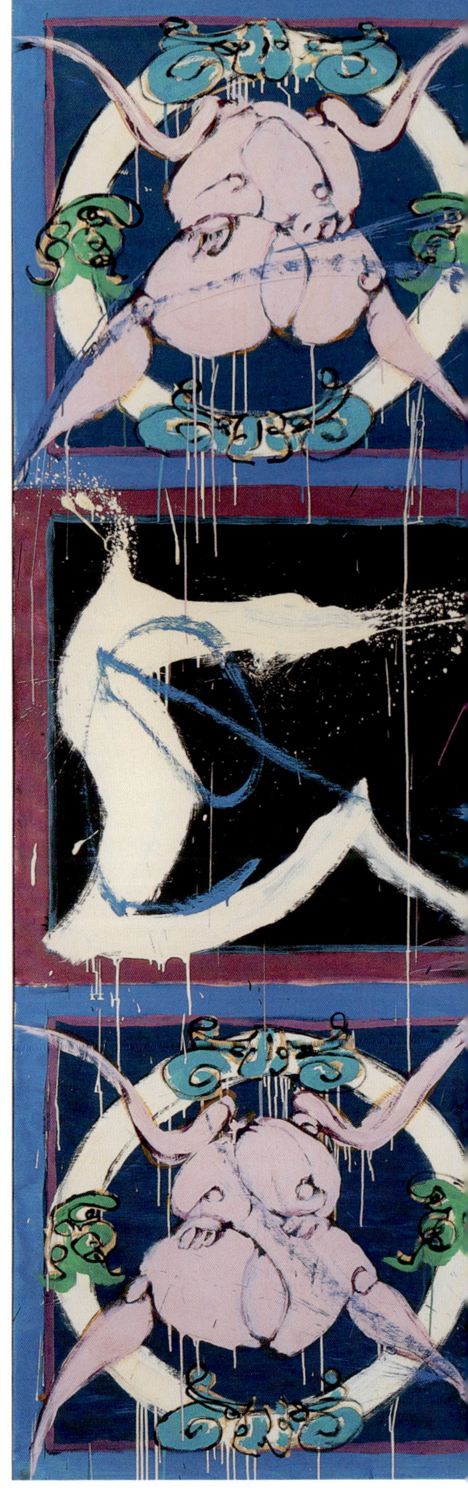

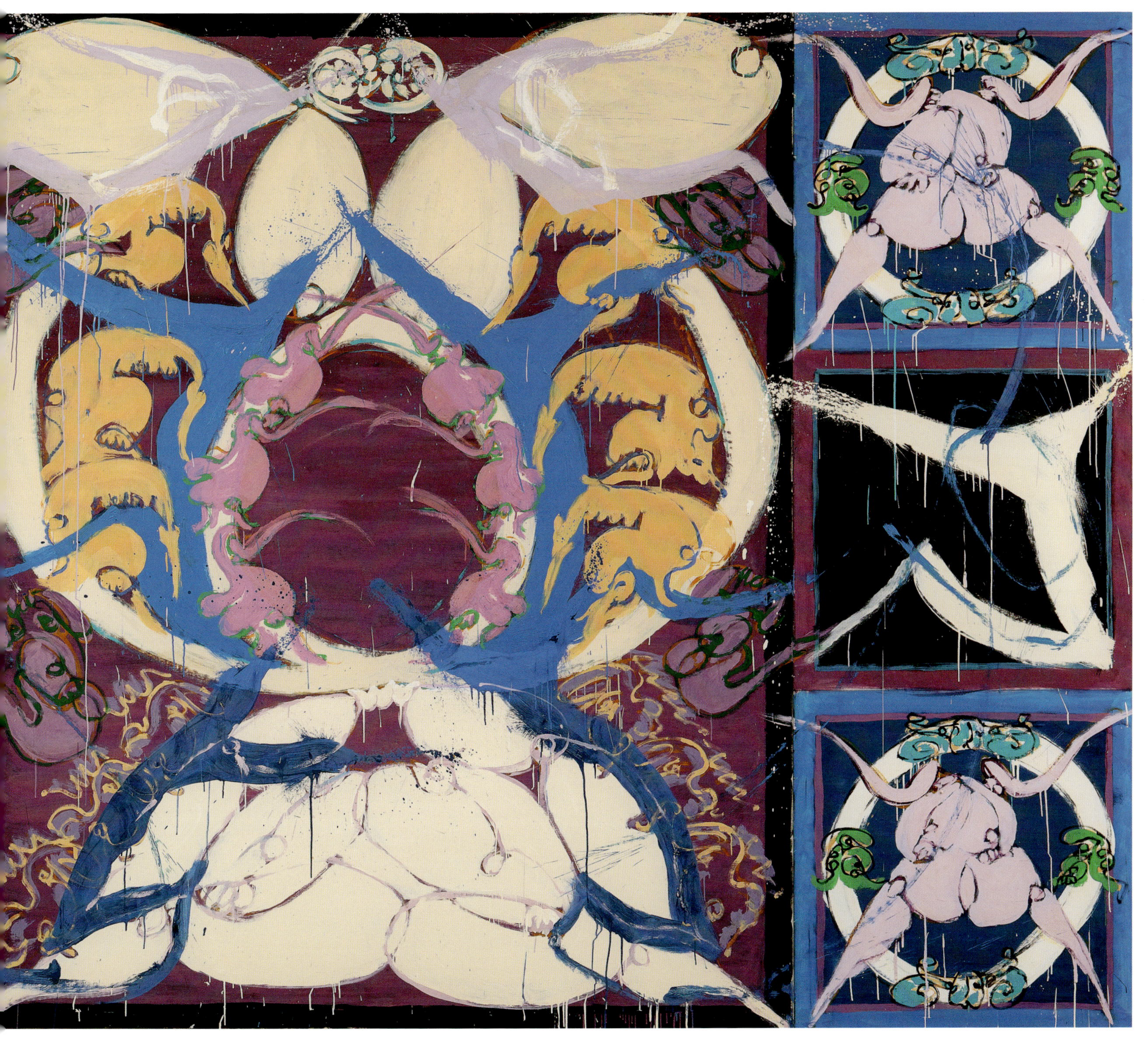

Plate 77

Siberian Chant, 1993
Oil on canvas
Triptych, 96 × 141 in. (244 × 358 cm) overall
The Estate of Norman Bluhm

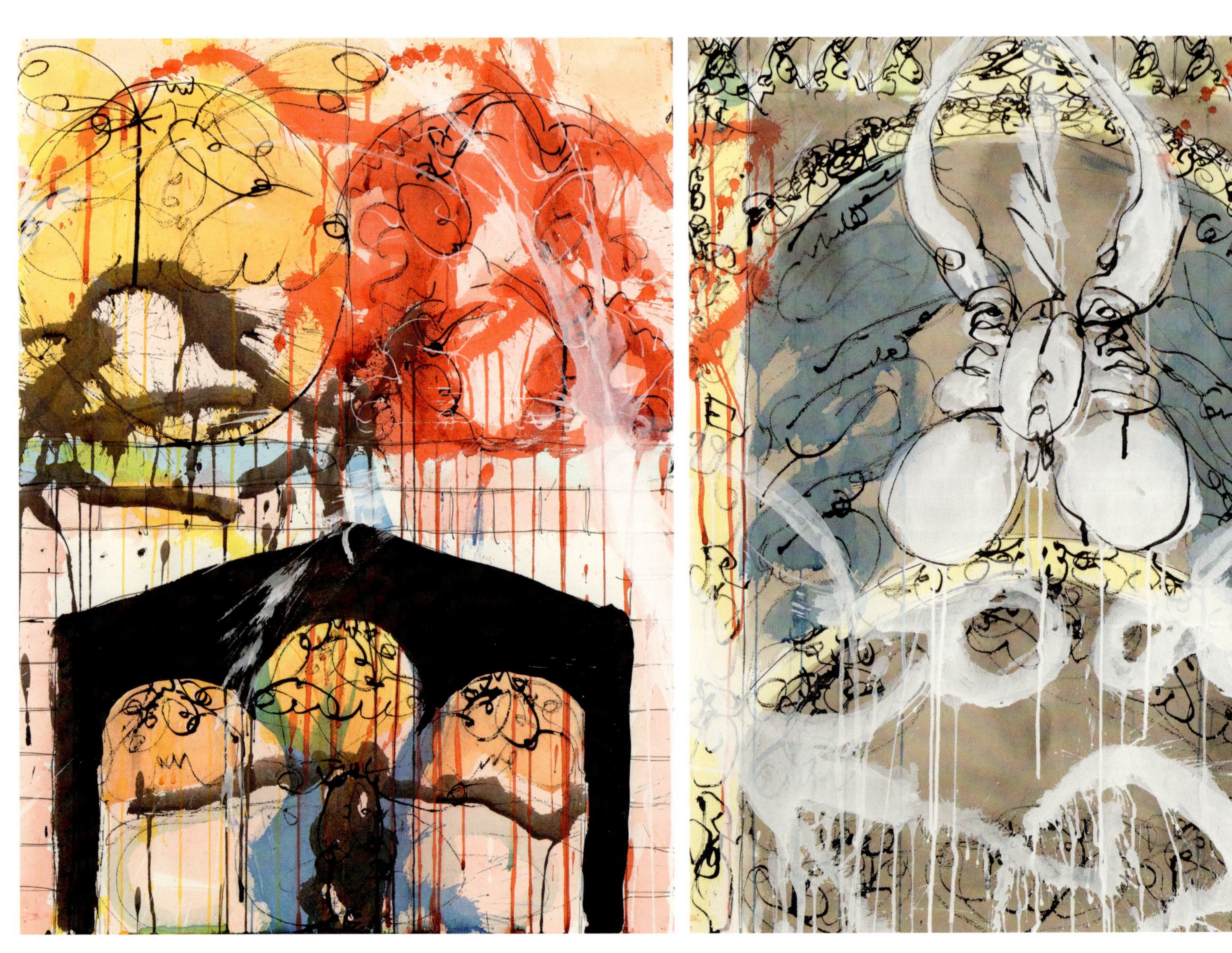

Plate 78

Untitled, 1996
Acrylic and ink on paper
Triptych, 30 × 66 in. (76.2 × 167.6 cm) overall
The Estate of Norman Bluhm

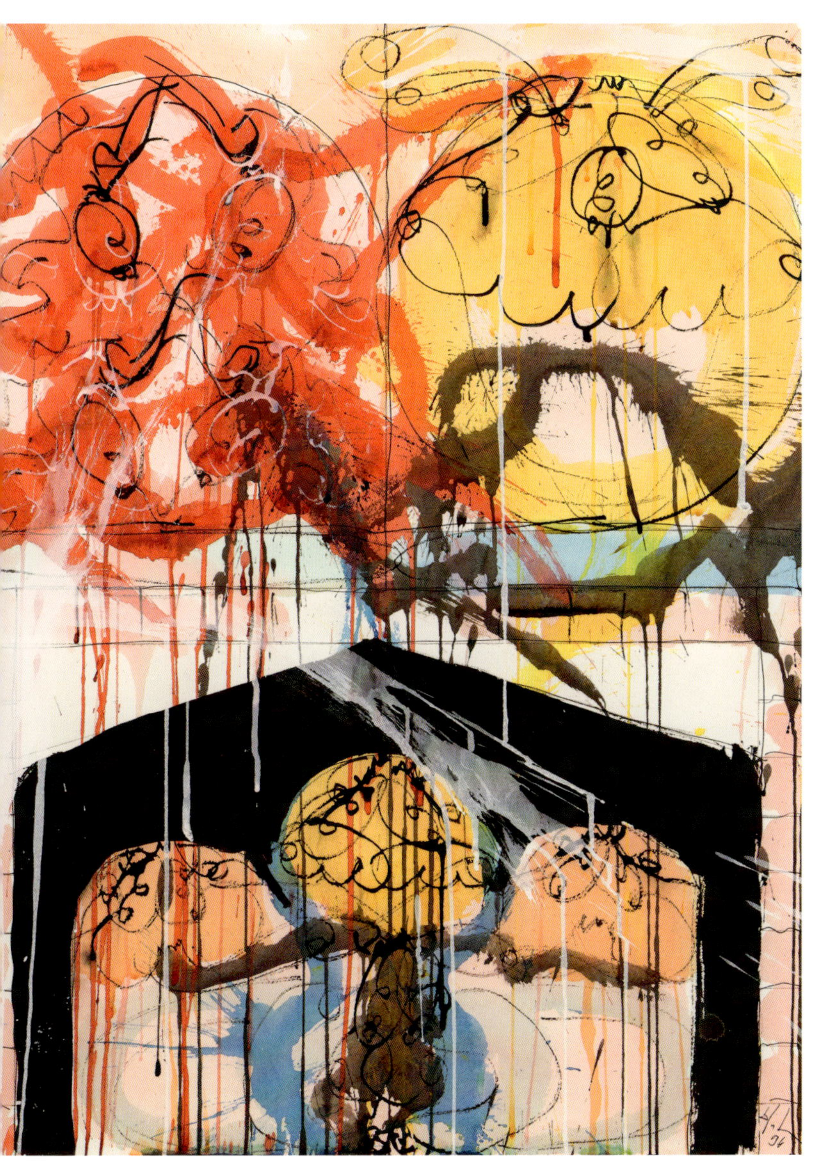

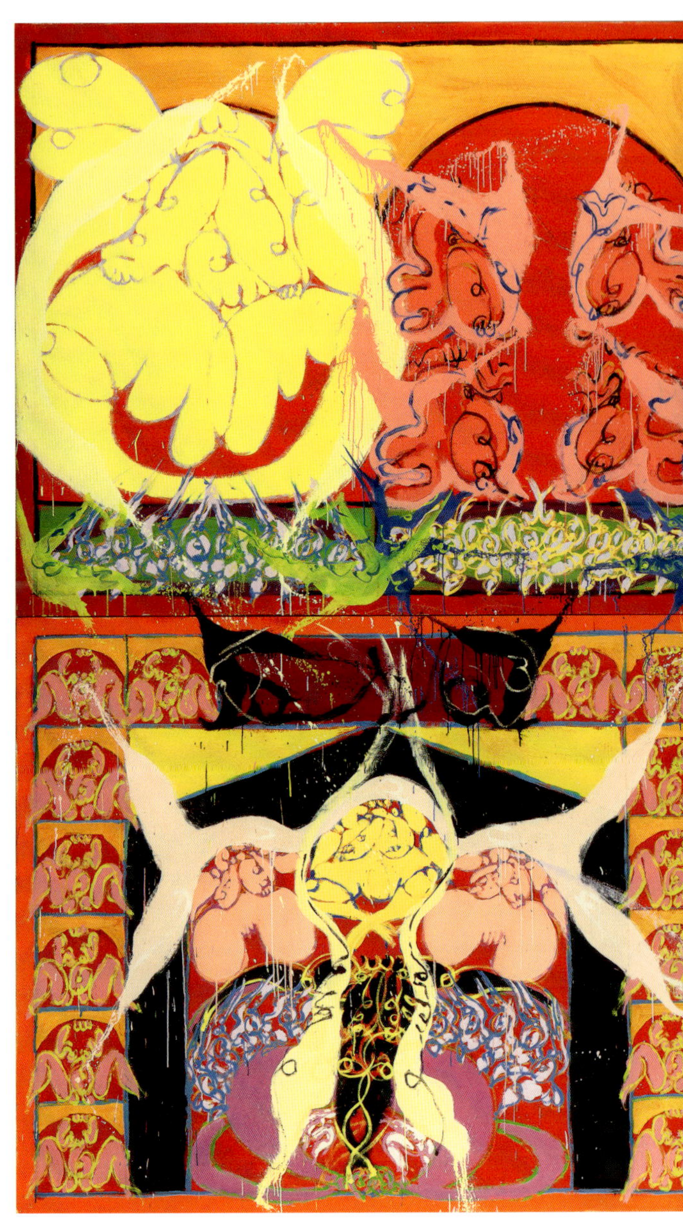

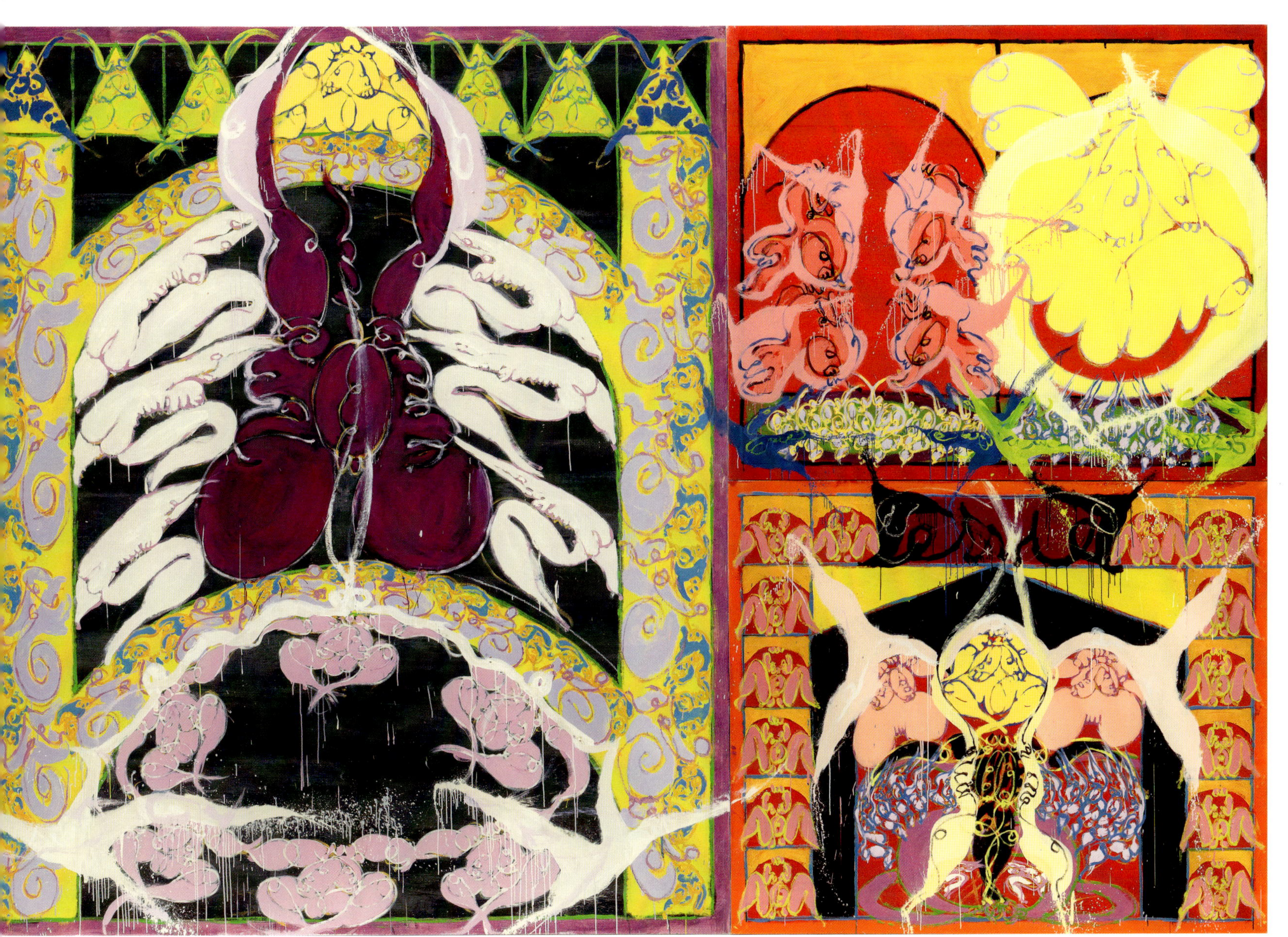

Plate 79

Cappella Ignota, 1997
Oil on canvas
Five panels, 120 × 244 in. (305 × 620 cm) overall
The Estate of Norman Bluhm

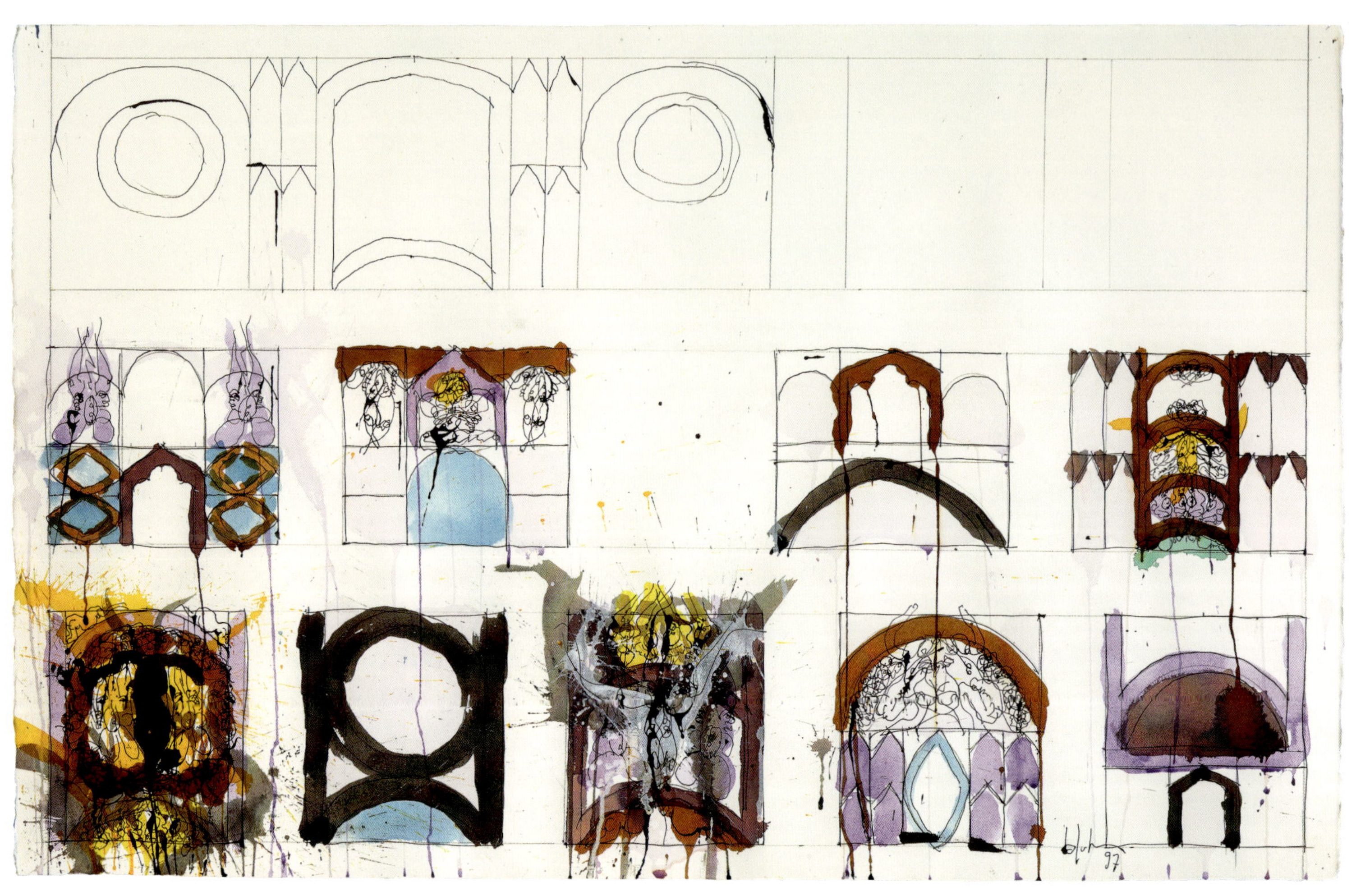

Plate 80

Untitled, 1997
Acrylic and ink on paper
26 × 40 ½ in. (66 × 103 cm)
The Estate of Norman Bluhm

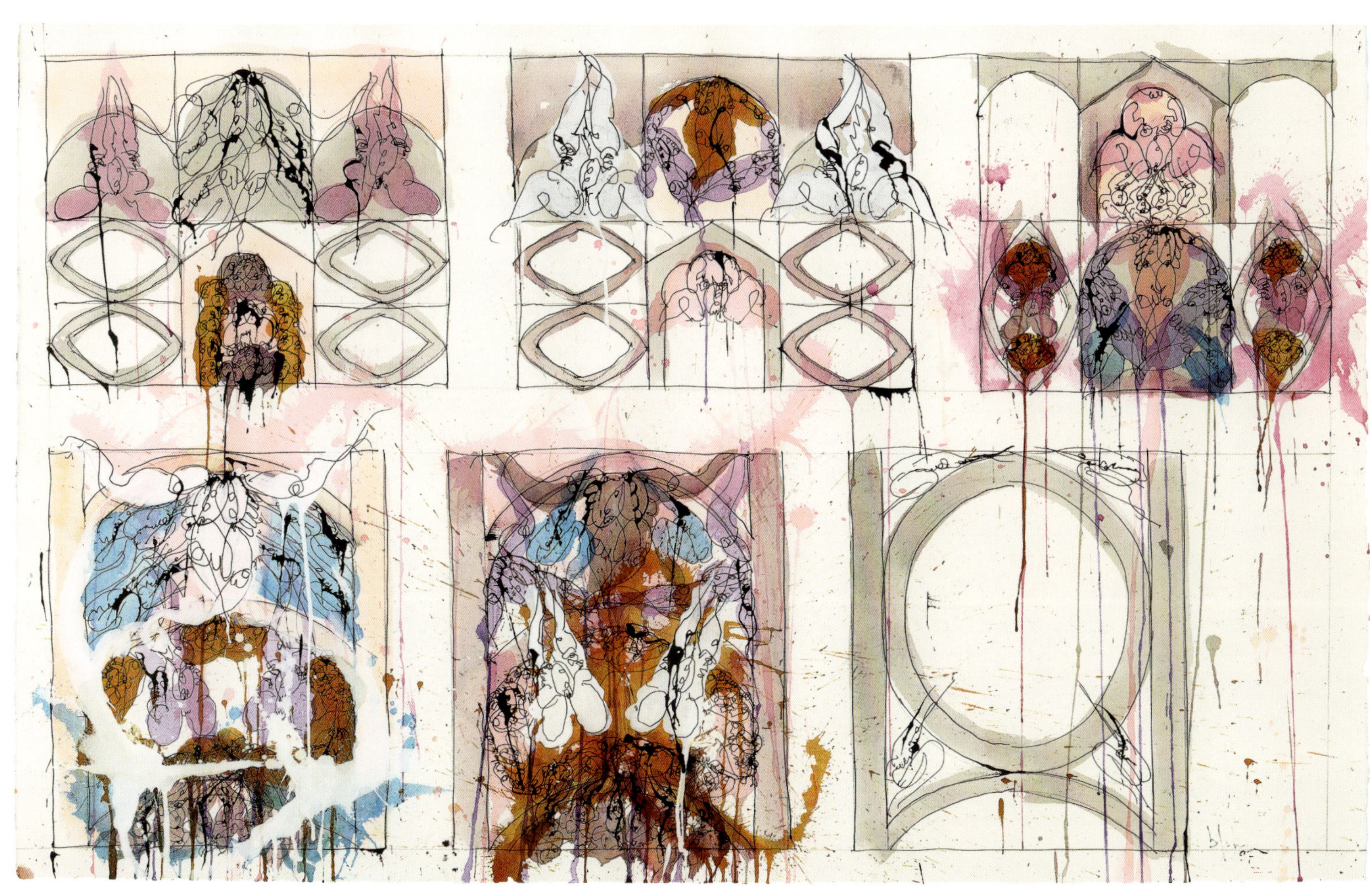

Plate 81

Untitled, 1997
Acrylic and ink on paper
26 × 40 ½ in. (66 × 103 cm)
The Estate of Norman Bluhm

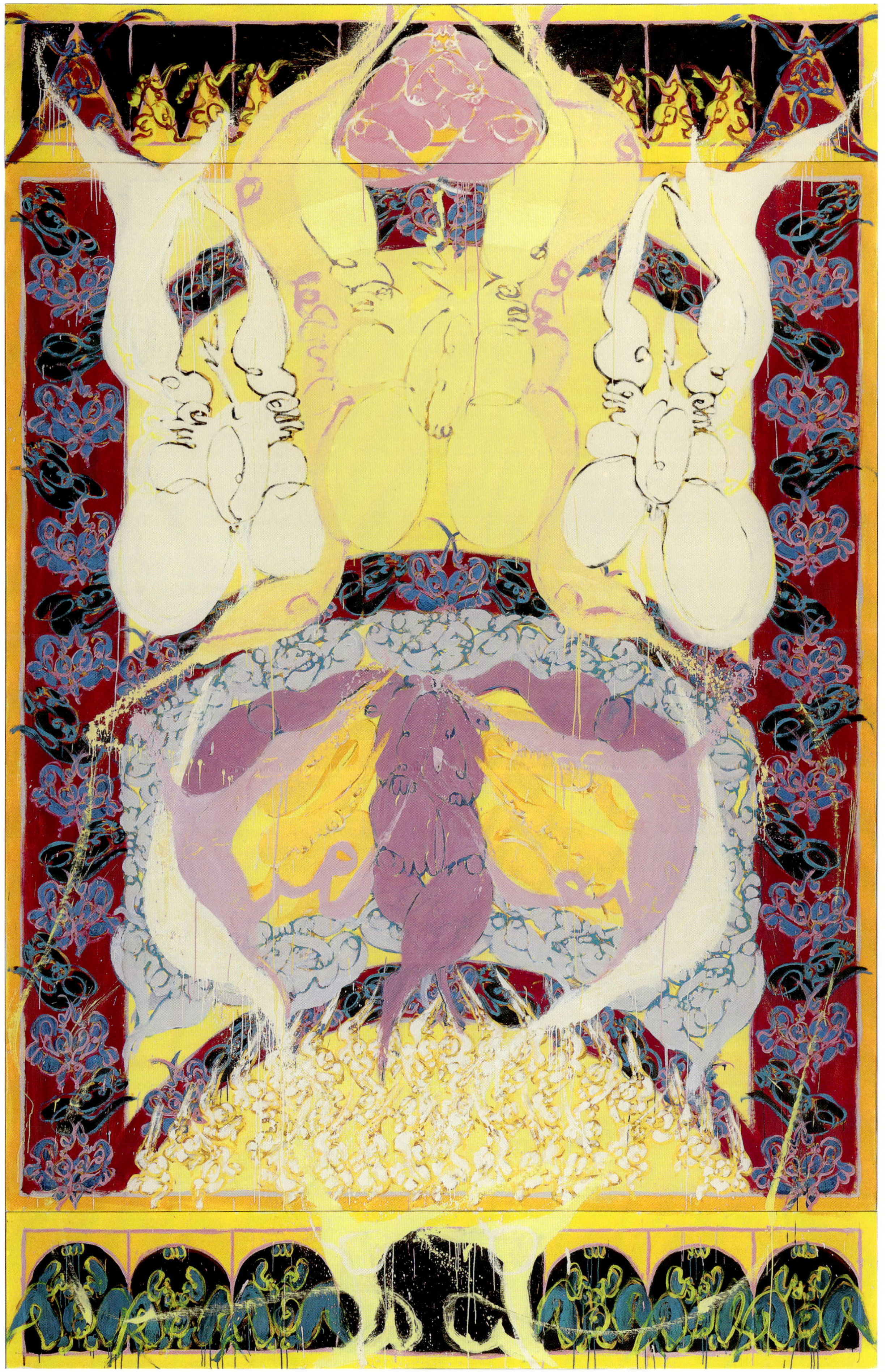

Plate 82

Ode to Apollo, 1997
Oil on canvas
156 × 100 in. (396.3 × 254 cm)
The Estate of Norman Bluhm

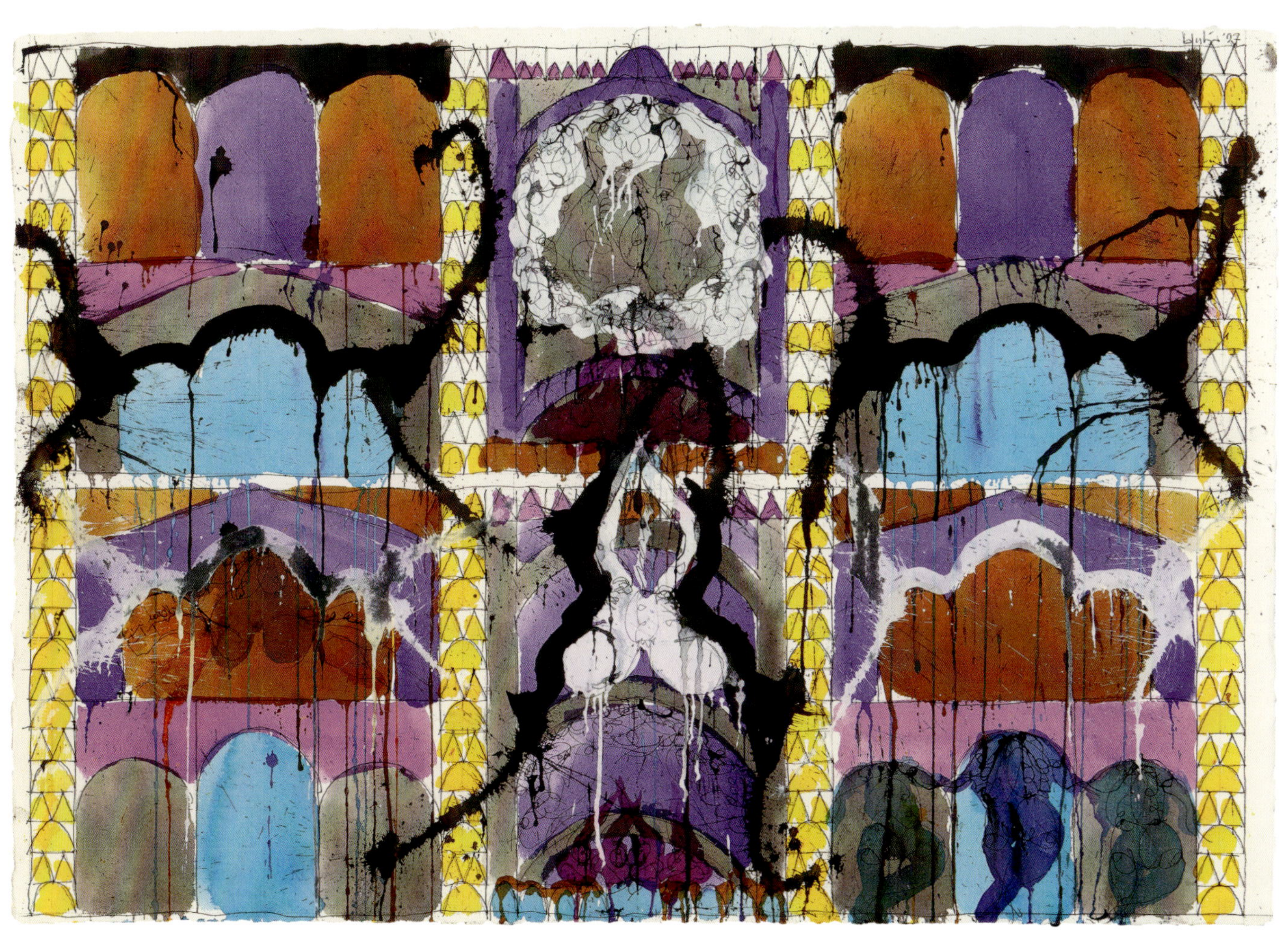

Plate 83

Untitled, 1997
Acrylic and ink on paper
29 ½ × 41 ½ in. (75 × 105.4 cm)
The Estate of Norman Bluhm

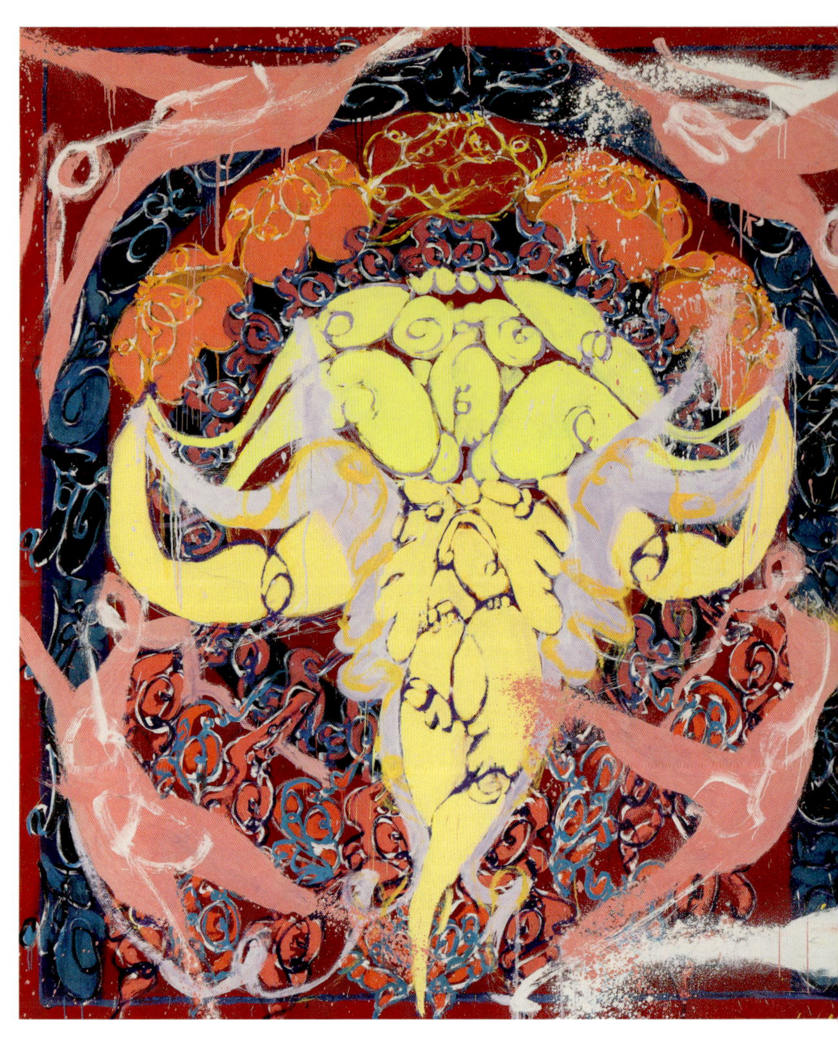

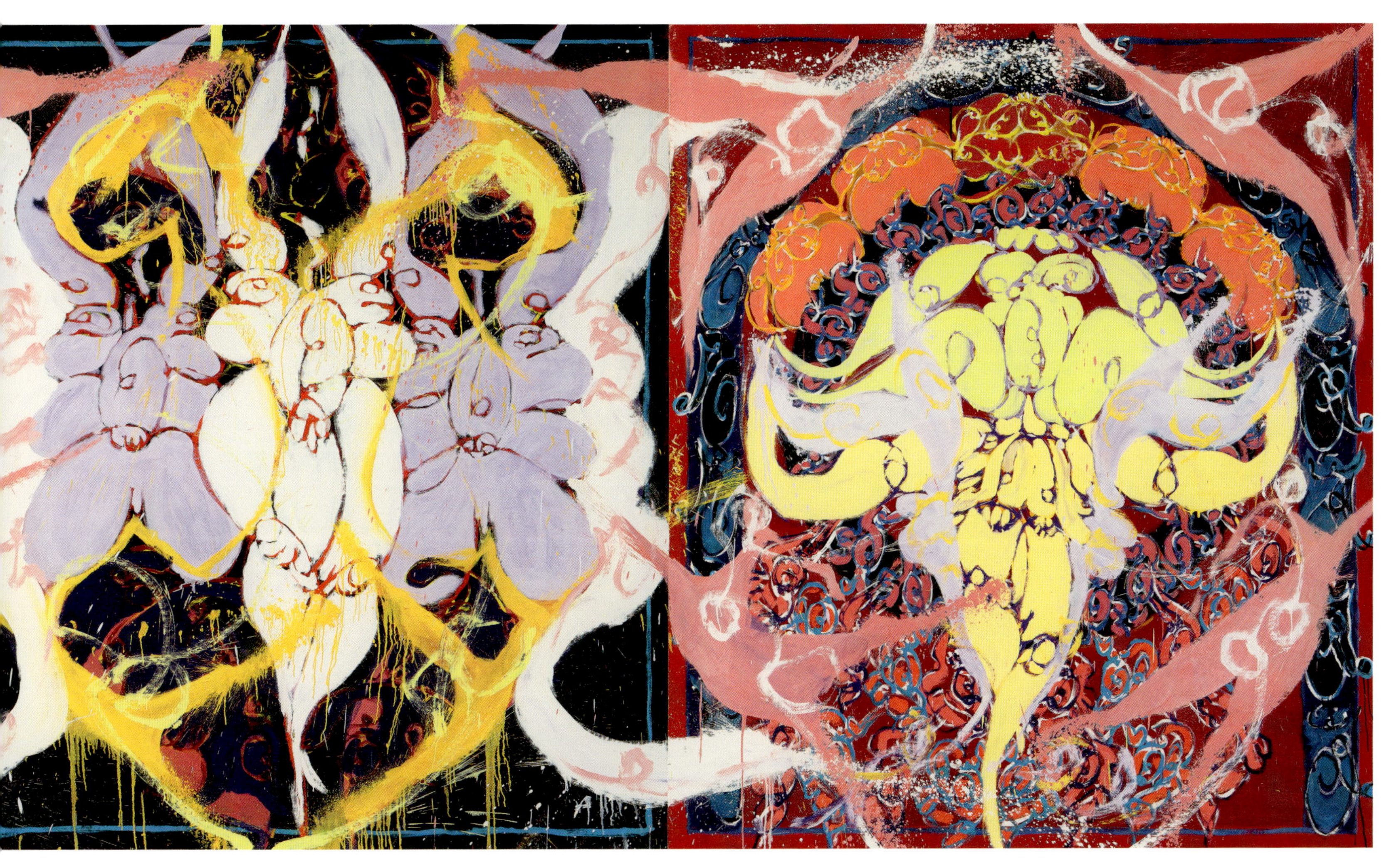

Plate 84

Calliope's Song, 1998
Oil on canvas
Triptych, 84 × 216 in. (213.4 × 548.6 cm) overall
The Estate of Norman Bluhm

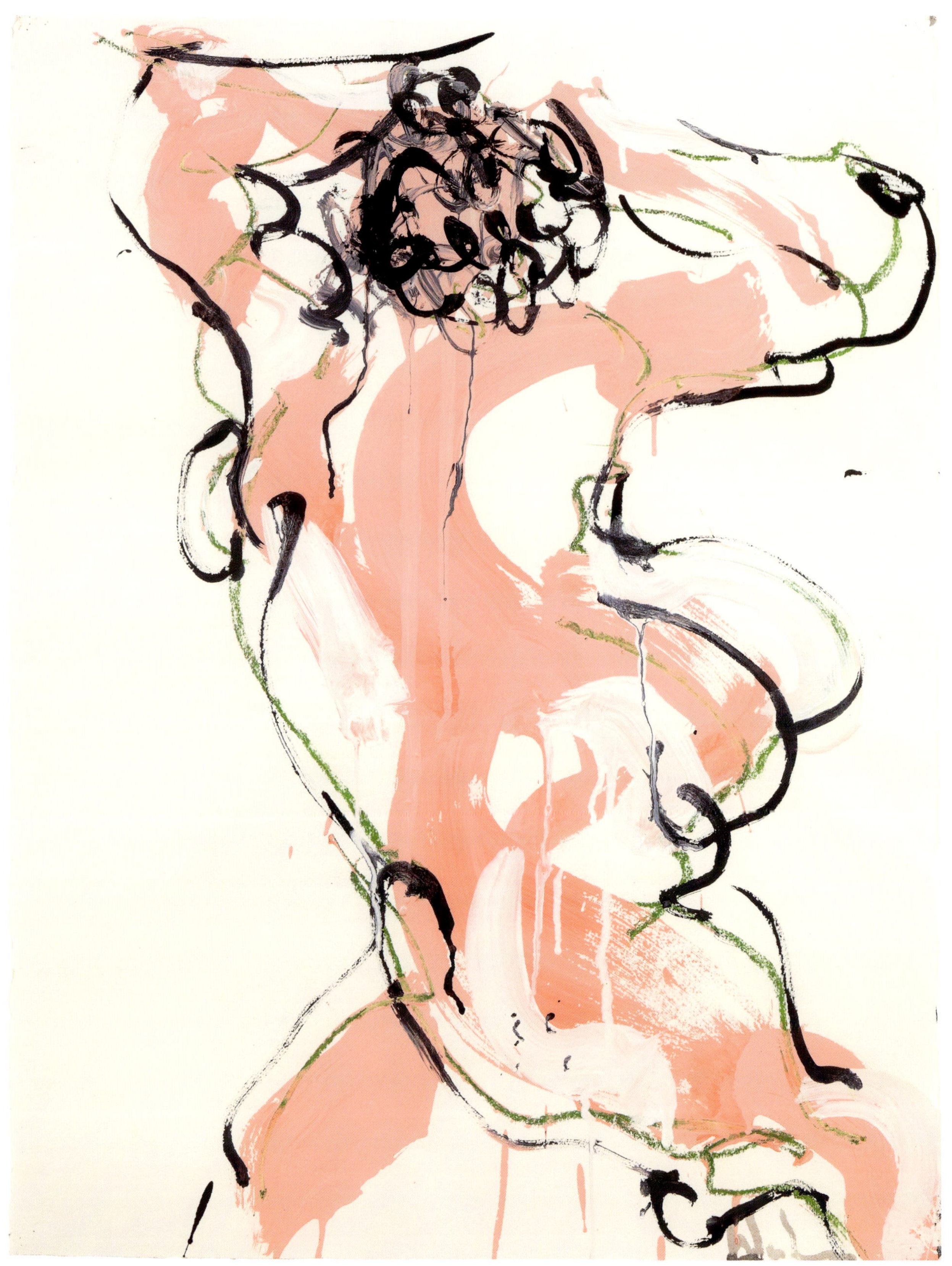

Plate 85

Nude, 1998
Acrylic, ink, and pastel on paper
30 × 22 ½ in. (76 × 57 cm)
The Estate of Norman Bluhm

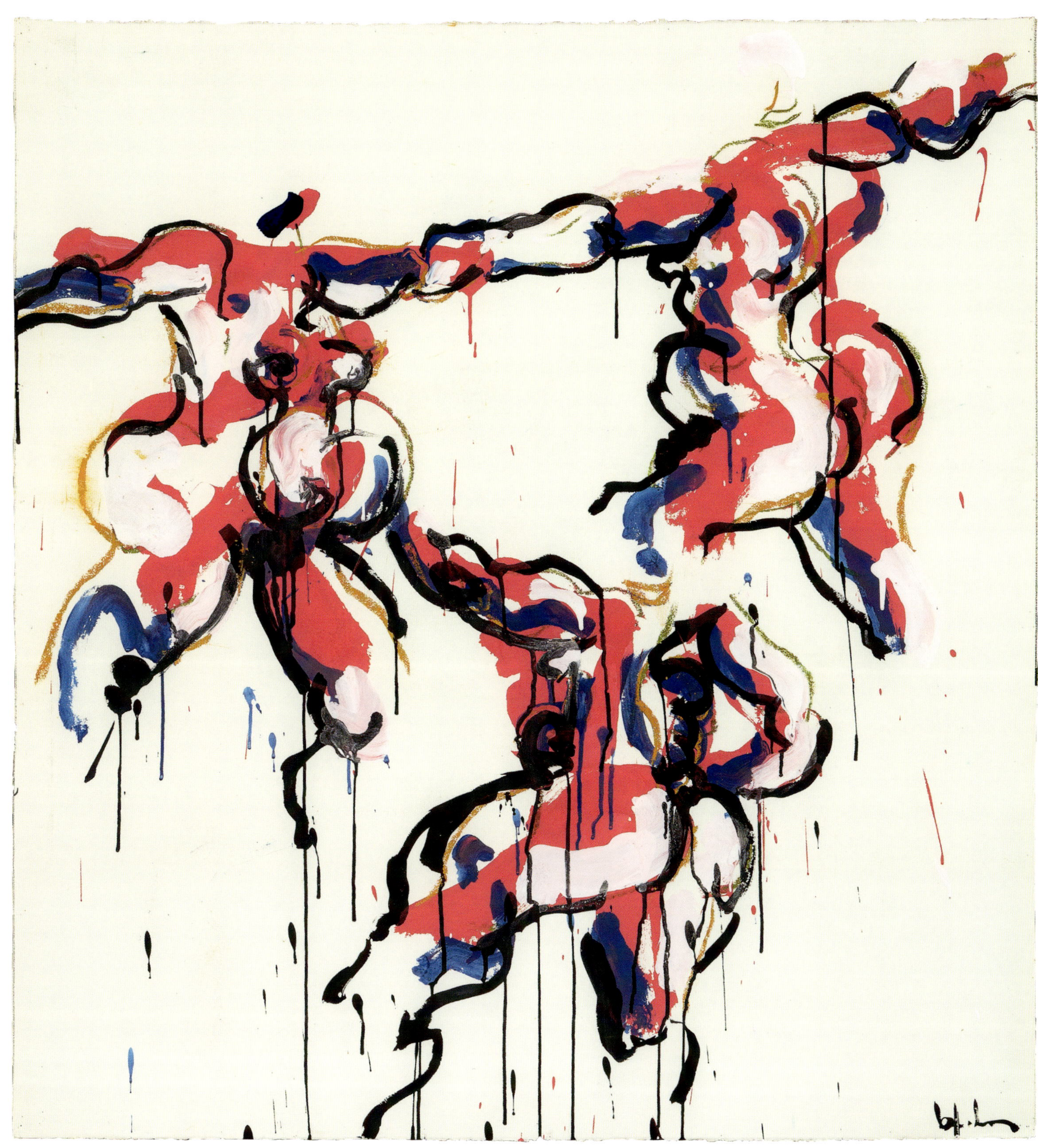

Plate 86

Nudes (*Tabitha Series*), 1998
Acrylic, ink, and pastel on paper
45 × 42 in. (114 × 106.7 cm)
The Estate of Norman Bluhm

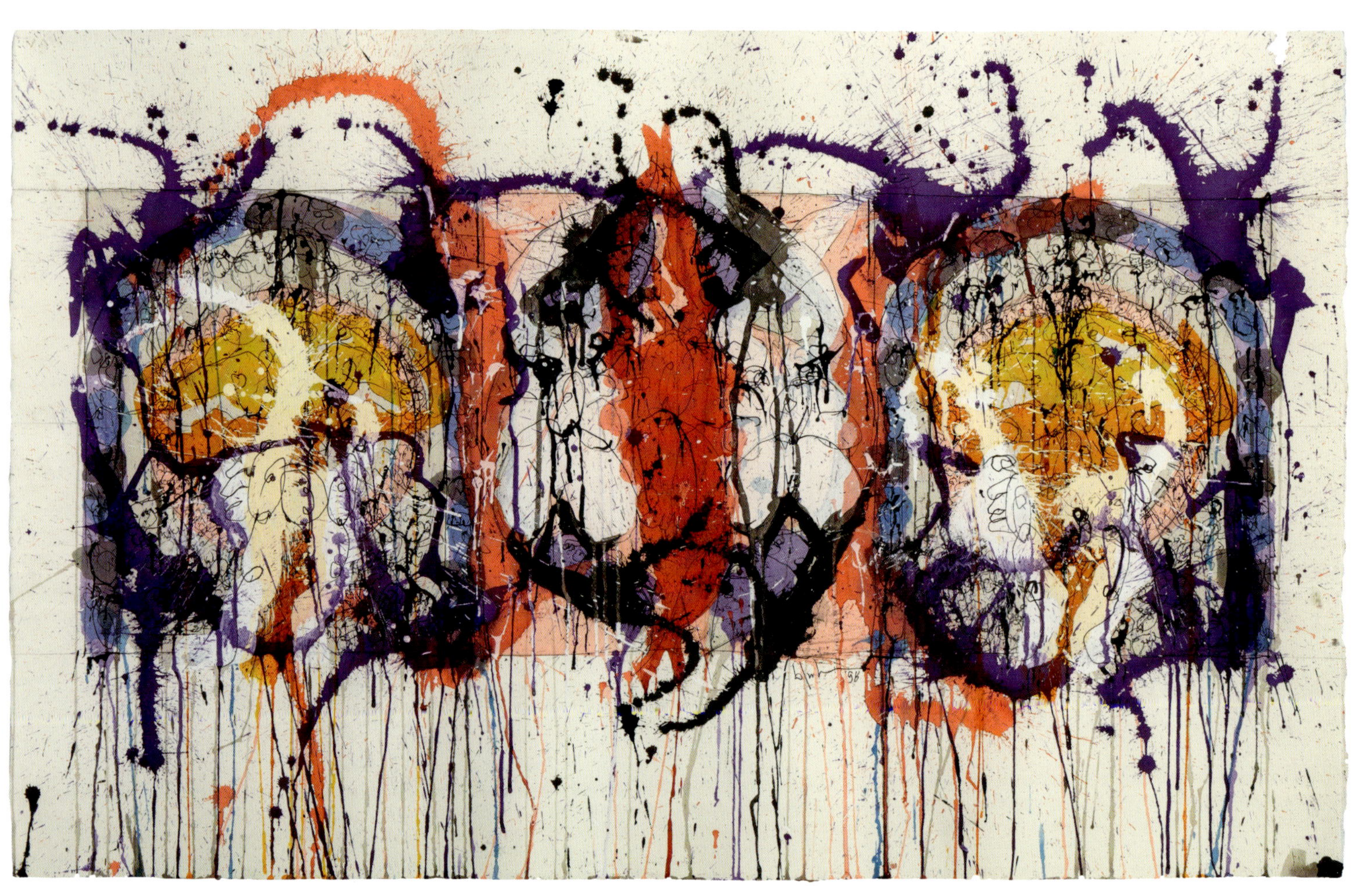

Plate 87

Untitled, 1998
Acrylic and ink on paper
26 × 40 in. (66 × 101.6 cm)
The Estate of Norman Bluhm

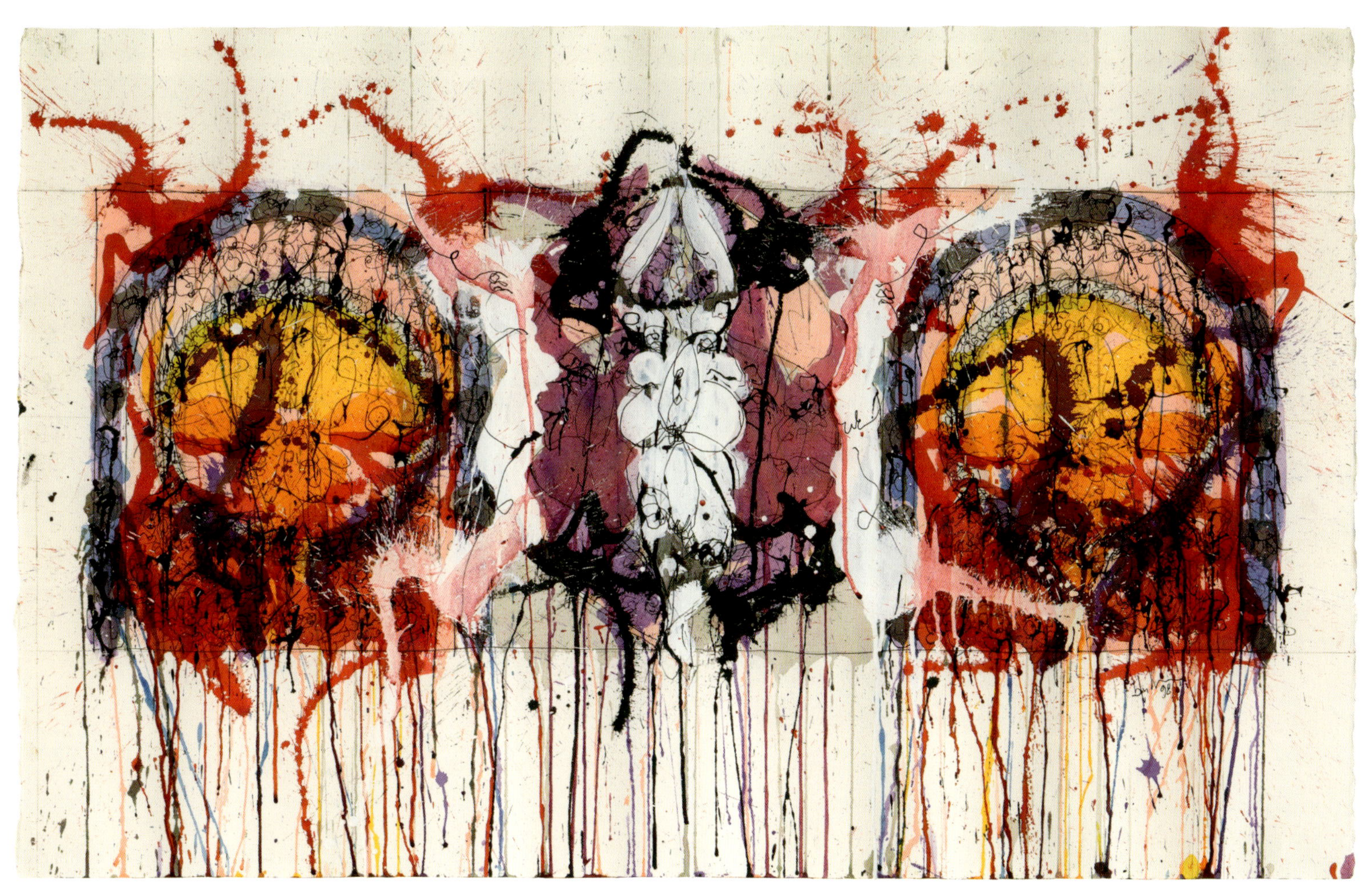

Plate 88

Untitled, 1998
Ink and acrylic on paper
26 × 40 ½ in. (66 × 103 cm)
The Estate of Norman Bluhm

Chronology

Fig. 26
Norman Bluhm, 1958, Springs, Long Island, with his 1929 Dodge. Photo courtesy of The Estate of Norman Bluhm

Fig. 27
Cary, Nina, David and Norman Bluhm leaving New York for France, June 1964. Photo courtesy of The Estate of Norman Bluhm

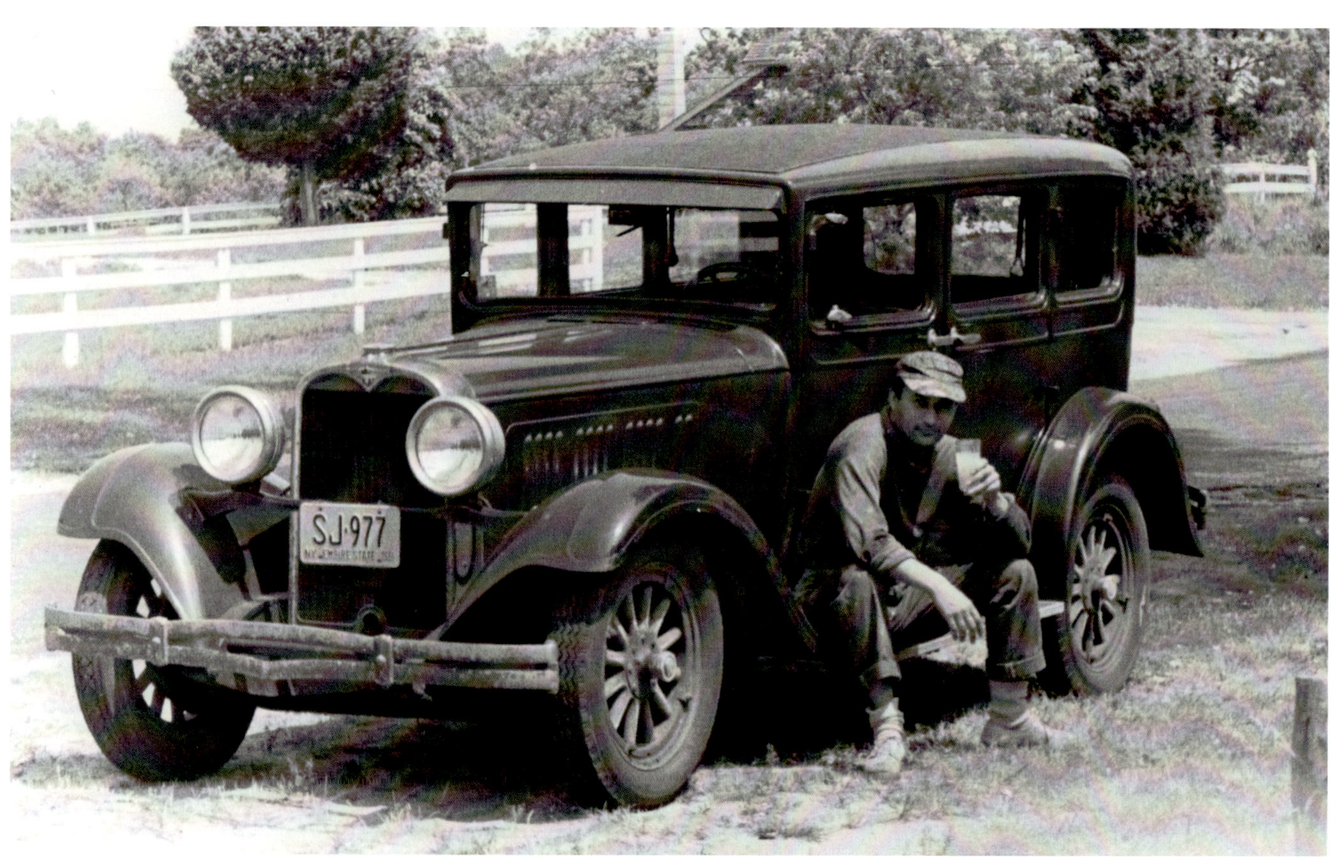

1920 Born March 28 in Chicago, Illinois, to Henry Bluhm and Rosa Goldstein; his birth certificate, obtained later, incorrectly lists his birth year as 1921

Late 1920s Lives in Florence, Italy, with his mother and his younger brother, William, while his father works on an engineering project in the Soviet Union

Early 1930s The Bluhm family returns to Chicago

1936–41 Studies architecture at Armour Institute of Technology. Mies van der Rohe becomes head of the department in 1938; Bluhm attends the first classes taught by Mies at Armour

1941 In late December, enlists in U.S. Army Air Corps, along with his brother William, who is later killed in action

1944 Discharged from the U.S. Army Air Corps

1945 Returns briefly to architectural studies at Armour, then decides to leave the field

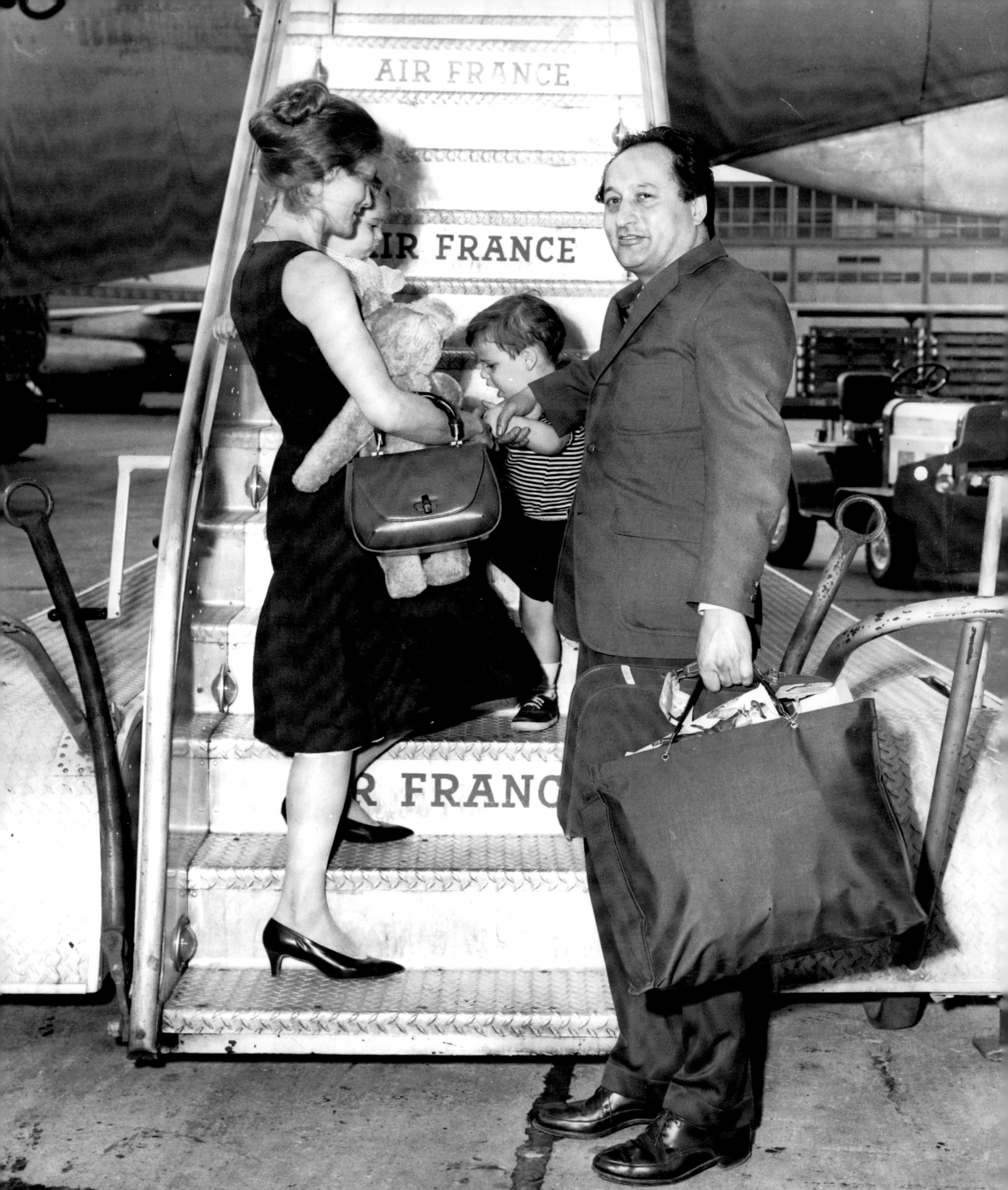
AIR FRANCE
IR FRANCE
R FRANC

Fig. 28
Norman Bluhm and Michael Goldberg in Bluhm's studio, 333 Park Avenue South, New York City, 1960. Photo by Rudolph Burckhardt. © 2019 Estate of Rudy Bruckhardt / Artists Rights Society (ARS), New York

Fig. 29
Norman Bluhm in his Millbrook, New York studio, 1973. Photo by Kerby C. Smith, courtesy of The Estate of Norman Bluhm

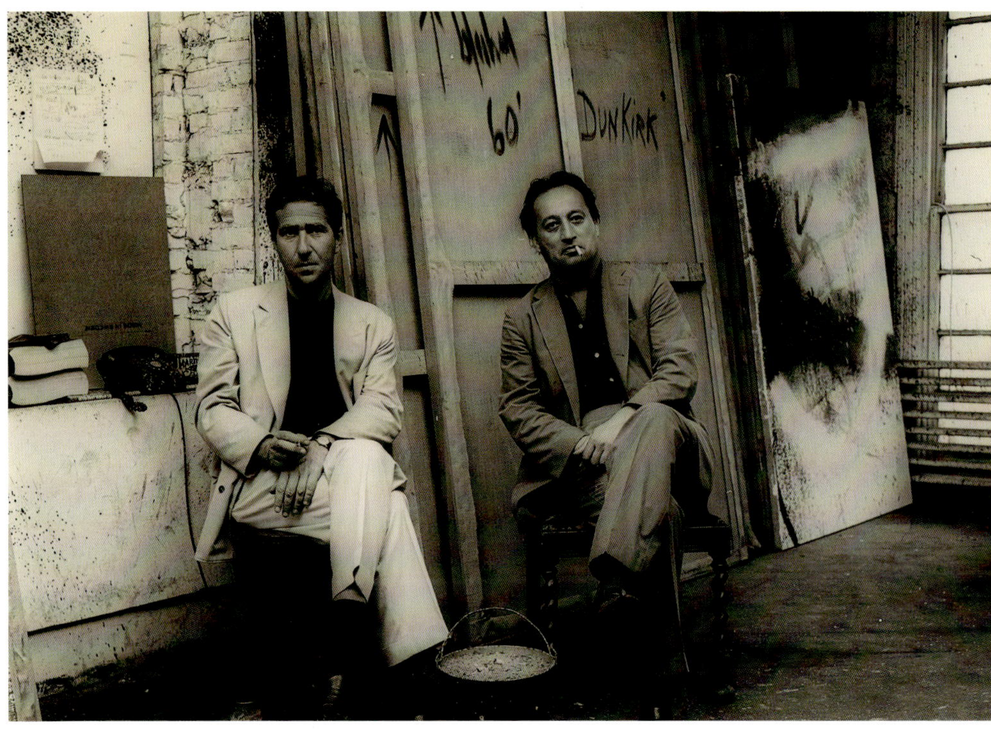

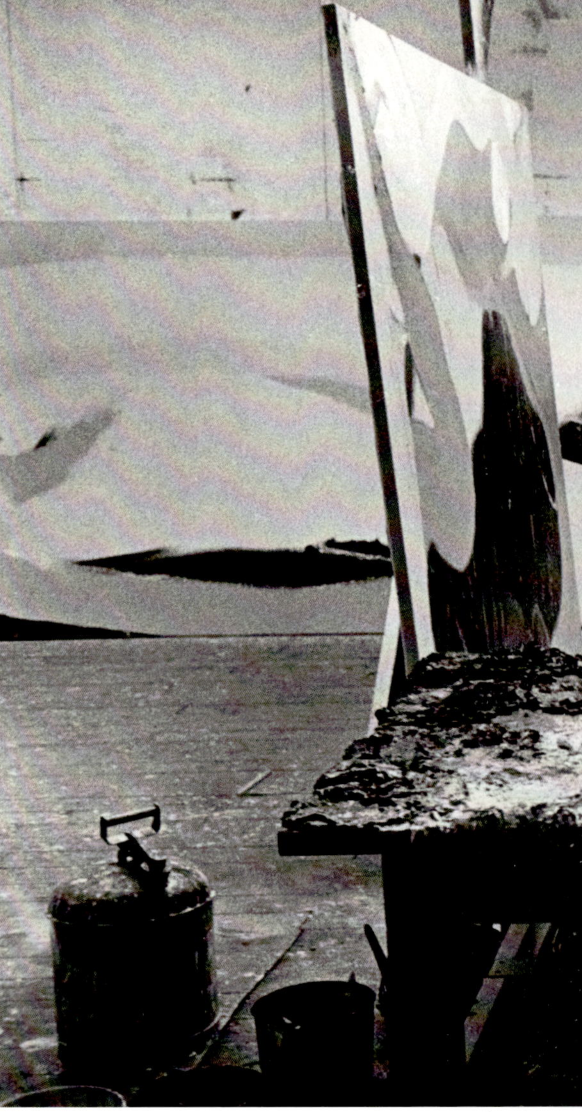

1946–47 Moves to Florence; studies fresco painting at the Accademia di Belle Arti

1947–56 Lives in Paris

Studies at the École des Beaux-Arts and Académie de la Grande Chaumière

1950 Marries Claude Souvrain, an artist with deep ties to the Parisian art world

Exhibits for the first time in a group show, at Centre Américain pour les Artistes, Paris

1953 Included in *Peintres américains en France* at Galerie Craven, Paris

1956 Divorces Claude Souvrain; moves to New York City

1957 Rents a studio at 333 Park Avenue South

First solo show at Leo Castelli Gallery, New York

1958 Rents a summer house in Springs, on the East End of Long Island, with Michael Goldberg across from Green River Cemetery

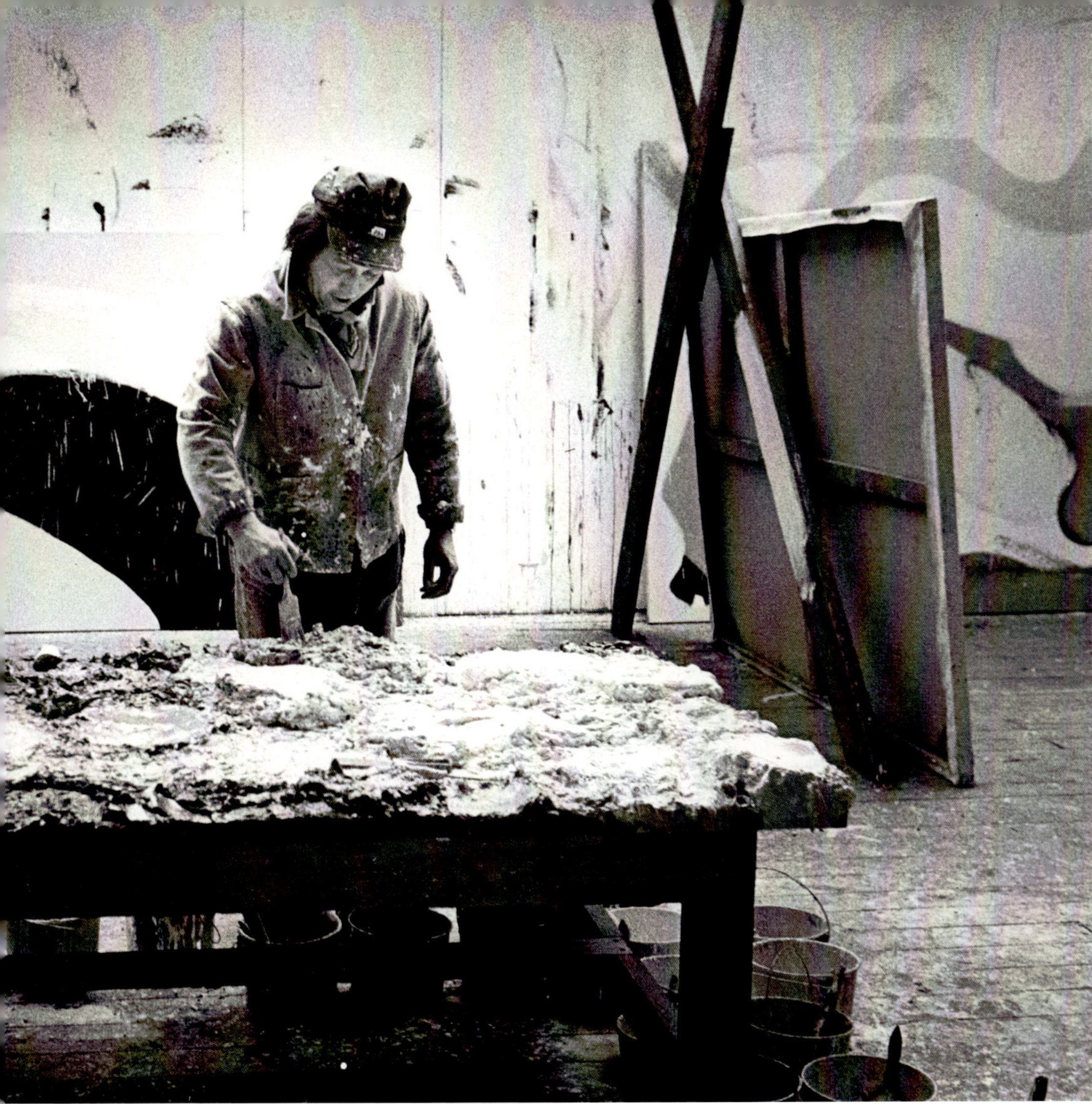

Fig. 30
Norman and Cary Bluhm on their wedding day in Norwalk, Connecticut, 1961. Photo by Mary Rittling, courtesy of The Estate of Norman Bluhm

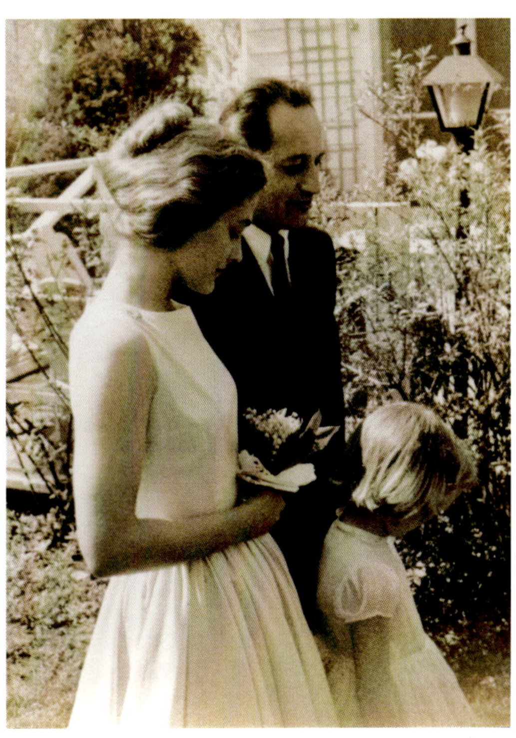

1958–59 Included in the Carnegie International, Pittsburgh; Whitney Museum Annual, New York; and Documenta II, Kassel, Germany. Also included in solo shows in commercial galleries in Los Angeles and Milan, and in group shows at Leo Castelli

1960 Meets Cary Ogle, who was working at Staempfli Gallery on East 77th Street; spends summer in Paris and uses Joan Mitchell's studio on Rue Frémicourt

Included in numerous surveys of contemporary art at American museums, most notably *Sixty American Painters* at the Walker Art Center, Minneapolis. Holds second solo show at Leo Castelli, but breaks off his relationship with the gallery shortly thereafter

1961 Marries Cary Ogle at Shirley Kaplan's mother's house in Norwalk, Connecticut, in May, followed by an extended honeymoon trip in Italy. Guests include Frank O'Hara, Mike Goldberg, Patsy Southgate, and Joe LeSueur

Included in the exhibition *American Abstract Expressionists and Imagists* at the Solomon R. Guggenheim Museum, New York; shows with Elaine de Kooning in a two-person exhibition at Graham Gallery, New York, organized by Joan Washburn

Fig. 31
Norman and Cary Bluhm, Millbrook, New York, 1973. Photo by Kerby C. Smith

Fig. 32
Norman Bluhm in Middletown Springs, Vermont, 1987. Photo by Terry Yank, courtesy of The Estate of Norman Bluhm

Fig. 33
Norman Bluhm in East Hampton, c.1980s, in front of *Easter Morning*, 1979. Photo by Cary Bluhm, courtesy of The Estate of Norman Bluhm

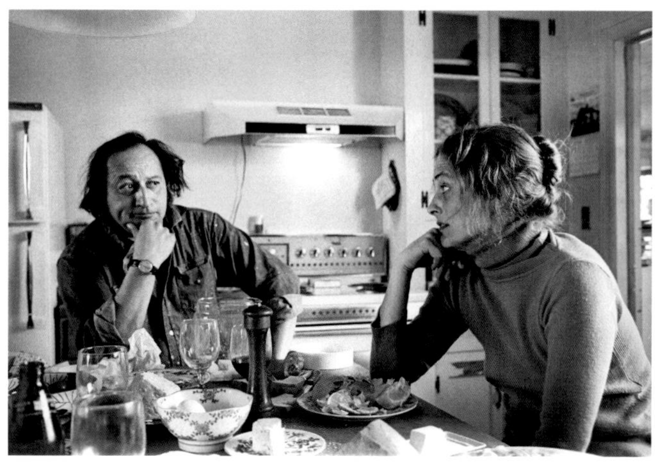

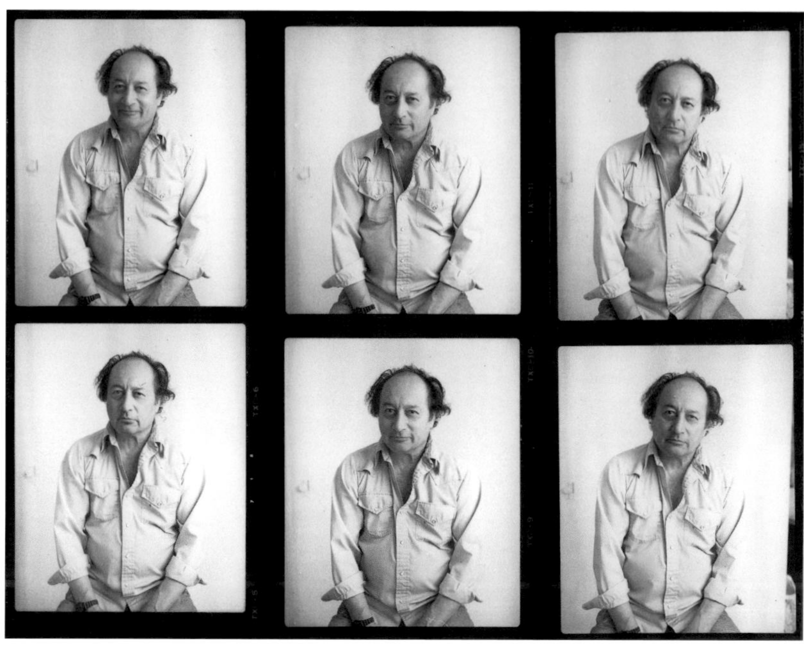

1962 Son David born

Solo show of paintings at David Anderson Gallery, New York

Solo show of watercolors at American Gallery, New York

1963 Daughter Nina born

Solo show at Anderson-Mayer Gallery, Paris; solo shows there again in 1964 and in 1965

1964–65 Moves to Paris with his family and works in studio owned by Galerie Stadler on rue Nationale

1965 Bluhm family returns to New York City

1968 First solo show at Galerie Stadler, Paris, opens during the 1968 student protests; has solo shows there in 1970, 1972, 1975, 1982, and 1988

1969 First monographic museum show at the Corcoran Gallery of Art, Washington, DC, of paintings from the 1960s, organized by James Harithas

Leaves New York with his family for Connecticut, but maintains New York studio

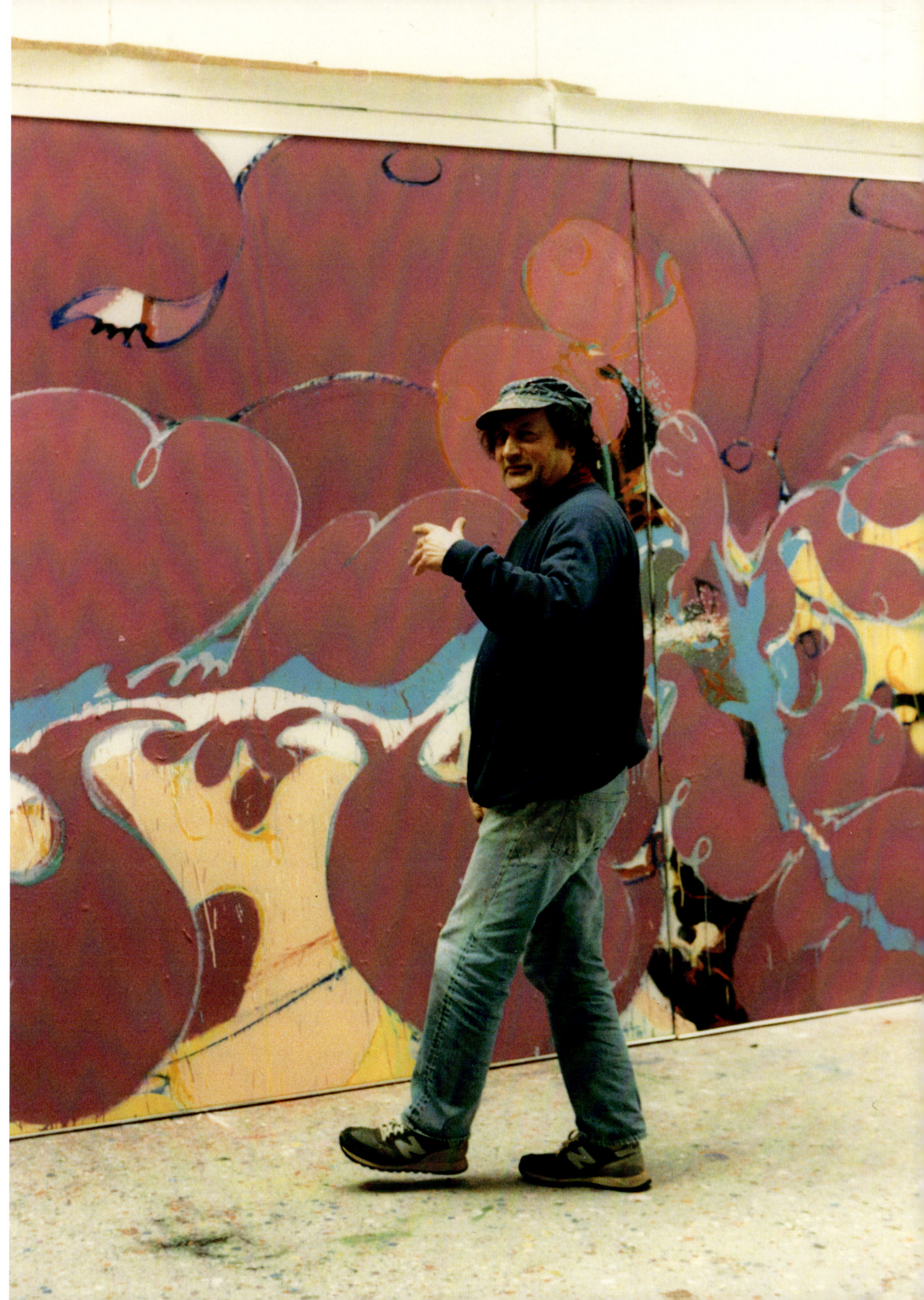

Fig. 34
Norman Bluhm and James Harithas at Bluhm's solo exhibition, Contemporary Arts Museum, Houston, 1976. Photo by Suzanne Paul

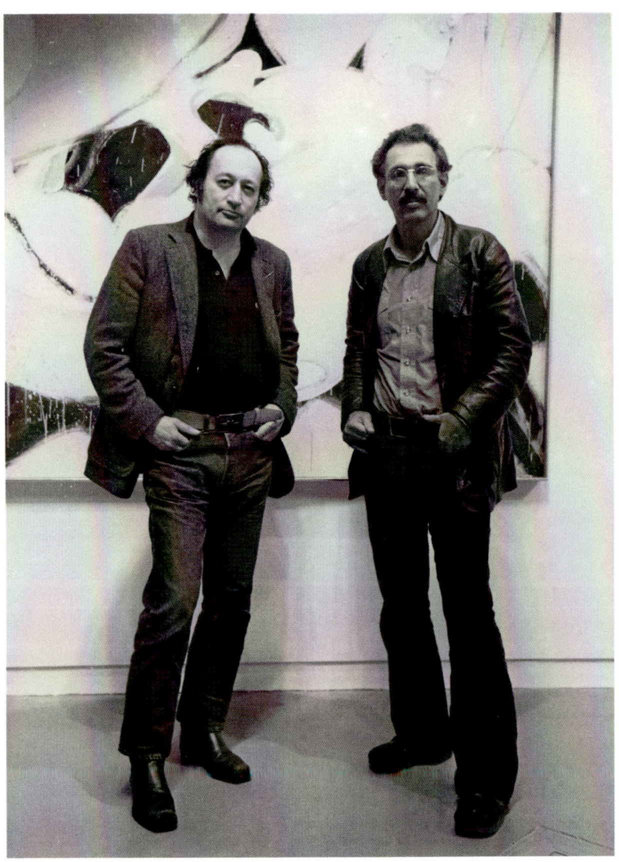

Fig. 35
Norman Bluhm in his Vermont studio with wall of nude drawings, early 1990s. Photo by Cary Bluhm, courtesy of The Estate of Norman Bluhm

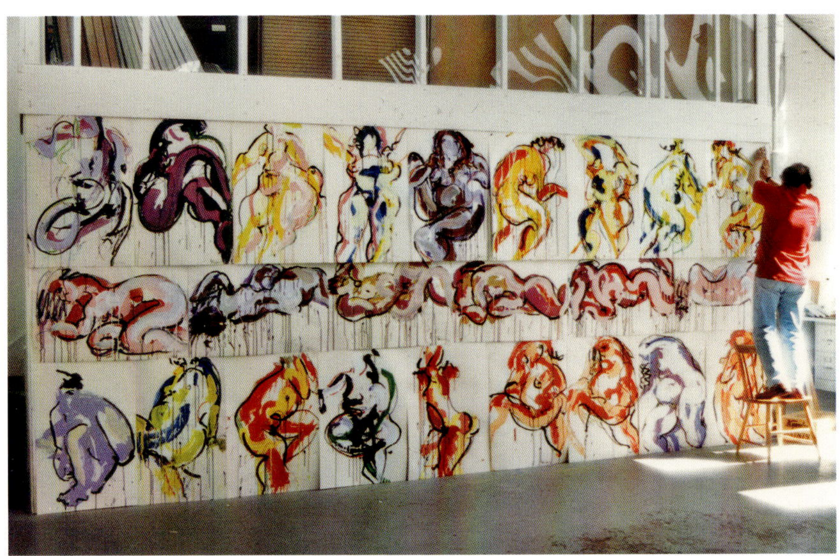

Fig. 36
Norman and Cary and their St. Bernards in East Wallingford, Vermont, 1990s. Photo by David Bluhm, courtesy of The Estate of Norman Bluhm

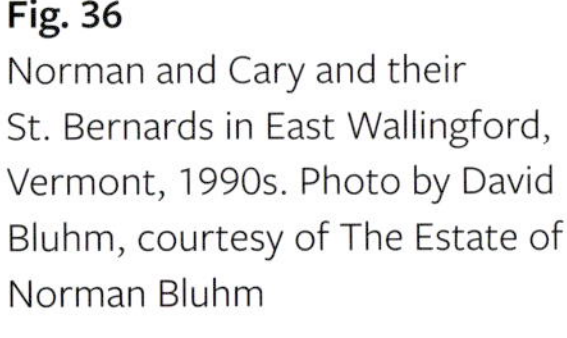

1970 Joins Martha Jackson Gallery, New York (David Anderson, director); has solo shows there in 1970, 1971, 1972, and 1974

Bluhm family moves to a former winery in Millbrook, New York; Bluhm sets up large studio in hayloft of an adjacent barn

1972 Included in the Whitney Annual Exhibition of American Painting

1973 Solo exhibition of recent paintings at Everson Museum of Art, Syracuse, New York, organized by James Harithas (director and curator)

Solo exhibition at the Palazzo delle Prigione Vecchie, Venice, arranged by gallerist Rinaldo Rotta

1976 Solo exhibition of recent paintings at Contemporary Art Museum, Houston, organized by James Harithas

1977 Solo exhibition of recent paintings at the Corcoran Gallery of Art, Washington, DC, organized by Jane Livingston

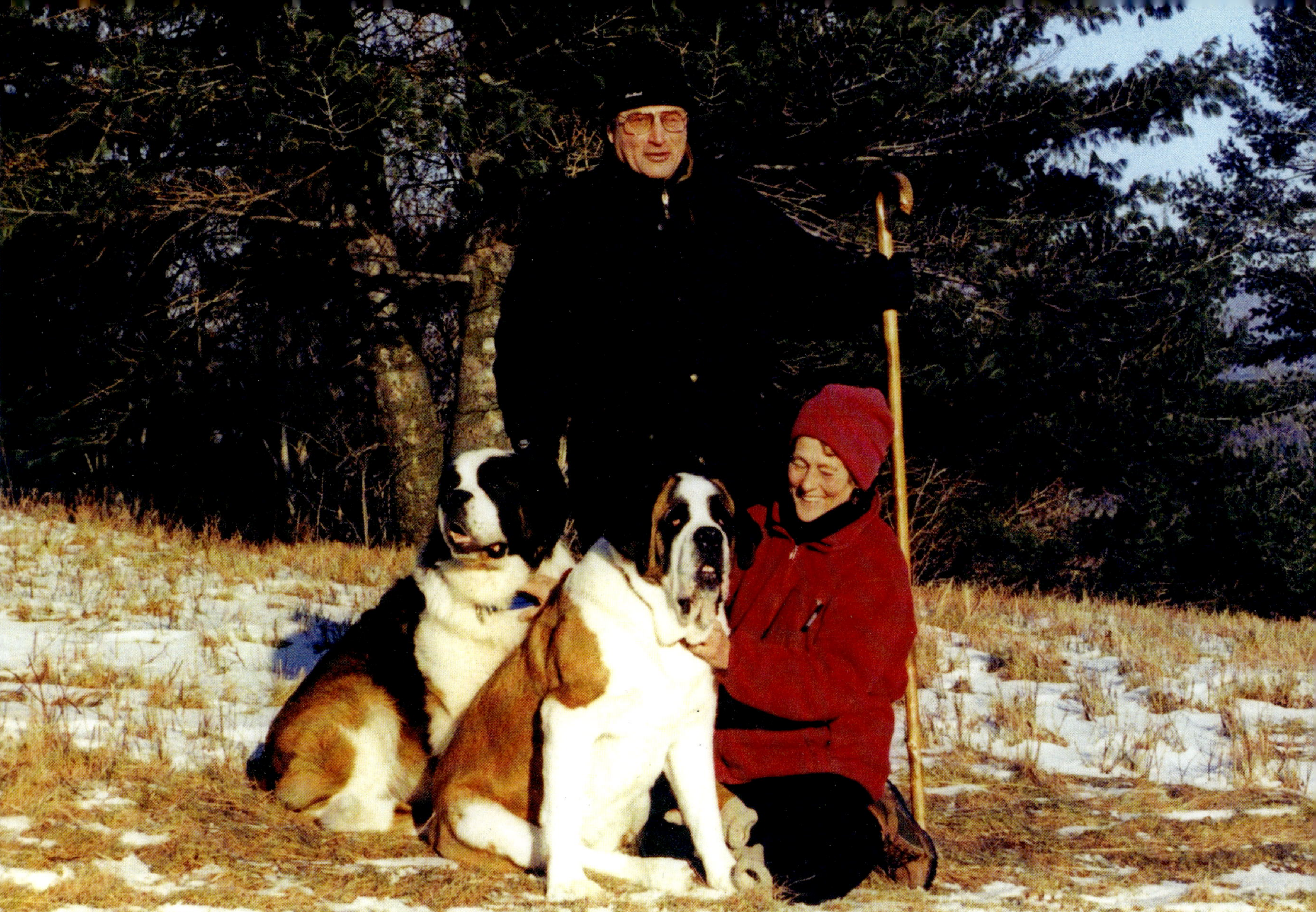

1981 Moves to East Hampton, New York; builds new house and studio

1984 Solo exhibition *Norman Bluhm: Seven from the Seventies* at Staller Center for the Arts, Stony Brook, New York, organized by Rhonda Cooper and Terence Netter

Included in the exhibition *Action/Precision: The New Direction in New York* at the Newport Harbor Museum of Art, California, organized by Paul Schimmel; the exhibition travels to five other venues

1986 Joins Washburn Gallery, New York; has solo shows there in 1986, 1989, 1990, and 1991

Moves to Middletown Springs, Vermont, with Cary

1987 Solo exhibition, *Norman Bluhm: Works on Paper, 1947–1987*, at Emerson Gallery, Hamilton College, Clinton, New York, organized by William Salzillo; exhibition travels to six other venues

1988 Moves to a renovated nineteenth-century house in East Wallingford, Vermont, and builds a large new studio

Fig. 37
Norman Bluhm on his Vermont studio steps with his St. Bernards, 1990. Photo by Cary Bluhm, courtesy of The Estate of Norman Bluhm

Fig. 38
Norman Bluhm in Bangkok, Thailand, c. 1995–96. Photo courtesy of The Estate of Norman Bluhm

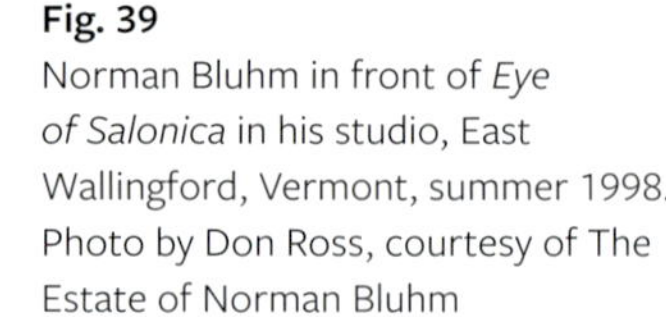

Fig. 39
Norman Bluhm in front of *Eye of Salonica* in his studio, East Wallingford, Vermont, summer 1998. Photo by Don Ross, courtesy of The Estate of Norman Bluhm

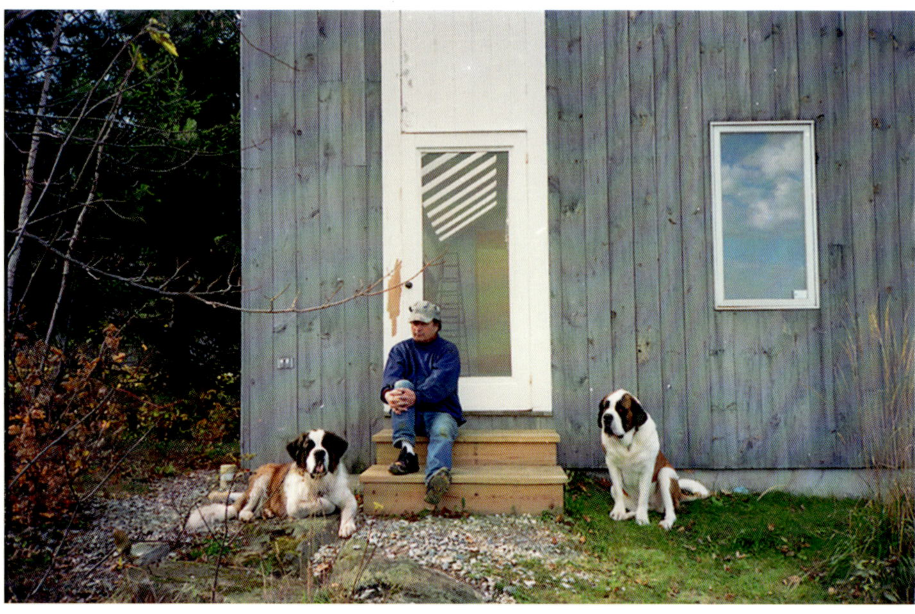

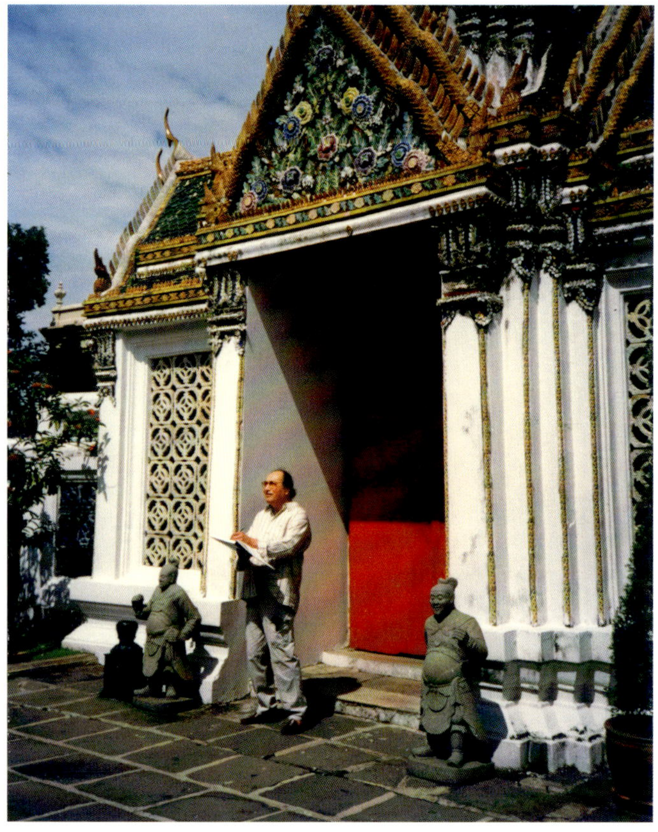

1992 Joins Galleria Peccolo, Livorno, Italy; has solo shows there in 1992, 1995, and 1998

Solo show at David Anderson Gallery, Buffalo, New York

1994 Solo shows at Ace Gallery, New York and Los Angeles

1999 On February 3, Bluhm dies unexpectedly at his home in East Wallingford

The Butler Institute, Youngstown, Ohio, exhibits *Norman Bluhm: A Tribute Exhibition*, organized by Louis Zona and Jim Harithas

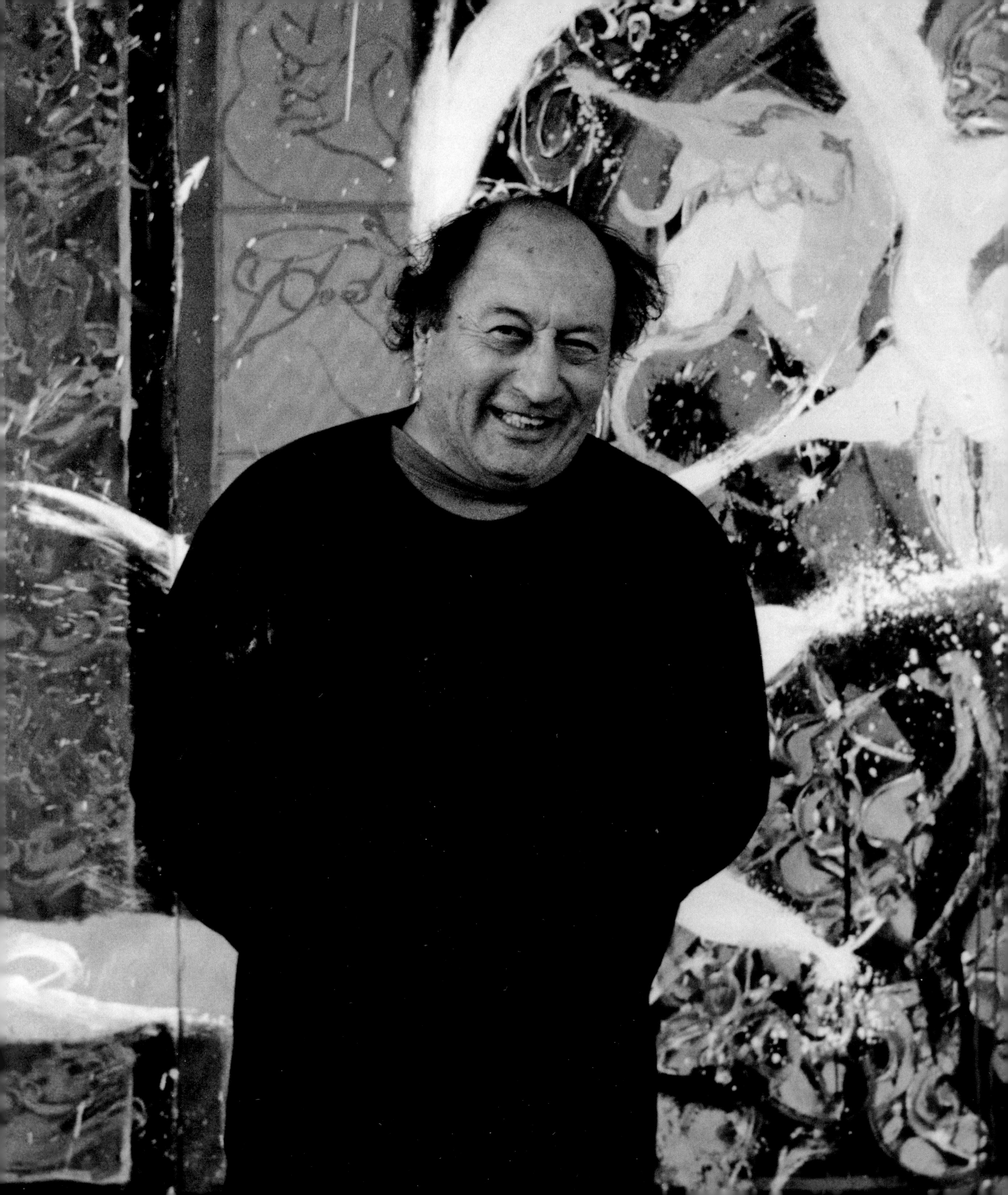

Exhibition Checklist

Cimitière de Montparnasse, 1947
Oil on canvas
32 ½ × 39 ½ in. (82.5 × 100.3 cm)
The Estate of Norman Bluhm

Untitled (*Two Seated Nudes*), 1949
Ink on paper
12 ¼ × 17 ¼ in. (31.1 × 43.8 cm)
The Estate of Norman Bluhm

Notre Dame, 1950
Ink and watercolor on paper
15 × 22 in. (38 × 56 cm)
The Estate of Norman Bluhm

Rooftops, 1950
Ink and watercolor on paper
22 × 15 in. (56 × 38 cm)
The Estate of Norman Bluhm

Untitled, 1952
Watercolor on paper
8 ½ × 10 ½ in. (21.6 × 26.7 cm)
The Estate of Norman Bluhm

Bleeding Rain, 1956
Oil on canvas
51 ¼ × 64 in. (129.5 × 162.5 cm)
Herbert F. Johnson Museum of Art, Cornell University, Ithaca, New York
Gift of Katherine Komaroff Goodman
77.074.001

Stained Glass Landscape #10, 1957
Watercolor on paper
Triptych, 30 × 66 in. (76 × 167.6 cm) overall
Private collection

Squall, 1958
Oil on canvas
72 × 96 in. (183 × 244 cm)
Collection of the Neuberger Museum of Art, Purchase College, State University of New York *1970.02.04*

Study for Clouds of Magellan, 1958
Watercolor on paper
30 × 22 in. (76 × 56 cm)
The Estate of Norman Bluhm

The Anvil, 1959
Oil on canvas
84 × 72 in. (213.3 × 183 cm)
Whitney Museum of American Art, New York
Purchase, with funds from the Friends of the Whitney Museum of American Art *60.22*

Untitled, 1959
Ink and gouache on brown paper
47 ½ × 39 ½ in. (120.6 × 100.3 cm)
Metropolitan Museum of Art, New York
Purchased by Longview Foundation Inc., in memory of Audrey Stern Hess, 1977 *77.368*

Norman Bluhm and Frank O'Hara
It's Raining, 1960
Gouache and ink on brown paper
48 × 40 in. (122 × 102 cm)
Metropolitan Museum of Art, New York
Gift of Mr. and Mrs. Norman Bluhm, 1984 *84.333*

Peacock, 1964
Oil on canvas
90 × 78 in. (228.6 × 198 cm)
The Newark Museum of Art, New Jersey
Purchase 1987 Special Acquisition Fund *87.40*

Himalayas, 1966
Oil on canvas
Triptych, 72 x 108 in. (183 x 274.3 cm) overall
Courtesy of Manny Silverman Gallery, Los Angeles, Graham Shay Gallery, New York, and The Estate of Norman Bluhm

Study for Brizo, 1967
Acrylic on paper
30 × 22 ½ in. (76 × 57 cm)
The Estate of Norman Bluhm

Untitled, Study for Isaac Commenus, 1967
Acrylic on paper
30 × 22 ½ in. (76 × 57 cm)
The Estate of Norman Bluhm

Untitled, 1967
Acrylic and ink on paper
30 × 22 ½ in. (76 × 57 cm)
The Estate of Norman Bluhm

Untitled, 1967
Acrylic on paper
29 ½ × 23 ¼ in. (75 × 59 cm)
The Newark Museum of Art, New Jersey
Gift of Ruth Bowman, 1996 *96.6.1*

Theodora, 1967
Oil on canvas
90 × 80 in. (228.6 × 203 cm)
The Estate of Norman Bluhm

Nude, 1970s
Acrylic and pastel on paper
24 × 18 in. (61 × 46 cm)
The Estate of Norman Bluhm

Nude, 1970s
Acrylic and pastel on paper
24 × 18 in. (61 × 46 cm)
The Estate of Norman Bluhm

Philomela, 1972
Oil on canvas
96 × 108 in. (244 × 274.5 cm)
The Estate of Norman Bluhm

Untitled, Studies in Blue, White, Gray, 1975
Oil on canvas
Four panels, 48 × 240 in.
(122 × 609.6 cm) overall
The Estate of Norman Bluhm

Sooty Lady, 1978
Oil on canvas
76 × 106 in. (193 × 269.2 cm)
The Estate of Norman Bluhm

Golden Flaxen Maiden, 1978
Oil on canvas
89 × 76 in. (226 × 193 cm)
Collection of Mr. Anthony Scotto

Nude, 1979
Acrylic, ink, and pastel on paper
24 × 36 in. (61 × 91.5 cm)
The Estate of Norman Bluhm

Nude, 1981
Acrylic, ink, pastel on paper
36 × 24 in. (91.4 × 61 cm)
The Estate of Norman Bluhm

Nude, 1982
Acrylic, ink, pastel on paper
36 × 24 in. (91.4 × 61 cm)
The Estate of Norman Bluhm

Dante's Promenade, 1984
Oil on canvas
Triptych, 84 × 216 in.
(213.4 × 549 cm) overall
The Estate of Norman Bluhm

Nude, 1985
Acrylic, ink, and pastel on paper
36 × 24 in. (91.4 × 61 cm)
The Estate of Norman Bluhm

Drawing #7, 1985
Acrylic and pastel on paper
49 ½ × 60 in. (125.7 × 152.4 cm)
The Estate of Norman Bluhm

Fresco #13, 1987
Acrylic and pastel on paper
60 × 50 in. (152.4 × 127 cm)
The Estate of Norman Bluhm

Fresco #15, 1987
Acrylic and pastel on paper
60 × 50 in. (152.5 × 127 cm)
The Estate of Norman Bluhm

Norman Bluhm and John Yau
Sam Spade Haiku #1, 1987
Acrylic, ink, and pastel on paper
26 ¼ × 59 ¾ in. (66.7 × 152 cm)
The Estate of Norman Bluhm

Aegean Angel, 1988
Oil on canvas
66 × 66 in. (167.6 × 167.6 cm)
The Estate of Norman Bluhm

Reine de Provence, 1989
Oil on canvas
72 × 144 in. (182.8 × 365.8 cm)
The Estate of Norman Bluhm

Study II, 1990
Acrylic and pastel on paper
58 × 44 ¾ in. (147.3 × 113.6 cm)
The Estate of Norman Bluhm

Untitled, 1994
Ink on paper
22 × 30 in. (56 × 76.2 cm)
The Estate of Norman Bluhm

Untitled, 1994
Ink on paper
22 × 30 in. (56 × 76.2 cm)
The Estate of Norman Bluhm

Persephone, 1995
Oil on canvas
Triptych, 120 × 300 in.
(305 × 762 cm) overall
The Estate of Norman Bluhm

Untitled, 1997
Acrylic and ink on paper
29 ½ × 41 ½ in. (74.9 × 105.4 cm)
The Estate of Norman Bluhm

Ode to Apollo, 1997
Oil on canvas
156 × 100 in. (396.3 × 254 cm)
The Estate of Norman Bluhm

Eye of Salonica, 1998
Oil on canvas
Triptych, 72 × 252 in.
(183 × 640 cm) overall
The Estate of Norman Bluhm

Untitled, 1998
Ink and acrylic on paper
26 × 40 ½ in. (66 × 103 cm)
The Estate of Norman Bluhm

Nudes (*Tabitha Series*), 1998
Acrylic, ink, and pastel on paper
45 × 42 in. (114 × 106.7 cm)
The Estate of Norman Bluhm

Selected Bibliography

Selected Monographs and Gallery Catalogues/Brochures for Solo Shows

1959 O'Hara, Frank, and Dore Ashton. Milan: Galleria del Naviglio.

1961 Tapié, Michel. *10 Dipinti de Norman Bluhm*. Turin: Associazione Arti Figurative.

1965 Hess, Thomas. Paris: Galerie Anderson-Mayer.

1967 Berkson, Bill. *Poem-Paintings by Frank O'Hara and Norman Bluhm*. New York: New York University/ Loeb Student Center.

1968 Schneider, Pierre. *Norman Bluhm*. Paris: Galerie Stadler.

1969 Agee, William C. *Paintings by Norman Bluhm at the Corcoran Gallery of Art, Washington, DC*. Baltimore: Garamond/ Pridemark Press.

1973 Hess, Thomas, and James Harithas (preface). *Norman Bluhm at the Everson Museum of Art, Syracuse University*. Syracuse: Everson Museum of Art.

1974 Schjeldahl, Peter. *L'evoluzione di Norman Bluhm*. Milan: Il Cerchio Galleria d'Arte Moderna; and Venice: Palazzo delle Prigione Vecchie.

1976 Harithas, James, and Paul Schimmel. Houston: Contemporary Arts Museum.

1977 Livingston, Jane. *Norman Bluhm*. Washington, DC: Corcoran Gallery of Art.

1984 Myers, John Bernard. *Norman Bluhm: Seven from the Seventies*. Stony Brook: Fine Arts Center, State University of New York.

1986 Washburn Gallery, New York

1987 Salzillo, William, and John Yau. *Norman Bluhm: Works on Paper, 1947–1987*. Clinton, N.Y.: Hamilton College.

Yau, John. *Poem Prints: Norman Bluhm and John Yau*. New York: Cone Editions.

1989 Washburn Gallery, New York

1990 Washburn Gallery. *Norman Bluhm: The 1950s*. New York: Washburn Gallery. Reprinted Frank O'Hara poem.

1991 Washburn Gallery. *Norman Bluhm: Paintings, 1960–65*. New York: Washburn Gallery. Reprinted Bill Berkson poem.

1992 Rubinstein, Raphael. *Norman Bluhm: Works on Paper, 1967–1991*. Livorno: Galleria Peccolo.

1995 Tedeschi, Francesco. *Norman Bluhm: Opere, 1993–1995*. Milan: Studio d'Arte Zanoletti.

1998 Ferdani, Roberto, and Norman Bluhm.*Norman Bluhm: Opere, 1959–1967*. Livorno: Galleria Peccolo.

1999 Harithas, James. *Norman Bluhm: A Tribute Exhibition*. Youngstown, Ohio: The Butler Institute of American Art.

2000 Harithas, James, Raphael Rubinstein, and Luigi Sansone. *Norman Bluhm*. Milan: Mazzotta. Extensive biographical and bibliographic notes compiled by Cary Bluhm.

Harithas, James, and John Yau. *Norman Bluhm: Opere su carta, 1948–1999*. Milan: Mazzotta, Padiglione d'Arte Contemporanea di Milano.

2005 Finnerty, Amy. *Works on Paper from the 70s, 80s and 90s from the Estate of Norman Bluhm*. New York: James Graham & Sons.

2009 Yau, John. *Norman Bluhm: A Retrospective of Works on Paper*. New York: Jacobson Howard Gallery; Houston: Robert McClain Gallery.

Norman Bluhm: Gestural Structures, 1960–1965. Berlin: Kunsthandel Wolfgang Werner.

2011 Yau, John. *Norman Bluhm: Paintings, 1967–1974*. New York: Loretta Howard Gallery.

2015 Grimm, Jay. *Norman Bluhm: Divine Proportion*. New York: Christie's.

2019 Yau, John. *Norman Bluhm: The 70s*. New York: Hollis Taggart Gallery.

Selected Books and Periodicals

The 1958 Pittsburgh International Exhibition of Contemporary Paintings and Sculpture. Pittsburgh: Department of Fine Arts, Carnegie University, 1958

Abrams, Amah-Rose. "Why Haven't You Heard of Norman Bluhm?" *artnet news*, June 8, 2016, https://news.artnet.com/art-world/norman-bluhm-496676.

Aesthetics of Graffiti. San Francisco: San Francisco Museum of Modern Art, 1978.

Alloway, Lawrence. "Gesture Into Form." *ARTnews*, April 1972, pp. 41–44.

Artner, Alan G. “Norman Bluhm at Zolla/Lieberman.” *Chicago Tribune*, October 30, 1986, sec. 5, p. 13.

Ashbery, John. “Norman Bluhm at Anderson-Mayer, Paris.” *New York Herald Tribune*, *Paris* March 13, 1963, p. 5.

———. “Norman Bluhm at Anderson-Mayer.” *New York Herald Tribune Paris*, May 4, 1965, p. 5.

Ashton, Dore. “Art: Group Show at Martha Jackson.” *New York Times*, April 12, 1957, p. 29.

———. “Art: A Local Anthology; ‘New York’ at Castelli.” *New York Times*, May 8, 1957, p. 75.

———. “Art.” *Arts and Architecture*, July 1957, pp. 4, 33, http://www.artsandarchitecture.com/issues/pdf01/1957_07.pdf. [Review of Castelli show]

———. “Art: Norman Bluhm at Castelli.” *New York Times*, October 3, 1957, p. 26.

———. “Art: Group Show at Castelli.” *New York Times*, October 28, 1958, p. 70.

Baker, Kenneth. “Second Generation: Mannerism or Momentum?” *Art in America*, June 1985, pp. 102–11.

Berkson, Bill. “Bluhm Paints a Picture.” *ARTnews*, May 1963, pp. 38–42, 50.

Bluhm, Norman. “Statement.” *It Is*, no. 2 (Autumn 1958): 41; Plates 4, 15.

———. “Is There a New Academy?” *ARTnews*, Summer 1959, p. 37.

———. “A Cahier Note.” *It Is*, no. 5 (Spring 1960): 40.

———. *Yugen*, no. 7 (1961): 64. [Cover illustration]

———. *In Memory of My Feelings: A Selection of Poems by Frank O’Hara*. Edited by Bill Berkson. New York: The Museum of Modern Art, 1967. [Illustration of O’Hara poem]

———. *Big Sky*, no. 6 (1973). [Cover illustration]

———. *Parenthèse*, no. 4. (1975): 204, 206. [Illustration of two poems]

———. *Saturday Night: Bill Berkson Poems, 1960–61*. Berkeley: Sand Dollar, 1975. [Cover illustration]

———. *Paul Auster, Fragments from Cold*. Rhinebeck, N.Y.: Open Studio Print Shop/Parenthèse, 1977.

———. “Homage to Frank O’Hara.” *Big Sky*, no. 11/12 (1978). [Illustrations of Bluhm-O’Hara poem-paintings]

———. *O-Blék: A Journal of Language Arts*, no. 4 (1988). [Cover illustration]

———. *Avec*, no. 4 (1991). [Cover illustration]

“Bluhm at Castelli.” *New York Herald Tribune*, February 2, 1960, p. 20.

Brumer, Miriam. “Norman Bluhm at Martha Jackson.” *Arts Magazine*, May 1970, p. 59.

Case, Richard. “Look, but Don’t Label Art.” *Syracuse Herald-Journal*, March 31, 1973.

Connor, Russell. “Group Portrait: Four Artists of New York State” (videotaped interview). *Cable Arts Foundation*, 1974.

Cotter, Holland. “Norman Bluhm at Washburn.” *Art in America*, October 1989, pp. 213–14.

———. “Obituaries: Norman Bluhm Is Dead at 78; Abstract Expressionist Painter.” *New York Times*, February 6, 1999, p. A16.

Creeley, Robert. “Love’s Labor Won: Norman Bluhm’s Art.” *Artspace*, September/October 1992, pp. 42–42.

Crehan, Hubert. “Norman Bluhm at Castelli.” *ARTnews*, January 1960, p. 13.

Cummings, Paul. “Oral History Interview with Norman Bluhm, Archives of American Art, Smithsonian Institution,” October 23, 1969.

Dannatt, Adrian. “Obituary: Norman Bluhm.” *Independent* (London), February 20, 1999, https://www.independent.co.uk/arts-entertainment/obituary-norman-bluhm-1071937.html.

Davis, Douglas. “The Painters’ Painters.” *Newsweek*, May 13, 1974, pp. 106–07.

de Kooning, Elaine. “5 Participants in a Hearsay Panel: Mitchell, Elaine de Kooning, O’Hara, Goldberg and Bluhm.” *It Is*, no. 3 (Winter/Spring 1959): 59–62.

Documenta II. Volume 1, Malerie. Cologne: M. DuMont Schauberg, 1959.

Edgar, Natalie. “Norman Bluhm at American Gallery.” *ARTnews*, November 1963, p. 13.

———. “Bluhm’s Light.” *ARTnews*, Summer 1967, pp. 48–49, 76–77.

Ferguson, Russell. *In Memory of My Feelings: Frank O’Hara and American Art*. Los Angeles: The Museum of Contemporary Art, 1999.

Fielder, Garland. “The Late Paintings of Norman Bluhm at the Station Museum.” *Glasstire*, April 7, 2007, https://glasstire.com/2007/04/07/the-late-paintings-of-norman-bluhm-at-the-station-museum/.

Forgey, Benjamin. “Norman Bluhm at the Corcoran.” *Washington Star*, June 5, 1977, pp. F20–21.

Frank, Peter. “Norman Bluhm at Martha Jackson.” *Art in America*, July/August 1974, pp. 89–90.

Frasnay, Daniel. *The Artist’s World*. New York: Viking Press, 1969.

French, Christopher. “Norman Bluhm at the Station Museum, Houston.” *ARTnews*, October 2007, p. 221.

Friedman, B. H. "Passages: Young American." *Artforum*, April 1999, p. 30.

Glueck, Grace. "Norman Bluhm at James Graham & Sons." *New York Times*, March 25, 2005, p. E31.

Grimm, Jay. "Interview with Norman Bluhm" (unpublished). March 1992, Norman Bluhm archive, Newark Museum Library.

Gruen, John. "Norman Bluhm at Martha Jackson." *New York Magazine*, April 27, 1970, p. 65.

———. "Norman Bluhm at Martha Jackson." *New York Magazine*, January 18, 1971, p. 49.

Hofmann, George. "Interview with Norman Bluhm." Artists Research Group, Hunter College Oral History Project, July 21, 1997, https://huntercollegeart.org/artists-research-group/norman-bluhm/.

Huntington, Richard. "The Courage to Explore a Drama in Paint." *Buffalo News*, December 30, 1989, https://buffalonews.com/1989/12/30/the-courage-to-explore-a-drama-in-paint/.

———. "Giant Abstract Paintings Reveal Emotions in Full Bluhm." *Buffalo News*, May 24, 1992, https://buffalonews.com/1992/05/24/giant-abstract-paintings-reveal-emotions-in-full-bluhm/.

Johnson, Ken. "Norman Bluhm at Ace." *Art in America*, February 1995, pp. 91–92.

Johnson, Lincoln L. "Corcoran Show of Bluhm's Works Suggests 'A Memory of a Caress.' " *Baltimore Sun*, July 14, 1977, p. B1.

Judd, Donald. "Norman Bluhm at American Gallery." *Arts Magazine*, December 1963, p. 62.

———. "Issues and Commentary." *Art in America* (September 1984): 9–19.

Kimmelman, Michael. "Norman Bluhm 1960–1965 at Washburn." *New York Times*, June 21, 1991, p. C20.

Kline, Katherine. "Perennial Bluhms." *ARTnews*, April 1969, pp. 34–37.

———. "Norman Bluhm at Martha Jackson." *ARTnews*, April 1970, pp. 12–13.

Kramer, Hilton. "Norman Bluhm at Martha Jackson." *New York Times*, January 9, 1971, p. 23.

———. "Norman Bluhm at the Corcoran Museum." *New York Times*, July 12, 1977, p. 37.

Kuspit, Donald. "New York Today: Some Artists Comment." *Art in America*, September/October 1977, pp. 78–79.

———. "Norman Bluhm at Stony Brook." *Art in America*, February 1985, pp. 146–47.

Küster, Ulf. *Action Painting*. Basel: Fondation Beyeler, 2008.

Lichtblau, Charlotte. "Norman Bluhm at Martha Jackson." *Arts Magazine*, February 1971, p. 58.

Long, Robert. "'Norman Bluhm' published by Mazzotta." *East Hampton Star*, June 21, 2001, sec.3, p. 8.

Lowenstein, Drew. "Norman Bluhm at James Graham & Sons." *artcritical*, May 1, 2008, http://www.artcritical.com/2008/05/01/drew-lowenstein-on-norman-bluhm/.

McDarrah, Fred W. *The Artist's World in Pictures*. New York: E. P. Dutton, 1961.

Moser, Charlotte. "Bluhm at CAM Houston." *ARTnews*, May 1976, p. 96.

Mott, Helen D. "Norman Bluhm at Castelli." *Arts Magazine*, February 1960, p. 64.

Muck, Gordon F. "Bluhm Show Major." *Syracuse Post Standard*, April 9, 1973, p. 17.

O'Hara, Frank. "Three Airs (to Norman Bluhm)." *Evergreen Review*, Summer 1959, p. 34.

———. "Art Chronicle." *Kulchur*, no. 5 (Spring 1962): 80–86.

Olson, Craig. "Norman Bluhm at Loretta Howard Gallery." *Brooklyn Rail*, December 11, 2009, https://brooklynrail.org/2009/12/artseen/norman-bluhm-a-retrospective-of-works-on-paper-1948-1998.

Pagel, David. "So Luscious and Lascivious; Bluhm at Manny Silverman Gallery." *Los Angeles Times*, June 29, 2007, p. E29.

Peccolo, Roberto. "Norman Bluhm: Io, F. Kline e W. de Kooning." *Cahiers d'Art*, January/February 1998, pp. 6–17.

Perrault, John. "Poem-Paintings by Norman Bluhm and Frank O'Hara at N.Y.U. Loeb Center." *ARTnews*, February 1967, p. 11.

Peterson, Valerie. "Norman Bluhm and Elaine de Kooning at Graham Gallery." *ARTnews*, April 1961, pp. 36–38

Preston, Malcolm. "Abstracts of Norman Bluhm at SUNY/Stony Brook." *Newsday*, July 25, 1984, sec. 2, p. 43.

Preston, Stuart. "Norman Bluhm at Castelli." *New York Times*, January 30, 1960, p. 19.

———. "Art: 3 Abstract Painters; Norman Bluhm at David Anderson Gallery." *New York Times*, March 30, 1962, p. 36.

Ratcliff, Carter. "NY Letter: Norman Bluhm at Martha Jackson." *Art International*, September 20, 1970, pp. 90, 92.

———. "NY Letter: Norman Bluhm at Martha Jackson." *Art International*, Summer 1972, pp. 74–75.

Raynor, Vivien. "Seven Abstractions by Norman Bluhm on L.I." *New York Times*, July 13, 1984, p. C17.

Richard, Paul. "Norman Bluhm's Powerful New Art." *Washington Post*, June 4, 1977, p. 3.

Rose, Barbara. "Second Generation: Academy and Breakthrough." *Artforum*, September 1965, pp. 53–64.

Rosenberg, Harold. "Tenth Street: A Geography of Modern Art." *ARTnews Annual* 28 (1959): 120–37, 184.

Rubin, William. "Pittsburgh: The Carnegie International." *Art International*, February 1959, pp. 19–22.

Rubinstein, Raphael. "Bluhm's Day." *Art in America*, October 1992, pp. 136–41.

———. "Nine Lives of Painting." *Art in America*, September 1998, pp. 90–99.

———. "Virtuosity in Crisis: Norman Bluhm, Sam Francis and Joan Mitchell Circa 1969." In *Blanton Museum of Art: American Art Since 1900*. Austin: Blanton Museum of Art, University of Texas, 2006.

———. "Reviews; Norman Bluhm at the Station Museum, Houston." *Art in America*, October 2007, p. 220.

———. "Norman Bluhm." *The Silo*, February 12, 2013, https://thesilo.raphaelrubinstein.com/artists/bluhm.

Russell, John. "Norman Bluhm at Martha Jackson." *New York Times*, May 11, 1974, p. 27.

———. "Norman Bluhm at Washburn." *New York Times*, June 13, 1986, p. C32.

Sandler, Irving. "Norman Bluhm at David Anderson Gallery." *ARTnews*, March 1962, p. 13.

Sawin, Martica. "Norman Bluhm at Castelli." *Arts Magazine*, October 1957, p. 59.

Schimmel, Paul. *Action/Precision: The New Direction in New York, 1955–60*. Newport Beach: Newport Harbor Museum, 1984.

Schjeldahl, Peter. "A Dead Style? Bluhm Seems Not to Have Heard." *New York Times*, May 3, 1970, sec. 2, p. 3.

———. "Bluhm's Progress." *Art International*, May 20, 1974, pp. 31, 35, 58.

Schneider, Pierre. "Art News from Paris: Norman Bluhm at Galerie Anderson-Mayer." *ARTnews*, May 1963, p. 46.

———. "Pierre a vu: Norman Bluhm a Galerie Stadler." *L'Express*, June 8–14, 1970, p. 28.

Schuyler, James. " 'New Work' at Castelli." *ARTnews*, May 1957, p. 10.

———. "Norman Bluhm at Castelli." *ARTnews*, October 1957, p. 17.

———. " 'Three: Bluhm, Rauschenberg, Dubuffet' at Castelli." *ARTnews*, April 1959, p. 13.

Schwabsky, Barry. "After the Great Separation." *Arts Magazine*, November 1985, pp. 22–25.

———. "Norman Bluhm and the Eternal Feminine." *Arts Magazine*, Summer 1986, pp. 45–47.

———. "At the End of the Fifties: Four Abstract Painters and the Search for Structure." *Arts Magazine*, Summer 1987, pp. 22–24.

———. "Norman Bluhm; 1960s Paintings at Washburn." *Arts Magazine*, September 1991, p. 61.

———. "Norman Bluhm; A Conversation." *Tema Celeste*, Summer 1992, pp. 70–71.

———. "Norman Bluhm at Ace." *Artforum*, February 1995, pp. 89–90.

Shaw, Lytle and Brian Reed. *Frank O'Hara Now: New Essays on the New York Poet*. Liverpool: Liverpool University Press, 2010.

Shirley, David L. "Rice and Hamburger." *Newsweek*, April 8, 1969, p. 91.

Spada, Sabina. "Recensioni: Norman Bluhm a Studio Zanoletti, Milano." *Tema Celeste*, Spring 1996, p. 66.

Tannous, David. "Norman Bluhm at the Corcoran." *Art in America*, November/December 1977, pp. 139–40.

Tillim, Sidney. "Month in Review: Abstract Expressionists and Imagists at the Guggenheim Museum." *Arts Magazine*, December 1961, pp. 42–43.

The Vincent Melzac Collection. Washington, DC: Corcoran Gallery of Art, 1971.

Wallach, Amei. "A Brawler In Paint." *Newsday*, September 2, 1984, Part II, pp. 1,5,19.

Westfall, Stephen. "Six of the New York School Look Back." *Art in America*, June 1985, pp. 115–17.

Whitney Museum of American Art Annual Exhibition. New York: Whitney Museum of American Art, 1959.

Whitney Museum of American Art Annual Exhibition. New York: Whitney Museum of American Art, 1972.

Wilson, William. "Norman Bluhm at Ace Contemporary." *Los Angeles Times*, March 30, 1994, p. F1.

Yau, John. "Norman Bluhm at SUNY/Stony Brook." *Artforum*, November 1984, pp. 105–06.

———. "Action/Precision: The New Direction in New York, 1955–60." *Artforum*, May 1985, p. 105.

———. "Norman Bluhm at Washburn." *Artforum*, September 1986, pp. 133–34.

———. "Norman Bluhm at Washburn." *Arts Magazine*, October 1989, p. 80.

———. "Norman Bluhm: 1960–1965 at Washburn." *Artforum*, November 1991, pp. 131–32.

———. "Norman Bluhm at James Graham & Sons." *Art on Paper*, July/August 2005, p. 66.

Yau, John, and Jon Gams. "26 Things at Once . . . " *Lingo*, no. 7 (1997): 10–18.

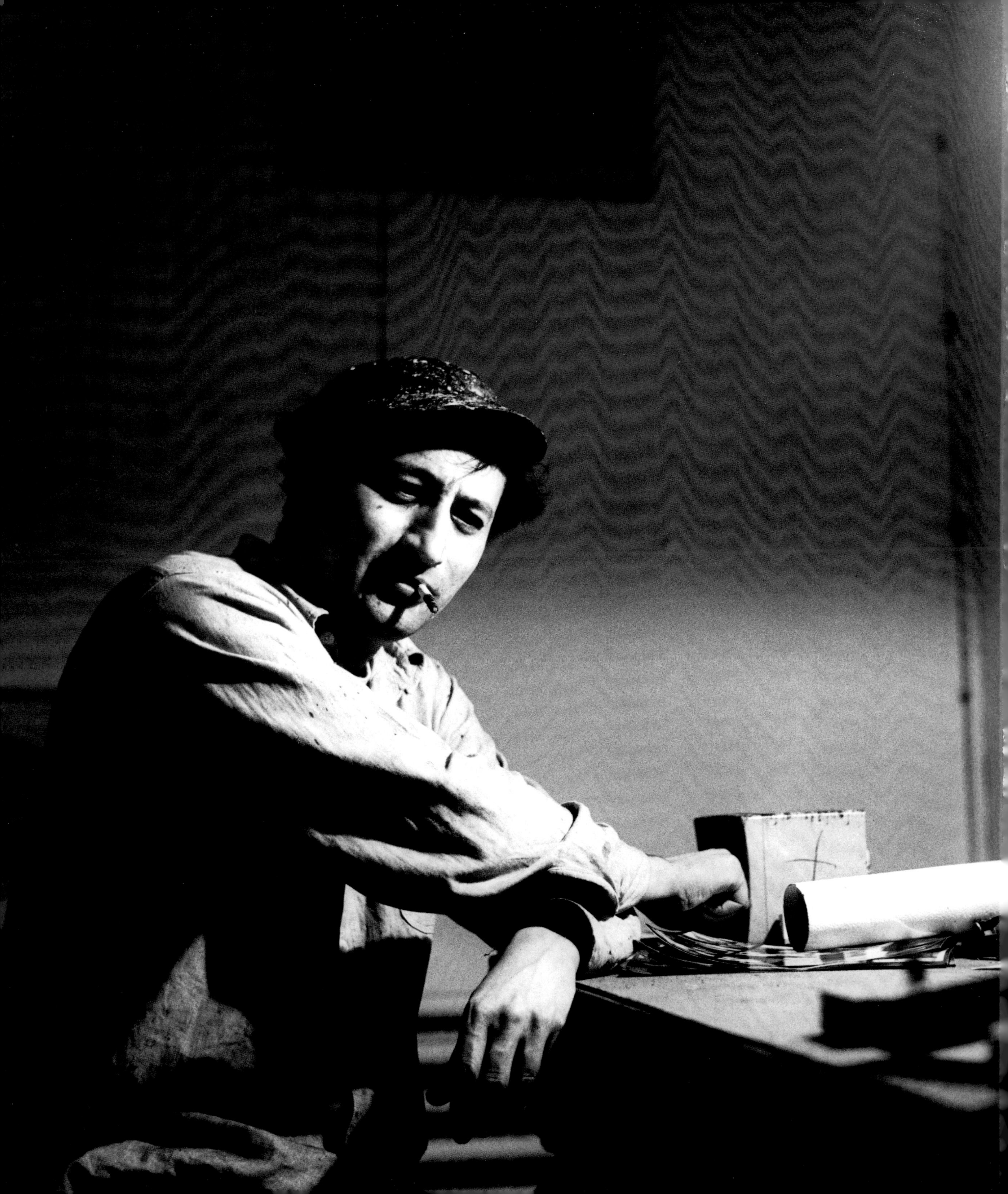

Index

Page numbers in *italics* indicate illustrations. All artworks are by Bluhm unless otherwise stated.

Fig. 40
Norman Bluhm in New York City, 1958.
Photo by George Moffett – Lensgroup, courtesy of The Estate of Norman Bluhm

Photo Credits

All new photography of works by Norman Bluhm by Richard Goodbody

Plates 9, 21, 22, 23, 42, 43, 58, 60, 61, 68, 71, 72, 73, 75, 76, 78, 85
Photos by Don Ross

Plates 10, 33, 35, 36, 40, 41, 44, 47, 69
© 2015 Christie's Images Limited

Plate 2
Photo courtesy of the Herbert F. Johnson Museum of Art, Cornell University

Plate 3
Digital image © Whitney Museum of American Art / Licensed by Scala / Art Resource, NY

Plate 13
Photo by Studio Fotografico Gonella 2007 Reproduced by permission of the Fondazione Torino Musei

Plate 26
Photo courtesy of Bridgeman Images

Plate 28
Photo by Jim Frank

Plate 29
Photo by Don Freeman

Plates 30, 31
Images courtesy the Metropolitan Museum of Art. Image Source: Art Resource

Plate 34
Photo by Jordan Huffer, David Owsley Museum of Art